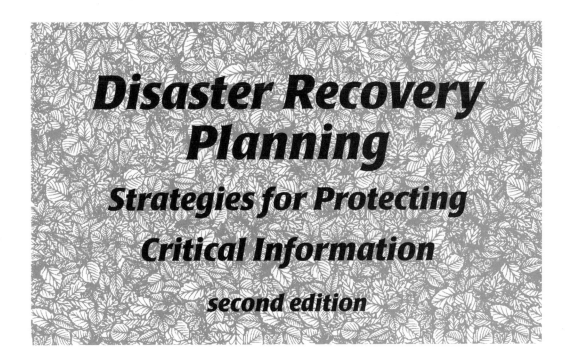

Disaster Recovery Planning
Strategies for Protecting Critical Information
second edition

Jon William Toigo

with illustrations by
Margaret Romao Toigo

PH
PTR

Prentice Hall PTR
Upper Saddle River, New Jersey 07458
www.phptr.com

ISBN 0-13-084506-X

90000

9 780130 845061

Library of Congress Cataloging-in-Publication Data

Toigo, Jon William
  Disaster recovery planning: strategies for protecting critical information / Jon Toigo.
    p. cm.
  ISBN 0–13–084506–X
  1. Data recovery (Computer science)--Planning. 2. Data protection. 3. Emergency
management. I. Title.
  QA76.9.D348 T653 2000
  658.4'--dc21   99-053827

Acquisitions editor: *Tim Moore*
Cover designer: *Anthony Gemmellaro*
Editorial assistant: *Julie Okulicz*
Cover design director: *Jerry Votta*
Buyer: *Maura Goldstaub*
Marketing manager: *Bryan Gambrel*
Project coordinator: *Anne Trowbridge*
Compositor/Production services: *Pine Tree Composition, Inc.*

 © 2000 Prentice Hall PTR
Prentice-Hall, Inc.
Upper Saddle River, New Jersey 07458

Prentice Hall books are widely used by corporations and government agencies for training, marketing, and resale.

The publisher offers discounts on this book when ordered in bulk quantities. For more information contact:

  Corporate Sales Department
  Phone: 800–382–3419
  Fax: 201–236–7141
  E-mail: corpsales@prenhall.com

  Or write:

  Prentice Hall PTR
  Corp. Sales Dept.
  One Lake Street
  Upper Saddle River, New Jersey 07458

Printed in the United States of America
10 9 8 7 6 5 4 3 2

ISBN: 0–13–084506–X

Prentice-Hall International (UK) Limited, *London*
Prentice-Hall of Australia Pty. Limited, *Sydney*
Prentice-Hall Canada Inc., *Toronto*
Prentice-Hall Hispanoamericana, S.A., *Mexico*
Prentice-Hall of India Private Limited, *New Delhi*
Prentice-Hall of Japan, Inc., *Tokyo*
Pearson Education Asia Pte. Ltd., *Singapore*
Editora Prentice-Hall do Brasil, Ltda., *Rio de Janeiro*

Robert Cantor once noted that the Chinese expression for the word "disaster" consists of two symbols. One is the symbol for danger, the other for opportunity. *Disaster Recovery Planning* is an effort to minimize the former, while maximizing the latter.

Meeting the unthinkable with courage, principles, audacity, and wit makes all the difference in life as in business. This I learned from Esther and Bill Toigo, and it is to you, my parents, that this edition is dedicated.

Contents

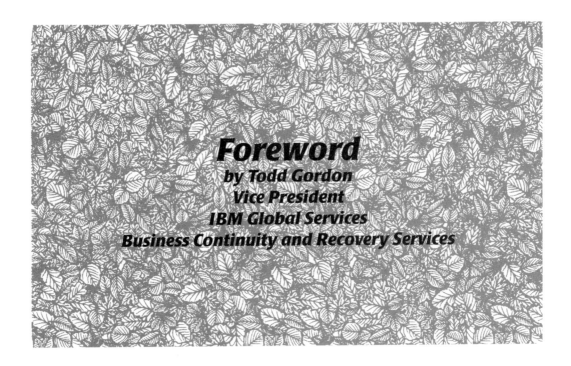

Foreword
by Todd Gordon
Vice President
IBM Global Services
Business Continuity and Recovery Services

Today's Internet-driven e-business economy, with its global, round-the-clock requirements, is raising a whole new set of disaster recovery challenges. Hacker intrusions, network attacks, viruses, spamming, and line failures now can pose greater risks to Information Technology (IT) operations than hurricanes, floods, power outages, and the like. And recovery can depend more on restoring applications than on fixing hardware.

Gone are the days when disaster recovery focused on protecting the data center—the heart of a company's heavily centralized IT structure. This IT model began to shift in the 1990s with the growth of distributed computing and client/server technology. At the same time, information technology became embedded in the fabric of virtually every business. Computing was no longer something done in the back room. Instead, critical business data could be found on desktop PCs and departmental LANs across the enterprise, as well as in the data center. Now this information is available around the world and around the clock at the click of a mouse—and businesses depend on it.

There is more at stake than ever before. Because electronic transactions and communications take place so quickly, the amount of work and business that can be lost in an hour far exceeds that of previous decades.

Losses can be staggering, particularly for businesses conducting high numbers of transactions (i.e. brokerage operations, credit-card sales authorization systems, automated teller machines). Losses from major system outages in these industries and others can range from thousands to millions of dollars per hour. Even minor outages can result in thousands of dollars in losses. For instance, a faulty RAID drive or a software glitch that impacts a critical business function can cause the same level of loss as a cable cut or power outage.

There are more risks today as well. Distributed, Internet-based applications (customer service, EDI, Enterprise Resource Planning, supply chainmanagement, e-mail, intra/inter company collaboration) provide increased access to corporate IT infrastructures for partners, suppliers, customers, employees—and hackers. This greatly increases the risk of malicious or unintentional acts that can cause major IT disruption. Operating a website also introduces the risks from interdependencies with organizations and systems that fall outside of a company's control. These include ISPs, telecommunications carriers and the hundreds of millions of users on the public network.

Today, vendors and companies alike are addressing these issues by shifting the emphasis from planning for traditional disaster recovery to assuring continuity of business applications and processes amid major or minor disruptions. Traditional disaster planning focused on recovering computer systems (namely, data centers) in the event of major natural or man-made catastrophes, and relied on IT executives to establish and maintain safeguards such as off site storage of nightly data backups and alternate computing facilities. While these measures remain important in overall disaster planning, they are not enough to protect today's distributed computing environments where recovery is a more complex, more urgent proposition.

Distributed applications, supply chain management, e-commerce and the Internet not only are making information more critical, but also diffusing it across networks and organizational boundaries. Recovering distributed applications that provide information is a complex process that can involve resynchronizing data and applications across hundreds of servers located around the world.

There is a greater sense of urgency with regard to recovery as well. Organizations today require continuous access to business-critical networked information and resources and customers demand 24-hour, global access totheir favorite Internet businesses. Most businesses cannot afford to be without information for minutes, let alone hours or days and those that depend on web e-commerce must be up 24 hours a day, seven days a week, or customers will simply click onto another site.

With these levels of exposure, business continuity (the ability to conduct business as usual, no matter what) takes on a much broader perspective, encompassing IT in all its parts—including software, hardware, infrastructure, networks, distributed systems, call centers, and service providers, among others. Clearly, protecting business processes, with all their complex interdependencies, has become as critical as safeguarding the data itself.

Investing in business continuity planning can bring positive returns, as well as reduce exposure to risks. This planning will assure that critical systems and networks are continuously available in the event of deliberate or accidental disruptions. In addition, companies can leverage their preparedness as a competitive advantage by assuring reliability to prospective customers and prospects. Good planning also can qualify a company for better insurance coverage and reduced premiums.

Companies today must be proactive in their approach to continuity-planning. This means engineering availability, security and recovery into their business processes from the outset, rather than retrofitting disaster recovery on existing systems or applications. And the best managed companies are spreading the responsibility for critical process continuity across all managers and employees.

No organization has the resources or the time to recover every functional area equally in the event of a disaster. In fact, any company that has implemented a single recovery solution for the entire organization is likely underprepared or spending money unnecessarily. The goal of business continuity is to identify those processes and information system components that are critical to the business, then put in place the measures necessary to recover them as quickly as possible.

Effective continuity planning begins with a Business Impact Analysis. This provides a thorough evaluation of a company's business environment and identifies the processes, applications, technologies and resources most critical to meeting customer expectations. Businesses also need information on the frequency, impact and causes of downtime that allows them to identify and rank the most vulnerable business activities. This knowledge helps to determine the maximum outage that each business process can sustain and to prioritize recovery of the most critical business functions. Once this is determined, companies can identify the technologies, resources and business recovery strategies appropriate for each IT component. Companies can balance overall recovery costs with acceptable risks and develop a workable recovery strategy that provides the basis for a business continuity and disaster recovery plan. Once the plan is in place, it is important to test it regularly.

While IT executives are central to the recovery equation, the responsibility for assessing business impact must ultimately belong to the managers of each business unit. These are the individuals who know best what their recovery point and recovery time objectives should be. Managers must work with IT colleagues to develop a business continuity plan that moves beyond traditional disaster recovery to cover all needs, including contingency actions.

The endorsement and support of senior management is equally important. Without buy-in at this level, it is unlikely that companies will be able to define recovery goals, objectives and assumptions or secure the resources necessary to implement an effective plan.

But despite the advantages of investing in approaches that assure continuity of business applications and processes, many senior executives and business managers remain wedded to traditional disaster recovery planning. A recent Gartner Group survey revealed that while 85 percent of Fortune 1000 companies have disaster recovery plans in place, 80 percent of those plans are limited primarily to data center resources. Only about half of the companies surveyed have plans covering their networks, and less than 35 percent have plans that would protect the data on their PC LANs.

Far fewer companies appear to have any means of recovering their Internet transactions. A recent IBM survey of 226 business recovery corporate managers revealed that only eight percent of Internet businesses are prepared for a computer system disaster. Yet doing business on the Internet means exposing a wide range of business-critical applications to a host of new risks!

Without continuity planning, e-businesses are at great risk of losing customers, investor confidence, stock value and profits. Internet companies that suffer disruptions of online business routinely make headlines in the next day's financial press. Ultimately, those that incur enough downtime can fail altogether.

There are legal implications as well. For instance, contracts today can require suppliers to deliver services or products promised, with no exceptions. In these cases, corporate executives can be legally liable for the consequences of business interruptions or loss of business-critical information. Moreover, adequate protection of data may be required by law, particularly for a public company, bank, utility or government agency.

It's clear that, in the Internet-driven worldwide market in which business never sleeps; traditional disaster recovery strategies are no longer enough. Downtime or business interruptions can no longer be handled simply by recoveringthe data center. Companies today that cannot do business as usual—no matter what—run the risk of losing time, money, and customer confidence and can even face business failure. In this demanding market, a proactive approach aimed at assuring continuity of business processes and applications amid major and minor disruptions is absolutely essential.

Todd Gordon
Vice President
IBM Global Services
General Manager
Business Continuity and Recovery Services

Foreword
by George Ferguson
HP Business Recovery Services

Businesses today depend heavily on access to electronic information, so when disaster strikes the computer network, it strikes the heart of the company. A disaster that cracks this foundation can generate huge losses. In some cases, it can compromise the survival of the company. It doesn't matter whether the crisis is a fire or flood, a computer virus or power outage, a strike or disgruntled employee; the impact on the business is the real disaster. Ensuring the continuity or recovery of IT-supported business processes, in the face of disaster, is essential.

The dependence on computing assets to sustain critical business functions continues to spur the need for disaster recovery support, particularly among new "e-services" companies, medium-size and large enterprises. Reliance on local and wide area networks, the rise of personal computing and the emergence of software for initiatives such as enterprise resource planning (ERP), supply chain management and e-commerce all are driving demand for disaster recovery planning and services.

Further, the overall faster pace of business has prioritized *quick* recovery. The high rate of technology refresh, expanding boundaries of business operations, new competitors, rapid deployment of new customer services, and the demand for around-the-clock services all are driving this trend.

TIME IS BOTTOM LINE

As recently as the late 1970s, companies could survive system interruptions of two to six days without significant revenue loss or disruption to operations. Today, in contrast, a two-day outage would undercut operations so seriously as to threaten the organization's market position. For certain kinds of companies, such as banks, brokerages, airlines and Web-based businesses, outages of even a few hours can cripple the organization's ability to do business or maintain credibility in the marketplace. This point is supported by the U.S. Bureau of Labor, which reported 93% of companies that suffer a significant data loss are out of business within five years.

The concept and practice of business recovery began some 30 years ago, and the evolution of the discipline has paralleled the evolution of business computing generally. Historically, disaster recovery meant restoring mainframe operations after a catastrophe. As businesses have moved to distributed client/server computing since the mid-1980s, disaster recovery has evolved to focus on recovering the client/server systems, applications and data that have become the seat of mission-critical business processes. To put this shift in perspective, at least 20% of mission-critical applications migrated off the corporate mainframe and onto the enterprise network during the 1990s.

However, few organizations have deployed high-availability client/server architectures. In addition, creation of disaster recovery plans for client/server systems has not taken off as rapidly as the technology itself. This point is troubling in light of the reliance on client/server technology for fundamental business processes via application suites for manufacturing resource planning (MRP), enterprise resource planning (ERP) and customer relationship management (CRM). The movement to these kinds of applications was strong throughout the 1990s and shows no sign of abating, making the need for disaster recovery plans even more intense. Similarly, the growing use of client/server architectures for e-commerce—where critical functions ranging from sales and marketing to supply chain management leverage the power of distributed computing and the Internet—makes it essential to be prepared for disaster.

As the client/server computing model evolves into more of an Internet-based computing model, vendors face the all-to-important challenge

to provide recovery services that affordably reduce the time it takes to recover from a natural or man-made disaster. To address this challenge vendors will need to partner with other service providers to develop global
portfolios of recovery services. IT managers and their executives will need
a continuum of recovery services that match specific IT-supported business processes to a recovery time windows. Similarly, vendors will need
to offer packaged services that affordably address heterogeneous IT environments. Bottom line: vendors will need to lower the entry cost of recovery services by financing the initial capital outlay while committing to
business-recovery windows worldwide. This way we can both satisfy the
CFO's bottom line and allay the CEO's worst fears.

GLOBAL PERSPECTIVE

Businesses worldwide strive to protect their technology infrastructures
from operational disruptions. The major sources of these disruptions
vary. For example, in the United States a leading cause of interference
with information systems (IS) operations can be attributed to storms and
everyday workplace mishaps. In South Africa, a major challenge to
smooth IS functioning comes from the lack of skilled workers and the frequency of lightning strikes. In Japan, a major concern is the chance of
large earthquakes interrupting IS activities. In Western Europe and South
America, telecommunications is a continuing problem, and civil unrest
causes ongoing concern in Indonesia. Whatever the cause of disruption,
businesses must protect their technology infrastructures and themselves
by having a current contingency plan.

Disasters can be grouped into a variety of categories, and vary within
specific geographic regions, climates, and countries. The most common
types of interruptions worldwide are those incidents which affect only the
system: the introduction of a devastating computer virus, an interruption
in power, a crashed disk, a telecommunications malfunction, a system upgrade that goes amuck or maybe even a customer's misguided intentions.
In addition, there are crises that affect only a single company: a fire in the
building, flooding from broken pipes, fumes. While these types of disasters can occur anywhere, they are of special concern to countries plagued
with poor standards of construction.

International contingency planning must include protection against
potential disasters that may be rare in the United States, but a viable
threat elsewhere in the world. Language barriers and cultural differences
could be a factor, too. For example, in the U.S. a hotsite equals a fully-

equipped and available IS alternative, while in England it means complete disk mirroring only. Even though these two countries share a common language, these implicit differences can lead to ineffective business recovery when it matters.

Having a global perspective to disaster recovery planning and services is imperative for current international businesses and those with aspirations of having global operations. IT managers will need to work with vendors that can deliver standard services worldwide; that have an understanding of the different approaches and techniques needed to deal with cultural differences and language barriers; and that have experience working within an individual country's information system's regulations.

COST OF DOWNTIME

Wherever and whatever the form the disaster takes, today's businesses cannot afford downtime of critical systems; every minute of downtime means losses that range from tens of thousands to millions of dollars. The business environment depends on IT for the business' bottom line: for productivity, cost savings, a competitive advantage and a strategic advantage. For example, banking and securities firms depend on information systems to conduct trades, monitor the stock market, respond to changing market conditions or to process payments. Telecommunications service providers depend on computer systems to support, manage and control their networks. And e-commerce vendors are dead in the water if their IT systems fail.

According to Contingency Planning Research, the average financial impact of just one hour of data center downtime is $6.5 million for a retail brokerage firm and $2.6 million for credit card sales authorization. Although these statistics represent the high end of the range, other kinds of operations also suffer serious financial damage when disasters disrupt normal processes. Contingency Planning Research's figures peg losses accrued from an hour of downtime at $199, 500 for infomercial 800-number promotions; $90, 000 for retail catalog sales centers; $89, 500 for airline reservation centers; and $69, 900 for a telephone ticket sales operation.

Any outage—whether it hits an isolated department, a network or an entire system—directly affects user productivity and ultimately revenue. Besides lost sales and opportunities, there are indirect costs, such as negative publicity, loss of customer satisfaction, overtime pay or loss in stock price.

Internet-based businesses that sell, broker or auction goods and services are particularly sensitive to outages. For example, immediately after a 22-hour outage at electronic auctioneer eBay in June 1999, the company's stock plunged 18 percent. Observers estimated that eBay lost $3 million to $5 million as a consequence of the outage.

More than ever, IT strategy and business strategy are closely aligned. The emerging Internet-based computing model brings about the age of instant comparison shopping, in which our customers' competitors are just a click away. In light of the key role the information technology infrastructure plays, and its vulnerability to interruption, companies have no logical choice but to plan for recovering systems and data when disaster strikes. Increasingly, disaster recovery vendors are recognizing this basic need and the spectrum of service requirements within it.

GRADATIONS OF SERVICE

As senior management has come to understand the impact of disasters on IT operations and on mission-critical business processes, as well as the financial risk that ineffective disaster recovery poses, the market has started to demand more of disaster recovery providers. Chief financial officers and chief operating officers—not IT managers—have become the decision makers for determining criticality.

To address the varying criticality requirements of businesses, HP and other vendors have started to specify estimated recovery timeframes for the offerings in its disaster recovery service portfolio and assign prices accordingly. The portfolio addresses differing recovery time objectives for various business processes.

Above and beyond recovery time objectives, businesses are in need of operational management services that blur the distinction between recovery services and more traditional outsourcing services. Manageability is a crucial, but often forgotten subject relating to disaster recovery. Below are two examples.

With the exception of full data replication environments, wide area recovery networking is typically only used once a year during disaster rehearsals. However, following a disaster telecommunications volume typically increase four times standard volume, and non-dedicated communications lines are overwhelmed. The Internet age has demonstrated the importance of networks to business operations, communication and productivity. Recovery service providers need to address businesses' needs for well-managed, fast and reliable bandwidth on demand during disaster rehearsals and real disasters.

Another manageability issue businesses have to plan for is the people aspect of operations management following a disaster. As an example, a Los Angeles-based company approached HP and asked us to manage their SAP environment for up to five days following a disaster. Understandably, the company believes that following a major earthquake, their employees' attention would rightfully be focussed on their family's needs—not the needs of the company's customers.

These two examples underlie the ever-evolving recovery demands of businesses. Vendors' abilities to successfully address these new demands with gradations of services or new packaged services will separate the winners from losers. Just as the Internet has changed selling and buying models, the Internet and new business models are changing the business recovery services market.

Clearly, the dynamics of how businesses use information technology are generating new levels of risk when it comes to disaster-related system interruptions. But at the same time, more and better disaster recovery resources are available to reduce these kinds of outages and to contain the damage they cause. By learning about the risks that disaster poses for IT systems and about strategies to avoid or limit interruptions, IT management can assure that their company's most valuable asset, its information technology, will survive.

George Ferguson
Marketing Manager
Hewlett-Packard Business Recovery Service

Preface

This book is scheduled for publication on the eve of a new Millennium, as described in Western calendars. Indeed, for the past five years, "Year 2000 issues" have dominated discussions at every level of business and government—at least in the world's developed countries. Building to a crescendo of nearly deafening proportions by the end of 1999, the mainstream press has allocated millions of column inches to Y2K, creating a kind of mystique around a rather arbitrary date.

January 1, 2000 has been positioned as a watershed event in human history. Somehow, it is more than just another wintery pause in the seasonal cycles that determine agricultural prosperity, more than just another New Year's Day spent recovering from the Bacchanalian excesses of the previous evening's celebration, certainly more than just another Saturday spent working in the yard or watching TV or attending religious services.

For many, the date is loaded with symbolic significance. Year 2000 conjures to mind the conclusion of ten centuries of fast-paced technological innovation that has changed forever the society and culture in which we live. In just the past 100 years, we have witnessed the harnessing of the electron, the atom, the microwave, and the photon to meet the needs of everyday existence. The Industrial Revolution has come to flower, given way to a Computer Age, and now, courtesy of the global Internet, World

Wide Web, and the ubiquitous Web browser, morphed analog reality into digital reality of the Information Age.

Doubtless, there are good reasons to select a day on which to pause and reflect on the past, to consider the present, and to prepare for the future. Some psychologists argue that the human mind requires bookmarks, milestones, and "closure events" to remain centered and healthy. One supposes that, to this end, January 1, 2000 is as good a date as any other.

However, Y2K has acquired a second symbolic meaning that is much less grounded in the psychological revolution that gave us Vatican II, no-fault divorce, and the self-help books of the 1980s. To many, the millennium is a mystical event, touching on a deeply rooted superstitious stratum seemingly present in the human psyche since the dawn of man. For a variety of reasons, Y2K is viewed as a harbinger of doom, a signal that some cataclysmic event is in the offing.

Hollywood understands the phenomenon and has provided a steady fare of disaster movies as the decade of the 1990s draws to a close. Recent wildly popular films have enabled audiences to "experience, " courtesy of Industrial Light and Magic and other computer graphic effects studios, the havoc and devastation caused by natural, man-made and even extraterrestrial disasters. With apologies to Bruce Willis and others, the acting and plot of these films do not explain their success. The real draw of the films appears to be the disasters themselves: tornadoes, volcanoes, earth-asteroid collisions, viral outbreaks, nuclear terrorism, and infrastructure collapse based on computer hacking. They satisfy a need in the viewers to confront their own mortality, if only vicariously.

Some of the movies are rooted in real-life disaster events, which seem to some observers to be coalescing as the end of the century approaches.

- The World Trade Center and Oklahoma City federal building bombings underscored the reality of terrorism for a heretofore-insulated North American audience.
- The eruption in 1980 of Mount Saint Helens, following a 128-year dormancy, and powerful earthquakes in California, including Loma Prieta/San Francisco earthquake of October 1989 and the Northridge/San Fernando Valley earthquake of January 1994, have stimulated concerns about geological disasters and their frequency. The National Earthquake Information Center of the U.S. Geological Survey is quick to point out that "while it may seem that we are having more earthquakes, earthquakes of magnitude 7.0 or greater have re-

mained fairly constant throughout this century and, according to our records, have actually seemed to decrease in recent years."

- The 1990s also gave the North America the costliest hurricanes in its history. While 1969 Hurricane Camille was the most powerful storm to date, Hurricane Andrew in 1992 racked up $26 billion in damage—the highest costs associated with any natural disaster on record to that point. As this book goes to press, experts are still calculating the costs accrued to 1999's Hurricane Floyd, which may well top Andrew's record. Between these devastating storms have been a steady wave of less powerful but very destructive cyclone events.

- Some may say that life imitates art. Following the success of the movie, *Twister*, Bridge Creek, Oklahoma experienced a real-life encounter in May 1999 with an F5 tornado, a so-called a "Finger of God".[1] This and many other severe storms, made the 1999 tornado season the most active since 1992. In part because of the movie, these storms commanded the full attention of the media, which subtly attributed the tornadoes, hurricanes, floods, and ice storms of the last decade to humanity's destruction of the environment and nature's reprisal. In some reports, the tornadoes were incorrectly correlated with the El Nino/Southern Oscillation effect.[2] According to government tornado watchers, the number of tornadoes have increased as the century draws to a close, but this phenomenon does not correlate to El Nino/El Nina weather patterns in any statistically meaningful way.

- The possibility of near-earth-orbit (NEO) asteroids and comets colliding with the earth has been part of science fiction lore since the Golden Age of the genre in the 1950s. As the millennium approaches, concerns about this threat have been fueled by several events. One was the 1994 collision of Comet Shoemaker-Levy 9 with Jupiter, which was photographed in brilliant color using NASA's Hubble Space Telescope and published in magazines and newspapers worldwide. The other was the hyperbole surrounding 1997 XF_{11}, an asteroid originally thought to be on a collision course with Earth, but later determined to be no threat when it passes the planet at a comfortable distance in 2028. The mistaken estimate sent many millennium watchers to their underground shelters and found NASA asking for authority to censor such predictions until they could be properly verified.

- One man-made disaster potential that has seen a marked increase as the millennium approaches is the computer virus. Bearing such innocuous names as Melissa, Chernobyl, and ExplorZIP, 1999's crop of viruses have already resulted in greater dollar losses than has malicious programs introduced in any previous year. Experts expect this trend to continue for three basic reasons. First, the widespread use of the Internet for email and file transfers provides a perfect mechanism for spreading viruses. Second, the increased sophistication of programming tools is enabling even novices to create powerful virus programs. Third, the increased complexity of common desktop applications, such as word processors, spreadsheets, and browsers, are providing a "target-rich environment" for exploitation by hackers and other malicious code writers.[3]

- According to the FBI and the Computer Security Institute, virus-related costs are only a subset of a growing trend in crime directed at companies and enabled by computers and networks. Directed against critical infrastructure systems, such as the power grid, telecommunications, air traffic control systems, and so on, malicious programs and computer terrorism could potentially be as devastating as nuclear weapons.

Given the perception in many minds that disasters are coalescing as the millennium approaches, it is easy to understand how Y2K has become so closely associated with Armageddon. However, upon more sober analysis, few indicators point to a cataclysmic end to human existence on the first Saturday in January. It is a safe bet that the day will come and go without the seas boiling, dogs and cats living together, or any other apocalyptic nightmares being realized. If we are wrong in this conclusion, then this book will have a rather short shelf life.

What we may have to look forward to on January 1, 2000 (and possibly for several months after) is a set of irritating, and in some cases hazardous, interruptions in services that are supported by information systems and networks. These interruptions will have nothing to do with Nature's wrath or Judgment Day. They will be linked to simple, software-based, date calculation errors.

The Y2K bug exists in many older software programs, those written at a time when programmers did not consider how programs would behave when the calendar turned over from 99 to 00. Some of the software is compiled to execute on computer systems. In other cases, the software is embedded in microchips that are installed on computing and networking devices themselves.

Obviously, government and industry have known about the Y2K problem for some time. Significant investments in Y2K code remediation efforts began in the mid-1990s in most developed countries. In 1998, however, validation and verification of these efforts by independent third parties revealed that substantial numbers of errors still existed in remediated code. The persistence of errors is attributed to the shortcomings of early Y2K code remediation tools and the failure of organizations to test adequately the code fixes that had been implemented. In a surge of effort and spending, many companies have addressed the problem in three ways:

- Continued remediation of persistent date calculation errors.
- Increased attention to contingency and disaster recovery planning to mitigate the operational impact of unresolved errors.
- Lobbying for liability caps in Y2K-related lawsuits that are expected to appear in droves as interruptions begin to occur.

As situations presently stand, the GartnerGroup, in testimony to the U.S. Senate,[4] predicts that 25% of Y2K code problems will manifest themselves in the months preceding January 1, 2000, 55% during the first year of the new millennium, and 15% in the year 2001. Unremediated errors in chip-embedded software will likely manifest themselves immediately with the date change at 12:59 PM on December 31, 1999.

According to the analyst, only 10% of Y2K bug-related failures will occur within the first two weeks of 2000. Of the failures that occur, only 10% will result in service downtime for a period of three days or more. Finally, one out of 100, 000 chips will fail due to Y2K bugs.

GartnerGroup's findings are echoed by other industry analysts, with a few criticizing the findings as too conservative or "feel good." Whether the numbers are exact is beside the point. The analysts agree that, despite the advanced knowledge of the problem, most companies did not build momentum to address date calculation issues until 1998. At that point, they were already behind the curve. As a consequence, the situation has taken disaster recovery planning from the backwaters of IT system stewardship—an audit checklist item—and elevated it to a managerial concern of the highest priority in many companies.

In a sense, Y2K has done what no other common-sense disaster recovery argument could do. It has crystallized for management the dependency of their businesses upon information systems and networks. Moreover, it has increased management's perception of the threat of unmitigated disasters—not only to business operations, but to corporate profits as well.

While government has acted to limit corporate liability and the deep-pocket lawsuits that Y2K outages were sure to generate, it did so after much debate. One issue that received much attention was the importance of due diligence as a modifier of corporate responsibility.

Due diligence mandates that a business, knowing that a potentially damaging situation exists, must take steps to rectify the situation or mitigate its consequences. With other disaster potentials, such as floods, fires, hurricanes, and earthquakes, the comparative rarity of the disaster potential manifesting itself into an actual disaster has limited the liability of most companies to lawsuits. The exception is in cases where legislative mandates required disaster recovery planning and testing of plans (in the financial sector, for example). In fact, shareholders and consumers can be pretty forgiving if a hurricane impacts a business and interrupts normal operations for a period of time.

In the case of the Y2K bug, the compassion of shareholders and consumers was likely to be much less forthcoming. U.S. lawmakers decided that shareholders and consumers would more likely to look for someone to blame and to sue. They would ask why, if business managers knew that a disaster was in the offing, did they do nothing to prevent the disaster from happening? And if the Y2K bug could not be excised from code in time, why didn't the company have a contingency plan that would minimize the impact of the disaster potential they could not prevent? Those questions go to the heart of due diligence and were central to the government's debate over Y2K liability limits.

Shortly after this book is published, Y2K—both the bug and the calendar change—will be ancient history. Interruptions resulting from the Y2K bug will become what many disaster recovery planners regarded them as all along: just another series of interruptions of business processes owed to software-related causes.

However, for some disaster recovery planners, Y2K—for all of its danger—will have also provided an opportunity. The sum of all of the practical and superstitious concerns about the millennium and the Y2K bug has, for a time, focused attention on the dependency of business on its information systems and their vulnerability to unplanned interruption. For now, DR planners are enjoying a bit of "face time" with corporate management. Used wisely, this increased level of awareness could be cultivated into an ongoing component of the corporate culture.

In this time of concern, disaster recovery planners would be well served to conduct themselves professionally and to vest all of their skills, knowledge, and experience to assisting their senior management in coping with the Y2K bug (as well as any millennium superstitions they may harbor). A well-developed plan will provide protection against a much more varied set of disaster recovery scenarios, of course. However, by emphasizing Y2K issues as a planning objective, DR planners will identify themselves to management as intelligent and competent resources who can be depended upon to support business objectives. This political capital can serve the DR planner well as he or she works to address the broader spectrum of business process protection.

Welcome to the world of disaster recovery planning.

ENDNOTES

1. F5 refers to the Fujita Scale for tornado classification. A class five, or F5, tornado, sometimes called "the Finger of God," is extremely rare.
2. Despite the tendency of movies and the popular media to assign a correlation between tornadoes and El Nino, this does not stand up to scrutiny. See "The Relationship Between El Nino, La Nina, And United States Tornado Activity," Joseph T. Schaefer, Storm Prediction Center, Norman, OK, and Frank B. Tatom, Engineering Analysis Inc., Huntsville, AL, Preprints, 19th Conf. Severe Local Storms, Minneapolis, MN, October 1999.
3. Daniel Sforza, "New Terror Lurks in Computer Mailboxes," *The Record*, June 12, 1999 and Robert Gebeloff, "On-Line Perils, Pitfalls Growing for the Unwary," *The Record*, June 12, 1999.
4. Lou Marcoccio, "Year 2000 International State of Readiness: Expert Testimony of Lou Marcoccio, March 5, 1999 to the U.S. Senate Special Committee on the Year 2000 Technology Problem, Washington, D.C.," GartnerGroup, 1999.

Acknowledgments

It has been ten years since the author first set pen to paper on the first edition of this book. *Disaster Recovery Planning: Managing Risk and Catastrophe in Information Systems* was written out of practical necessity.

The MIS Director for a large financial company (and my boss at the time), Mary Kern, first placed me in the role of disaster recovery coordinator. The job was made extremely difficult both by Mary's desire to be an "early adopter" of distributed systems technology, and by the general lack of information available in print on the subject of disaster recovery for mainframes, let alone distributed information systems. The technical challenges were surpassed only by the political ones.

Fortunately, I discovered a band of "fellow travelers"—other MIS and IT personnel tasked with DR planning, as well as a few vendors of DR-related services. Together, we shared ideas and developed approaches and techniques that strengthened the plans we developed for our respective companies.

In time, this core group formed a organization for businesses located on Florida's West Coast called the Disaster Avoidance and Recovery Information Group (DARING) that, together with one or two others throughout the United States, set the trend for the large national and international contingency planning associations that exist today.

We have since moved on to new adventures, but the fellowship and advice from Judith Brugner, John Flint, Joan Kobernick, Tom Little, Ross Markley, Pat O'Connell, Judy Ryan, Steve Glantz, Kevin Hephner, and Mark Sher contributed much to both the first—and now the second—edition of this book. The author wishes you well, wherever you are.

Staying current with the industry requires practice. DR books can't be written based on vicarious experience. The author wishes to extend special thanks to Frank McIntire, Craig Jensen, Charlie Fox, Jim Nowah, Milt Maughan, and many other friends at the ACP-Utah Chapter, as well as editors Ceil Perry, Tony Strattner, and Charlie Simpson for providing me with opportunities to keep in touch with disaster recovery planning. Thanks to them, I have had ongoing assignments in the field—consulting on plans for a broad range of businesses, speaking at DR planning conferences, reporting firsthand on actual post-disaster business recovery efforts, and documenting my findings in the trade press. There are no experts in disaster recovery planning, but experience is a great teacher. You, my friends, have provided the means for me to continue to learn and grow.

Edward Yourdon is also owed a debt of gratitude for contributing a structured approach to the first edition, which continues in this version. Special thanks to Philip Jan Rothstein, as well, for serving as a reviewer of the second edition and contributing many insights that helped to improve the scope and content of the work.

The author was also fortunate to have a champion in the person of Tim Moore. He and his staff merit special recognition for bearing with my delays and seeing this book through another Prentice Hall edition. Thanks also to Patty Donovan and company at Pine Tree Composition. It is always a pleasure to work with you folks, and the results are marvelous.

Margaret, Alexandra, Maximilian, Mercedes, Vincent, and the entire Toigo and Romao clans kept the author alert, healthy, and positive about the effort. Tony Romao and his Nerd Herd filled my email inbox with jokes each day, while Lori provided babysitting services at critical times, freeing up the author to write the words and Margaret to do the graphics.

Last but not least, the author wishes to thank the many vendors, analysts, and DR planners who contributed information and interviews to this project. A special thanks also goes to the many readers who sent me their comments on the first book, and also to the college professors, who continue to use the now-out-of-print first edition, photocopied with my permission, as a text in their classrooms.

To think, disaster recovery planning is now a college-level discipline! Quite a change from a decade ago.

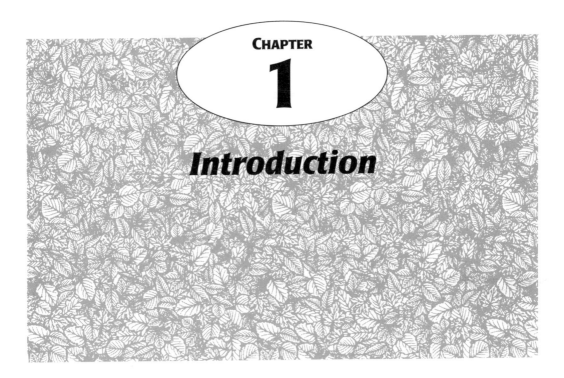

CHAPTER 1

Introduction

The history of business automation is fascinating and vast. For the purpose of this study, however, one aspect of the history is especially important. Driven by the incentives of cost efficiency and competition, business has placed more and more of its critical information assets into automated systems and networks. This, in turn, has made business dependent upon the uninterrupted function of the machine, a dependency rarely perceived by those within the corporation who have no direct contact with the information technology (IT) infrastructure itself. The consequences of a loss of access to the IT infrastructure to the business may never be considered—until a disaster occurs. By then, it is often too late.

Recent business experience is replete with examples of companies that failed to recover from a disaster. Some were consumed by a flood or fire that demolished offices and data centers, leaving skeletons of twisted metal and smoking rubble. Others died gradually over several years, after being crippled by a catastrophe from which they could never fully recover.

However, in the same historical experience, there are also examples of companies that suffered disasters of the same magnitude and survived.

They emerged from the crisis, with critical operations intact, to regain their position in the marketplace and to continue their commercial pursuits.

One must ask the reason for the different outcomes. Why do some companies survive when others fail? Is it simply fate or chance that determines success or failure in disaster recovery?

The word *disaster* connotes chance or risk. It is derived from the Latin word for "evil star"—a metaphor for a comet, once thought to be a harbinger of some impending doom. While the word embodies a fatalistic view of the unavoidable and inexplicable nature of disaster, it also contains a positivist tone: forewarned is forearmed. Knowing in advance that a disaster might happen provides the ability to prepare and to mitigate its consequences.

The insights of the ancient Romans continue to hold truth for modern corporations. Mounting evidence supports the contention that companies can take measures that will improve the likelihood of full recovery following a disaster. Companies that plan for the possibility of a disaster—that implement preventive measures to avoid predictable events and formulate strategies for recovering critical business processes in the wake of events that cannot be prevented—generally do survive disasters.

WHAT IS DISASTER RECOVERY PLANNING?

This book is about disaster recovery planning. As defined here, disaster recovery planning consists of a set of activities aimed at reducing the likelihood and limiting the impact of disaster events on critical business processes.

This preliminary definition may raise a few eyebrows. In the past few years, there has been an effort in some quarters to distinguish the concept of disaster recovery from a related concept, business continuity planning.

To some commentators, disaster recovery pertains to a specific domain of disaster events: recovery from natural disasters such as floods, hurricanes, and earthquakes. Business continuation planning, some argue, covers a broader domain of events, many of which may be less cataclysmic and life threatening in nature. Software viruses, hard disk failures, malicious attacks on systems and networks by hackers or disgruntled employees, and many other factors can and do cause interruptions in normal business processes without necessarily resulting in the widespread regional damage that might be left in the wake of a hurricane.

At the level of semantics, there is a measure of clarity in the term "business continuity planning" that may not be present in the term "disaster recovery planning." Business continuity more concisely describes the objective of this type of activity, which is to sustain mission-critical business processes during an unplanned interruption event. In contrast, some would argue, disaster recovery is semantically flawed. By its nature, a disaster is a nonrecoverable event. If recovery is possible, due to the implementation of some planned strategy, then an unplanned interruption event does not, strictly speaking, constitute a disaster.

This book does not seek to contribute to the semantic debate. Suffice it to say that the use of the term disaster recovery planning in this book encompasses the objectives attributed to all of the other forms. Namely, it is a set of activities intended to prevent avoidable instances of unplanned interruption, regardless of cause, and to minimize the impact of interruption events that cannot be avoided.

PURPOSE OF THIS BOOK

This book is designed to equip company planners with the background knowledge and skills they need to develop an effective disaster avoidance and recovery capability for their companies. It is also intended to serve as a primer for information technology managers and business executives in the critical and sometimes mysterious discipline of disaster recovery planning. It may be useful as a guide for managing the activities of the planning project, whether such a project is undertaken by internal personnel or outside consultants. Finally, it is a pragmatic reference describing the products, practices, and politics of the disaster recovery industry that has emerged over the past three decades.

Once having read this book, the reader will understand the principles of disaster recovery planning and will be equipped with a generic model for a DR planning project that he or she may emulate to develop a workable disaster recovery plan. Along the way, the reader will be exposed to some of the current debates and emerging technologies of disaster recovery as well as firsthand experiences of numerous business planners in both the preparation and implementation of disaster recovery plans. All that will remain is for the reader to select and apply what has been learned to develop a workable plan for his or her own company.

A WORKING DEFINITION OF DISASTER

The term *disaster,* as used in this book, means the unplanned interruption of normal business processes resulting from the interruption of the IT infrastructure components used to support them. This definition includes information systems and networks and their hardware and software components as well as data itself.

Of IT infrastructure-related business process interruptions, those resulting from a loss of data itself are arguably the most devastating. Whether a loss of data results from accidental or intentional erasure and/or the destruction of the media on which data is recorded or from any of a number of manmade or natural phenomena, data is the most difficult of all infrastructure components to replace. As a result, interruptions of business processes resulting from data loss may be the most difficult to surmount.

In addition to data loss, business process interruptions can also result from a loss of IT infrastructure components used to transport, process, and/or present data for use. A broad range of factors can lead to infrastructure component loss. These may include events that cause the destruction of key system, network or storage hardware or software, such as fires or floods. Component "loss" may also be the by-product of disruptions in regional infrastructure supports such as power or telecommunications outages.

These infrastructure interruptions have the potential to wreak as much havoc within a company as the loss of the data itself. However, their effects can generally be minimized through the application of recovery or continuity strategies that are the result of advanced planning and preparation.

The above description of disaster may suggest that only a major calamity—a terrorist bombing, an earthquake, or even a war—would qualify as a disaster. The term *disaster* conjures to mind a smoking data center at Goliath, Inc., rather than an accidental hard disk erasure at the small business office down the block. In either case, if the result is an unplanned interruption of normal business processes, the event may be classified as a disaster. Disasters are relative and contextual.

THE TIME FACTOR IN DISASTER RECOVERY

However, with all of their contextual diversity, there are some constants about disasters. One is time. Because of business's growing dependency on customized information systems and networks, alternatives to system-provided functions and information cannot be implemented readily. Yet, for a business to survive a disaster, the time factor for restoration of system functions is critical.

In the past, interruptions in normal processing could be withstood by most companies for a protracted period of time. A 1978 study by the University of Minnesota depicted the resilience of business to system interruptions, suggesting that most companies could survive interruptions of two to six days in length.[1]

Given the increased dependency of business today on information technology, it is hard to imagine a company withstanding an outage of more than 48 hours without incurring serious difficulties for its market position. Indeed, for companies ranging from brokerages and banks to e-commerce vendors and just-in-time manufacturers, the costs associated with even short duration system or network interruptions may be extremely high.

This is underscored by data from the Fibre Channel Industry Association, describing the cost of downtime by application type. Some applications with the most expensive per-hour downtime costs are described in Figure 1–1.

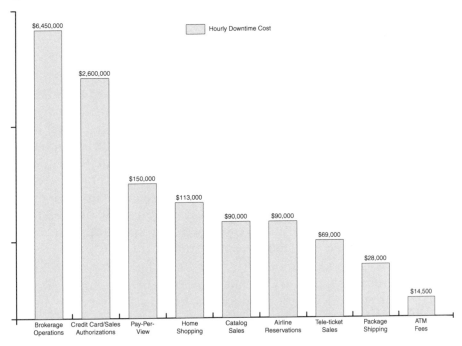

FIGURE 1–1 Cost of downtime by application. (*Source:* The Fibre Channel Industry Association San Francisco, CA. www.fibrechannel.com)

While industry- and application-specific averages for downtime cost are poor indicators of specific business vulnerabilities, they do point out the growing dependence of business processes on IT infrastructure. In view of business' dependence upon its information technology infrastructure and its vulnerability to an unplanned interruption of normal information processing activity, it makes sense for a company to plan and prepare for this possibility.

Recent events attest to the fact that those who plan for unplanned interruptions fare better than those who do not. A brief listing of some disaster recovery successes illustrates this point. In the last decade of the twentieth century, publicized business process interruptions included:

- A 1996 data center fire at Humana Inc. headquarters in Louisville, Kentucky.
- A 1998 roof collapse and flooding at Landstar Systems in Jacksonville, Florida.
- A tornado hit on Bank of America Corporation's Nashville, Tennessee operations center in 1998.
- A 1999 pipe break and flood at Charles Schwab and Company offices in San Francisco, California.
- The 1998 Hurricane Georges evacuation of Degussa Corporation in Theodore, Alabama.

The above examples, and many others, provide empirical evidence of the efficacy of disaster recovery planning. In each case, companies that experienced potentially devastating disasters implemented tested contingency plans and survived to continue operating in the marketplace.

By contrast, according to press accounts, more than 150 companies without disaster recovery plans received a death blow in February 1993, when a bomb wracked the World Trade Center in New York.[2] These firms learned too late that when a company does not have a tested set of procedures for reacting to and recovering from a catastrophe, it places all of its other plans and objectives in jeopardy.

Business Continuity Planning Consultant Philip Jan Rothstein correctly observes that documented information about the outcomes of system or network interruption events, both in the presence and absence of recovery plans, remains very limited. He bristles at the use of gross estimates of downtime cost as a substitute for factual industry statistics.[3] The point is well taken, especially as it pertains to business failures following disaster. In many cases, the relationship between a disaster event and business failure is not discussed publicly at all. Moreover, failures of businesses that are rooted in a disaster event may not occur until several years after the event, making the relationship difficult to document.

Based on available evidence, the time required to recover critical business processes following an interruption is a universal determinant of successful recovery. Unplanned interruption can cost a business dearly in revenues, reputation, customers, and investors. The objective of DR planning is to recover mission-critical processes as quickly as possible following the interruption event to mitigate its duration and costs.

However, evidence also suggests that interruption costs do not remain constant following a disaster event. They may rise exponentially, then decline over time. Assuming that a company can sustain itself through the initial high-cost interruption period, even those without tested DR plans may be able to recover their operations and live to fight another day.

While this may seem to contradict the recovery time factor argument cited above, in fact it confirms it. Companies can elect to expend time, effort, and resources in advance of a disaster to reduce the risk of business failure, or they can do nothing, accept the risk, and hope that their IT infrastructure can be repaired "on the fly" following an unplanned interruption.

Even in the absence of a statistical DR planning *nirvana*—the availability of exacting data on outage costs and business failure rates that would provide an airtight case for planning—numerous case studies can and do make a persuasive argument. Proactive planning can avoid certain risks and mitigate the impact of others.

THE NEED FOR DISASTER RECOVERY PLANNING

The need for disaster recovery planning is usually self-evident to an IT professional. Who, after all, has a more personal stake in the survival of a company's information systems than the manager whose position, prestige, and salary are directly dependent upon system performance?

In addition to self-interest, information managers often manifest a protective, almost parental attitude toward "their" systems. This is especially true when systems have been developed in-house. Effective IT managers and Chief Information Officers (CIOs), like good parents, take a personal interest in the safety and health of their charges.

Beyond self-interest and psychological factors, the IT professional has an ethical mandate to protect data integrity and ensure system and network survivability. Service level agreements between the IT department and company's end user departments are one manifestation of this commitment to quality and excellence in IT services. Contingency plans must exist if service level agreements are to be made in good faith.

Given all the compelling arguments for undertaking disaster recovery planning, it may seem redundant for auditors and federal law to require it. Unfortunately, a 1998 survey of 4255 IT and information security managers conducted by Ernst & Young and *Computerworld* revealed that over half had no disaster recovery plan in place for their companies.[4] The study further showed a decline in attention to disaster recovery planning generally, despite increasing downtime-related costs:

> While over 59% of this year's respondents said they experienced financial loss due to system downtime or failure within the past 12 months, only 41% of the organizations surveyed have a [disaster recovery] plan, compared to 55% last year; of that number, 34% have never tested the plan. In approximately 45% overall, there was no budget for [DR planning] activities.... In 45% of the organizations surveyed, there were no full-time employees dedicated to [DR planning], while 26% had none last year. The number of part-time employees allocated has also decreased: in 1997, 20% had no part-time [DR planning] employees; this year it is 53%."[5]

One year before the Ernst & Young survey, the Meta Group interviewed 100 of its Fortune 1000 company clients and discovered that fewer than 5% had "back-to-front" disaster recovery plans in place. Missing were provisions for the recovery of client/server systems, even in those companies that were in the process of migrating mission critical legacy applications onto distributed platforms.[6]

In the absence of effective planning, it has fallen to auditors, and in some cases legislators, to apprise corporate information managers of disaster recovery planning requirements and to enforce them as a matter of law.

THE AUDITOR'S VIEW

Auditors tend to view disaster recovery planning as a facet of an organization's efforts to guarantee the security and integrity of its data processing capability. While in the past auditors may have been content with a regular schedule for off-site storage of backup tapes and a paper plan gathering dust on the IT manager's bookshelf, their level of sophistication has grown. Documented and tested disaster recovery plans are increasingly regarded by IT auditors as a necessary component of business operation integrity.

Internal auditors are also taking a more active role in helping develop business recovery plans, often to ensure that corporate management (for whom they serve as the "eyes and ears") is not exposed to lawsuits or regulatory censure in the event of a disaster. Another reason for their interest is a well-founded concern that the integrity and security of corporate information assets will be maintained as contingency plans are rolled out and critical business applications and data are transitioned to backup platforms. The importance of this aspect of contingency plan auditing was underscored in the late 1990s as auditors and IT managers alike troubled over the possibility of hacker attacks during the recovery of Y2K-related application failures.[7]

External auditors, especially the "Big Five" consulting/accounting firms—Deloitte Touche Tohmatsu, Arthur Andersen, Pricewaterhouse-Coopers, KPMG International, and Ernst & Young, offer disaster recovery planning services to clients. The auditor-as-contingency-planner opens some controversial issues that will be explored later in this chapter.

IT audit handbooks now contain chapters devoted entirely to auditing the IT department's disaster recovery plan. Auditors are paying increasing attention to the following areas as they examine a company's disaster recovery plan.

- **Plan revisions**. While IT auditors may have no way to determine a plan's solvency or workability (unless they are invited to participate in an actual test), they may look to see when the plan was last revised. They are also interested in procedures providing for the regular review and revision of the document and for the regular reporting of system changes that must be accommodated within the plan. A list of revision dates should appear in the back matter of the plan document to answer these questions.
- **Plan test schedule and results assessments**. An untested disaster recovery plan cannot be assumed to provide an adequate measure of recoverability to corporate data assets. Tests provide the means for assessing the workability of strategies for evacuation and recovery that appear to work well on paper but may not perform well in real life. A schedule of regular testing and documentation of methods and results are important indicators to the auditor of management's

attentiveness to the disaster recovery requirement. This is also typically added to the back matter of the plan.

- **Training and awareness**. It is often said at IT Security and Disaster
  Recovery Planning seminars that DR plans are "living documents."
  A disaster recovery plan addresses two time frames: the future time
  frame, when the plan will be implemented to cope with some man-
  made or natural catastrophe, and the present time frame, when the
  plan is maintained and tested, plan participants are trained, and
  every corporate employee is made aware of the principles of disaster
  preparedness and prevention. This dual focus of disaster recovery
  planning presumes an ongoing training effort. Thus, auditors may
  ask to see a schedule indicating the dates, topics, and attendance by
  key recovery personnel at training sessions covering the many aspects of the plan. They may also wish to see evidence of provisions
  made to increase safety awareness within the company as a whole.
  Awareness posters in dining areas and elevators, handouts for new
  employees, and even designated "disaster awareness days" may be
  some of the ways that this audit requirement can be satisfied.

In addition to these general items, there are many specific requirements of a disaster recovery plan that may be checked or verified by the
auditor. These may include:

- A fully articulated planning rationale, providing an overview of
  threats and exposures and prioritization of risks based on potential
  business impact and other factors (e.g., likelihood of occurrence),
  plus a discussion of mitigation strategies considered and selection
  criteria applied.
- Effective disaster prevention and mitigation measures for all critical
  business process infrastructure components, including strategies for
  system, network, and end user work area recovery and evidence that
  these measures can be implemented in whole or part in response to
  various interruption scenarios.
- Documentation of relationships with other companies for backup of
  system platforms in the event of a facility disaster, including contracts with vendors of system backup facilities and services (hot sites,
  shell sites, mobile recovery facilities, etc.).
- Contracts and schedules for regular off-site storage for paper files
  and magnetic media backups, schemes for electronic tape vaulting,
  and/or remote data mirroring with off-site entities.

- Provisions for network recovery including contracts with network vendors for on-demand rerouting or automatic switching of voice and data communications services to a designated alternative work site.
- Specifications for fire protection systems, power continuation systems, water detection systems, and automated detection and alarm systems for other contingencies (disaster prevention capabilities).

AN IMPERFECT LEGAL MANDATE

In many industries, the dictates of common sense and audit requirements are supplemented by legal mandates for disaster recovery planning. The U.S. government has enacted legislation or issued regulations that require a broad range of contingency planning and related activities to be undertaken by businesses. A partial list of these provisions is provided in Table 1–1. In addition, many states are currently deliberating legislation pertaining to contingency planning, and some, including Florida and Maryland, have already passed laws requiring demonstrated disaster recovery capabilities for certain industry segments. Readers are urged to consult a lawyer specializing in computer and business law to determine the requirements that pertain in their respective states.

Federal mandates for disaster recovery planning affect various industry segments unevenly. Financial institutions, particularly those participating in the various components of the federal banking system, must comply with a well-rooted regimen of regulations on DR.

National banks, for example, must comply with Comptroller of the Currency Banking Circulars and Federal Financial Information Examination Council (FFIEC) guidelines that require them to develop means to reduce the impact and/or risk of losing IT support for business-critical applications.

In many cases, bank management is made directly responsible for determining critical functions at the bank, assessing the risk and potential impact of a loss of IT support for those functions, and developing plans to reduce the risk and/or impact of such a loss. Moreover, boards of directors are obligated to review the plans of bank management annually, approve them, record their approval in the board minutes, and provide the minutes for review by the bank examiners. The intent is to make both the board and bank management legally liable for a bank failure arising from inadequate preparation for an IT outage.

Table 1–1   Business Recovery Regulatory Profile

Regulation	Industry	Description
Comptroller of Currency BC-177 (1983, 1987)	Banking	Amended since original in 1983; requires banking institutions to develop and maintain Business Recovery Plans
Federal Home Loan Bank Bulletin R-67	Banking	Follows intent of BC-177
Inter-Agency Policy from Federal Financial Institutions Examination Council (FFIEC—1989, 1996)	Banking and any related service bureaus	Requires businesswide resumption planning for banking institutions and extends regulation to require contingency plans from any service bureaus or outsourcing companies that service such banks.
Financial Institution Letter from Federal Financial Institutions Examination Council (FFIEC—1997)	FDIC supervised banks	Emphasizes to the board of directors and senior management the importance of corporate business resumption and information systems contingency planning functions, also addresses issues that management should consider when developing a viable contingency plan.
Inter-Agency Statement from Federal Financial Institutions Examination Council (FFIEC—1998)	Banking and any related service bureaus	Guidance concerning contingency planning in connection with year 2000 readiness.
Fair Credit Reporting Act	Reporting agencies	Ensures credit information is accurate and up-to-date.
Foreign Corrupt Practices Act (1977)	Cross-industry	Management accountability through record keeping.

Regulation	Industry	Description
IRS Procedure 86-19	Cross-industry	Legal requirements for computer records containing tax information
IRS Procedure 97-22, Cumulative Bulletin 1997-1	Cross-industry	Compliance requirements for electronic storage systems used to maintain record-keeping information
IRS Procedure 98-25, Internal Revenue Bulletin 1998-11	Cross-industry	Requirements for documentation of machine-readable record-keeping system processes
Federal Response Planning Guidance (1994) FRPG 01-94	Federal departments and agencies	Outlines responsibilities and objectives of recovery planning
GAO/IMTEC-91-56 Financial Markets: Computer Security Controls	Financial	Guidelines for stock markets
GAO/AIMD-10.1.19 Year 2000 Computing Crisis: Business Continuity and Contingency Planning August 1998	Cross-industry	Guidelines for Y2K preparedness
GAO/AIMD-10.1.21 Year 2000 Computing Crisis: A Testing Guide. November 1998	Cross-industry	Guidelines for Y2K testing
GAO/AIMD-10.1.14, Year 2000 Computing Crisis: An Assessment Guide. September 1997	Cross-industry	Guidelines for Y2K validation
Accreditation Manual for Hospitals (1994)	Healthcare	Guidelines for information management established by JCAHO
Clinical Laboratory Information Act (1988)	Healthcare	Requires protection of critical laboratory data

Source: U.S. Government sources and William P. Dimartini, "What Drives Business Recovery Planning—The Carrot or the Stick?," *Contingency Planning & Management Magazine,* March/April 1996, © 1996 Witter Publishing Corp.

Other banking regulations extend management accountability for disaster recovery planning to include the performance of service bureaus. Banks using service bureaus to process information are required to investigate the financial condition of their servicers annually and to develop alternate processing strategies if the servicer's financial condition is deteriorating or unsound. They are also required to prepare their own contingency plans for mitigating exposure to a failure of the service bureau's processing capability.

The focus of federal regulators on the disaster preparedness of financial institutions in particular originated in the wake of an actual disaster. Following a computer failure at the Bank of New York in 1985, senior officials of the bank were summoned to appear before a Congressional investigating committee that, at one point in its hearings, considered the possibility of removing senior managers from their positions for not adequately preparing for a disaster.[8]

Bank of New York, reputedly the state's largest broker for government securities, experienced an IT outage that lasted approximately 27 hours. To continue operations, the bank was forced to borrow $22 billion from the discount window of the Federal Reserve Bank. It did so at an interest rate well below prime. The huge loan briefly destabilized the weighted rate of federal funds and cost the bank (or its insurer) $4 to $5 million in interest.[9] While Congress did not remove management in this case, the Federal Reserve did issue a circular that set the rate for borrowing in the face of an IT failure at prime plus two.

Not all federal regulations are reactive, however. In the late 1990s, the Year 2000 problem focused the attention of some regulators on corporate contingency planning as a proactive measure—a hedge against widespread economic calamity.

The Securities and Exchange Commission, for example, required all publicly held companies to disclose the details of their Y2K remediation projects, including contingency plans, as part of their SEC filings. Presumably, this requirement was intended to pressure companies to deal with their Y2K vulnerabilities by making the status of their preparedness a matter of public record.

The regulation cajoles companies to perform Y2K remediation by providing prospective investors with an additional criterion for making investment decisions. It may also provide a basis for shareholder lawsuits in the wake of Y2K outages if false claims are made by companies about their preparedness.

The regulation further incites companies to remediate their application code or risk being dropped as suppliers by business customers who depend upon their products within their own supply chains. As the 1990s drew to a close, many companies were actively reviewing their supply chain providers and selecting new, Y2K-ready providers for critical supply sources.

The close attention paid to the disaster preparedness of the financial industry (and to Y2K remediation across all industries) by federal lawmakers and regulators is not indicative of a comprehensive DR planning mandate, however. In many cases, disaster recovery planning requirements must be interpreted from legal language pertaining to recordkeeping requirements.

The Foreign Corrupt Practices Act of 1977, for example, requires only indirectly that companies to undertake contingency planning. The post-Watergate-era legislation was conceived as a mechanism for prosecuting companies that routinely used bribes to obtain business advantage in foreign markets. However, the recordkeeping provisions of the law are sweeping and have been adopted by the SEC and applied to all publicly held companies.

The recordkeeping provisions of the Act require companies to keep and safeguard records that clearly indicate how their assets are used. The original intent was to eliminate vaguely labeled accounting entries, such as "slush funds," which investigators found were often used to disguise bribery payments. According to the legislation, any accounting system that fails to indicate clearly how money is disposed of violates the Act. The SEC has since used the Act in several cases to prosecute wrongdoers who have not engaged in bribery of foreign officials, but whose actions technically violate the Act's accounting requirements (much like the federal government has used tax laws to prosecute organized crime figures whose "real" crimes cannot be proven).[10]

The Foreign Corrupt Practices Act pertains to any company using manual or computerized ledger, accounts receivable/accounts payable, or other accounting systems. Under the law, a business must take measures to guarantee the security and integrity of its recordkeeping system—a provision that has been widely interpreted as a requirement to undertake contingency planning. The Act further provides the means to prosecute individual managers and corporate executives who fail to comply with the Act. By legal extension, management can be prosecuted for failing to plan adequately for recordkeeping system recovery following a disaster.

Individual fines of up to $10,000, five years in prison, and corporate penalties of more than $1 million have been established. To date, however, no penalties have been exacted under the provisions of this law against companies or their executives simply for failing to develop disaster recovery plans.

Another government regulation, from the Office of Management and Budget, requires government agencies to take adequate measures to safeguard the operations of their IT processing facilities. This rule has been interpreted to extend to government contractors and subcontractors and is being rigidly enforced as a matter of national defense. Proponents of the regulation argue that because the design and production of military equipment and other contracted goods are being conducted or controlled using computer systems, the inadequate safeguarding of these systems represents an economic and military threat to the security of the United States. Plans must be made by federal contractors and subcontractors to ensure the availability and integrity of these systems.

The assignment of the ultimate responsibility—in legal terms—for the protection and preservation of corporate assets to corporate management has precedents. The Internal Revenue Service (IRS), for example, has articulated a number of strict rules pertaining to secure storage of business records. Management is often liable if IRS rules have not been observed and the records are lost.

For example, IRS Procedure 64-12 requires that recorded and reconstructible data be maintained in accordance with the Internal Revenue Code of 1954 and that program and source documentation be securely stored so that an audit trail from source documents to final accounting balances and totals may be demonstrated in the event of an IRS audit.[11] IRS Ruling 71–20 goes further to describe the requirements for retaining and safeguarding machine-readable records (including punched cards, disks, and other machine-sensible data media) that may become material in the administration of any IRS law.[12] Corporate officers are subject to penalties if these rulings and regulations are not observed.

Besides making provisions of disaster recovery and secure storage of data, the U.S. government further requires all businesses to safeguard the health and safety of employees and to refrain from activities that could harm the community in which facilities are located. The Occupational Safety and Health Administration (OSHA) and the Environmental Protection Agency (EPA) have issued enforceable codes and regulations aimed at "disaster avoidance" that make company management prosecutable if avoidable disasters occur.[13] At the state level, numerous agencies and departments have followed the federal government's lead with fire, building, and emergency management codes that impact on disaster avoidance and recovery planning.[14]

BUILDING MANAGEMENT CONSENSUS
FOR DISASTER RECOVERY PLANNING

This brief survey demonstrates that the disaster recovery planning project is propelled by a number of considerations, ranging from a common-sense business impetus to safeguard corporate assets from loss or damage to a natural desire to reduce legal exposure and personal loss. This is not to say, however, that corporate management is aware of all of the legal penalties, or even the risks, associated with not having an effective disaster recovery capability. In some cases, a management consensus must be cultivated by an information manager or auditor.

Even after a consensus is built to support the planning for business interruption and recovery, sustaining the consensus when it comes time to implement the paper plan—to install the recovery capability—can be difficult. The reasons for the breakdown of the consensus are numerous. In some cases, management exhibits reluctance to spend money acquiring the services and products that are intrinsic to the plan. This often occurs when management does not fully understand the risks and exposures a company faces without a recovery capability.

To address this dilemma, DR consultants recommend that a formal risk analysis process be undertaken early in the disaster recovery planning project. An assessment should be made of the impact of unplanned interruption events on the business as a whole—including a detailed assessment of tangible and intangible costs accrued to the unplanned interruption of each automated application that supports a mission-critical business process.

As an adjunct to this analysis, any legal requirements that compel management to undertake planning should be cited and clearly communicated. Where the law does not directly mandate disaster recovery planning, other strategies have to be found to convince reluctant senior managers of plan benefits. Effective strategies are often difficult to find.

Convincing corporate management to shoulder the costs of a disaster recovery capability can often be a greater challenge than surmounting the technical problems involved in backing up critical systems and networks. In the final analysis, however, management will play the most critical role in the planning effort—the role of underwriter.

Following are some typical problems reported by the information managers who had to sell their plans to senior management, and the successful strategies they developed to overcome them.

- *"You haven't cost-justified the plan."*

This criticism usually reflects the disaster recovery planner's failure to document adequately the exposures and risks of not having a plan. Often, planners first encounter this objection when they seek management approval to conduct an analysis of risks and exposures. That is, management may ask the planner to cost-justify the plan before they have authorized an investigation of whether such a disaster recovery capability is necessary!

How does one cost-justify a capability that, in the best circumstances, will measure its success in nonevents? A good disaster recovery plan, after all, sets the stage for disaster avoidance by providing the means to detect and react to potential problems, in many cases, before they become disasters. Strategies for successfully addressing this problem generally fall into two categories.

One strategy for responding to this criticism is to assign a dollar value to an hour of downtime. Calculate the average hourly earnings of employees who use an application that provides a business process for which a recovery capability will be planned. This provides an estimate of the cost of an hour of lost productivity were an application outage to occur. Assuming that the data could be entered at a later time without other adverse consequences, repeat the above calculation for one hour of average overtime salary (i.e., the amount of time all system users would need to work to make up for lost time). Then, add the two dollar costs as the total average labor cost for one hour of downtime.

For applications used by greater numbers of end users, this number by itself could be sufficient to demonstrate the benefit of a disaster recovery capability that would avoid outages or minimize the duration of un-avoidable outages. By multiplying the number to reflect 10 hours, 24 hours, 48 hours, and so on, the statistic could be quite compelling.

This approach, while simplistic, can be augmented by citing any documented costs associated with outages that have previously been experienced by the company. However, the planner must keep in mind what was said earlier about the tendency of outage costs to decline over time.

In some cases, the better case can be made by referencing intangible costs. The loss of customer satisfaction, the abrogation of service level commitments, potential legal liability, lost sales opportunities, negative press, and a host of other non-dollar-based factors may hold significant meaning for management. Arguments based on these nonquantifiable factors may actually be more compelling than cost-justification and other quantitative methods. The latter are inherently flawed, in any case, by the lack of reliable data on the likelihood of occurrence for any given disaster potential.

Another way to justify the plan is to demonstrate the collateral benefits of such a plan. An effective disaster recovery capability can actually reduce business insurance costs in some situations. Premiums for facility or business interruption insurance may be substantially reduced in many cases where disaster recovery planning identifies the specific coverages required and blanket insurance policies are replaced with targeted and less-expensive plans.[15]

Some disaster recovery capabilities, such as uninterruptible power supplies (UPS), actually do double duty. They can sustain critical business systems or network devices for a time so that organized shutdowns can be accomplished or independent generators started up in the event of a disastrous power outage. In addition to its use in a disaster, the UPS also supports equipment during the occasional surges, dips, and flickers of a typical business day. In so doing, the UPS can actually prolong the useful life of connected equipment.

Another dual-use scenario may apply to a enduser or workgroup operations center—a facility designed to house users if the main business facility becomes uninhabitable for a period of time. Such a facility may also be used during nondisaster periods as a training or conference facility.

Dual-use benefits can usually be discerned for most disaster recovery plan components, given sufficient time and creative energy. When a particularly compelling benefit cannot be found to outweigh a cost, the impact of the cost may be softened if it is examined from the perspective of tax deductions, health and safety of personnel, or good corporate citizenship.

- *"Our insurance will cover an outage, so why do we need the plan?"*

Even if a consensus exists for developing a plan on paper, management may resist spending money for implementation, especially if the disaster recovery capability is viewed as just so much more insurance. According to spokespersons for two data processing insurers, the right insurance policy will cover operating costs that are above the normal costs of business operations, provided that the appropriate "extra" costs are spelled out in the policy. This business interruption insurance, however, should not be viewed as business resumption insurance.[16] An information manager may need to educate management in the following facts.

Insurers can readily cover the costs of facility damage (and, in some cases, replacement), and they can provide coverage for hardware and media. However, while insurers are willing to underwrite the *reconstruc-tion* of data lost to a natural or man-made disaster, it would be cost pro-hibitive to the client to underwrite the *value* of the data.

Without a disaster recovery plan, the client would be hard pressed to estimate the cost of reconstructing data or to buy adequate insurance for doing so. In all likelihood, without a disaster recovery capability, there would be nothing with which to reconstruct the data: no extant records, no systems, no location for personnel to work. Purchasing extra coverages under these circumstances would be pointless.

In a disaster situation, a company protected only by business inter-ruption insurance is placed in the unenviable position of relying on the progress of the claims adjustment cycle to drive the recovery. While top insurers generally provide excellent turnaround on disaster claims and may even provide support services to facility the insured's recovery activ-ities, this is generally less desirable than controlling recovery within the business itself and capitalizing on the determination and commitment of trained recovery teams who are employees of the company.

If management does not understand the problems inherent in de-pending on insurance to recover from disaster, planners should provide information about the experience of companies that have experienced dis-asters firsthand. The aftermath of Hurricane Andrew—the subsequent flight (and, in some cases, bankruptcies) of property and casualty insurers from the State of Florida—attests to the impact of a regional disaster on insurance companies as well as the potential problems companies con-front in obtaining the timely handling of insurance claims.

The bottom line is that business interruption insurance is properly regarded only as a supplement to a tested disaster recovery capability. It is never a substitute for planning.

- *"The purpose of the plan is to satisfy the auditors."*

While it may seem blasphemous, managers often express this senti-ment in spoken or unspoken terms. One manager of a national financial concern remarked, off the record, that the best disaster recovery plan he could get his company to fund was an up-to-date resume. Sadly, in the absence of rigidly enforced laws, auditors' comments are often the only incentive for management to undertake disaster recovery planning. Audi-tors seldom have the power to compel management to do anything it is not inclined to do.

One strategy for surmounting management indifference is to barrage corporate officers with news clippings about business disasters, although this may ultimately cost the sender some prestige or power. The object of this strategy is not to aggravate or frighten, but to create awareness in senior management that disasters do happen and that those who prepare for them generally recover normal operations far more readily than those who do not.

Another method for reducing senior management indifference is to demonstrate that the planner understands and participates in management's priorities and objectives. This may be reflected in the methods used to create and articulate the plan. For example, every effort should be made to maximize the plan's protection while minimizing its cost. Despite his or her personal investment in systems and networks, the planner should strive to assess IT resources dispassionately for their criticality to the corporation. Certain applications are more vital than others, a fact that is underscored by a careful analysis of the impact of an unplanned interruption on business applications. It needs to be clearly communicated to senior management that the plan will target the largest share of budget expenditures for the most important applications.

Furthermore, plans must ultimately encompass not only the recovery of IT and network resources but also the user departments. It makes little sense to restore applications if no provision is made to restore the user community. By involving the managers of user departments in the planning project, the planner may be able to cultivate a corporate climate of support for disaster recovery planning. This, in turn, may reinforce senior management's perception of the value of the disaster recovery planning effort and result in a more comprehensive and effective recovery capability.

The Y2K Bug, and the legal exposure it creates for a company, has not escaped the attention of senior management. In a sense, Y2K has provided an opportunity for DR planners to demonstrate to senior management that what they do is motivated by concern for the business and for management. While Y2K is merely another software-related disaster potential, it can be leveraged by the savvy DR planner to gain political capital with management that may be used later to expand the scope of DR planning into other areas.

These are only a few of the common problems and strategies used by DR planners to obtain senior management approval for disaster recovery planning costs. Other problems may develop that reflect the particular circumstances of a business, the distribution of information systems, or even the individual personalities of senior managers themselves. Whenever possible, disaster recovery planning should be depoliticized and depersonalized. Since the initial focus of the planning effort is on information systems, the information manager will play an important role in setting the stage for the entire corporate disaster recovery plan.

WHO SHOULD WRITE THE PLAN?

Once the decision has been made to undertake disaster recovery planning, the information manager must first determine the method to be used to develop the plan. One option is to hire a consultant to perform this task. Another is to develop the plan in-house. Valid arguments exist to support each option.

At first glance, hiring a consultant with X years of experience in developing this type of project may seem the best choice. Indeed, this approach has several distinct advantages.

First, the disaster recovery planning project is just as complicated as a major system development project and, in fact, parallels the systems development life cycle (SDLC). (Figure 1–2 depicts the similarity.)

Like a system development project, a disaster recovery planning project begins with analysis. A risk analysis process is undertaken to identify potential threats and vulnerabilities, while business impact analyses and application impact analyses are undertaken to identify critical business processes and their IT infrastructure supports and to discern recovery priorities, objectives, and requirements.

Recovery strategies are then outlined and tasks are prioritized much in the way that an analyst would set forth a general system design. This general design is subjected to user review and, if it is approved, a detailed system description is articulated. At this point, development costs are specified and a project time-and-money budget is developed.

In systems development, the project would be approved by management, and coding would begin. Similarly, the disaster recovery planning budget is presented to senior management and, if approved, vendors are contacted, products and services purchased, and recovery procedures developed and documented.

Plan testing and user training follow, just as comparable activities would follow the conclusion of coding. Finally, when the system is released or the plan is placed into effect, it is integrated into a change management system to provide for periodic review, revision, and maintenance.

An information manager, realizing the scope and complexity of the planning project, may decide that a consultant is needed to manage it. The

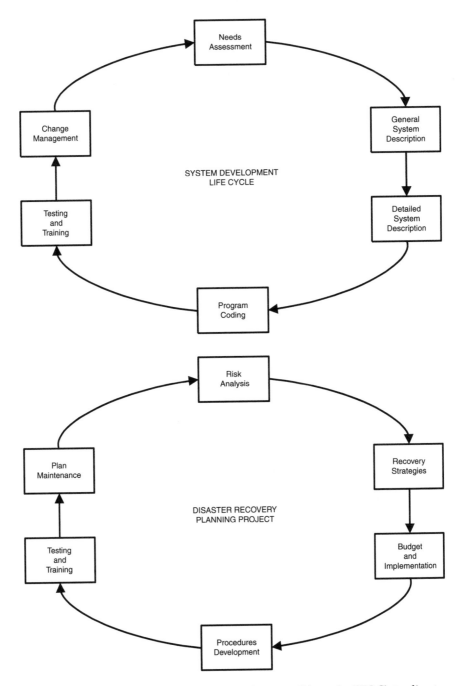

Figure 1–2   Comparison of systems development life cycle (SDLC) to disaster recovery planning project.

information manager either cannot reassign an employee to manage the project or feels that no employees are equal to the assignment. There may also be other factors that favor the consultant option:[17]

- Consultants bring specialized knowledge to the planning project that may facilitate the speedy development of an effective plan. An experienced consultant knows how a disaster recovery plan is constructed, knows the right questions to ask, and typically knows who's who in the disaster recovery products and services industry. Consultants who work within a specific industry may combine an understanding of the industry with a methodology for disaster recovery planning. This reduced learning curve, in turn, can help to speed plan development.

- Consultants can bring a fresh eye to the project, noticing recovery requirements that may be overlooked by someone who is too close to the data center he or she is seeking to protect. One consultant relayed a story about a client who had hired her to perform a risk analysis of a data center. In conferences, the client confidentially reassured her that all vital processing equipment had been identified. Then, during a preliminary visit to the data center, the consultant nearly tripped over an ancient time card reader. She asked what it was and learned that no payroll checks could be generated without its use. A vital piece of equipment, yet it had not been mentioned anywhere in the lists that otherwise documented completely the state-of-the-art hardware installed in the shop.

- Consultants are expensive. While this may be viewed as a drawback of the consultant option (and will be discussed later in this chapter), it may actually favor plan development in certain cases. Disaster recovery planning requires the interaction of users and information systems and network technical personnel. Within a large information systems shop, where rivalries frequently exist among applications support personnel, systems administrators, and operations, disaster recovery planning will also require the interaction of these groups. Often the only way to get all of the relevant parties to sit down as a group and discuss critical issues to make it clear that a great deal of money is being spent for the consultant's time. Similarly, senior management, having invested a considerable sum of money for a consultant-developed plan, may be less inclined to withdraw support for the implementation of the plan.

Consultant-driven plans are similar to computer hardware acquisitions; they are usually available with a maintenance agreement. For a fee, the consultant will return on a semiannual basis to aid in the testing and updating of the original plan. Furthermore, since the plan usually reflects the "favored" (read "proprietary") methodology of the consultant, many consulting firms offer a training service to educate personnel in the client company who will maintain or use the plan.

Good consultants usually produce good plans and provide competent maintenance and training services. Unfortunately, not all consultants are good consultants. As of this writing, the disaster recovery planning consultancy is an unpoliced field. In the late 1960s, there were only handfuls of disaster recovery consulting firms. Since that time, the number has increased exponentially. It is not uncommon for consulting firms to open and close their doors within the same year. This bodes ill for the industry as a whole.

Consultants may attempt to demonstrate their competence by referencing a certification from a DR planning certification body. Several certification organizations have evolved over the past decade with the stated objective of training novice planners and, for a fee, "certifying" the skills of those who have learned their trade "on the job." Contrary to the view of many who have obtained certifications, the kindest thing that this author has to say about certification programs is that, at present, they provide little assurance about the capabilities of those who hold them.

This assertion is likely to draw fire from several quarters, so it merits further discussion. In the early 1990s, the originator of one of the first certification programs for DR planning contacted this author to solicit his participation in promoting a "marketing concept": disaster recovery certification. The proposal consisted of selling certifications for a fee to anyone who could pass a multiple-choice test consisting of easy-to-answer questions such as the meanings of familiar acronyms and the definitions of DR-specific concepts such as "dial backup" and "hot site." Not to be exclusionary, DR practitioners would also be invited to participate. They would be "grandfathered in"—that is, provided the certification without testing in exchange for dues payment. The fellow was clearly delighted with the concept, which he viewed as a "sure money maker" on three grounds:

1. Many individuals responsible for disaster recovery planning for their organizations suffered from a lack of confidence. They feared that they were not as professional as consultants who developed DR plans for many companies. The certification program would not

make them better planners, but it would give them the appearance of professionalism when they interacted with other professionals and with management. Basically, the certification program was a confidence game.

2. The certification program would become a discriminator between consultants in a highly competitive and totally unregulated disaster recovery consulting industry. The revenue potential for the program based on "grandfathering" fees alone was enormous, even if the certification program was meaningless.

3. The certification program would be a great way to amass the world's best database of DR planner names and addresses, which could subsequently be resold to vendors of DR products and services, producing another revenue stream.

Demonstrating a lack of business acumen, the author declined to participate. Nevertheless, the program was launched and became one of the most successful certification programs today.

Recently, an acquaintance of many years, who had retired as the chief disaster recovery planner for a major financial institution, complained that he was required to obtain a certification before he could join the consulting group of a major systems integrator. The fellow was told that in spite of his extensive experience in DR planning, his intimate familiarity with planning methods and tools, his thorough knowledge of vendors and their offerings, his former senior role within a major disaster recovery planning user group, and his numerous references, he was unmarketable without the letters of a certification program following his name on his business card. Rarely has there been a more clear-cut case of a Grand Panjandrum.

While numerous organizations, including the well-respected National Fire Protection Association, are working to develop objective DR planning standards, the present state of this endeavor is as much art as science. Effective planners require a broad base of knowledge across a variety of technologies and business practices. For this reason, disaster recovery planning is not a skill set that is easily tested.

Thus, it is the contention of this book that, despite the fact that a consultant's business card contains an acronym for a disaster recovery certification body, this alone is insufficient evidence that the consultant is competent to do an acceptable job for the business client. Some of the best consultants in the field do not have letters following their names on a business card or brochure.

Speaking of credentials, over the past decade, many "Big Five" accounting firms entered the contingency planning business. In other words, the same firm that performs the company's annual audit probably offers a disaster recovery planning service as well.

Despite claims by these organizations that their audit and planning organizations are entirely separate, it is not uncommon, following an audit that discovers a missing or inadequate disaster recovery plan, for a representative of the planning services arm of the firm to pay a impromptu courtesy call on the IT manager, CIO, or other business manager. The accounting firms argue that there is nothing incestuous about this practice, but concerned observers have asked how an auditor can objectively assess an DR plan bearing the label of his or her own firm.

Undoubtedly, there are good and bad consultants in "Big Five" accounting firms just as there are in the "pure" disaster recovery consultancies. The business or IT manager should use the same criteria when evaluating either type of consulting service. The following guidelines may be useful when considering the hiring of consultants to develop the disaster recovery plan.

1. **Check the qualifications of the consultant.** It is important to know the name and background of the consultant who will be providing services. Find out how many and which companies the consultant has served and check directly with the clients for recommendations and criticisms. Be wary of using an inexperienced consultant, even if he or she reputedly has access to more experienced hands. Ideally, the consultant will be able to demonstrate a knowledge of the IT and network technology used at the prospective client's company, will understand the specific requirements within a prospective client's industry, and will have developed satisfactory disaster recovery plans for at least two other businesses within the same industry.

2. **Ask for a project roadmap.** Ask for a proposal that shows the phases and tasks of the planning project. The consultant should not view this as an illegitimate request. Over the past few years, with the increasing availability of excellent DR planning project models and improved information on the techniques and methods of recovery planning, consultants have been hard pressed to portray what they do as secret, mysterious, or otherwise beyond the reach of nonconsultants. Most consultants have planning methodologies that they adapt to accommodate specific client requirements. All the manager needs is enough information about techniques and methods to evalu-

ate the validity of the methodology. (For this reason, even if a manager elects to use a consultant, this book will help the manager to evaluate the applicability of the consultant's planning methodology.)

3. **Check and validate proposed time and cost estimates.** Read consultant proposals carefully and note first whether time and dollar cost estimates have been assigned to parts of the project. Unless consulting services are packaged as fixed price contracts, there is no way that a consultant can develop meaningful time and cost estimates. The manager should be especially wary if the consultant quotes exact prices or times before knowing anything about the particular requirements of the company.

Estimates provided by the consultant can be of value to the information manager in other ways. For example, valid time and cost estimates can provide a useful benchmark for comparing various consultant proposals, especially if each consultant states that he or she is basing estimates on similar projects performed for similar businesses. This is about the only way "comparison shopping" can be performed for this type of service.

To ensure that the data being collected from each candidate is not skewed by anything other than unknown factors, ask whether all predictable costs, including the consultant's travel and lodging, are reflected in the estimated cost.

Information managers should be aware that some consultants tend to push their premium service initially, and offer less-expensive shared responsibility approaches only if they sense that they may be pricing themselves out of a contract. Faced with the prospect of losing a prospective client, some consultants can often be very creative in finding cost-saving measures. One manager reported that he cut the cost of consultant-aided plan development in half by offering to provide "administrative assistance" (someone to do word processing, etc.) to the consultant, and by allocating one of his employees to work with the consultant on a full-time basis, replacing the assistant to be provided by the consulting firm. Other managers have discovered that they could purchase the consultant's PC-based disaster recovery planning tool and utilize the consultant's personal services only in the up-front analysis and data collection phases of the project. Substantial cost reductions resulted in each case.

Another manager reported that the business ethics of the consultant could be discerned from the way in which he reacted to the manager's reluctance about costs. In one instance, a consultant offered to reduce costs by dropping the final two phases of the proposed project. These phases consisted of training personnel who would play key roles in the plan and maintenance of the plan document itself. Implied in this offer was the consultant's willingness to develop a paper plan that would sit on a shelf and satisfy a casual audit but provide no meaningful recovery capability!

Cases such as the one described above are certainly the exception rather than the rule. No stereotyping of disaster recovery consultants is intended—some other the author's best friends are disaster recovery planners.

4. **Ask about the consultant's relationships with vendors of disaster recovery products and services.** Managers who are considering the use of consultants also need to be aware that many consulting firms have formal or informal relationships with vendors of disaster recovery products and services. These relationships can profit the consultant's client in some cases. Using a particular consultant, for example, may qualify the client for discount rates on fire protection systems, off-site storage, or hot sites (subscription-based system backup facilities).

There is, however, a potential for misuse of these relationships. An unethical consultant may be willing to sacrifice the objective analysis of client requirements in favor of recommending a product or service from which the consultant receives a kickback. It is valuable to know whether and with whom the consultant has marketing agreements, and how these agreements may result in price advantages for the client. Most vendors will openly admit to any special arrangements, particularly when they may profit the client and improve the marketability of their service. Some consultants argue that it is partly their extensive knowledge of the disaster recovery industry that qualifies them for the rates they command.

Should the manager decide to use a consultant, whether or not the consultant admits having special marketing arrangements with vendors, he or she should pay particular attention to soliciting competitive bids for any product or service that the consultant recommends.

For many managers, the cost of a consultant-driven disaster recovery plan is the major drawback. Plans can range from $20,000 to upwards of $120,000. This is generally perceived as a cost over and above the cost for in-house plan development. Consultants respond that their price is reasonable from many perspectives.

A company electing to use in-house personnel to develop a plan must patiently wait for the novice disaster recovery coordinator to acquire knowledge that the consultant already possesses and finance the coordinator's education and pay his or her salary while doing so. Plan development is a slower process when performed by a novice in the field. In the meantime, the company's vital information asset remains exposed. Consultants also point to the fact that most plans begun by in-house personnel are never completed.

Despite these arguments, many companies elect to use in-house personnel. Even consultant plans ultimately require that in-house skills and knowledge be developed. Someone must coordinate plan revisions and maintain the plan between visits by the consultant. In addition, much of the consultant's work must be overseen by in-house personnel since the consultant is essentially an outsider who does not participate in day-to-day business operations. Also, in-house personnel must perform all evaluations of products and services to be used in the plan, partly to ensure the honesty of the consultant.

Finally, in-house personnel now have access to information about disaster recovery planning techniques and methods through special training courses, published articles and books, the Internet and World Wide Web, and by participating "sharing" groups. So, the learning curve for the in-house planner is drastically reduced.

Generic PC-based planning tools are also now available, and several consulting firms market their own software package containing their proprietary planning tool. These tools provide a structured approach to planning for common equipment configurations. They need to be modified by the purchaser to account for specific applications, networks, decentralized processors, and other characteristics peculiar to the customer site.

Although the PC-based planning tool does not provide comprehensive answers for the novice planner, it can offer valuable models that the planner can imitate when customizing the plan to meet his or her requirements.

Another change that is supporting the development of disaster recovery plans by in-house personnel is the improvement of project management skills across all industries and business activities. The development of a disaster recovery capability is essentially a project with discrete tasks, milestones, resources, and budget. Once the principles peculiar to disaster recovery planning are understood, any person skilled in the techniques of project management can develop a competent disaster recovery plan. Many, including this author, have found that the only tools they require are old-fashioned research and communication skills; email and web browser; a word processor; and a generic, off-the-shelf, spreadsheet, database, or PC-based project management software package.

A final word on the consultant versus in-house development strategy is suggested by consultant Philip Jan Rothstein, who notes that there are other roles for consultants than performing or managing the plan development process. Consultants can be used in connection with in-house planning efforts "to perform or support certain planning phases" (such as analysis or testing) with specialized methods or techniques, "or to serve as a *true* consultant—meaning, a knowledge base or coach."[18]

Given the right consultant, such an approach has the potential to deliver the best of both the in-house and the consultant-driven planning project models.

A STRAIGHTFORWARD, PROJECT-ORIENTED APPROACH

A straightforward project-oriented approach to DR planning comprises the subject of this book. Each chapter provides cogent, practical information about the major tasks involved in developing a disaster recovery capability. Each chapter clearly defines the objectives of a development task, describes typical methods used to realize objectives, defines what resources are typically required, identifies sources for specific products and services, and discusses methods for evaluating task fulfillment.

In some cases, the IT manager or his or her designee serves as the disaster recovery coordinator for the company. In other cases, planning is undertaken by a group of users representing both information systems and the user community. If planning is undertaken by a group, however, it will need a person who will serve sometimes as researcher, sometimes as data collector, sometimes as honest broker, and ultimately as the person responsible for maintaining the plan in the face of almost daily shifts in recovery requirements. All these responsibilities are implied in the title DR coordinator.

In many cases, the IT or business manager will either hire a new employee to serve as disaster recovery coordinator or transfer an employee to fill the position full-time. The critical phrase is *full-time.* In very small companies, the IT manager is likely to serve as disaster recovery coordinator. In medium to large companies, developing and maintaining the disaster recovery plan is a full-time job.

Who is the ideal disaster recovery coordinator? There is no pat answer to this question. The coordinator does not require the highly technical skills set of a programmer, network analyst, hardware specialist, or systems administrator, but it is important that the candidate be able to communicate with technical staff and correctly interpret what they say in order to communicate it effectively to nontechnical users in reports, procedures, and other documentation.

It is important that the coordinator be organized, detail-oriented, and a competent writer. The candidate should be able to work methodically through complex problems and issues and be experienced in managing vendors and evaluating product offerings. He or she should also be fluent in project management principles and techniques. In addition to these skills, the coordinator will need highly developed qualities of patience, perseverance, and diplomacy.

There is a common theme in meetings of organizations for disaster recovery coordinators. Regardless of the initial level of enthusiasm and team spirit participants bring to the disaster recovery planning project, a substantial effort will be required to keep participation levels high. Planners need to cultivate enthusiasm and constantly reaffirm the buy-in of plan participants. Unless participants see the plan as their creation, nearly everyone will develop a resentment of the planning process.

DR planning is demanding work. IT operations personnel can easily come to view the coordinator's insistence on routine backups as an unwarranted interruption of their already overcrowded processing schedules. They need to be applauded for the work they are doing to safeguard the corporation's most important asset, information.

Similarly, application developers may be put off by the DR requirement that they pause periodically to document changes made to programs and systems so that work can be reconstructed in the event of disaster. Reinforcing the importance and value of their work—known in the vernacular as stroking their egos—may ensure their continued enthusiastic cooperation.

User departments may develop an intense dislike of the coordinator's constant testing and probing for possible gaps in their preventive and protective measures. The coordinator needs to work with users and ensure that they regard the procedures involved as their own effort, rather than a task that is being imposed on them from outside.

Senior management may even come to disdain spending money on a project that delivers little tangible return on investment. Coordinators can diffuse this trap before it occurs by exploring every possible dual-use or dual-value opportunity for disaster avoidance and recovery components.

The relationship with management works both ways. To supplement the skills that the coordinator brings to the job, the IT or business manager will have to provide the coordinator with authority to make decisions and to quell dissent, visible (and budgetary) support and enthusiasm for the planning effort, and personal support for the coordinator's ego.

No statistics are available to demonstrate the stress level associated with the position of disaster recovery coordinator, but considering the nature of the job—the need to confront the dark side of business survival daily and make the safety and security of fellow employees one's personal concern—the coordinator's stress level must rate somewhere between that of a dentist and a Middle East peace negotiator. The manager needs to recognize this and compensate for it, not only in salary, but by freeing the coordinator from other tasks and giving personal recognition and reinforcement for the valuable work that the coordinator is performing.

The above may convey the impression that fulfilling the role of DR coordinator is a thankless task. Before readers rush to put this book back on the shelf, it should be observed that there are few business roles that are more compelling and challenging than disaster recovery planning. Creating an effective team, working across the exclusive territories established by business units, developing innovative strategies to fit requirements, and playing the ombudsman for corporate safety and continuity comprise a dynamic set of tasks that appeal to one's creativity and provide an enormous sense of accomplishment.

A NOTE ON METHODOLOGY

A cursory examination of the literature will confirm that there are as many methodologies for developing disaster recovery plans as there are plan authors. This book seeks to find common ground by returning to the fundamental methodology of project management.

Fortunately, disaster recovery planning is too young an endeavor to have spawned argumentative schools of adherents to this or that guru's methodology. There are no gurus except, perhaps, those who have experienced and recovered from an actual disaster. Having talked with many of them in research for this book, they are wiser and somewhat modest about their accomplishment. Hardly the guru type.

This is not to say that there are not pretenders. In certain facets of disaster recovery plan development, one is almost certain to run up against a vendor representative, a plan author, or a risk manager who is convinced he or she has all the answers. The best policy is to listen. They may, after all, have a few worthwhile observations.

In the meantime, there are far more important and basic skills to master. One of the most important is one's ability to think systematically about the planning task. This is no mean feat: One must, after all, super-impose rationality on an event that is inherently chaotic—disaster.

It cannot be overstressed that disaster recovery planning is not some-thing that one can do perfectly the first time. Only by putting the plan on paper and testing it can its errors be realized and corrected. The only method is trial and error.

There are a few other points to make about the approach of this book to its subject. As previously observed, developing a disaster recovery plan is a project entailing the performance of many discrete tasks and the allo-cation of fixed resources. The end product of the effort is less a plan docu-ment than a recovery capability. The plan is only a roadmap for yet another project: recovery from an actual disaster.

To help the reader understand the objectives and alternative strate-gies that must be considered in the formulation of the plan, it is some-times necessary to describe in detail how the plan will be implemented in a disaster recovery project. To help the reader, a simple diagrammatic dis-tinction has been made between the planning project and the recovery project. When this book describes the plan development project, the ac-companying illustrations use the techniques of data flow diagramming. When the recovery project is described, flow charts are used.

Data flow diagrams, or DFDs, seem appropriate to the description of the plan development project since the project generally consists of ac-quiring, processing, and presenting information.[19] Figure 1–3 provides the context for the disaster recovery planning project. It shows the plethora of organizations—including corporate departments, professional groups, and regulatory agencies—that shape the environment of the planning en-deavor and form the reality against which plan adequacy is judged.

From this simple diagram, however, little can be discerned about the components of disaster recovery planning. Thus, in the coming chapters, the reader will find other DFDs that illustrate the major activities involved in the planning project.

For example, Figure 1–4 is a DFD depicting data flows and activities described in Chapter 1. Information resources, such as industry stan-dards, published disaster accounts, and legal mandates, are used to de-velop a rationale for the plan development project for presentation to senior management. Data from these sources is used to define methods (consultant or in-house development) and to create project outlines. Other inputs and outputs are also presented to account for the numerous tasks involved in the initial start-up phase of disaster recovery planning.

DFDs do not necessarily show precedence or chronological order of tasks. They are flexible, spatial constructs that the reader, it is hoped, will

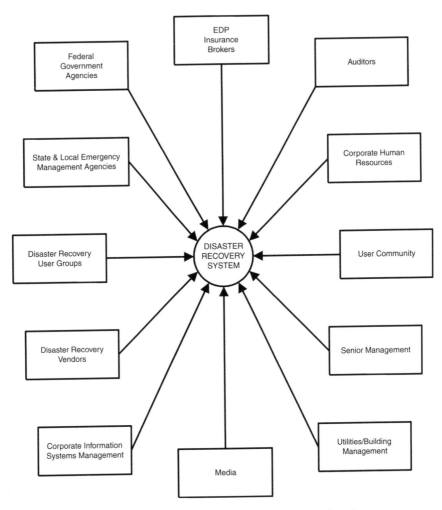

Figure 1–3   The context of disaster recovery planning.

find easy to apply to his or her planning requirements. As such, DFDs are preferable to the linear and rigid structure of a flow chart depicting tasks and milestones in the plan development project.

Elsewhere in this book, the reader will encounter flow charts that provide examples of master plans for various aspects of the recovery project. These flow charts attempt to superimpose order and sequence on recovery events. Flow charts are not intended as models to be rigorously followed, but as guides for creating and organizing one's own implemen-

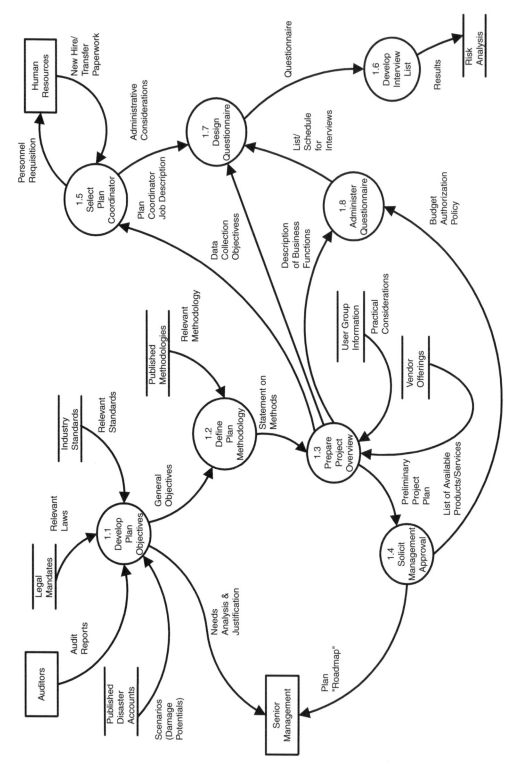

Figure 1–4 Initialization phase data flow diagram.

tation plan. A concatenated flow chart is provided at WWW.DRPLAN-NING.ORG, a web site that has been established to serve as a "living appendix" to this book.

It is hoped that this distinction in illustrations will help to clarify any confusion that may arise between the planning project and the implementation project that is its product.

ENDNOTES

1. D. O. Aasgaard, et al., "An Evaluation of Data Processing 'Machine Room' Loss and Selected Recovery Strategies," *MISRC Working Papers* (Minneapolis, MN: University of Minnesota, 1978).
2. Thomas Hoffman, "Denial Stalls Disaster Recovery Plans," *Computerworld*, 2/23/98.
3. Philip Jan Rothstein, Rothstein Associates, Brookfield, CT, comments to the author, 07/99.
4. Gary H. Anthes, "Lotsa Talk, Little Walk," *Computerworld*, 09/21/98.
5. *6ᵗʰ Annual Information Security Survey*, conducted in conjunction with *Computerworld*, Ernst & Young LLP, 1998.
6. Jaikumar Vijayan, "Client/Server Disaster Plans Fall Short," *Computerworld*, 11/03/97.
7. Bruce Caldwell, "Homestretch," *Information Week*, 07/19/99.
8. Eddy Goldberg, "DP Nightmare Hits N.Y. Bank," *Computerworld*, 12/02/85.
9. *Ibid.*
10. Dale Stackhouse and Kenneth T. Ungar, "The Foreign Corrupt Practices Act: Bribery, Corruption, Recordkeeping and More," *The Indiana Lawyer*, 04/21/93.
11. William Perry, "The Auditor, EDP, and the Federal Government," in *Data Processing Management* (New York: Auerbach Publishers, 1979).
12. *Ibid.*
13. *Ibid.*
14. Interview with Inspector Roy Williams, St. Petersburg, FL Fire Department, 9 January 1987.
15. Interviews with Maar Haack, EDP Underwriter, The St. Paul Insurance Companies, and Tom Cornwell, CHUBB Insurance Company, December 5–6, 1987.
16. *Ibid.*
17. Jon Toigo, "Alternatives for Disaster Recovery Plan Development," *Data Security Management* (New York: Auerbach Publishers, 1988).
18. Rothstein, *op. cit.*
19. Data flow diagram (DFD) standards taken from Tom DeMarco, *Structured Analysis and System Specification* (New York: Yourdon, 1979).

Just as a systems development project responds to user needs, a disaster recovery planning project responds to an organization's needs for survival and business resumption in the wake of a disaster. In disaster recovery planning, defining corporate needs is synonymous with identifying risks and exposures. This is accomplished through a series of analytical procedures.

- The business processes of a company need to be identified, together with the components of the IT infrastructure used to support each process. IT infrastructure components may include application software; servers and operating systems; data and data storage systems; local and wide area networks; and client systems including PCs, thin client devices and terminals. Key peripheral devices, such as printers, must also be identified.

- With business processes and their IT resources identified, disaster recovery planners need to turn their attention to the measuring the impact of unplanned interruption on each business process. This is done for two reasons: first, it provides insights that are of use in justi-

fying measures that must be taken to safeguard or provide continuity for the process, and second, the analysis assists in gauging the relative criticality of business processes to overall business continuity
so that recovery efforts can be prioritized.

- Most analyses also include the development of a list of threats and
the ranking of threats according to some rational strategy (i.e., likelihood of occurrence, depth or breadth of impact on company business
processes, anticipated cost to company, etc.). One benefit of a threat
assessment is that it can help guide the development of a plan so that
the plan can be implemented flexibly—in whole or in part—in response to a broad range of disaster scenarios.

This description covers considerable territory. It embraces concepts
and activities that some DR methodologians prefer to break down into
discrete practices such as Business Impact Analysis, Application Impact
Analysis, Threat and Exposure Analysis, and Risk Impact Analysis. To
avoid becoming identified with any of the rarified or proprietary methodologies that exist in the field, this discussion subsumes all of the preceding
activities under a single rubric: risk analysis. In the broadest sense, risk
analysis assesses what is vulnerable, the causes of vulnerability, and what
needs to be given priority for recovery.

Figure 2–1 is a DFD showing typical inputs and outputs of a risk
analysis. As one can readily see, risk analysis is key to the development of
objectives for many of the disaster recovery tasks that will follow. Its
many activities involve interviewing company IT personnel and users,
collating responses into a comprehensive view of the corporate information asset—segregated by business processes and their associated resource requirements, and formulating criteria and objectives for the plans
that will be created to safeguard this asset.

THE PURPOSES OF RISK ANALYSIS

Risk analysis is perhaps the single most misunderstood aspect of disaster
recovery planning. To many, the term is vague and mysterious, connoting
rarefied techniques and unintelligible calculations known to only a very
few privileged practitioners. To others, risk analysis is perceived as an irritating process of formalizing what is self-evident or obvious to anyone
with a modicum of horse sense.

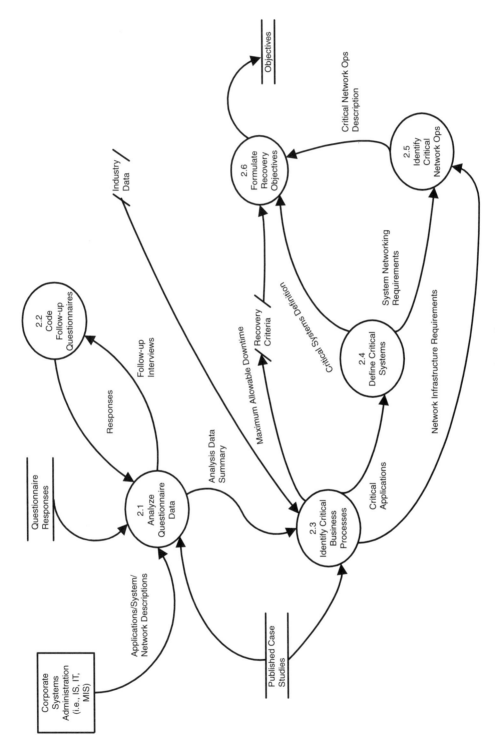

Figure 2–1 The analysis phase.

As one information manager put it, "There is a generally accepted statistic that places the likelihood of a major disaster for any business at right around one percent per year. This is the risk. And when you have a disaster, you either have one or you don't. That's the exposure. That's all the risk analysis that you need. You just prepare for the worst."

This is an oversimplification, of course, but the meaning is clear. Risk analysis is a big term for what is essentially a straightforward application of good research and common sense. This is indicated by the three basic objectives of risk analysis:

1. Identify business processes and their associated IT infrastructure re-source requirements (that is, the data, applications, systems, and net-works that are used in delivering the business process). Prioritize business processes according to time sensitivity and criticality.
2. Identify existing threats to business processes and infrastructure re-sources.
3. Define objectives for strategies to eliminate avoidable risks and to minimize the impact of risks that cannot be eliminated.

IDENTIFYING AND PRIORITIZING ASSETS AND FUNCTIONS

Risk analysis consists of two basic operations: *data collection* and *data analysis*. The data collected in risk analysis should include a comprehensive list of business processes and their infrastructure supports, including computer and network hardware and applications, databases, and system software. From these data, business process flow diagrams are created and annotated to show resource requirements. Additionally, planners need to collect information about the amount of activity, traffic, or use of infrastructure resources to deliver each business process during a normal business hour, day, week, or month.

Typically, the data listed above is collected from end users and IT personnel, often through the use of a paper questionnaire. Other collection methods may include in-person interviews, on-line or diskette-based surveys, and so on.

Users are in an excellent position to identify work procedures and overall business process criticality (see below). Technical personnel can usually address more specific questions such as operational hardware configurations, locations of data stores, and network connections. They also have access to data on numbers of transactions, traffic volumes, and other measures of business process activity.

The ultimate purpose of the questionnaire is to collect information on each business process and its infrastructure supports so that the criticality and recovery requirements can be assessed. Secondarily, the planner uses the data to develop a deeper understanding of dependencies that may exist between business processes.

With this data collected and analyzed, risk analysis can commence. Risk analysis seeks to identify which business processes and related infrastructure resources are critical to the business, what threats or exposures exist to unplanned interruption of business processes, and what costs accrue to an interruption based on duration.

The ability of a company to cope with the interruption of a business process determines the *tolerance* of the business process. In practical terms, tolerance may be expressed as a dollar value—the cost to the company if the business process is interrupted for a period of time.

It is worth noting that not all assessments of tolerance and cost are necessarily expressed as dollar values. Some organizations may be concerned about outages of applications for reasons other than lost dollars. Business processes that maintain customer service levels, support reputation in the market, or provide some other intangible value to the company may be deemed just as critical as business processes whose interruption results in dollar costs. Planners need to be sensitive to this fact and avoid classifying all business processes based only on a dispassionate assessment of their dollar value. For this discussion, cost is used as a straightforward indicator of business process value.

If there is a very low tolerance within the company to the interruption of a business process (typically the result of an infrastructure resource outage), this low tolerance is typically expressed as a high dollar value or cost. If, on the other hand, the company can tolerate to a significant extent the interruption of a business process, this high tolerance is typically expressed as a low dollar value or cost.

This concept cannot be overemphasized. The dollar value to the company of a given business process may have little to do with the dollar cost of the hardware or software used in the system. A PC, using an off-the-shelf spreadsheet package and a few hundred bytes of corporate financial data, may actually support a low-tolerance/high-cost business process. The corporation might more keenly feel its loss than the loss of any application running on an expensive network or mainframe platform.

Applications or equipment whose loss or outage would impact low tolerance business processes and entail great costs for the company are termed *critical.* Conversely, infrastructure resource supports for high-tolerance/low-cost business processes may be regarded as *noncritical.*

For example, the loss of a telemarketing company's telecommunications switch would represent a low-tolerance or high-dollar loss. For each minute that the switch is down, the company is unable to perform mission critical business processes, resulting in serious dollar losses. The telecommunications private branch exchange (PBX) switch, therefore, would be regarded as a critical system.

If, on the other hand, the same telemarketing firm were to lose the function of a computer application that is used to generate random telephone numbers, a noncritical business process, the financial impact of the outage would be very different. Since the company could readily change over to a manual system of random number generation, this application would not cost the company nearly as much as a telecommunications outage of the same duration. Thus, the application could be considered noncritical.

Of course, most companies have numerous business processes that depend upon a variety of systems, networks, and applications whose loss or interruption can be tolerated to varying degrees. Thus, a spectrum of tolerances exists between those systems or applications that are critical and those that are noncritical. For this reason, business process criticality is often expressed in a ranking or scale. This may be reflected in the end-user questionnaire, which might ask the respondent to rate the criticality of a business process and explain the reasons for the ranking.

With many business processes, tolerance to an outage or interruption is contingent upon the length of the outage or interruption. In an electrical power company, for example, customer billing processes may be sustainable for a brief period of time by reverting to manual methods. However, because a large part of the customer base for a power company is transient (i.e., the customers associated with a given meter may change several times over the course of a month), the efficiency of manual billing processes may be degraded over time. It may become difficult to keep pace with the changes, driving up the costs of the interrupted business process. Hence, over time, the utility's tolerance for the interruption of the normal business process may decrease, and the criticality of the process may increase.

Variances in tolerance may also be linked to the time of the day or month an interruption occurs. For many companies, a loss of their payroll process for a two-week period at month's end may be devastating. However, if the same interruption occurred at mid-month, tolerance might be far greater. Risk analysis, in general, assumes that an outage will always occur at the worst possible time.

COLLECTING INPUT FROM END USERS

It is not uncommon for users to identify mitigating factors, such as the timing of a disaster, when they assess the criticality of their applications. Applications are increasingly engineered to provide discrete business processes. Where this is the case, application may be used as a synonym for a business process.

To end users, time is a dynamic determinant of tolerance, for both economic and psychological reasons. Confronted with the news that an application is unavailable for use, the question that many users first ask is not why, but for how long. An outage of any length represents, in most cases, a need to make up time later—under stress or in costly overtime.

It is also quite common for users to begin a criticality assessment by stating that *all* of their applications (i.e., business processes) are critical—precisely because they are *their* applications. This categorization may seem like flagrant egotism, but it may reflect something quite different. Perhaps obtaining approval for application development was an uphill battle, or the development project itself took a deep personal toll. Whatever the rationale, few users (or systems administrators) like to believe that the work they do, or the applications they use, are anything less than critical to the company.

Planners are well advised to avoid provocative questions or insinuations when collecting end-user data. The criteria used to classify the criticality of applications must be clearly explained. The questionnaire should ask not how critical an application is but what steps a user would take to perform the same business function if the application were unavailable. Placed in this context, the determination of application criticality usually becomes less problematic for the questionnaire respondent.

More than one disaster recovery coordinator who has used the questionnaire method to gather information has discovered that users will provide a surprisingly fair assessment of their applications' criticality. One planner reported that three factors contributed to the success of a user poll at his company: First, each participant realized that other users were making similar concessions and complying with the classification scheme. Second, in group meetings held as a follow-up to the questionnaires, individuals who had displayed creativity or resourcefulness in developing coping strategies to deal with a hypothetical outage were given special praise or recognition by the coordinator. Third, everyone quickly realized that the classification of "his or her" business process or application as less-than-critical applied only in the event of a disaster. The coordinator stressed that, under normal conditions, every system or application played a necessary, vital role in the achievement of company goals.[1]

Critical applications are often defined as such because, regardless of duration of the outage or the time of month in which an outage occurs, there are no substitute methods for providing the functions of the application. Electronic commerce applications used by on-line brokers, for example, are clearly mission critical.

In April 1999, an outage of less than two hours at on-line broker, E-Trade, and its subsequent reportage on the front page of the *Wall Street Journal*, resulted in a 50% drop in the company's stock price and a 330% increase in complaint calls to the Securities and Exchange Commission concerning on-line investing.[2] According to George Ferguson, Hewlett Packard Company's Business Recovery Services Marketing Manager, this phenomenon has generated a "push in the mission-critical industry."

> The first generation of e-commerce/e-services companies don't have service level objectives in place. Their customers are early adopters and are more tolerant of outages. But, this is changing quickly. The customer drives the requirement to bring up the service level. The next generation companies are entering a much more competitive market. Consumers are demanding more. They have a much lower tolerance to outages and interruptions and it is less costly for them to simply switch to another vendor if the one they normally use has an outage.[3]

This example illustrates clearly how the criticality of an application/business process may be directly linked to market forces. And e-commerce is not the only application area where this connection holds, according to Tony Martinez, General Manager for IBM Business Continuity and Recovery Services. He points to the trend in many companies to migrate business-critical applications from mainframes to client/server Enterprise Resource Planning (ERP) software suites in response to legacy Y2K concerns.

Says Martinez, the criticality of ERP to managing the total supply chain for the company is driving new recovery technologies designed to eradicate downtime completely. These include wide area disk storage mirroring as a replacement for tape backup. Mirroring, in theory, can provide automatic, near instantaneous recovery of multiterabyte ERP databases at an alternate location in the event that access to data at the normal production facility is compromised. The expense of such a technology can only be cost-justified based on the absolute criticality of ERP business processes, according to Martinez.[4] The benefits and potential drawbacks of mirroring are discussed in greater detail in Chapter 4.

The criticality of a business process extends to its infrastructure supports, such as a database in Martinez's ERP example. In most cases, it is safe to categorize certain infrastructure components, including electrical power systems, air conditioning systems, communications network "local loops" (connections between the company premises and the telecommunications provider's local point of presence or central office), and other fundamental resources required by all business processes, as critical. Without backups or manual means of control, a loss of any of these systems *at any time* may represent a total cessation of normal business operations.

In engineering terminology, these resources are sometimes described as *single points of failure.* Within any complex system, there are usually components or processes that, if not replicated or otherwise backed up by redundant capabilities, represent points of failure for the entire system. A large part of disaster avoidance planning comes down to identifying single points of failure wherever they exist and eliminating them. This may include complex arrangements to secure alternate utility providers for the corporate data center to simple plans to eliminate notebook computer "docking stations" that can impair recovery efforts. (Docking stations provide desktop attachment points for some types of portable computers, providing such functions as auxiliary hard disk drives, LAN connectivity, and AC power when the computer user is in the office. Typically, docking stations are unusable when a power outage occurs and may prevent access to vital auxiliary disk-based data and LANs while the portable computer operates in battery power mode.)

In addition to fundamental infrastructure supports, other infrastructure components, including hardware, software, and networks, derive their criticality from the support they provide to a specific critical business process. Often criticality can be determined by asking end users a pointed question: How would you deal with an application interruption that was one hour in duration, or 24 hours, or 48 hours, or 72 hours? If no coping strategies can be identified by the respondent, and if tolerance to interruption is low, the application and its infrastructure resources are likely to be critical.

A CRITICALITY SPECTRUM

In the context of conventional information processing, applications may be defined on the following spectrum of tolerance:

- **Critical.** These functions cannot be performed unless identical capabilities are found to replace the company's damaged capabilities.

Critical applications cannot be replaced by manual methods under any circumstances. Tolerance to interruption is very low and the cost of interruption is very high. Thus, for critical systems and applications, the company would need to arrange to have access to hardware comparable to its own, and in an emergency, plan to transfer the application to the backup hardware in order to resume processing.

- **Vital.** These functions cannot be performed by manual means or can be performed manually for only a very brief period of time. There is somewhat higher tolerance to interruption and somewhat lower costs, provided that functions are restored within a certain time-frame (usually four or five days). In applications classified as vital, a brief suspension of processing can be tolerated, but a considerable amount of "catching up" will be needed to restore data to a current or usable form.

- **Sensitive**. These business processes can be performed, with difficulty but at tolerable cost, by manual means for an extended period of time. Sensitive applications, however, require considerable "catching up" once restored.

- **Noncritical.** These applications may be interrupted for an extended period of time, at little or no cost to the company, and require little or no "catching up" when restored.

Figure 2–2 illustrates this spectrum of tolerances. It should be noted that this classification scheme may be extended from business processes to their infrastructure resources, including hardware, software, networks, and even to data itself. Classification schemes employed by planners will vary from company to company. As previously noted, the basis for categorizing a specific business process as critical may have more to do with corporate culture than with prospective dollar losses accrued to an unplanned interruption. The important thing is to document the rationale used to assess criticality so that auditors and others can understand them.

Disaster recovery service providers, such as Hewlett Packard Business Recovery Services and IBM BCRS, are working on similar business process criticality assumptions to define appropriate services for their customers. In the case of Hewlett Packard, this takes the form of a "portfolio of services," which the company unveiled in 1999. According to Ferguson, "Certain business processes are worth every dime spent to recover them, while others are not so critical."

At the very high end, we will offer data replication and other technologies designed to keep business processes available through all circum-

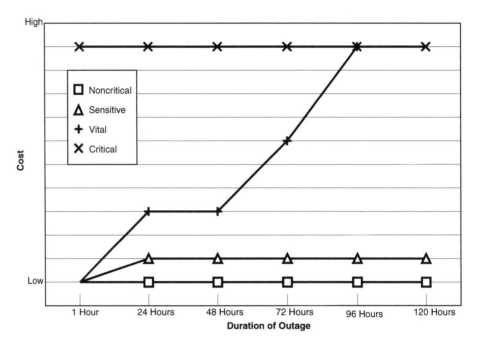

Figure 2–2   Relative tolerances to business process interruptions.

stances. Companies may be looking at $750,000 per year to achieve high availability uptime solutions. For other business processes, there are three lower availability solutions that extend recovery intervals to between eight hours and three days. The pricing reflects that. From $750,000, there is a huge price drop to below $100,000 per year for a lower availability solution."[5]

HP's example, which is likely to take hold industry-wide, underscores the importance of risk analysis. Choosing the appropriate services from a disaster recovery vendor will become increasingly tied to a customer estimate of business process criticality. One goal of risk analysis is to apply a classification scheme to each company process or asset that the disaster recovery plan will seek to protect.

COLLECTING DATA ON OUTAGE COSTS

In cases where business process interruptions may be measured in terms of dollar cost, the questionnaire analysis method can be harnessed to compile some compelling cost justifications for disaster recovery planning. In addition to asking users to classify their application's criticality and identify strategies for coping with outages, another question should be asked during initial data collection: What would outages of the specified duration cost the company?

User departments are often able to compile accurate estimates about the cost of downtime. They may have documented the impact of past interruption events or they may have compiled data describing normal operations costs for use in demonstrating departmental performance. Many times this data can be adapted to show the value of the work that would be lost if an interruption occurred.

For example, a marketing manager might keep data on the department's average daily sales of product in order to set sales goals for the next sales period. Using this statistic, the loss of on-line ordering systems for two days could be evaluated as a dollar loss.

The permutations, as those who regularly perform risk analyses have observed, can be quite ingenious. They can also be useful in addressing budgetary concerns that often arise when it comes time to fund disaster avoidance and recovery capabilities.

IDENTIFYING THREATS TO ASSETS AND FUNCTIONS

Once the criticality of business processes has been assessed, another objective of risk analysis is to identify what threats exist to normal business operations.

There are a variety of schemes for classifying threats, with most endeavoring to create a taxonomy for use in analysis. One scheme classifies threats by causal origin, either man-made or natural. Another classification scheme uses locational scope, with distinctions drawn between facility and regional disasters.

These taxonomies have little merit in planning, and the distinctions they introduce tend to obfuscate more than they clarify. The dividing line, for example, between man-made and natural disaster potentials is often unclear until long after the disaster event has passed. Whether a fire was started by a negligent employee or by a bolt of lightning is, practically speaking, irrelevant to disaster recovery.

Similarly, the regional-versus-facility distinction provides a poor analytical tool. Practically speaking, a regional disaster, such as a hurricane, may have a no less debilitating effect on business operations than would a facility disaster (and, in fact, a regional disaster will in many cases also damage the facility).

The best method for identifying threats is to look at the phenomena, regardless of root cause, that typically interrupt normal business processes. These may include:

- Water damage (whether from leaky pipes or floods)
- Fire (heat) damage (whether from arson, equipment overheating, environmental contamination, lightning strikes, etc.)
- Power failure (originating at the customer premises or across the power grid)
- Network failure (LAN or WAN, whether component or line based)
- Mechanical hardware failure or software failure (whether due to human error, short circuits, normal parts wear and tear, or building collapse following an earthquake)
- Accidental or deliberate destruction or corruption of hardware, software, or data (by hackers, disgruntled employees, industrial saboteurs, terrorists, or misbehaving software)
- Other causes (including forced evacuation for environmental hazards, aircraft crashes, etc.)

Many novice planners become mired down in an effort to define every conceivable risk scenario. A preferred strategy is to plan for a worst case scenario, one that portends an interruption of all business processes, and to develop a plan with such a scenario in mind. Organizing recovery procedures rationally—by business process, for example—provides for flexible implementation and enables the plan to be activated, in whole or in part, in response to a number of disaster events.

THE PROBLEM WITH PROBABILITY

If there is one debate in the disaster recovery planning field that equates to the "How many angels can dance on the head of a pin?" argument, it centers on which type of disaster occurs most frequently. Many planners wish that there was an actuarial table or set of probability statistics that could be used to assess the precise risk posed by each disaster potential. There isn't, and this fact has created more pointless discussions in DR circles than virtually any other issue.

Information security professionals point to the computer virus as the culprit behind the greatest number of business interruptions. Natural disaster statisticians point to the much greater dollar cost per incident of major hurricanes, earthquakes, floods, and tornadoes.

The Federal Emergency Management Agency points to fires as the number one disaster potential, but quickly adds that floods are in second place. Floods account for nine out of ten presidential disaster declarations and cause property damage in excess of $1 billion per year.[6]

Hard disk drive manufacturers, who equate disaster with data loss, blame user and software errors for the preponderance of drive failures. By contrast, data recovery vendors, such as Ontrack Data International, place the blame squarely at the feet of the hard disk manufacturers, claiming that 44% of the data recovery jobs they receive are the result of hardware malfunctions (see Figure 2–3).[7]

Reliable business disaster data, organized by type of disaster, are difficult to obtain for a variety of reasons. For the purposes of this book, it will suffice to say that each of the disaster potentials addressed in the above list is a cause of significant interruptions each year in mission-critical operations. Having said this, some statistical information may be useful, not to evaluate threat probability, but to aid in building management awareness or to sensitize company employees about threats.

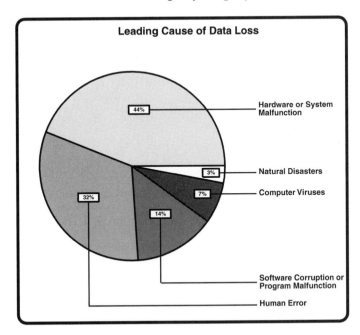

Figure 2–3   Leading causes of data loss. (*Source:* Ontrack Data International, Inc., Eden Prairie, MN. Reprinted with permission.)

A FEW COMPELLING STATISTICS

It was the position of major EDP insurers about a decade ago that, because of improvements in fire detection and suppression systems and increased industry awareness to the threat of fire, flooding (water) was the number one threat to corporate data processing.[8]

Water damage frequently results from fire-fighting techniques, but fires themselves claimed an annual average of 1239 data centers and telephone switch rooms annually from 1980 to 1996, according to the National Fire Protection Association (NFPA). The direct property damage to facilities averaged $24.98 million in the same period.[9]

NFPA provides additional information on structure fires that were started by electronic equipment but did not originate in equipment rooms themselves (e.g., fires in user work areas, rather than data centers). These fires averaged 990 in number, causing damage estimated at an average $20.47 million per year from 1992 through 1996, though the preponderance of events (320 in the period covered) originated in one- or two-family dwellings.[10]

The study goes on to point out that only 28% of the fires originating with electronic equipment were in facilities with automatic suppression equipment (such as sprinkler systems or other extinguishing agents).[11] This continues a "tradition" of unprotected user work areas that contributed to a fire at the U.S. Postal Service headquarters in October 1984. In that instance, fire claimed more than 500 PCs in user work areas and cost the U.S.P.S. approximately $20 million. Disaster recovery planning and disaster prevention did not extend to user work areas where PCs were in great use.[12]

In addition to fires, floods, and other disaster potentials, power failures, mechanical breakdowns, software malfunctions, network outages, and computer sabotage, hacking and viruses account for the balance of the IT disasters that business suffers in any given year.

According to a survey conducted of 500 small businesses by Los Angeles, CA-based Impulse Research, 90% of those interviewed reported experiencing at least one power outage in 1998. Of this group, 26% reported two outages in the period, while 12% indicated that they had experienced five or more outages. The preponderance of interviewees attributed power outages to storms and lightning, but more than 50% blamed at least one of their power outages on problems at their power company. Of the outages blamed on the power company, further investigation revealed that accidents or construction accounted for 18% of blackouts; floods for 8%; with electrical fires, earthquakes, and strikes taking the blame for the balance.[13]

A June 1999 survey of more than 800 commercial and industrial companies by energy industry analyst E SOURCE gleaned an outage record bordering on insanity. Said respondents, their companies had sustained an average of nearly 15 outages during a twelve-month period, at a total cost of more than $7 billion per year. Bill LeBlanc, Vice President of E SOURCE remarked, "This is a huge level of loss for U.S. and Canadian businesses to sustain. If you look beyond the seven sectors surveyed in our study, national outage costs could be five to ten times as high." He also noted a growing market for uninterruptible power supplies (UPS), battery backups for commercial power that provide a hedge against momentary power outages.[14]

Like power outages, public telephone service outages also take a toll on business process availability annually. The Federal Communications Commission (FCC), concerned about a series of lengthy and extensive outages in 1991, created the Network Reliability Council in 1992 and issued a requirement for carriers to report outages lasting 30 minutes or longer and impacting 30,000 or more customers. Together with the Alliance for Telecommunications Industry Solutions (ATIS), the NRC began collecting data from carriers and generated a report in 1996, classifying telecom outages by cause.

Between 1992 and 1995, the leading causes of outages were line dig-ups, other line-related problems, and hardware failures. Procedural problems and software design errors filled out the causal list. The average number of reported failures between 1993 and 1994 was 180. This climbed to 280 in 1995, owing mainly to increases in dig-ups and hardware failures at telco facilities.

Dig-ups, especially of fiber optic cable trunks (cable conduits carrying tens of thousands of fiber optic cable strands), required on average six hours to repair in the 1992-to-1995 period. Switch related problems climbed steadily from an outage duration of 1.2 hours in 1992 to 2.5 hours of downtime per event in 1995.[15]

Analysts speculated in 1997 that increased demand for Internet access would increase trunking requirements (the number of communications lines—copper or fiber optic—that the telco needs to deploy and maintain) and place even greater loads on switches. This, in turn, could lead to a dramatic increase the number of outages attributable to carrier overloads.[16] The many outages that have affected the Internet and World Wide Web through the end of the decade appear to bear out these predictions.

The occasional stoppages of the Internet may have an upside, however, as they offer a temporary respite from the seemingly endless barrage of email viruses that became an almost weekly occurrence in 1999. Even as the reasonably benign "Happy99.exe" and "Melissa" Microsoft Word macro virus were becoming a memory, industry analysts were speculating in mid-April that mutant strains of Melissa, carrying destructive payloads, might be in the offing.

First "Chernobyl", then "Pretty Park," and in June, the extremely destructive "Explore.Zip" worm appeared. In response to the Explore.Zip worm infections, PricewaterhouseCoopers, Boeing, and Microsoft Corporation, among others, were forced to take their Internet email systems offline for nearly 6 hours. Experts projected that the problem would worsen as 2000 approached, with many virus program writers seized upon January 1 as a "trigger date" for the activation of hidden viruses.[17]

According to a 1998 Computer Virus Prevalence Survey from the International Computer Security Association (ICSA), the rate of virus attacks has been growing steadily since 1996. Encounters with viruses grew from approximately one infection per 1000 PCs annually in 1994 to 31 per 1000 PCs annually in 1998 (see Figure 2–4). [18]

Common sources of viruses in 1998 consisted of infected diskettes brought to the workplace from home by employees (36%) and infected email received via the Internet (32%) (see Figure 2–5).[19] Experts agree that Internet email has now become the leading source of infection. Finally, in

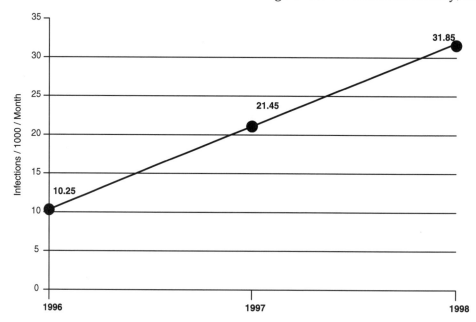

Figure 2–4   Virus infections per 1000 computers per month, 1996–1998. (*Source: ICSA 1998 Computer Virus Prevalence Survey,* International Computer Security Association, Carlisle, PA.)

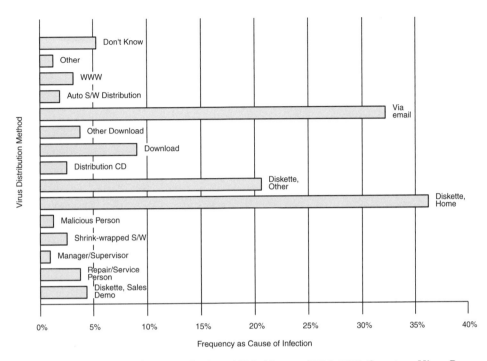

Figure 2–5   Sources of virus infection, 1998. (*Source: ICSA 1998 Comptuer Virus Preva-lence Survey,* International Computer Security Association, Carlisle, PA.)

1998, ICSA says that the cost per incident was approximately $2400 and complete recovery took on average 45.6 hours per infection.[20]

Again, the purpose of citing industry statistics on disaster potentials is not to suggest that they are predictors of actual disasters. In risk analysis, it is valuable to know what the threats are in order to develop scenarios that will serve as the basis for planning prevention and recovery strategies. For example, it is valuable to know at what temperatures various media burn (see Table 2–1) in order to assess the protection afforded by fireproof cabinets of various ratings.

On the other hand, there is a hardcore group of risk managers and analysts who take this investigation to the extreme by quantifying the likelihood of each threat and expressing this percentage as a corporate financial exposure. However, the admonition of the information manager quoted earlier should be observed: "Either you have a disaster or you don't." Hence, the practical value of threat identification is twofold: (1) It serves to point out where disaster avoidance measures (such as fire suppression systems, security access systems, and power protection systems)

Table 2–1   Temperatures at which Damage
                Begins to Occur

Computer Equipment	175°F
Magnetic Tape/Diskettes	100–120°F
Magnetic Disk	150°F
Paper/Punch Cards	350°F
Microfilm/Microfiche	225°F (with steam) 300°F (without steam)

may be needed; and (2) it identifies specific vulnerabilities that plans and procedures must specifically address.

Another benefit of the threat identification process is less methodological than psychological. Focusing a group's attention on the threat potential can increase members' awareness and sensitivity. It can also facilitate group cohesion and unity in the disaster recovery planning effort because it helps the group recognize the importance of the work it will perform. This is extremely important, since there is much in the risk analysis process, including the classification of system criticality, to divide the group.

Threat identification may also serve to make participants more aware of the interdependencies that exist among them and build team unity by clarifying shared vulnerabilities. In this way, threat identification can set the stage for cost sharing in expensive threat avoidance systems and cooperation in other essential areas.

DEVELOPING PLAN OBJECTIVES

Having classified business process/application criticality, assigned costs to outages of various duration, and identified threats to systems and data, it remains to analyze this data to formulate a set of specific objectives to guide the development of the recovery capability. The goal is to eliminate exposures that can be eliminated and to minimize the effects of those that cannot be eliminated.

This analysis does not lend itself readily to "group think," although follow-up interviews with users and system administrators may help the disaster recovery coordinator better understand requirements and set objectives. In fact, certain exposures may not fall under the aegis of the disaster recovery coordinator and, thus, require coordination with the security manager, auditor, or other authorized persons.

Threats related to the intentional abuse by persons who are not corporate employees are typically viewed as security threats. Obviously, if a hacker demolishes a network or erases critical data, these activities may have an impact equivalent to a disaster. Security planning is a companion discipline to disaster recovery planning, and the two functions must work together to accomplish their respective goals.

To address effectively the other threats to normal operations, such as fire and flooding, the disaster recovery coordinator will need to work with individuals at practically every level within the company. This is because of the nature of the planning project.

As Figure 2–6 illustrates, the objectives of disaster recovery planning are to develop both a plan and a permanent, ongoing disaster prevention and recovery capability. Installation of a fire prevention system will require the cooperation of the data center manager or department manager in whose area the system is being installed. Similarly, the coordination of a regular schedule of off-site storage for important records, storage media, and microfiche will require the full participation of those who create and use these items.

A set of clearly stated objectives, identifying the conditions, tasks, and standards for each protection or recovery strategy, is often a prerequisite for justifying the strategy to those who will have to absorb the cost and/or modify their existing procedures. Representatives of the affected department and senior management will want to know what the coordi-

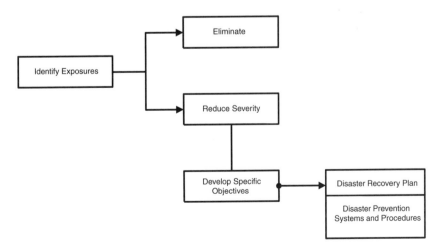

Figure 2–6   Objectives development in risk control.

nator is specifically seeking to do and will want to see how all of the objectives fit together in a comprehensive recovery strategy.

The following is a generic, but by no means comprehensive, set of objectives that may result from a risk analysis. Each objective assumes that sufficient information has been collected to justify the need for the tasks. Objectives are organized under section titles that define the function or area that the objectives are designed to address. (If the objectives seem a little bit like a job description for the disaster recovery coordinator, this is only because they reflect the assumption made at the outset: Disaster recovery planning is a full-time task.)

Company Policy

1. The disaster recovery coordinator will develop and seek senior management approval for a company policy for the protection of people, property, and assets (within a specified timeframe) that meets current company standards and format for documentation.

This objective addresses itself to the need to undertake disaster recovery planning, to obtain management approval and support, and to generate a paper plan within a set timeframe. It also assigns responsibility for the task to the disaster recovery coordinator.

Plan Maintenance

2. The disaster recovery coordinator will develop a schedule for periodic review and maintenance of the plan and advise all personnel of their roles and the deadline for receiving revisions and comments.
3. The disaster recovery coordinator will collate reviewer revisions and comments and update the plan within 30 days of the review date.
4. The disaster recovery coordinator will arrange and coordinate scheduled and unscheduled tests of the disaster recovery plan to evaluate its adequacy.
5. The disaster recovery coordinator will participate in scheduled plan tests that will be performed X times per year on (specific dates). For all scheduled and unscheduled tests, the coordinator will write evaluations of test results and integrate test results into the disaster recovery plan within 30 days.
6. The disaster recovery coordinator will develop a schedule for training recovery personnel in emergency and recovery procedures as set forth in the disaster recovery plan. Training dates should be scheduled within 30 days of each plan revision and scheduled plan test.

7. The disaster recovery coordinator will maintain records of plan maintenance activities (testing, training, and reviews) and submit these for examination by internal and external auditors.

This section sets forth the objectives for maintaining the plan and empowers the disaster recovery coordinator to initiate and supervise plan maintenance activities. It will be the IT manager's job to ensure that the disaster recovery coordinator is provided with the authority to fulfill these responsibilities.

Physical Environment

8. The disaster recovery coordinator will collect information regarding company facilities and assess existing structures and facilities for their susceptibility to earthquake-, fire-, and water-related damage, as well as criminal intrusion, and will report the findings in memoranda to senior management, IT management, and departmental management.

This objective specifically seeks to assess facility-related risk factors so that they may be addressed in the disaster recovery plan or through the development of loss prevention capabilities. (Facility-related risk factors are explored in greater detail in Chapter 3.) Obviously, the results of the departmental risk analyses are provided to those persons who will need to underwrite the costs of acquiring a specific avoidance or recovery capability. Risk factors and potential costs are typically communicated as a part of a cost-justification for the capabilities that are being proposed.

Organizational Control

9. The disaster recovery coordinator will work with departmental managers or system/network administrators to develop informational programs to advise all employees within the department of the assets and functions they are expected to safeguard, the events they are to note and/or report, and the immediate actions they are to take in response to disaster events.
10. The disaster recovery coordinator will work with departmental management to develop a formal "ownership" program in order to assign responsibility for each and every resource to individual employees within the department.

This section provides the means for employees and managers to aid the disaster recovery coordinator in the early detection and correction of potentially hazardous or debilitating conditions or practices. The disaster recovery coordinator may be called upon to draft these disaster avoidance procedures, or the task may be assigned to the department manager once the specific procedures and guidelines have been identified.

The second objective, to establish an "ownership" program, may be familiar to security planners, with whom the concept originated. However, system or application ownership has relevance in the context of disaster recovery planning as well.[21] The practice of assigning ownership of equipment or functions to employees is tantamount to giving the employee "owner" the right to say who may use the resource. At first glance, this may seem to invite friction and disputes among employees. However, the experience of many organizations that use ownership programs demonstrates that the opposite effect typically results.

Ownership programs often help employees become more attentive to the secure and qualified use of "their" resources. Abuse of systems or misuse due to inadequate training may be spotted sooner so that the detection and correction of errors can be undertaken before the problem creates an outage.

Human Resources

11. The disaster recovery coordinator will work with the human resources department to develop procedures for notifying IT managers of pending employee terminations or separations.

12. The disaster recovery coordinator will work with the human resources department to develop procedures for maintaining a telephone directory to be used in contacting recovery team members in the event of a disaster.

13. The disaster recovery coordinator will work with the human resources department to develop a program designed to foster safety awareness among employees of the company.

The human resources connection is a vital one for a variety of security and disaster recovery-related reasons. In some companies, human resources will be responsible for making employees aware of where to go to continue work in the event of a disaster.

Human resources may also be called upon to set a policy providing for the immediate dismissal of employees who abuse systems and to set into motion a procedure that will see a terminated employee's access passwords and file permissions revoked and company property reclaimed.

Human resources may also be asked to assess the psychological strengths of employees who will be called upon to provide key recovery functions. Knowing how an employee is likely to behave under stress and having access to the employee's personal data (marital status, home address, home and emergency contact telephone numbers) can be critical for evaluating his or her suitability to participate directly in recovery or salvage activities.

14. The disaster recovery coordinator will work together with systems administrators and network management personnel to coordinate data backup programs.
15. The disaster recovery coordinator will identify all documentation and forms required for continuation of normal operations following a disaster and ensure that adequate supplies are inventoried in a secure, access-controlled location.
16. The disaster recovery coordinator will document network and system integrity control measures.
17. The disaster recovery coordinator will ensure that master and/or firmware passwords and/or encryption/decryption standards are recorded and stored in a secure, access-controlled location.

Operational and access control measures are typical features of data processing or network operations; they are the backbone of security in normal, day-to-day operations. However, they can present a nightmare for disaster recovery. If systems administrators or network operations personnel cannot be located at the time of a disaster, it is possible that the recovery of impacted business processes will be delayed because master passwords or data encryption keys, known only to the administrator, are unavailable. A related concern: the lack of procedural or software documentation or preprinted forms used in normal operations can also delay recovery.

Applications Development

18. The disaster recovery coordinator will develop and implement a schedule of routine backup and documentation for applications under development.

Applications development projects, which represent a substantial investment of company time and resources, should be backed up to prevent disastrous loss. If industry-accepted documentation standards are observed and enforced, this objective may have already been met. However, the disaster recovery coordinator should verify this.

Systems and Networks

19. The disaster recovery coordinator will quantify, to the extent possible, the dollar loss potential to the company of business process/application outages of fixed duration for every business process/application in the company, identifying infrastructure components including mainframe, mini-, and microcomputer-based systems, telecommunications systems, and data networks.

20. The disaster recovery coordinator will develop a disaster recovery capability that provides for recovery of critical applications within X hours.

21. The disaster recovery coordinator will document responsibilities of key recovery personnel in the event of a disaster.

22. The disaster recovery coordinator will develop minimum acceptable configurations for systems and networks that will provide emergency service levels for X hours, or until normal operations are restored.

23. The disaster recovery coordinator will develop strategies for the replacement of business process infrastructure resources by manual or automated means for a period of X hours in the event of a disaster.

24. The disaster recovery coordinator will develop sufficient alternative vendors or sources of supply for each resource required for business process recovery in a minimum acceptable configuration in order to provide in an acceptable level of risk mitigation.

These objectives begin to approach tasks that are generally recognized as the exclusive domain of disaster recovery planning. They set a timetable for recovery of interrupted business processes in emergency mode. This number is expressed as a goal: Critical applications will be up and running at emergency service levels within X hours.

Furthermore, the tentative recovery timeframe is set forth: Recovered applications will need to be operated at emergency levels for X hours/days, which is the estimated time required to relocate to the original or to a new permanent operating site.

The term "minimum acceptable system configuration" in the above objectives is also significant. It refers to the fact that recovery systems and networks need not be mirror images of predisaster systems and networks.

If only critical application service levels are being provided, for example, end-user client workstation requirements might be drastically reduced. Also, storage capacity requirements may not be as great if the amount of data required by partially restored systems is reduced.

For voice and data communications, a smaller telecommunications switch might suffice to replace a full-sized private branch exchange (PBX). An analysis of capacity requirements might reveal that critical communications activity can be adequately sustained with fewer incoming trunks and fewer wide area service lines.

Whatever strategies are developed for system or network recovery, they must be cost-justified by demonstrating how much it would cost the company if it did not have the capabilities in the event of a disaster. The backup strategies and configurations that are formulated must be documented in advance, the documentation must be made available to those who will rebuild systems in an emergency, and provisions must be made for two or more sources to supply hardware and supplies that will be needed for reconstruction.

Backup/Off-Site Storage

25. The disaster recovery coordinator will assess and contract with a qualified vendor of off-site storage services according to the guidelines set forth by PRISM International (formerly, the Association of Commercial Records Centers), or some comparable body.

26. Having documented the criticality of data, applications, systems, and networks, the disaster recovery coordinator will identify the following resources for backup and/or removal to off-site storage:
    a. Hard copies of system documentation, user manuals, operating procedures, vital paper records, disaster recovery plans, and other documentation that might be useful or essential to recovery.
    b. Critical, vital, and sensitive data stored on magnetic or photographic media.
    c. Stocks of forms and supplies that are necessary for recovery and subject to delays in resupply.

27. The disaster recovery coordinator or designate will inventory materials stored off-site at 60-day intervals and periodically audit materials for completeness and integrity in accordance with the latest update of the plan.

28. The disaster recovery coordinator will assess options and recommend strategies for system and network backup that meet business process recovery requirements in the most cost-effective way.

29. The disaster recovery coordinator will make all advance arrangements that are necessary to facilitate the logistics of the transition from normal system operation to emergency system operation, including the transportation of resources, the acquisition and delivery of emergency supplies and materials, and the rerouting or activation of telecommunications networks.

These objectives go to the heart of the disaster recovery capability. When realized, they provide the means for recovery and the methods for implementing the recovery strategy.

Emergency Action

30. The disaster recovery coordinator will document all procedures and policies of civil or government organizations that might impact on the company's recovery strategy.
31. The disaster recovery coordinator will develop procedures that provide for the monitoring of all alarm sources, including fire alarms and weather and emergency radio.
32. The disaster recovery coordinator will develop clear decision trees (decision-making flowcharts) that assign specific personnel responsibility for invoking the disaster recovery plan. These procedures will fully identify the criteria for decision making.
33. The disaster recovery coordinator will document the notification procedure that will be observed when the plan is invoked.
34. The disaster recovery coordinator will develop sound evacuation and immediate action procedures and train all personnel in their use. Periodic drills in evacuation will be conducted with the consent of department managers.
35. The disaster recovery coordinator will develop a strategy/facility for management command, communication, and control of recovery efforts in the wake of a disaster.

The orderly evacuation of facilities is prerequisite in disaster recovery planning, which seeks first and foremost to safeguard human life. In addition to the need (and legal requirement) to assign evacuation routes and drill employees in their use, it is also necessary to identify how and by whom the disaster recovery plan will be invoked to initiate recovery strategies.

Some disasters occur suddenly and without warning. Others, such as hurricanes, may develop over a period of time, allowing for a last-minute backup and an orderly shutdown of systems. These differences would be reflected in the logic of a decision tree included in the plan.

Furthermore, the procedures for warning and evacuating populations used by civil government authorities can have a direct impact on the implementation of the disaster recovery plan. In hurricane-prone areas, for example, it is not unusual for businesses in vulnerable areas to be evacuated while a storm is still quite distant and has a very small chance of striking anywhere in the vicinity of the business. Evacuation orders employ the logic of mass population movements, not of business resumption. Thus, the timetable with which government emergency managers work may be very different from the timetable of the disaster recovery plan.[22]

Finally, this section introduces the idea of an Emergency Operations Center (EOC), a facility (physical or virtual) from which senior management will be able to monitor and manage the recovery effort.

Articulating Objectives

These thirty-five objectives are very general and generic. Those developed for a particular company will reflect the company's specialized needs in the area of disaster recovery. Once developed, plan objectives should be articulated to those who will provide spending authorization and those who will actually develop strategies and procedures based on the objectives.

Procedures development can be a lengthy process involving hours of research, consulting, writing, reviewing, and rewriting. During this process, the coordinator should take some immediate steps to provide basic protections for the data centers and user departments. These protective measures are the subject of Chapter 3.

ENDNOTES

1. Kenneth N. Myers, "Avoiding a Crisis," *Datamation*, 1/2/86.
2. Stacy Collett, "E-brokers' Snafus Provide Lessons," *Computerworld*, 4/12/99.
3. Interview with George Ferguson, Marketing Manager, Hewlett Packard Company Business Recovery Services, Palo Alto, CA, June 1999.
4. Interview with Tony Martinez, General Manager, IBM Business Continuity and Recovery Services, Sterling Forest, NY, June 1999.
5. Ferguson interview.

6. Federal Emergency Management Agency, "Backgrounder: Floods and Flash Floods," FEMA Publication, Washington, DC, January 1998.

7. Interview with Stuart Hanley, Vice President of World Wide Operations, Ontrack Data International, Eden Prarie, MN, June 1999.

8. Interview with Maar Haack, EDP underwriter for St. Paul Fire and Marine, St. Paul, MN, January 1987.

9. John R. Hall, Jr., *Special Analysis Package: Computer Equipment and Computer Areas*, National Fire Protection Association, Quincy, MA, February 1999.

10. *Ibid.*

11. *Ibid.*

12. Interview with Steve Skolochencko, data security branch, US Postal Service, Washington, DC, August and October 1987.

13. "Power Outages Cost Small Business Big Bucks," *Power Online*, 3/24/99.

14. "Electricity Outages Cost Corporations Billions And It Also May Make Them Run From Their Current Utility," E SOURCE Press Release, E SOURCE, Inc., Boulder, CO, 6/10/99.

15. Alliance for Telecommunications Industry Solutions, Network Reliability Steering Committee, "Fixing Facility Outages: Building Tools to Make It Happen," ATIS Facilities Solution Team Report, November 1997.

16. William Taren, "How Reliable Is the Public Network?," *Internet Telephony*, 2/10/97.

17. Dick Satran, "Users Feel Bite In Year Of Computer Bug," Reuters, 6/15/99.

18. "ICSA 1998 Computer Virus Prevalence Survey," International Computer Security Association, Carlisle, PA, September 1998.

19. *Ibid.*

20. *Ibid.*

21. Security Assessment Questionnaire, IBM Data Security Support Programs, May 1985.

22. Jon Toigo, "Storm Alarms Sound," *Databus*, 8/86.

CHAPTER
3

Facility Protection

Formulating the strategies and documenting the procedures for disaster recovery may be challenging and time-consuming processes. However, there are usually a number of action items, identified during risk analysis, which may be undertaken while procedures are being developed. These include the purchase and installation of systems to safeguard against certain avoidable disaster potentials, such as fire and flooding.

Figure 3–1 is a DFD showing many of the generic activities that aim at securing disaster avoidance capabilities for a company's user departments and information-processing facilities. As the chart suggests, the evaluation, selection, cost-justification and installation of these capabilities may be undertaken concurrently with the development of the paper plan.

As depicted in the data flow diagram, planning for disaster prevention capabilities requires, first, an evaluation of existing vulnerabilities and a survey of any existing prevention measures. Tests and inspections as well as consultations with civil emergency planners, fire protection officials, security professionals, police, and other experts facilitate threat assessments. Based on these assessments, objectives can be articulated that will be useful when identifying suitable preventive systems and when evaluating the proposals of vendors.

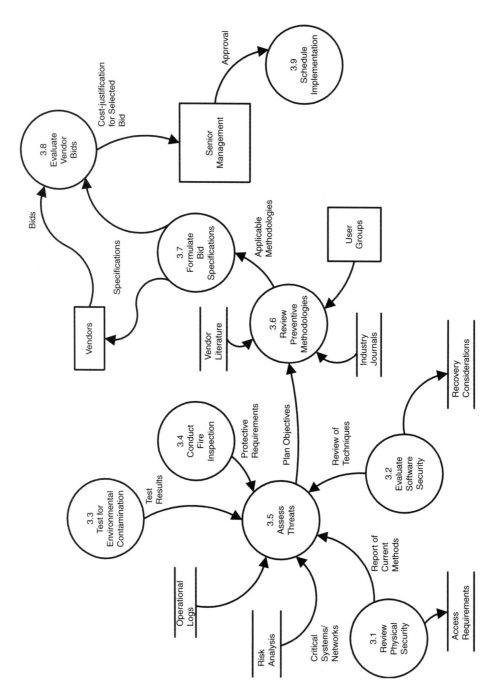

Figure 3–1 Disaster prevention system selection and implementation.

This chapter focuses on a specific set of preventive measures. These include:

- Systems for water detection that can provide early warning of leaks and other water-related hazards.
- Systems for the detection of preignition gases, smoke and other indicators of impending fire to enable proactive response that will ensure the health and safety of personnel and prevent the loss of data and equipment to fire.
- Systems for the detection of airborne contamination levels that are associated with employee illness, data loss, equipment malfunction, and fires.
- Systems for the suppression of fires.
- Systems for the continuation of electrical power in the presence of a utility power outage.
- Systems for the physical security of corporate computing and telecommunications facilities.

A conscious decision has been made to exclude two additional disaster prevention systems from this discussion. The first is computer/network security systems. A complete discussion of this topic would require a book of its own, and several excellent ones are already available. Moreover, many organizations have planners who are already tasked with computer and network security functions. DR coordinators should make every effort to develop working relationships with their peers in the security area and to include corporate computer and network security representatives on their disaster recovery planning teams. The second prevention system that is not included in the above list is a corporate data backup/restore system. This topic is covered in Chapter 4.

The purpose of disaster avoidance systems is to provide an automated mechanism for detecting certain disaster potentials (and to respond to them, where possible) before they develop into unplanned interruptions of normal business processes. The acquisition of disaster avoidance systems is rarely a simple matter of cutting a purchase order. Vendors must be identified, products evaluated, bids solicited, costs justified, and expenditures approved.

Furthermore, depending on the type of system, there may be an additional set of tasks to coordinate system installation (with the data center or user department), schedule work, prepare the installation site, or provide for the interruption of normal operations for training or installation work. Preparatory steps differ depending on a number of factors, ranging from the type of disaster avoidance system being installed to the work schedule of the affected department.

Under ideal circumstances, systems are installed during the preparation of new company quarters. However, more often than not, disaster avoidance capabilities are add-ons to existing facilities and must, to the extent possible, be implemented around normal business activities.

The following sections discuss several common disaster prevention and protection strategies that can be implemented to provide a disaster avoidance capability.

WATER DETECTION

As noted previously, flooding poses a significant threat to data processing and records management facilities. Annual costs to companies resulting from water damage are in the millions of dollars.

Some encounters with flooding are sudden and catastrophic. Landstar Systems, a transportation broker in Jacksonville, FL, learned about water damage firsthand in 1998, when six inches of rain, weighing an estimated 150 tons, collapsed the roof of its data center. Noting a trickle of water in the data center, the night operator managed to place one call to the Vice President of IT before the flood moved from the second floor into the data center directly.[1]

Leaks can also develop slowly and, if detected and rectified in time, can be prevented from resulting in a facility outage. For example, a water pipe sharing the same channel as the building main electrical bus at Charles Schwab's Montgomery Street office building in San Francisco, CA, may have been leaking for some time before it finally broke in February 1999. The leak was not detected, however, until the pipe burst on Friday morning, spilling a torrent into the bus cabling, shorting out the building electrical system, and forcing the evacuation of 550 employees. Repairs to the pipe and the bus required two weeks while Schwab personnel operated from other company-owned space in the Bay Area.[2]

Water can intrude into sensitive information processing and storage facilities, as well as user work areas, in a variety of ways and from a variety of sources. Some common sources of flooding are:

- **Facility plumbing leaks.** Although well-designed data processing or storage facilities should be located away from building plumbing, they often are not. Water and sewer pipe leakage, particularly in multistory buildings, can travel along pipes and duct work and drain into data centers, records storage centers, communications equipment closets, or electrical panels.

- **Air conditioning.** In data centers, spot coolers and subfloor air conditioning plants can produce water, either through leakage or condensation. Roof-mounted air conditioners and improperly sealed building rooftops are also a potentially dangerous combination.
- **Water cooling systems.** Some larger mainframes are cooled, not by air, but by water. Leaks in the cooling system can show up as underfloor puddles in raised floor environments.
- **Sprinkler systems.** Sprinkler heads or piping can be damaged by workers carrying ladders or performing construction or repair work in crawl spaces or on facility ceilings and walls. Leaks may not be obvious for a protracted period of time.

Some hardware vendors suggest that their equipment is impervious to water damage and it is not uncommon to hear a sales representative state assuredly that water poses no threat to de-energized equipment. If the computer is de-energized and becomes wet, says the rep (or service technician or field service agent), just disassemble it, dry it out, put it back together, and it will work properly.

This presumes that the information manager or computer operator will have the prescience to know when water will enter the facility, contacting energized equipment. With the exception of the times when facilities are intentionally evacuated in response to natural threats, such as hurricanes, storm surges, or rising water, there is rarely a clear indication of imminent water intrusion. Thus, it is likely that water will contact energized equipment, causing short circuits and damage.

Even if it were true that electronic components are waterproof if de-energized (and according to a U.S. Air Force study, this is certainly not the case[3]), there are several problems with vendor optimism. For one, even if equipment is not energized, the presence of water may represent a shock hazard to personnel. The health hazard represented by the combination of water and electronics should be paramount in any discussion of the subject.

Secondly, if equipment is recently powered down prior to contact with water, components will still be warm and subject to warping due to uneven cooling. Restarting a system with warped circuit cards will likely result in untrustworthy performance.

Third, the contaminants present in sprinkler systems and other sources of water intrusion, more so than the water itself, represent a continuing threat to the operation of electronic equipment. Even if water-laden components are dried perfectly, the evaporated water will likely leave behind a noxious mixture of organic and metallic particulate that, in turn, will leave components vulnerable to failure.

Fourth, insurance, warranties, and service agreements may be invalidated if equipment has gotten wet, is restarted, and fails.

Finally, even in the best-case scenario, when wet equipment is salvageable, the period required to dry and test components before re-energizing them is likely to be protracted. Thus, the claims of many vendors about the tolerance of their hardware to water intrusion may be a moot point. Disasters are disasters in part because they interrupt critical business processes for an unacceptable period of time.

To anticipate water intrusion before it contacts energized equipment, and in some cases, before a leak can become a disaster, planners may wish to consider any of a number of water detection and annunciation systems presently available on the market. Detection systems—ranging from simple battery-operated alarms to sophisticated sensing cables and ceiling grids—are available to detect the presence of water wherever it is found and either signal an audible alarm or relay hazard alert messages to a system or network management console.

Figure 3–2 provides a schematic drawing of one water sensor product that can be deployed either as a standalone unit or as part of a cabled

Figure 3–2   Water Alert® Sensor Schematic View. (*Source:* Dorlen Products, Milwaukee, WI.)

Figure 3-3   A Tracetek® cable asembly. (*Source:* Raychem HTS, Tyco International, Ltd., Menlo Park, CA.)

sensor network. Placed in strategic locations, the simple, battery-operated device deploys two metal contacts against the mounting surface. If a film of water touches both contacts, a circuit is completed and a buzzer sounds.

Another product, appropriate for applications ranging from structural risers to raised-floor environments, features a sensing cable consisting of a braid of wires and a fluoropolymer conductor, available in 3- to 50-foot lengths (see Figure 3–3). One or more cables can be connected together and deployed in a snakelike pattern to enable the coverage of a broad area of subfloor, wall, or other surface. Multiple cable branches can be deployed to provide coverage for different areas.

The branches return to an alarm and locating module, which provides both annunciation of the detected leak and a display of its exact lo-

Figure 3-4   A Tracetek® data center deployment. (*Source:* Raychem HTS, Tyco International Ltd., Menlo Park, CA.)

cation. When the system is deployed around subfloor air ducts, pipes, and fixtures in a raised-floor environment such as a data center, it can provide ongoing monitoring of moisture conditions and localize detected leaks to their source. In addition to signaling leakage with an alarm, systems can also provide the means for automatically de-energizing equipment when water intrusion is detected. Figure 3–4 depicts a common installation.

FIRE SUPPRESSION

Fire is typically the disaster scenario of choice for DR planning. Fires present very directly the prospect of life safety issues and total property destruction that necessitate a total disaster recovery capability.

According to the National Fire Protection Association, fires can be prevented from resulting in smoke-and-rubble disasters through a combination of prevention, detection, and suppression. Fire prevention begins with facility design and construction. Fire-resistant construction materials, firewall placement, and facility compartmentalization can play major roles in limiting the scope, duration, and destructiveness of a fire. Also, when fire codes are observed in facility construction, many building-related fire hazards can be minimized or eliminated.

However, despite the existence of some very thorough building and fire codes (Disney World's EPCOT code being one of the most advanced), state laws differ in enforcing contractor adherence to the codes. Some states have adopted National Fire Protection Association standards *in toto*, while others have adopted only part of the NFPA code. Even in states that have adopted NFPA codes, nearly all lack sufficient enforcement personnel to inspect all new and existing construction for code adherence. Code violations often become evident only after a fire occurs.

A good starting point for the disaster recovery coordinator interested in installing fire prevention is to contact the local fire department. Fire inspectors are generally willing to visit a site and provide practical (and legal) insights into the adequacy or inadequacy of existing detection and suppression capabilities.

The inspector may find code violations in the building structure that will need to be rectified, regardless of the type of fire suppression system being considered for installation. However, few inspectors will penalize facility owners or tenants for less-than-life-threatening code violations discovered in an investigation prompted by an invitation, provided that they are remedied within a reasonable period of time.

The inspector can make recommendations regarding detection and suppression capabilities that can be used to support the case for spending money on an effective system. The inspector's comments should be requested in writing.

Another way in which fire departments (or fire protection engineers, consultants specially trained and certified in fire prevention methods and technologies) may assist during disaster recovery planning is by identifying the techniques that will likely be used if a fire occurs. More than one company has learned, to its chagrin, that the expensive, "clean-agent"-based fire suppression system it purchased proved useless in the case of a major fire originating in another part or on another floor of the building.

Clean agents are replacements for Halon™, a thirty-year-old fire suppression workhorse that was determined to be hazardous to the Earth's ozone layer and banned by international treaty in 1993. The Environmental Protection Agency (EPA) enforces the ban on new production of Halon in the United States and is monitoring the phasing out of existing Halon systems. Companies with Halon systems already deployed may retain them, but may not perform live tests of the systems, nor recharge them once used.[4]

The Halon ban prompted a quest for effective, environment-friendly alternatives, especially for data centers and certain industrial applications. To date, the EPA under its Significant New Alternatives Program (SNAP) has approved four alternatives (see Table 3–1).[5]

As with Halon in the past, the new crop of "clean" fire suppression agents must reach a certain concentration within the atmosphere of the protected environment (i.e., a data center, telecommunications equipment room, etc.) in order to be effective. Thus, the environment must be sealed. Fire-fighting techniques, however, may require that the integrity of the protected environment be violated by breaking windows or opening sealed doors.

Fire inspectors can often advise, based on facility design and probable fire-fighting techniques, whether a clean-agent system is appropriate for a given facility. In the case of one facility, an inspector observed that the data processing department's system would be useless: "We'd just

Table 3–1 Clean Agent Replacements for Halon

Trade Name	Chemical Name	Manufacturer
Inergen™	IG-541	Ansul Fire Protection
FE 13™	HFC-23	DuPont Company
FM-200™	HFC-227ea	Great Lakes Chemical
CEA-410™	FC-3-1-10	3M Specialty Chemicals

open the doors at one end of the building and hose everything through the doors at the other end, and on into the parking lot. Computers, cubicles, chairs, the works."

This is not meant to imply that clean-agent systems are inappropriate in all cases. Brian Pung, President of Protective Systems, Inc., observes that the objective of a clean-agent system (as with Halon previously) is to stop electrical fires originating with electronic equipment from spreading.

> The intent is to limit fire to a specific component. The systems are designed to hold a sufficient concentration of the agent in a room so that people can shut down intelligently and exit safely, rather than doing these things reactively. We deploy systems so they will provide at least ten minutes [of protection]. The national average for fire protection response is six minutes. These systems are not for building protection. Sprinkler systems are used for that. They are for fire protection in data centers and similar types of environments.[6]

In addition to advice on the selection of fire suppression systems and the determination of facility fire code compliance, fire inspectors can often identify fire hazards within company offices and recommend corrective measures. The coordinator should accompany the inspector through the facility and note any comments he or she may make. Some common observations and concerns may include:

- **The presence of combustibles located near potential ignition sources.** In a computer environment, for example, this may include cartons of paper located in close proximity to heat-generating hardware.

- **Exceeding the UL rating of extension cords and utilizing electrical devices that lack UL approval.** The Underwriting Laboratory rates a wide range of products for, among other things, their fire hazard potential. Many products do not bear the UL label and this may be a factor in determining fire risks.

- **Company smoking policy.** Lighted tobacco is an obvious hazard. However, in addition to the immediate danger of a fire, cigarette smoke can also invade and damage sensitive storage media and drives. Workplace smoking is obviously on the decline in most companies, either as a function of company policy or of local indoor anti-smoking ordinances.

- **Fire-related health hazards posed by certain types of fabrics and materials.** Some fabrics and materials, when burned, can release poisonous particles and gases into the atmosphere. Phosgene, hydrogen chloride, and hydrogen cyanide may be released by the burning of common plastics, while PCBs may be released from fires involving transformers and older electronic equipment that some companies may still have in service. These toxic by-products can not only result in the loss of human life, but they can also delay reentry into the facility following a fire.

Besides hazards within the facility, a fire inspector is often in a position to warn the disaster recovery coordinator about neighbors with high potential for disaster. In multistory buildings, it may be valuable to know the lines of business of other occupants. If a neighbor engages in an activity that poses a substantial fire risk, this might affect the selection of fire avoidance systems. Such information may also be a springboard for opening discussions with fellow tenants in a shared office building setting. With cooperation, tenants can watch out for each other in the area of fire detection and physical security.

Also, if a facility is located near a firm engaged in toxic chemical or other volatile product manufacturing or storage, the fire inspector usually knows this and can notify the disaster recovery coordinator.

Knowledge is power. However, knowing the risks does not necessarily mean that all threats can be eliminated. Just as the disaster recovery coordinator may have no control over the initial construction of the facility, he or she may have no control over where the facility is located in relation to high potential risks. The best one can do is to eliminate potential risks that can be eliminated and minimize exposure to those that cannot.

This strategy involves both preventive and prophylactic measures. Protecting against fires means identifying possible causes and controlling or eliminating them.

CONTAMINATION REDUCTION

An important and often overlooked root cause of fire in facilities where electronic equipment is used is environmental contamination. The entry of airborne contaminant particles into electronic equipment can cause short circuits and even flash fires in electronic equipment. Moreover, contamination has been the indirect cause of more IT downtime than all the fires, floods, hurricanes, earthquakes, and disgruntled employees combined.

Contaminants are microscopic particulate bearing such grandiose names as crystallines, carbonaceous particles, organic and synthetic fibrous particulate, and metallics (such as zinc). Without a degree in chemistry, an DR planner can be unimpressed by the reports and analyses conducted by research labs that explain how contaminants effect sensitive disk media, circuitry, and microswitches. Also, due to the minute size of many contaminants, industry specialists report that they are often hard pressed to convince a business manager that a contamination problem exists.

Concern with the destructive potential of contamination has long been an issue for agencies of the U.S. government. In the late 1960s, the General Services Administration issued federal air standards for clean rooms and workstations in federal agencies. These were revised in 1973 and issued by the GSA under the unassuming title, *Federal Standard 209B*.

209B set forth three scientific classifications of environmental contamination and mandated that certain federal agencies and contractors comply with them. Class 100 facilities included certified clean rooms, such as those employed by NASA and the Department of Defense for the development of sensitive electronic devices. Class 10,000 facilities included government hospital operating theatres. Class 100,000 facilities included all federal data processing centers.

The classification nomenclature—100, 10,000, and 100,000—referred to particulate concentrations. It was determined that environments having less than 100,000 particulate (no larger than 0.5 microns in size) per cubic foot of air were optimal for data processing hardware.

209B was revised several times in the 1980s and in 1992 became *Federal Standard 209E*. The revised standard included classes of air cleanliness by metric measurements as well as newly defined criteria for ultrafine particles.[7]

While the 209 standards have not been enforced stringently in the private sector (except in the case of certain defense contractors and within certain facilities regulated directly by the federal government), the inclusion of an air standard for data centers does suggest the correlation the government has drawn between environment and system integrity. 209E specifies techniques for sampling air in the facility and for determining the concentration of contaminant particles it contains. Effective measurement requires multiple tests conducted at different locations in the room. Some of the more popular testing methods include:

- **"White-glove" method.** As the name suggests, this method assesses the level of contamination by wiping the exposed surface of a piece of equipment with a white glove. The particulate on the glove is analyzed to determine the type of contaminant in the center environment.

- **Petri-dish method.** With this method of checking contamination, a petri dish is used to collect particulate that fall out of the air.[8] After a period of time, the contents of the dish are analyzed to determine the amount and type of fallout.

- **Aspirating pump.** This method involves the installation of a pump in an area where air quality is to be measured. Air samples are collected through an air intake, and the contents are analyzed following several hours of operation.

- **Electronic particulate counter.** The electronic counter is one of the most advanced method of airborne contaminant data collection. Most units are about the size of cellular phones, except that the "antenna" is actually a sensing tip that counts the number of particles that it contacts over a period of time (see Figure 3–5). To analyze the contaminants themselves, counter probes are wiped with a swab and the swab is then microscopically examined.

Figure 3–5   Electronic airborne particulate counters. (*Source:* Biotest Diagnostics Corporation, Denville, NJ.)

None of the above methods alone provides a means to both count and analyze the contents of airborne contamination. Hybrid systems are appearing in the market that count particulate moving with room air flow, while at the same time sampling the contaminants with special filters, so that it can be analyzed. The analysis can often reveal the sources of contamination so they can be corrected, if necessary.

Once the presence of contamination in the data center has been demonstrated and the threat it poses to personnel and equipment is understood, next it is necessary to develop strategies for eliminating or reducing contamination levels. A good way to begin is to answer the question: How are contaminants introduced into the clean environment of the data processing facility?

While certain contaminants are carried in by operators (including clothing fibers, hair and skin particles, and even cigarette smoke and ash), most particulates are airborne and, in data centers or other raised-floor environments, are transported into sensitive equipment through the computer room subfloor air supply. Examples of the more common contaminants follow.

- Cement dust, sand, plaster, and brick dust may be produced by the gradual erosion of the subfloor surface beneath a data center's raised floor. Even if the subfloor has been properly sealed with polyacrylic sealants, the dust that was generated during raised floor installation may settle on the subfloor. This cement dust, propelled by air conditioning, can enter bottom-cooled equipment at high velocity and damage board components.

- Urban pollution, including carbon/coal dust, can enter the subfloor air supply by way of the air conditioning system. The wearing of drive belts or printer components and the release of laser printer toner can also introduce these contaminants to the DP area. These particulate are a special problem since they can conduct electricity and cause short circuits and cross-tracking.

- Electrically conductive metallic particulate can often be traced to equipment wear, wear of the air-conditioning plant, floor and ceiling suspension systems, and even to old-fashioned rust (iron oxide). Metallic contaminants are even more dangerous than carbon residue because they tend to "plate out" on components where they will cause the most damage.

Nearly any contaminant can conduct electricity—even paper dust. If the contaminant can absorb moisture, it can wreak the same sort of damage as the "bug" of computer legend that, when it straddled two poles of an open switch with its legs, made a circuit and short-circuited the first computer. As in the case of the first bug, it is almost impossible to determine the cause of the short circuit since fiber or paper particles disintegrate in the heat generated by the short.

Fortunately, there are several steps that the information manager can take to eliminate certain types of contamination and to minimize the impact of contaminants that cannot be completely eliminated. The good news is that most of these steps do not require that the equivalent of a NASA clean room be established in the data center or telecommunications switchroom.

1. Forbid cigarette smoking inside the data center or switch room. If smoking is now permitted, smoke particles and tar are already harming the health of computer equipment.

2. Remove wastepaper baskets and bulk paper containers from the computer room. These are prime sources of fiber and paper dust, which is a highly water-absorbent, therefore conductive, particulate.

3. Invest in a handheld vacuum that is fitted with brushless rotors and microstatic filters for use in general cleanup of paper handlers and printers in the center. Most portable vacuum cleaners add more contamination than they remove. Especially dangerous are the metallic particles from the motor brushes that are expelled in the vacuum exhaust and collected by sensitive equipment in the center.

Most modern data center grade vacuum cleaners feature "H.E.P.A." exhaust filtration. H.E.P.A. stands for High Efficiency Particulate Air (or Arresting) and a H.E.P.A. rating indicates that the filter media used on the vacuum is certified by the U.S. government to comply with a specific filtration efficiency. The efficiency of a H.E.P.A. filter is evaluated in two ways. One measure is the proportion of particulate that the filter will trap: government-certified H.E.P.A. filters operate at 99.97% efficiency. The second measure of filtration efficiency is expressed as the smallest particle size that will be filtered: Particulate of 0.3 microns or greater are filtered by a certified H.E.P.A. filter.

Only those filters with the "S-CLASS H.E.P.A." printed on the filter are the genuine article. The periods between the letters in the acronym are important. Vendors who offer vacuum units emblazoned with the terms "true HEPA" or "HEPA type" are not certified. Of course, H.E.P.A. filters are not the only media on the market that are effective for removing computer-killing contaminants. Independent laboratories have certified the 3M FILTRETE™ hospital filter, for example, with a filtration efficiency of 99.95% dust free at 0.1 microns. However, the media loses effectiveness as it is used.

Both H.E.P.A. and other high-efficiency filtration vacuums are expensive because of the frequency with which the filters must be changed. Replacement filtration media itself is costly. An alternative is to invest in a central vacuum system that empties its exhaust outside of the equipment room.

4. If space permits, move printers—especially laser printers—out of the vicinity of CPUs, tape drives, telecommunications switches, and disk drives. Ideally, computer and telecommunications equipment should be compartmentalized and printers should be in a separate room with separate air handling.

5. Observe proper computer floor tile maintenance practices, as recommended by the manufacturer. For example, perform all tile alterations outside the raised-floor environment. Cutting a tile inside the center will flood the environment with fiber and aluminum contaminants. In addition, always replace a tile in the same direction as it was removed. Replacing tiles incorrectly can cause them to wobble and wear, depositing contaminants into the plenary air supply below the raised floor.

6. Ensure that all equipment is fitted with the best filters that the equipment vendor can provide. This will not eliminate contamination altogether, but it will keep some of the larger particulate out of older drives and switches.

   Most drive manufacturers insist that their disk products are safe from the airborne contamination that surrounds them because they are sealed. With the latest disk drives, this is likely the case. To achieve extremely high-storage capacities (a function of the areal capacity of a disk drive), vendors are using magnetoresistive heads that are very sensitive to particulate contamination and corrode easily. Moreover, in order to read more densely packed data from the disk platter, most vendors are reducing the head-fly height in their disk drives. Read/write heads fly approximately 2 to 3 microns above the media.

   With such close tolerances, drives need to be sealed away from external contamination. Otherwise, catastrophe can result. Think of a 747 airplane flying at 400 miles per hour three feet off the ground and encountering a boulder four feet tall. This is actually a fair metaphor for current drive read/write heads (the airplane), disk platters (the runway 3 microns below) and a small particulate of four microns. The result can be a head crash.

With some older disk drives that may still be in service, however, contamination remains a threat to drive media. Previous generation drives featured so-called "absolute" filters or "breather" filters designed to vent heat or provide pressure equalization inside and outside the drive assembly during shipping. In some cases, particles that were small enough to pass through absolute filters were still large enough to cause disk crashing (see Figure 3–6).

Furthermore, even when contaminants did not pass through the filter, but instead built up on its outer surface, they caused tempera-

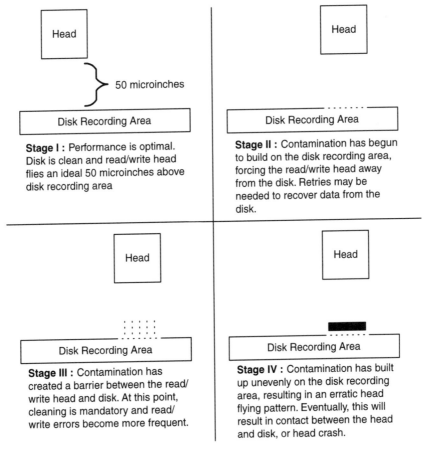

Stage I : Performance is optimal. Disk is clean and read/write head flies an ideal 50 microinches above disk recording area

Stage II : Contamination has begun to build on the disk recording area, forcing the read/write head away from the disk. Retries may be needed to recover data from the disk.

Stage III : Contamination has created a barrier between the read/write head and disk. At this point, cleaning is mandatory and read/write errors become more frequent.

Stage IV : Contamination has built up unevenly on the disk recording area, resulting in an erratic head flying pattern. Eventually, this will result in contact between the head and disk, or head crash.

Figure 3–6   Chronology of a head crash. (*Source:* Jon William Toigo, "Environmental Contamination: Averting a Microscopic Threat to Data Center Operations," *Data Center Operations Management* (Auerback Publishers: New York, 1987).

tures to build up in the drive to a point at which disk media was affected. Platter *warble* (or warping) occurs when heat inside the drive exceeds the upper limits for the disk media. When this happens, the media undergoes a molecular change that warps its surface. As with contamination buildup, an irregular surface caused by warping can lead to head crashes.

Frequent disk crashes were often cited as harbingers of environmental contamination. With newer drives, hermetic sealing largely eliminates the possibility of contaminants affecting disk media directly. Indirectly is another matter however.

Dust and contamination can still create heat problems for systems, switches and disk drives, causing shutdowns and failures. According to Eric Williamson, President of Worldwide Environmental Services, contamination is still a threat to hard disks and other electronic systems,

> Generally speaking, although it is true that the hardware is more reliable today than previous technologies, the environment, including contamination, is still a major issue, partly because availability requirements are so much higher today. [Vendors may have sealed their] hard disk assemblies against the introduction of external particulate. Unfortunately, there are still many components within the drives that CAN be affected by contamination. The mechanism for problems is sometimes quite complicated, but two ways that contamination can affect hardware are:
>
> a) Depending on its makeup, airborne contamination flowing through the drives may eventually coat hardware components, applying an insulative coating, and reducing the unit's ability to adequately shed its heat load, increasing the temperature, and leading to reduced mean time to failure (MTBF).
> b) Conductive particles can cause shorts or voltage aberrations on sensitive electronic components. Power supplies are particularly vulnerable to this phenomenon, and much has been written in recent years about this issue. [Disk drive vendors] are fully aware of this problem.[9]

The buildup of contaminants and dust on the filters covering power supply cooling fans remains a major source of disk problems today, according to Stuart Hanley, Vice President of World Wide Operations at OnTrack Data International.

> There is plenty of evidence that heat is a disk drive's worst enemy (see Figure 3–7). The first generation of 10,000 RPM

Drive Reliability Typical Temperature Sensitivity

Figure 3–7   Heat and hard disk drive reliability. (*Source:* IBM.)

drives had a major heat problem, though the newer ones run cooler. From a data recovery standpoint, we still see system cooling failures, usually poor or blocked ventilation of the system cabinet, that lead to hard disk crashes. Some box manufacturers have started adding temperature strips to their system cabinets [to check whether hard disk failures are the result of heat].[10]

Hanley further observes that root cause analysis is rarely performed on damaged drives. Therefore, the cause of a failure is usually listed as "mechanical problems," when blame should probably be placed on contamination-related heat in some cases.

7. For data centers and equipment rooms, consult an engineer to determine how (and at what cost) a positive pressure air system can be established. In a positive pressure air system, air blows outward when the integrity of the room is violated (e.g., when a door is opened). If air blows outward, airborne contaminants are less likely to find ready access to the facility.

8. Remove all ion-generating air purifiers from the center environment. Also, deinstall any humidifiers or "toaster-element" space heaters and set up a schedule for thorough maintenance and inspection of air

conditioners. All of these are major contributors to the contamination of environments where they are present. Ion-generating purifiers, nicronic wire heating elements (like those in a kitchen toaster), and the electrostatic precipitators found in some older model air conditioning units produce electrostatic particulate that seek out electronic components like guided missiles.

9. Perhaps the most important step to take to control contamination is to contract with a reputable computer room maintenance company to perform routine cleaning.

Unfortunately, a number of firms claim to be competent in the field of computer room cleaning, and selecting one requires some savvy about the causes of environmental contamination and proper cleaning techniques. For example, many janitorial companies are more than willing to clean a company's computer facility using the same techniques that they use to keep other office areas neat and clean. The fact is that contracting with one of these services could well add to the problem of contamination.

Stories abound of janitorial services that wax and buff tile floors, creating a wax barrier that impairs the static grounding ability that was part of the floor's design. Another company found piles of sawdust under the computer room floor, deposited there by janitors to absorb water. More than one firm has experienced costly damage because janitors took up 20 or 30 raised-floor tiles at the same time to clean the subfloor beneath them "more efficiently."

According to industry specialists, most janitorial services do not know enough about the raised-floor environments to provide a service that will effectively reduce contamination. They use improper techniques and equipment that do more harm than good and possibly cause even more contamination-related downtime.

What should an IT manager or DR coordinator look for in a cleaning vendor? First, the best cleaning companies use only shielded, brushless-rotor equipment to avoid releasing ferromagnetic pollutants into the atmosphere and to prevent electromagnetic interference from affecting data processing equipment.

Furthermore, the cleaning company should clean tiles using OSHA-approved, nonionic solutions and lint-free towels, and should clean equipment exteriors with silicon-treated cloths that leave a silicon film that repels dust.

As with most service providers, companies are well served by asking for and checking provider references. The vendor should have a reputation for quality work and a pedigree of experience.

PRECOMBUSTION DETECTION

In the final analysis, the solution to the problem of contamination-related equipment failure and downtime will never be a comprehensive one. At best, an informed DR planner or IT manager, aided by a competent high-technology environmental maintenance service, will be able to reduce the amount of costly downtime and greatly offset the possibility of fire from this cause.

In addition to fire prevention through facility design and maintenance, it is necessary to take other measures to detect and suppress non-preventable fires. Detection systems are required by most states to counter the threat to human life posed by fire. Legal requirements for installing suppression capabilities vary widely, however.

The telltale signs of fire are, of course, heat and smoke. These by-products of fire can do substantial damage in an area, such as a computer facility or records storage area, that is never touched by flame itself. Heat can destroy CPUs and storage media. Furthermore, heat in the presence of water generates steam that can destroy microfilm and fiche at a substantially lower temperature than heat in the absence of steam. Finally, smoke can render equipment unusable, and corrosive gases can make the facility uninhabitable.

Protective Systems recommends that detectors be placed every 125 square feet in computer and switch rooms, and at least every 900 square feet in user work areas. Heat and smoke detectors are available in a variety of types, shapes, and sizes to alert personnel to hazardous conditions. Some types are:

- Photoelectric detectors, which detect the smoke produced by smoldering fires and fires that involve PVC insulation.
- Ionization detectors, which detect fires involving more flame than smoke.
- Temperature detectors, which detect heat in excess of a preset value.
- Rate of rise heat detectors, which monitor rates of heat increase and do not actuate alarms unless heat increases at a rate exceeding a preset threshold (useful in environments subject to significant ambient temperature changes such as nuclear power generation facilities or heavy manufacturing environments).
- Air sampling detectors, which detect the invisible by-products of materials as they degrade during the pre-combustion stages of fire. According to Vision Systems, detectors that capitalize upon this fact can

shorten response times to fire events and even prevent them before combustion occurs (see Figure 3–8). The VESDA air sampling detection system continuously draws samples of room air into a "monitored environment"—a sampling pipe network—with the aid of a high-efficiency aspirator pump. There, the dust particles are filtered out and the sample is exposed to a high-intensity and broad-spectrum light source, such as a laser. The incident light scattered from smoke particles in the air sample passes through a series of optical components to a solid state light receiver, where it is analyzed for signs of precombustion. Depending upon smoke levels and the preprogrammed alarm levels, the appropriate output signals are generated and sent to a monitoring station or annunciator (see Figure 3–9).

It is advisable to select, purchase, and position detection devices on the advice of a fire protection official or a knowledgeable fire protection contractor—preferably a certified fire protection engineer with experience in computer room environments. This recommendation cannot be empha-

"All escalating fires have four stages: Incipient (pre-combustion), Visible Smoke, Flaming Fire, and Intense Heat. The incipient stage of smoldering fires provides the widest window of opportunity to detect and control the spread of fire, before it develops into devastating stages. VESDA LaserPLUS can be configured to generate multiple alarms within this window."—Vision Systems VESDA LaserPlus marketing literature.

Figure 3–8   The window of opportunity in fire detection. (*Source:* Vision Systems— VESDA, Hingham, MA.)

Figure 3–9   How VESDA® works. (*Source:* Vision Systems—VESDA, Hingham, MA.)

sized enough given the special environmental characteristics of data centers and switch rooms (air conditioning, air streams, etc.), which can actually impede the effective detection of hazardous conditions.

Once a hazardous condition is detected, the purpose of the detector is to alert on- and/or off-site personnel to the situation. Audible alarms are typically connected to signaling systems. Says Pung, modern detection/suppression systems also typically provide automated functions that may include:

> annunciating the alarm to the building fire alarm system, automatically shutting power down to equipment, activating dampers to block air conditioning airflows so that a clean agent release will reach its optimal concentration. In many cases, the alarm will also turn off security systems so that card keys or digital codes do not need to be entered in order to access the room.[11]

Pung points out that the many functions associated with fire suppression systems require that the DR planner select a qualified contractor to deploy an effective solution.

> The protective systems contractor serves as a general contractor. He should have five years minimum in the business, use nationally recognized products, and have a qualified distributor. Beyond that, he needs to be able to manage a mechanical contractor who will install air conditioning dampers, an electrical contractor to power the dampers so that they provide a fail-safe close in the event of a fire, and a security systems contractor who will connect the fire suppression system to the security system.[12]

In addition to the above, the fire suppression system contractor will also need to specify a system that will effectively suppress fire. Knowledge of the new "clean agent" technologies is particularly important (see Figure 3–10 for a simplified system layout diagram). These products are

Figure 3–10   A simplified FM-200™ fire suppression system layout.

still new in the market and substantial misunderstanding surrounds them, according to Pung and others.

For example, the EPA warns users of FM-200™ that frostbite may occur if a hand or other body part comes into contact with the discharge of the chemical. Similarly, it warns of reduced visibility following a discharge. In general, the use of most clean agents seems fraught with peril, based on EPA caveats and warnings.

In the case of FM-200, says Pung, "no frostbite will occur unless you stick your hand into the discharge, which lasts for about 10 seconds. The reduced visibility results from humidity in the air contacting the chemical and dissipates very quickly as the agent mixes with the air." He adds that FM-200 is at least as "people safe" as Halon and notes that it has been used for years as the propellant in asthma inhalers.[13]

An equipment room fire that breaks out in the presence of a properly installed and tested suppression system, according to NFPA statistics, results in damage costs 53% lower than fires in unprotected areas.[14] This is true whether the system uses clean agents or water.

Obviously, with the distribution of electronic equipment throughout user work areas of a company, including LAN servers, desktop PCs, departmental routers, switches and hubs, and even telecommunications systems, not every device can be adequately protected by clean agents. Sprinkler systems and handheld extinguishers remain the primary fire suppression mechanism for distributed systems.

Sprinkling does have drawbacks, including the potential damage they cause to electronic gear and the delay to facility reentry associated with their use. This may be perceived as one more argument for recentralizing servers and communications equipment into the glass house and deploying "thin client" devices on corporate desktops, with no local data storage. Centralization may make sense from a disaster avoidance standpoint (though it is offset to some degree by the advantages accrued to "target dispersal," as discussed in Chapter 6).

POWER FAILURE

Another cause of data center downtime is electrical power failure. Providing alternatives or backups for the facility power supply is one method to insulate the company against external conditions that are beyond its ability to control. Interruptions in electrical power can result from a variety of factors, such as:

- Transformer failure or line damage
- Natural disasters and damage from severe weather
- Utility company outages
- Inadequate power-handling capacity in multi- or single-tenant buildings
- Sabotage and terrorism

In addition to prolonged outages, most companies also confront a host of day-to-day power-related problems, including line dips and surges, transverse and common-mode interference or "noise," and in some areas, brownouts. All can bode ill for computer equipment.

As its name implies, an uninterruptible power supply (UPS) affords protection against both momentary and prolonged power outages. As previously mentioned, a UPS is a dual-value technology. It provides a hedge against disastrous data loss by supplying backup power for a sufficient amount of time to perform an organized shutdown of systems and other equipment. Additionally, a *power conditioning* UPS (a line interactive or on-line unit, see below) reduces the daily, power-related wear and tear on connected hardware and prolongs the useful life of hardware. Given this value proposition, planners often report that their recommendation to acquire UPS protection for key systems results in quick approval from senior management.

What is a UPS? Basically, it is an interface between critical electronic devices in a company (collectively termed the *critical load*) and the local power company (the *utility*). Rich Feldhaus, a product specialist with Chicago, IL-based UPS maker, TrippLite, explains that there are three types of UPS systems. As shown in Figure 3–11, the first type is an *off-line* system.

Feldhaus explains that vendors prefer to use the term stand-by, mainly because of the negative connotations of the term "off-line." (Why would anyone want to buy something that is off-line—that is, not used?) Semantics and political correctness aside, this type of UPS is among the most popular for use with desktop and server systems—mainly because of its power protection capabilities and low price.

Stand-by UPS systems are characterized as such because they remain outside of the path between the utility and the load in normal operation. A trickle charger draws some current from the utility source in order to maintain batteries at full power. That way, if utility power is interrupted, the load can be switched automatically to UPS battery power.

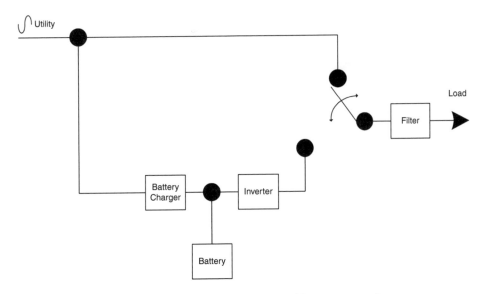

Figure 3–11   Stand-by uninterruptible power supply.

A few years ago, Feldhaus says, the time required to switch the load—called the UPS *transfer time*—was a concern. If a stand-by UPS did not switch quickly enough to meet the needs of the connected load, a failure would occur in the connected device(s). Says Feldhaus, "The current state of the switching power supply has made transfer time a non-issue."[15]

> Today's switching power supplies make servers and desktop systems much more resilient. They can wait 30 to 200 milliseconds for load transfer to occur before failing. Most UPS systems today can switch loads in a much shorter amount of time: 2 to 4 milliseconds on average for a 2 kVA UPS, 4 to 6 milliseconds for a 5 kVA system.[16]

The shortened transfer time is also a characteristic of the second type of UPS system: the *line-interactive* UPS. According to Feldhaus, line interactive UPS systems are a "hybrid line conditioner and stand-by UPS." As shown in Figure 3–12, the difference is that the UPS system unit filters the power supplied by the utility, even while the UPS itself is in stand-by mode.

Filtering circuitry conditions the power supplied to the load to remove electrical noise and to smooth surges and spikes. Additionally, this design provides low-grade voltage regulation by supplementing utility power with battery power if brownouts occur. Some experts claim that the price paid for this type of protection is shorter battery life in the line-

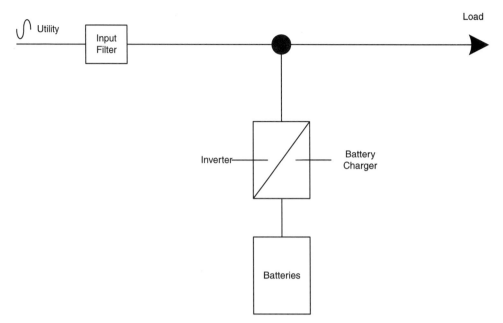

Figure 3–12   The line-interactive uninterruptible power supply.

interactive UPS than in either the stand-by or on-line UPS shown in Figure 3–13.[17]

With an on-line UPS, the UPS inverter and batteries are continuously used to deliver conditioned power to the load, effectively isolating the connected equipment completely from the vicissitudes of utility power. In operation, a rectifier circuit converts utility AC power into DC power, both to charge the UPS storage batteries and to supply the UPS inverter. The inverter converts DC power from the rectifier or storage batteries into a clean, continuous AC power supply for use in driving connected equipment.

On-line systems are commonly used with large systems whose load power requirements exceed 6 kVA, though some on-line units are available for much smaller loads. The on-line UPS also features a by-pass switch that serves as both a protective device, should the UPS itself fail, and as a mechanism for changing the load over to an alternative AC source such as a backup generator.

An on-line UPS remains in the line between the critical load and the power company at all times, while other types supply battery power only when switched. This configuration protects the load from transients that may be generated by the power switching process itself.

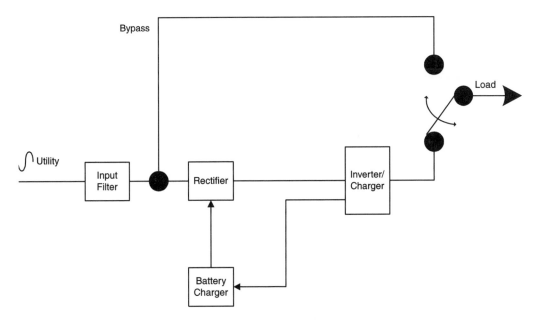

Figure 3–13   On-line uniterruptible power supply.

All UPS configurations share one thing in common: They provide a battery backup to commercial power. Typically, units will be selected based on the combined kVA requirements of the load, the length of time that emergency power will need to be provided, physical characteristics of the unit itself (i.e., footprint, environmental conditions, etc.), and cost. Units are available in a variety of kVA ratings and some feature rackmount configurations (see Figure 3–14) or modular battery designs (see Figure 3–15) enabling backup power durations to be extended.

Additional "intelligence" is also being added by UPS vendors in an effort to discriminate products from each other and from those of competitors. These features include:

- Simple Network Management Protocol (SNMP) support, enabling the transmission of information about UPS status to system or network management software
- Event logging, providing the means to store information about power events to facilitate the troubleshooting of power-related problems
- Temperature monitoring, capturing temperature information on UPS components as well as power outlets and signaling operators if preset thresholds are exceeded

Figure 3–14   A rackmount UPS. (*Source:* American Power Conversion, West Kingston, RI. For more information: www.apcc.com.)

Figure 3–15   The Powerware 9125 two-in-one form factor (rack or tower installation) with extended battery modules. (*Source:* Powerware Corporation, An Invensys Company, Raleigh, NC. www.powerware.com)

Intelligent features aside, selecting the right UPS strategy for a facility requires technical expertise. One question that may need to be addressed is whether a larger UPS (or several large units), providing protection at certain wall outlets, is better suited to requirements than would be the purchase of separate, stand-alone units for each device requiring protection. This decision must be part of an overall power backup strategy that takes into account such factors the intent of power backup and the management of power events.

Some UPS deployments are intended solely to insulate equipment from short duration (10-minute or less) power outages. This is a practical necessity for companies located in regions with frequent lightning storms. On the west coast of Florida, for example, thunderstorms roll inland from the Gulf of Mexico like clockwork during the summer months. Momentary power outages due to lightning are a predictable occurrence.

Another possible goal of power protection is to provide sufficient battery power to conduct organized shutdowns of hardware in the event of long-duration outages. This may be required to prevent data corruption or data loss.

In other cases, UPS power is provided to enable the smooth transition between alternate supplies. If a utility outage occurs, a company may need time to switch from one utility source to another, or to switch from utility power its own generator. The UPS supplies power while this switch-over occurs.

In addition to the intention of power backup, planners also need to consider the management requirements of their power backup alternatives. Deploying fewer UPS systems with larger load capacities may facilitate management, since the actual number of UPS systems that need to be maintained is smaller. However, implementing such a strategy can have a fairly large up-front cost in terms of equipment, installation, wiring, etc. Moreover, if company quarters are leased, rather than owned, this may be a consideration in determining the long-term value of a large UPS deployment.

By contrast, deploying many small UPS systems may negate certain up-front expenses, but introduces other potential drawbacks. One is increased asset management cost and potential for theft; another may be the difficulty entailed in keeping stand-alone UPS systems current with changing load power requirements (i.e., equipment upgrades).

Input from facility or electrical contractors, power company representatives, or vendor specialists may be useful in identifying options for consideration. Some of the factors to be addressed are the following:

1. **Load power requirements.** The first step in making a UPS acquisition is to identify the load to be supported and its power require-

ments, expressed as kilowatts (kW) or kilo-volt-amperes (kVA). Once the power requirements, which are specified by most equipment manufacturers on plates or tags connected to the hardware itself, have been determined, the size of the UPS can be calculated. For large heterogeneous, or nonstandard loads, additional factors such as momentary, transient, and peak load requirements must also be included in UPS sizing calculations.

TrippLite's Feldhaus notes that power consumption figures noted on most electronic devices are generally overstated and represent the requirements of the server or switch chassis when fully loaded and configured. Says Feldhaus, "This means that you may be buying too much UPS protection if you use manufacturer labels alone." In any case, it is a good idea to have an electrician verify the load calculations before shopping for a system.

2. **Reserve power**. Determine how much battery backup time is required based on the objectives of the power backup strategy that has been selected.

3. **Identify reliability requirements.** Depending on the quality and characteristics of utility power supplied to a company facility, a stand-by or line-interactive UPS may be called upon to support the critical load once, or 30 times, in a given day. This information is useful when determining the type of UPS best suited to an environment.

Other factors, including overload capacity, environmental and safety requirements, compatibility with load equipment, and the load imposed by the UPS itself on facility wiring, must also be considered in the selection of the right UPS.

The acquisition and installation of a centralized UPS is significantly more complex than the acquisition and deployment of multiple, smaller units. Facility preparation tasks may be extensive. Most vendors are extremely helpful with advice and information, and some even provide an installation planning team. Ensure that warranties and maintenance agreements are clearly understood and that thorough documentation and training are provided to those who will manage the system.

According to Kenneth Brill, a proponent of what has been termed "uptime management science," the UPS is only one of eleven power-related subsystems that must be installed and maintained in an information processing facility to prevent a power-related disaster. Others subsystems include: lightning protection, building switch gear (and utility-service entry), critical power buses, UPS air conditioning (without it, a large UPS will shut down), frequency conversion equipment, UPS batteries (considered a component of the on-line UPS described above), emergency generators, off-line testing, computer room power distribution, and, grounding. Overall reliability of power backup systems, according to Brill, is determined by the "weakest element" in this eleven-subsystem chain.[18] It is important, therefore, that power protection systems, like other disaster prevention systems, be inspected and tested regularly and maintained in top operating condition.

The need for UPS backup power underscores a larger issue of the current state of the U.S. power generation industry. Anyone who experienced the late summer heat wave of 1999, which drove electrical energy consumption rates in the midwestern and northeastern United States beyond all previous records, understands the supply and demand issues that confront producers of electrical power. According to the Energy Information Administration of the U.S. Department of Energy, the number of Americans grew by 82% from 1949 through 1998, but energy consumption expanded by 194%. As energy became increasingly accessible, the average amount used per person rose 62% during the period. In the face of such a growing demand for electricity, producers have struggled to keep pace.

"Struggled" is the appropriate term. The industry has had to cope with numerous shifts in the last decades of the twentieth century in the methods by which electrical power was produced. Coal has been largely replaced by oil and natural gas as the basic fuel for the turbines used in electrical power generation—this, at a time when the United States transitioned from self-sufficiency in these fuels to a significant supply shortages and increasing dependency on imports. A forty-year flirtation with electricity production via nuclear fission reactors topped out in 1995, with current production from these plants falling many points below the peak generation rate that once accounted for 22% of the country's total energy supply.

Changes in generation methods have also been accompanied by changes in government regulation. Increased regulation of the industry, especially in the area of environmental protection, has been followed by stepped-up efforts at forced deregulation of the industry to encourage competition among local power providers and lower prices to local consumers.

As the 1990s drew to a close, electric companies seemed to surrender to the fact that generation methods were unable to keep up with peak demand periods. New technologies are being brought on line and, combined with reduced consumer demand, are expected to shore up the situation in the early decades of the twenty-first century, according to the EIA.[19] In the interim, the energy demands imposed by the 1999 heat wave and the measures employed by businesses and electricity companies to cope with them may well be a harbinger of things to come.

In point of fact, the measures used to cope with the extraordinary energy demands of the 1999 heatwave were a combination of old and new techniques. One industry observer summarized them as a combination of:

1. On-site electric power generation.
2. Deliverable electric power generation.
3. Electric power loss insurance.[20]

Prior to the demand spike, many power companies were offering business customers on-site power generation equipment, a strategy that dates back to the earliest days of electric power before the rise of commercial electricity generation. In fact, power companies were originally founded by entrepreneurs in response to problems that early electricity users reported with on-site generation, including difficulties servicing, maintaining, and repairing equipment and the danger and expense entailed in operating equipment. According to one industry observer,

> [A] key difference between yesteryear and today...was that most companies using electric power would not suffer hugely expensive losses every time that power went out. Such is not the case today. According to a study by Impulse Research, small businesses alone lose an average of $7500 per day due to blackouts. For larger businesses the losses may be nearly incalculable. So, on-site generation used almost exclusively by hospitals, police, forestations, the government, and the military reappears on the front doorstep of the modern corporation.[21]

Just as consumers began purchasing bottled water despite the availability of water utility supplies, so there appears to be a trend toward self-generation of electricity to augment the electrical utility supply, which has come to be considered as unreliable during periods of peak use. An industry is springing up around this trend consisting of entrepreneurial vendors (in some cases, subsidiaries of power generation companies) offering self-generation packages sized to meet specific load needs that are operated and maintained by the provider.

For companies that prefer not to go into the power business or absorb the expense of purchasing a generator or small turbine, a second class of portable power providers has also appeared. These companies sell UPS systems and wiring services and a contract to appear on site with a portable generator (or to deliver power from a separate generating facility) in an emergency or during periods when utility outages are expected, that is, during certain holidays or under certain weather conditions. This strategy has the advantage of reduced expense when compared to self-generation, but may incur a steeper price tag than self-generation when the service is operated on a continuous basis in a seasonal scenario.

The third response to potential outages is insurance. A growing number of underwriters are developing policies that will compensate a business customer for losses incurred during a power outage. According to one observer, some firms may view the insurance option as "the easiest way out."

> It is certainly the simplest to administrate and the risks are significantly lowered. However, this area too can get a little tricky. First of all, you need to make sure that any policy you sign will cover any power loss for any reason. This makes the premiums go up. You may want to contract with a portable power provider anyway. This would make the premiums go down. Finally, you may want to break down and buy a generator after all. This would give you the best chances for never being down. In addition, your insurance premiums, if you decided to keep the policy, would go way down.[22]

An alternative to the above strategies—and one that may be preferred by traditional power generation companies—is to diversify power feeds. Most power companies distribute electricity across their operating area via a network of transmission lines and substations. Within each substation are several feeder transformers that are individually controlled by the power company's central computer. If a peak demand overload occurs, power companies may institute a pattern of "rolling blackouts" that turn feeder transformers on and off at intervals. When an outage hits a company's utility power during a peak period, this rolling blackout strategy may be to blame.

According to Garry Riley, Construction and Operations Manager for Florida Power Corporation, there are ways for companies to avoid being caught in the rolling blackout or other outages resulting from damaged transmission lines or transformers.

> One way is to diversify your utility feeds. Depending on geography, this may be done cost-effectively by purchasing two feeds from two different substations, or it may be possible to purchase two feeds served by different feeder transformers within one substation. You can contract with the power company to guarantee that both the primary and secondary feeder will not be shut off at the same time during a rolling blackout in order to ensure a constant power supply during this time.[23]

Riley observes that switching from a primary to a secondary power feed can be provided by power company computers or by on-site switching gear. He recalls one company, a pharmaceutical manufacturer, who found that transfer switching speeds were not fast enough to prevent systems from shutting down, causing momentary outages that resulted in the company processes "making the wrong kind of pills." To rectify the problem, the company purchased an on-site, custom-configured power transfer switch for between $15,000 and $20,000 and invested in a UPS to buffer the switching of power feeds. Since that time, says Riley, Florida Power Corporation's computerized switching systems have been redesigned to switch transmission facilities within one-twelfth of a second.

Power companies can deliver a broad range of solutions, says Riley, for any company's utility requirements. Given money to spend on electrical power, companies can still ensure a continuous energy supply. In any case, power companies can provide a wealth of insights that may be useful to planners working to mitigate the risk of a power-related interruption of mission-critical business processes.

PHYSICAL ACCESS CONTROL

Although commonly regarded as a security concern, facility access is another area with which the disaster recovery coordinator may need to become involved. An increasing number of disasters are the result of intentional or accidental damage to equipment and facilities by employees and others who have access to the corporate business offices and data centers. Disgruntled employees, corporate saboteurs, negligent users or vendors, and a host of others may cause fires, damage media, disrupt processes, or otherwise impair normal operations.

This has led to the installation of physical access control systems in many companies ranging from locked doors, security guards, and closed-circuit cameras to electronic card key systems and biometric access control systems. It is essential for the disaster recovery coordinator to fully understand systems that are already in place and to champion the physical security issue if inadequate access control methods are discovered.

The reasons for involving the disaster recovery coordinator in physical security matters are twofold. For one, effective access security can greatly reduce the risk of certain disaster potentials. The coordinator needs to document the capabilities that exist in the plan.

The second reason for the DR coordinator's concern with physical security is for post-disaster recovery. It is important to know how to *circumvent* security measures in the event of a disaster in order to evacuate personnel, to perform emergency equipment shutdowns, and to access and remove secure information that is at risk of loss or damage.

In a financial environment, for example, checks and other executable financial documents, printed on a daily basis, are often stored on-site in locked cabinets. Also, registers and logs, which are used to track the use of checks, may be stored in the cabinets where they can be accessed to record check processing runs. Assuming that a supply of checks is readily available from off-site storage or from vendors in the case of a disaster, the disaster recovery coordinator may see no reason to change the current security arrangement.

However, if the registers are important and irreplaceable, the coordinator may need to make provisions for accessing registers in order to remove them to a safe location in the event of an emergency.

The concept that disaster recovery planning may require security workarounds is sometimes difficult for security administrators to accept. Implicit is the threat that security-breaking methods will become common knowledge, and that expensive and time-consuming systems will be rendered impotent. Considerable diplomacy and common sense may be required to cultivate the cooperation of security managers in those areas where access control and disaster recovery priorities conflict.

A comprehensive discussion of physical access controls and security management is beyond the scope of this book. However, there are some very basic tasks for the DR coordinator to undertake in order to facilitate the integration of security with disaster recovery.

- **Become familiar with current security industry practices.** The World Wide Web is a good place to begin. Numerous security trade associations and practitioner societies host extensive sites on the Web filled with technical papers, case studies of security system designs, and detailed guides. Attending security-oriented tradeshows and seminars and reading up on the latest techniques and methods are also excellent ways to become conversant with the field and its jargon.

- **Consult with experts.** If the corporate office facility or data center is currently without an access control capability, consult with one of the many vendors of security products and services to provide a preliminary analysis of facility security requirements. If knowledgeable security professionals are not part of the corporate organization, DR coordinators may want to consult with a security professional prior to inviting vendors into any discussion. The American Society for Industrial Security (ASIS) is a good source for qualified security consultants.

- **Develop an understanding of security systems that are already in place**. If security consists of a locked door, cabinet, or drawer, find out who has the keys. Similarly, if a master card key, or special code number, or other device (sometimes called a *token*) exists that will open all doors, find out who possesses the token. The security administrator or a designee from the security organization should be a member of the recovery team. Not only will the individual be helpful in identifying current capabilities and security workarounds that may be needed for emergency response, a security professional can also contribute useful input about how security will be provided for business processes that are being operated in a disaster recovery mode.

- **Learn what is being safeguarded by security measures and determine if it is needed in day-to-day work at the facility or if it would be better stored in a secure, off-site location.** In some cases, companies have invested significant resources to secure sensitive documents and other private corporate materials from disclosure or theft, but have not considered their loss to fire, water damage, or other disaster potentials. Working with the security administrator, the DR coordinator may be able to find those materials a home in secure off-site storage, solving both their security and disaster recovery requirements.

- **Make provisions for the restoration of physical security at the recovery site.** It is important to ensure that security controls are reestablished at the same time as systems and networks are restored. Controls should also be established to safeguard data during evacuation and transport to the backup site.

The point is that physical security remains just as important in an emergency as it is during normal operations. Only by providing the means for replacing standard security procedures with emergency security procedures will the objectives of both security planning and disaster recovery planning be met.

In addition to physical security considerations, a host of application and network security measures may also need to be accounted for in the disaster recovery plan. These will be discussed in greater detail later in this book.

ENDNOTES

1. Hewlett Packard Case Study, 5/24/99, and Jeffrey Camp, "Flood Prods NT Move," *Computerworld,* 6/1/99.
2. Alan Radding, "Lights Out," *Computerworld*, 6/1/99.
3. "Report of Test Results: Halon 1301 vs. Water Sprinkler Fire Protection for Essential Electronic Equipment," Document ESL-TR-B2-28, Air Force Engineering and Services Laboratory (Tyndall AFB, FL: AFESL, 1982), pp. 75–76. Conclusions about water damage to computer equipment included: "water ... produced many deleterious side effects, primarily through corrosion and staining of sensitive electronic components" and that "considerable downtime [was required] to dry out the electronic equipment and repair water damaged components."
4. "Facts about Clean Agent Suppression Systems," The Fire Suppression Systems Association (FSSA), Baltimore, MD, 1994.
5. Significant New Alternatives Program Preliminary Findings, Environmental Protection Agency, Washington, D.C., 3/18/94.
6. Interview with Brian Pung, President, Protective Services, Inc., Hollywood, FL and Tampa, FL, 6/99.
7. Richard A. Matthews, "Cleanroom Velocity Not Subject to Outdated Standards," *CleanRooms*, 3/99.
8. According to studies published by the American Society of Heating, Refrigeration and Air Conditioning Engineers (ASHRAE), *Handbook of Fundamentals* (Atlanta, GA, 1986), particles have a calculable settling velocity. A particle one micron in size that is suspended in the air of a room eight feet tall, under ideal conditions of still air, will take nearly 19 hours to settle out. A .1 micron particle, under the same conditions, would take 72 days. In a typical data center—with doors opening and closing frequently, air conditioners blowing, and machines moving and generating electrostatic, thermal, and frictional influences—the settling rate would be very much prolonged. For this reason, contamination detection methods that rely on settled particulate are inherently flawed in their findings.
9. Interview with Eric Williamson, President, Worldwide Environmental Services USA Inc., Blue Bell, PA, 6/99.
10. Interview with Stuart Hanley, Vice President of World Wide Operations, OnTrack Data International, Eden Prarie, MN, 6/99.

11. Pung interview.

12. *Ibid.*

13. *Ibid.*

14. John R. Hall, Jr., "Special Analysis Package: Computer Equipment and Computer Areas," National Fire Protection Association, Quincy, MA, February 1999.

15. Interview with Rich Feldhaus, Product Specialist, TrippLite, Chicago, IL, 6/99.

16. *Ibid.*

17. "Uninterruptible Power Systems (UPS) Technology: Which UPS Is Right for My Systems?" Technical Paper, Powerware Corporation (formerly Exide Electronics), Raleigh, NC, 1999.

18. Kenneth G. Brill, "Keeping Up Your UPS," *Datamation,* 7/15/87.

19. Market Trends, from the web site of the Energy Information Administration, U. S. Department of Energy, http://www.eia.doe.gov/oiaf/aeo98/ele_pri.html#generating, 12/18/97.

20. Stephen Heiser, "Balance of Power: Summer Shortages and Opportunities," *Power Online,* A Verticalnet Community, 08/03/99.

21. *Ibid.*

22. *Ibid.*

23. Interview with Garry L. Riley, Construction and Operations Manager, Florida Power Corporation, St. Petersburg, FL, 08/99.

CHAPTER
4

Data Recovery Planning

Many experts believe that successful business recovery comes down to a simple axiom: Shorten the time to data. For the company experiencing an unplanned interruption in time-sensitive, mission-critical business processes, the primary objective is to reestablish access to application data quickly and by whatever means possible.

Time to data is a determinant of post-disaster business survival. Companies that go too long without key business process restoration quickly amass lost revenues, lost customers, lost market position, and eventually lose everything. How long this takes is a matter of conjecture because it depends so much on the unique sensitivities of the company.

For most firms, failure to recover mission-critical business processes within a week or two virtually guarantees business failure within five years. For companies that are extremely dependent upon technology to support business processes—especially those engaged in electronic commerce or dependent upon supply chain management or Enterprise Resource Planning (ERP) applications—the timeframe may be much shorter.

From an IT perspective, creating strategies to shorten time to data is the primary mission of disaster recovery planning. Once provisions have been made to minimize the likelihood of avoidable disasters, attention turns to developing strategies to restore infrastructure supports for critical business processes in the wake of disasters that cannot be effectively avoided.

THE PRIMACY OF DATA

Recently, significant attention has turned to electronic data and its storage infrastructure (rather than processors or networks) as the focal point for effective information systems design and integration. Data storage is increasingly recognized as the center of the IT universe. Extending this metaphor, networks of servers and client devices provide a system of satellites that orbit the storage platform.

The above is more than a metaphor. Companies are increasingly deploying large-scale, stand-alone storage disk arrays or storage area networks (SANs) to serve as a centralized repository for corporate data. These platforms provide the means to share data among multiple, heterogeneous processor platforms, usually via high-speed network interconnects such as SCSI, Fibre Channel, or even Gigabit Ethernet.

Many factors are driving this shift in the perspective of corporate IT architects and have been discussed in detail elsewhere.[1] For the disaster recovery coordinator, the relevance of the phenomenon is that data—its effective storage, management, and accessibility—is already a major concern for most businesses and their IT organizations. So, too, protecting data and assuring its availability for access following a disaster must be the central concern of disaster recovery. Without data, there can be no recovery at all.

Many disaster recovery planning product vendors have already come to this conclusion. They argue that, following a disaster, alternate system processors might be able to be found "on the fly," that network backup strategies might be "pieced together" *ad hoc*, and that temporary user quarters might be set up just about anywhere. Without the recovery of data, however, all the other logistics and strategies of disaster recovery plans are meaningless.

While one cannot discount the value of advance planning for other aspects of recovery, the importance of safeguarding data assets required for business process recovery cannot be overstated. To understand why, one needs only recall some of the issues discussed earlier in this text.

As discussed previously, business interruption insurance can provide only for the restoration—not the replacement—of data. Restoration frequently requires that copies of electronic datasets and the most current updates to them (whether in the form of electronic update files or paper-based input documents) be available to the recovery effort.

To guarantee that data copies and other update sources are not consumed in the same disaster that renders the production environment untenable, these items should be stored at a safe location, preferably off-site and at a facility other than the one that houses the production systems.

PLANNING FOR DATA RECOVERY

Maintaining secure, off-site data copies is not enough to assure recovery, however. The time to data requirement means that companies must be able to restore electronic datasets to an accessible form efficiently so they may be processed by the systems, networks, and end users who make them purposeful. How quickly datasets must be restored to a usable form is determined by the sensitivity of the company to the duration of an unplanned interruption. To address different degrees of sensitivity, several techniques of data restoral have evolved over time. These include:

- Routine data backup to magnetic tape using backup/restore software and the removal of backups to off-site storage. Restoral requires the retrieval of stored backup tapes, transport to system recovery facility, and restoration of data to a new storage platform via software.
- Routine data backup to an electronic "tape vault" via a wide area network (WAN) interconnect or the Internet. Restoral may require the physical retrieval of tapes and their transport to a systems recovery site, or restoral may be possible using a WAN link between the recovery system and the electronic tape vault.
- Remote mirroring of data to a second (or third) storage platform via a wide area network (WAN) interconnect. Restoral is unnecessary. The recovery system is connected via WAN links to the remote mirror array, or the remote mirror may be located at the system recovery site.

A modern data recovery strategy may include one or more variations of the above techniques. The major differences between them are the data availability timeframes they provide and, of course, their cost (see Table 4–1). Choosing the appropriate set of techniques is usually a matter of balancing the time to data requirement of the business process and the willingness of senior management to invest in the data protection strategy.

Table 4–1   Data Backup and Restoral Alternatives

Strategy	Description	Pros	Cons	Cost
Traditional Backup to Tape	Manual process of copying data from hard disk to tape and transporting to secure facility.	Simple-to-implement technology, multiple price-point devices/software available.	Manual transportation and storage prone to risk and error. Potentially long lead time to restoral. Not always practical given available "windows" of processing time.	Low to Medium
Backup to Electronic Tape Vault	Copying data from disk to a remote tape system via a wide area network link.	Data is accessible in shorter timeframe, services becoming standardized, WAN link prices falling, exposure to risk/errors in manual methods reduced.	WAN links can introduce latency into backup process; depending on e-vaulting provider, storage may be difficult to restore; data restoral times potentially lengthy.	Medium to High
Disk Mirroring	Copying data written to one disk or array of disks to a second disk or array of disks via a wide area network link.	Instantaneous restoral of access to data possible (depending on WAN link availability and synchronicity of primary and mirrored arrays).	WAN links can introduce latency into production system operations; some mirroring systems reduce production system performance; logic errors may be replicated from original to mirrored data sets.	High

Clearly, before a disaster recovery coordinator can approach senior management with a proposal for an expensive remote mirroring strategy, a careful analysis of data assets needs should be made. Despite improvements in data backup/restore technology, the underlying methods for determining what data assets need to be protected and how best to protect them have not changed significantly in the last decade or more. The data flow diagram in Figure 4–1 provides an overview of the complex network of activities involved in creating and maintaining an effective data recovery plan.

As suggested by the DFD, data recovery planning several activities. These include:

- The analysis and classification of data based on importance to recovery (and to the company)
- The review of existing backup procedures
- The evaluation and selection of a backup strategy
- The formalization of that strategy in the form of automatic and manual procedures for moving data to a secure, off-site location

Given its close relationship to system, network, and end-user recovery, data recovery planning is often undertaken concurrently with the development of other backup strategies and procedures in the disaster recovery planning project.

IDENTIFYING THE INFORMATION ASSET

For a data recovery plan to be meaningful, it must ensure the "right" data—data that will be used to reduce downtime and speed recovery—is identified and safeguarded against loss. This is a deceptively simple premise. Consider these facts:

- Data is growing at a rate of 100% or more per year in most corporations. Replicated data, "enhanced" data (e.g., document files with graphics, sound clips and other data objects embedded), and large program files account for some of this growth—perhaps as much as 50%, according to some analysts. However, the balance is new data that is constantly being created by end users and automated systems.
- A significant percentage (some argue as much as 80%) of the data stored on hard disk drives is never referenced again.

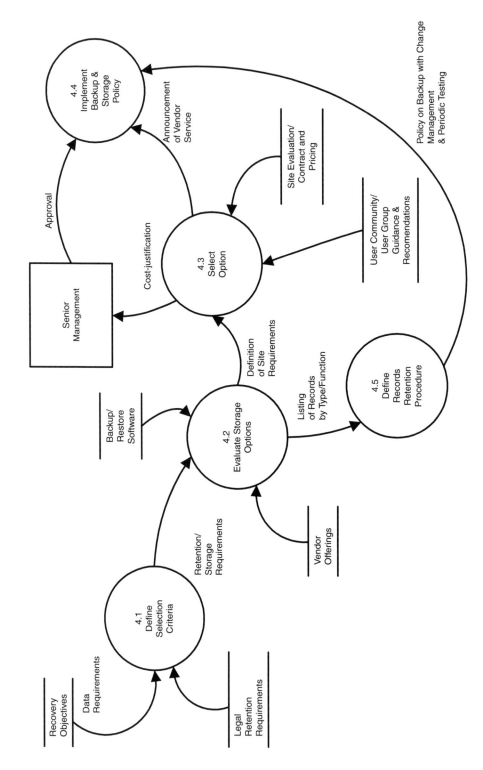

Figure 4–1 Data Recovery Planning.

- Databases measured in terabytes are becoming commonplace within Fortune 1000 firms, according to Dale Miller, Vice President with the Trilliant Group.[2] Even in medium-sized firms, says Miller, it is not uncommon to find databases sized in the 400 to 700 GB range.

- In most companies, policies and standards do not exist for the classification of data by its importance to the organization. According to the 1998 *Information Week*/PricewaterhouseCoopers Global Information Security Survey, 43% of the 1600 companies surveyed worldwide indicated that they never classify data and 14% classify their records only on an annual basis.[3] Says Nora Denzel, Senior Vice President of Product Operations with Legato Systems, "In many firms, a memorandum is sent out to employees, which usually gets discarded, instructing employees to copy important data to a particular directory or folder so it can be included in backups. The policy is not enforced, so no one does it. Companies that do enforce this policy generally do so because they have experienced a costly data loss at some point."[4]

Against this backdrop, it is clear that the DR coordinator may confront a major obstacle at the outset of data recovery planning: learning where the data is stored in the organization.

Trilliant Group's Miller states that this task can be facilitated through the use of software products that "autodiscover" volumes, databases, and files installed on networked devices.[5] In particular, Miller references Dallas, TX-based Sterling Software's SAMS:Vantage, Network Edition (see Figure 4–2) and Marlborough, MA-based HighGround Systems' Storage Resource Manager (SRM) (see Figure 4–3) as valuable tools for ferreting out data, determining its usage characteristics, and planning capacity requirements for backup.

Discovering the locations and usage characteristics of electronic files stored on PCs, server-captive storage arrays, stand-alone arrays, network attached storage (NAS) devices, and storage area networks (SANs) does not, however, define the criticality of the data or its suitability to a backup strategy. According to Legato's Denzel, culling through data sets to assess their importance and to set policies for backup can be a lengthy and challenging undertaking.

> To perform backups of distributed data effectively requires policy-driven management. Before you can set policy or [deploy an enterprise-wide data backup product tool like Legato NetWorker], you need to go through a three to four week planning exercise. Visit each depart-

Figure 4–2 Sterling Software SAMS: Vantage, Network Edition file distribution screen. (*Source:* Sterling Software, Inc. www.sterling.com)

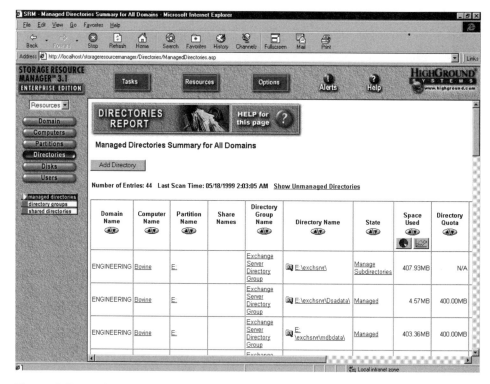

Figure 4–3 HighGround Systems Storage Resource Manager (SRM) file distribution screen. (*Source:* Highground Systems, Marlborough, MA.)

ment and identify critical data. Run reports and figure out exactly what they have. The process is more like interior decorating than buying a couch off the rack.[6]

In addition to electronic or machine-readable data, data recovery planning must also concern itself with identifying business critical information stored on paper and with the interdependencies that may exist among paper or other documentation, electronic data, source documents, and worker knowledge that make all data usable. This too can be a laborious and time-consuming task. To the list of information storage repositories that must be examined by the DR coordinator an assortment of safes, file cabinets, microfiche and microfilm storage racks, and old-fashioned desk drawers must be added.

Paper and microform continues to proliferate in most companies, to the dismay of naturalists and efficiency experts alike. One vendor of electronic document management systems summarizes the problems associated with these popular information storage media:

> Upwards of 90% of all corporate knowledge is stored on paper—but paper itself is never a profit center. Filing, storing, and retrieving paper documents is an enormous drain on a company's resources. . . . [Moreover,] paper documents and the data contained on them must be analyzed on a document by document basis. Sorting or searching for data is, practically speaking, impossible . . . 3% of a company's documentation is misfiled—and 3% is lost . . . 32% of a company's documentation is in use by a single user at any time—and is unavailable to any other users. The cost of locating a missing document is $6 to $120.[7]

These drawbacks of static storage media and the advantages of maintaining machine-readable copies is behind explosive growth in the knowledge management industry, which includes electronic document management systems, workflow management systems and related technologies. According to a joint survey of 500 IT managers by *Information Week* Research and Cap Ventures, total document management solutions spending jumped 38% in 1998 to $3.5 billion, up from $2.5 billion in 1997.[8]

If an organization has embraced electronic document management, the DR coordinator can leverage this effort to identify key documents for removal to off-site storage, of course. If not, disaster recovery may provide yet another justification to senior management for such an endeavor.

In the absence of an electronic document management capability, the DR coordinator may still be able to enlist the services of a corporate records manager, or clerical personnel at a departmental level to identify paper and microform-based information for inclusion in the data recovery strategy.

It is worth noting that, according to numerous studies, records managers are the forgotten asset in disaster recovery and security planning. These knowledgeable persons were members of recovery plans in fewer than 20% of plans reviewed in one 1997 survey. In another survey conducted in the same year, it was determined 70% of company executives excluded records managers from the process of assessing and mitigating risk to records—this despite the fact that 90% of businesses that lose their vital records are out of business within one year.[9]

CLASSIFYING CRITICALITY: INPUTS AND OUTPUTS

No data, whether paper-based or machine-readable, is critical in and of itself. It is only critical insofar as it supports critical business processes or satisfies other legal or financial requirements of the business. Critical data includes all information files, regardless of storage media, that provide inputs to and, in some cases, the outputs from critical applications. Thus, in formulating a data recovery plan, the coordinator needs to:

- Identify input (and output) data sources for those critical business processes that were identified as part of risk analysis.

  Inputs may comprise source documents that are coded or otherwise rendered machine-readable by system users. These source documents (or copies of them) should be identified for removal to off-site storage.

  Output documents, such as reports or summaries, may also be critical if they are auditable records, used in important historical analyses, or used by others in their performance of vital work (e.g., account histories used by customer service, shipping records for recent deliveries to customers, etc.). These documents and/or the media on which they are recorded should be listed for regular removal off-site.

  Of course, licensed programs and systems software, and as well as source code and compiled source for custom-developed applications software, should also be earmarked for off-site storage. Be sure to include any software license information and registration keys that may be required to make software function or to obtain vendor support. More than one disaster recovery effort has been held up when it was discovered that software keys were omitted from recovery requirements lists and applications could not be restarted without them.

- Identify ancillary documentation required for restoring business processes.

    In addition to application programs and input source data and documents, a number of other items must be stored off-site to facilitate recovery. These may include insurance policy information, asset inventories, and other documentation required for efficient processing of insurance claims; key operations and user manuals; preprinted forms such as blank check stock; and, of course, copies of the disaster recovery plan.

- Identify data that must be preserved to satisfy legal requirements and to reduce business loss.

    Auditors and records managers can assist in identifying data and documents that must be preserved to satisfy legal requirements. In addition, there may be a number of records—such as sales and marketing client contact lists and email directories, drafts of contracts, and intellectual properties such as designs for prototype systems—that would not be needed to restore vital business operations or to satisfy legal mandates, but which do represent substantial investments of company resources. These may be difficult, costly, or impossible to replace and would be a substantial business loss if destroyed. These files, too, are excellent candidates for secure off-site storage.

SETTING A POLICY ON DATA ASSET IDENTIFICATION, CLASSIFICATION, AND BACKUP

The identification of key business data is not a one-time undertaking. As information proliferates, an ongoing identification, classification, and protection strategy is required to keep the data protection plan in synchronization with the business. A formal policy or set of policies may need to be developed and enforced to facilitate data recovery requirements in the future. Elements of such a policy may include the following:

- Establish departmental "owners" of information. Make someone in each business unit, department, or workgroup responsible for providing the "brainwork" of data asset identification and classification on an ongoing basis.

- With the assistance of auditors, establish criteria for identifying the relative importance of records. The simplified method for classifying data criticality summarized in Table 4–2 may be adapted to the needs of virtually any company. As may be apparent, the same categories that are applied to applications in risk analysis may also be applied to classify the data required to restore the applications.

With the help of auditors and in-house experts, it may be possible to correlate certain types of documents (i.e., forms with specific form numbers, specific "named" reports, etc.) with the generic categories identified in Table 4–2. These and other classification aids can assist data owners in keeping their off-site storage inventories current.

Of course, classifying data may entail some of the same problems encountered when classifying application criticality during risk analysis. No one likes to believe that the data he or she "owns" is anything less than critical. However, most owners will concede that third-generation

Table 4–2   Simplified Data Classification Scheme

Classification	Definition
Critical	Data or documentation that must be retained for legal reasons, for use in key business processes, or for restoration minimum acceptable work levels in the event of a disaster.
Vital	Data or documentation that must be retained for use in normal business processes and that represents a substantial investment of company resources that may be difficult or impossible to recoup, but may not be required in a disaster recovery situation. Information that requires special secrecy or discretion may also fall under this category.
Sensitive	Data or documentation that is needed in normal operations, but for which alternative supplies are available in the event of loss. Data that can be reconstructed fairly readily but at some cost could also be classified as sensitive.
Noncritical	Data or documentation that can be reconstructed readily at minimal cost, or duplicates of critical, vital, or sensitive data that have no prerequisite security requirements.

copies of original documents are less critical than the originals, and many will comply with a definition of criticality that does not suggest that their work does not contribute to business success in day-to-day operations.

POLICY-BASED MANAGEMENT OF ELECTRONIC DATA VIA SOFTWARE

Management of ongoing data identification, classification, and backup tasks for electronic data can be facilitated through the use of a policy-based backup/restore software package. A number of worthwhile enterprise-, workgroup-, and server-class tools are available today, as might be expected of a software market segment that is experiencing a period of significant growth.

Leading packages currently include Computer Associates ARC-ServeIT™, Legato Systems NetWorker™, Veritas Software (formerly Seagate Software) Backup Exec™, Sterling Software SAMS: Alexandria™, Hewlett Packard Company OmniBack™, and IBM ADSTAR Distributed Storage Manager (ADSM). In a crowded field, these products stand out for having lengthy pedigrees and a broad range of deployment options. This does not mean that a new product that provides competitive features, or that a point product that supports a specific hardware configuration, would not provide an appropriate choice as well.

According to one Seagate Software (now Veritas Software) product manager, a comprehensive backup software solution is one that "provides logical views into data storage [and] that allows you to classify data and establish views of data on some logical basis (e.g., by the application that the data supports)."

> The package should also allow you to set policies on data backups and provide an event-correlating policy engine that enables the software to take certain actions when policy thresholds have been reached, such as forwarding alarms or backing up changed data automatically. [10]

Jeff Wells, Product Manager for SAMS: Alexandria at Sterling Software notes that the performance of the product, in terms of both its speed of operation and its CPU resource utilization, are also important considerations.

When Sterling acquired the Alexandria product, we went to existing customers and asked why they selected it. One of the largest telcoms was a user and their IT manager told us they bought the product because it could do everything that other packages could do, but on a smaller server—basically a desktop system. The others required high-powered servers. But, with Alex [sic], they could run it on a large server and still have some resource left over to perform other tasks important to the business. The difference is in the product's use of memory. Many products rely on remote procedure calls (RPCs), involving many memory-to-memory data copies. Alex is unique in that it uses an asynchronous memory scheme. It makes for extremely efficient data movements with low CPU overhead. That is something others don't tell you when they announce the results of terabyte backup "speed trials"—what their resource utilization was like.[11]

Computer Associates Product Marketing Manager Allan Mohess further defines appropriate solutions by their support for heterogeneous computing platforms. He notes that most enterprise-class products, including ARCServeIT, provide centralized consoles, "NT- or Java-based," that enable the management of backup activity on multiple, heterogeneous hosts and their storage platforms from a single location.[12]

Legato's Denzel agrees generally with this assessment, noting that her company's NetWorker product is "the Switzerland of backup and recovery products."[13] She adds that, given the large volume of data and multiplicity of systems that need to be included in a distributed system backup strategy, an open tape format that stores data together with "self-describing metadata" is key for efficient recovery. Moreover, she adds, a comprehensive solution needs to support a broad range of backup devices and strategies.

Says Denzel, "Most of our customers prefer to backup to tape rather than to mirror their data using disk. Partly, this is because of the cost of remote mirroring and its inherent problem: Mirroring replicates whatever logic problems that exist in the [original] data, creating two sets of bad data." She notes that, in Legato's experience,

Most companies use a tape autoloader to perform local backups [that are then removed off site]. Sometimes they copy to disk first, then to tape, in order to reduce latency. Other customers have begun to embrace electronic vaulting, backing up data directly to remote tape libraries or autoloaders. Whatever their strategy and their device preference, [a good backup software product] will support them with a common console, a tape backup solution, and a mirroring solution.[14]

PERFORMANCE CONSIDERATIONS
IN BACKUP SOFTWARE SELECTION

Denzel's observations cut to the heart of backup/restore software selection. In the past, organizations sought solutions for backup/restore that were consistent with available "backup windows." A backup window consisted of the time available within the normal operating schedules of systems and networks for performing large scale data movements from primary storage media (usually disk) to secondary storage media (usually tape). In the past, these windows were defined by application usage characteristics and network bandwidth availability.

Put another way, companies sought backup products that would enable them to copy mission-critical data to tape while on-line applications were not being used and networks were quiet. These conditions usually existed after working hours, when everyone except janitorial staff and night operators had gone home for the night or weekend.

This scenario is increasingly anachronistic in many companies. With the growth of the Internet and the trend to extend corporate applications for access by customers or business partners via extranets and the World Wide Web, applications tend to be active on a 24x7 basis. That means that systems and networks are rarely quiesced for a sufficient period of time to enable a window for backup. Moreover, the amount of data to be backed up has increased to the point in many organizations where large-scale data movements could not be accomplished within any predefined window of opportunity.

Andrew Gup, a Product Marketing Manager at Spectra Logic Corporation made a fascinating analysis of the problem in 1997.[15] He noted that terabyte-sized relational databases and 24x7 operating schedules had largely invalidated the traditional approach to off-line, or cold, database backup. In its place, database vendors enabled their products with application programming interfaces (APIs) that could be used to support "hot" backups (backups of active or in-use databases). Most leading backup/restore software vendors have since availed themselves of these APIs, which are also provided with many large ERP software suites.

In addition to hot backup API support, backup software vendors have added other capabilities to enable the performance of backups in a no window, multiterabyte world. It is difficult to create a taxonomy of these approaches because vendors tend to give their technologies brand names in order to discriminate their products from one another. Table 4–3 provides a seminal effort in this area.

The strategies discussed in Table 4–3 are only the beginning of a broad array of solutions that will likely be developed to facilitate high-speed, reliable, and comprehensive backups of distributed corporate data. In many cases, the technologies for backup have begun to merge with the technologies for disk mirroring, reflecting less the problem of backup window shrinkage than the dilemma of fast restore.

BACKUP OR RESTORAL PLANNING?

Many observers have pointed to restore as the critical part of the backup/restore solution. Rather than "windows for backup," they discuss backup/restore from the perspective of "windows of exposure" and emphasize both the impact of data loss and the time required to return data to a usable form following a disaster.[18]

While it is important to back up data accurately and with a minimal impact on the production environment, it is the speed of data restoral that is of key importance in a disaster recovery context. This premise is behind most of the recent technological improvements in backup/recovery software and also architectures for its deployment.

Throughout 1998 and 1999, the press releases of major backup/restore software vendors cited new "world records" for terabyte database recovery on an almost monthly basis. This was more than a marketing effort to best the opposition. It was a manifestation of the concern of business about the recoverability of such large and increasingly mission-critical data sets. Given the speed of popular tape devices in the midrange market (DLT 7000 Tape Drives from Quantum Corporation were the marketshare leaders), transferring a terabyte of data to or from tape at a rate of 7 MB/s seemed a dangerously slow proposition. Moreover, with DLT Tape, it was necessary to scan an entire tape to find a particular file to restore, which could dramatically increase time to data in a recovery setting.

Advances in tape technology, especially in the areas of interface speed, parallel multiplexing capability and tape RAIDing, provided a marked improvement in overall disk-to-tape data transfer rates. Backup/restore software vendors were quick to capitalize on these capa-

Table 4–3 Backup Strategy Taxonomy

Backup Strategy or Technology	Vendor	Functional Overview
IMAGE BACKUP		
Server Image Backup	Some vendors of backup software support variations of this method, which is probably the oldest method of electronic data backup on record.	Image backup creates a physical image of an entire disk. It operates at the physical disk level by transferring sectors or physical data storage blocks from hard disk to tape. Image backup delivers fast transfer rates by moving the hard disk head smoothly from one edge of the disk to the other as sectors are transferred. Complete server backup is a relatively simple process since the entire contents of the hard disk are moved as a unit. The image contains the entire disk contents, but requires the system to be quiesced prior to backup. Though a high-speed approach, the resulting backup tapes cannot be used to recover specific files, directories, or server specific objects (Bindery and DNS for NetWare and the system registry under Windows NT).
Snapshot or Versioning Backups	Originated by CrosStor Software (formerly Programmed Logic Corporation), this capability has been added to many backup software vendors' offerings.	Fast, block-level copies on a partition basis, enabled for fast incremental (changed data only) backups to facilitate high-speed versioning (see Figure 4–4).

(continued)

Table 4–3 *Continued*

Backup Strategy or Technology	Vendor	Functional Overview
FILE BACKUP		
Traditional Full Volume Backup on a File-by-File Basis	Most current vendors support this approach, which varies from an image backup in that data is recorded in accordance with the underlying file layout and structure of the host system controlling the disk volume.	Copy complete data sets via the production network to backup device(s) using a server-initiated, server-controlled process. The server maintains a database of file identifiers and provides monitoring and reporting on process completion, errors and exceptions, and other factors.
Traditional Full Volume Backup with Hot Backup API Support	Many vendors support Hot Backup APIs as either an integral function of their core product or as a modular add-on purchased on an as-needed basis by the customer.	Same as above, except that support is provided for database and application vendor application programming interfaces (APIs) that enable backup while active.
Traditional Full Volume Backup with Open File support	Innovation attributed to St. Bernard Software (see Figure 4–5), but variations are now widely available from different vendors.[16]	Open files are backed up to a "pre-write" cache, which is copied by the backup software instead of copying or skipping the open file entirely.
Incremental, Differential, or Delta File Backup	Most backup software supports the intelligent backup of data that has changed since the previous full or incremental backup. Methods for documenting changes and for facilitating file recovery vary from vendor to vendor.	Basically, file characteristics are compared to historical data (databases compiled in previous backup operations) to identify files that have changed since the last backup. Only changed files (and new files) are backed up. In some cases, differential differs from incremental backups in a subtle way. With differential backups, changed data files may be maintained as separate versions. With incremental backups, changed files replace their predecessors.

124

Backup Strategy or Technology	Vendor	Functional Overview
HYBRID IMAGE AND FILE BACKUP		
Full and Partial Backups Using Object Replication	Supported by products from Stac Software (Replica Tape) and others.	Object replication is a blend of file-by-file and image backup options. Logical objects are defined by the software, including disk partition tables, boot volume, security information, system volume, and user data volumes. All data on servers is treated as a single logical unit rather than as separate files, and all data can be copied at once. Object replication creates an exact copy of the entire server by saving it logically, block by block. Only data blocks that contain data are transferred.[17]
ARCHITECTURE ADD-INS		
Host-free Backup	Supported by Legato NetWorker following the company's acquisition of Intelliguard Software in 1999.	Using intelligent agents to initiate backups that then run independtly of the host or server system, saving server resources and enabling direct storage device to storage device copies (see Figure 4–6).
Full Backups with Parallelism Provisions	Essentially a hardware interconnect defintion that enables multiple hard disks or a multi-ported disk array to be connected to multiple tape drivers or multiported tape arrays/libraries. Backup software must support interconnect device drivers.	Speeds the backup of large arrays by creating multiple, parallel paths for data movement (see Figure 4–7). Some products, such as Ultera Systems', implement RAID striping and mirroring to facilitate multiple concurrent tape backups at high speed.

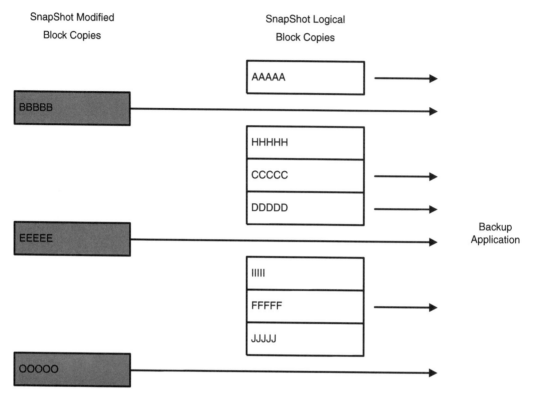

Figure 4-4   Snapshot technology. (*Source:* CrosStor Software, South Plainfield, NJ.)

bilities and added some tricks of their own to keep tape the dominant backup medium.

Beyond refinements and innovations in software and hardware, efforts to reduce time to data have also led to the reexamination of the traditional scenario for data recovery: tape backup with off-site storage. In this approach, the backup tapes and other documents needing backup are trucked off-site on a routine basis to a safe storage facility. In the event of a disaster, the tapes and other documents are collected from the off-site storage facility and transported via truck or airplane to a remote systems recovery facility, or hot site. There, the tapes are loaded into drives connected to the recovery platform, backup/restore software is loaded if necessary, and data is written from the tapes to the new storage devices on the backup platform.

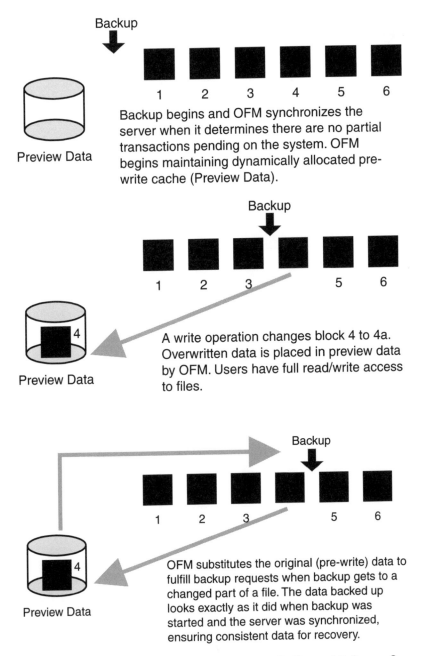

Backup begins and OFM synchronizes the
server when it determines there are no partial
transactions pending on the system. OFM
begins maintaining dynamically allocated pre-
write cache (Preview Data).

A write operation changes block 4 to 4a.
Overwritten data is placed in preview data
by OFM. Users have full read/write access
to files.

OFM substitutes the original (pre-write) data to
fulfill backup requests when backup gets to a
changed part of a file. The data backed up
looks exactly as it did when backup was
started and the server was synchronized,
ensuring consistent data for recovery.

Figure 4–5   Open file copy technology. (*Source:* St. Bernard Software, San
Diego, CA.)

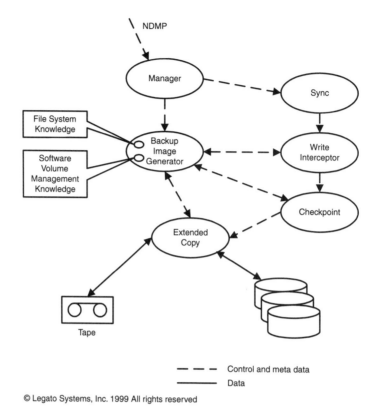

Figure 4–6 Celestra agent architecture. (*Source:* Legato Systems, Palo Alto, CA. www.sterling.com)

Figure 4–7 Expedited backup through support for parallelism and tape array striping and mirroring. (*Source:* Ultera Systems, Laguna Hills, CA.)

This procedure continues to be used as the primary data restoral method for the preponderance of companies that plan for disaster recovery. Upon closer examination, however, several steps may be removed from this procedure to save critical time to data.

Jim Grogan, Vice President of Alliances for disaster recovery facilities vendor SunGard Recovery Services, says that the complexity of modern client/server platforms—including ERP applications, with their often huge and unwieldy distributed databases—have motivated many organizations to look for ways to shave precious hours off their data restoral processes.

> This basically comes down to some sort of data shadowing or mirroring technology that eliminates the need to retrieve data from off-site storage and places it directly on-site at the recovery data center. In the past, this was a prohibitively expensive proposition because it would have cost a company ten times more than [the traditional scenario]. Today, with the deregulation in the telecommunications industry, the cost model has changed dramatically. Our first electronic vaulting customer was signed in 1992. It took until 1996 for a second customer to sign. Now, a significant percentage of our customers choose either electronic tape vaulting or remote mirroring as a component of their recovery contract.[19]

ELECTRONIC VAULTING

Electronic tape vaulting replaces the manual procedures for handling tape in and out of off-site storage facilities and for transporting tape between locations. A Wide Area Network connection is established between the company facility and a remote tape library using channel extension technology or some similar high-bandwidth network interconnect (see Figure 4–8).

Ideally, in a recovery situation, the company employing electronic tape vaulting should be able to access tape backups immediately from their storage locations at the system backup facility. In some cases, restores can be initiated and completed by the time recovery personnel arrive at the hot site—representing a significant time savings.

Of course, backups may be required on site at the corporate facility to recover failed systems and to restore business processes before they have a chance to evolve into disastrous interruptions. To facilitate both local tape backup and remote electronic tape vaulting, intelligent tape controllers, like Ultera Systems Reflection, may be of service (see Figure 4–9).

Figure 4–8   Electronic tape vaulting via channel extension. (*Source:* Computerm Corporation, Pittsburgh, PA.)

Products like shadowing or multiplexing controllers provide the capability to duplicate backup data streams to two or more tape devices simultaneously. By directing a data stream across one link to a local tape autoloader and another data stream across a high-speed WAN link to a remote autoloader, both a local and a remote backup can be made expeditiously. This controller-based solution is compatible with most backup/restore software products and with tape libraries and enables duplicate backup sets to be made in the amount of time typically required to make one backup.

REMOTE MIRRORING

Another alternative to traditional tape-plus-off-site storage may be found in remote disk mirroring. As suggested by its name, disk mirroring does not entail tape-based data copying at all. Instead, writes to one disk are duplicated in near real time on a duplicate disk volume.

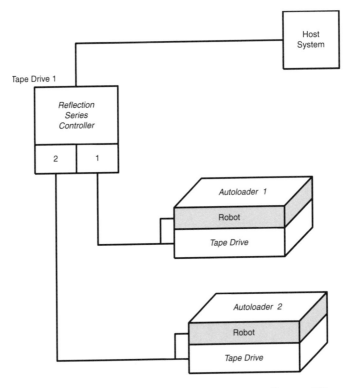

Figure 4–9   Mirrored tape backup operations. (*Source:* Ultera Systems, Laguna Hills, CA.)

Disk mirroring is not a new concept. In fact, it is a mainstay of Redundant Array of Inexpensive Disks (RAID) technology, affording RAID disk arrays an internal means of fault tolerance that is sometimes confused with disaster recovery backup.

With internal RAIDing, disks inside an array are mirrored as a safeguard against certain data loss scenarios. However, disasters can and do occur in which the building that houses the RAID disk array catches fire, loses power, or crumbles in any of a number of cataclysmic natural disasters, rendering the disk array—whether internally mirrored or not—inaccessible. In short, deploying mirrored storage within a data processing facility can contribute to the avoidance of certain types of disaster potentials, but it does not offer a comprehensive disaster recovery capability for the data asset.

Remote mirroring is essentially an extension of the concept of internal disk array mirroring. The idea is to perform duplicate writes to disks on identical (or at least similar) disk array platforms located some distance from the company facility—presumably far enough away so that the mirrored array is not consumed by the same disaster that affects the primary or production array.

In some cases, the mirrored array may be located at another site owned by the organization and remains a component of the organization's internal network. In other cases, the remote mirror may be located at a secure off-site storage facility. In still other cases, the mirror array may be located at a commercial system recovery facility that will be used to recover system platforms in the event of a disaster.

When the remote mirror is geographically distant from the production array, the two are typically connected to each other via a high-speed WAN link. As data writes are made to disk on the production array, they are replicated on the remote array.

In some mirroring arrangements, writes to production disks are placed in a holding queue while the system waits for the mirrored write to be completed and acknowledged. Known as synchronous mirroring, this technique introduces substantial latency into the production environment when mirrored arrays are located next to each other and share a high-speed interconnect. The problem worsens when arrays are separated by greater distances from each other and use slower WAN links for an interconnect.

For many years, extending the distance between mirrored arrays across hundreds of miles—say, between a corporate data center in California and a hot site facility in Pennsylvania—was the stuff of science fiction. The distance-related latency that would accrue to the production environment was enough to make remote mirroring a pipe dream. Over time, however, as the intelligence of disk array controllers improved, the speed and capacity of wide area networks increased, and the costs of high bandwidth WAN links declined, remote mirroring got a second look.

By the mid-1990s, vendors of large (sometimes called "mainframe class" or "enterprise class") array products were experimenting with new techniques for removing distance barriers to remote mirroring. One technique, quite simple in design, consisted of using three arrays instead of two. As illustrated in Figure 4–10, the idea was to use a surrogate mirroring array between the primary and remote array.

The surrogate array is "local" (within the reach of a high-speed serial link) to the primary array and affords protection against an equipment outage in the primary array. A second purpose of the surrogate array, however, is to initiate and manage a separate asynchronous mirroring process with a remote mirror array. The surrogate and remote arrays are linked via a WAN facility, and the latency of the mirroring operation be-

Figure 4–10   A surrogate mirroring configuration.

tween these arrays does not impact the primary array or the production environment at all.

Surrogate mirroring and other innovations in mirroring operation control and management began to move the technology out of the backwaters and into the mainstream of business continuity technology by the mid-1990s. Today, most hot site vendors offer a remote mirroring solution for customers. Vendors recognize that remote mirroring entails substantial costs, which might include the purchase of surrogate platforms and the cost of WAN links. However, many vendors have found that customers with "zero downtime" tolerance can justify these costs.

A variety of remote mirroring solutions are available to meet a variety of applications and price points. Some, like EMC Corporation's Symmetrix Remote Data Facility (SRDF), are closely coupled with a particular vendor's array products. As depicted in Figure 4–11, SRDF may be used to provide synchronous or "adaptive copy" mirroring modes. Synchronous modes are preferred for short distance mirroring, while adaptive copy—a technique for mirroring only changed disk tracks—produces smaller amounts of traffic and can save companies on bandwidth expense in wide area mirroring applications.

Most large hot site facility vendors have adopted the EMC SRDF solution as part of their disaster recovery offerings. This is attributable in part to EMC's market share leadership in the enterprise disk array market through the second half of the 1990s. If customers are deploying EMC Symmetrix platforms in their production environments, they will likely seek comparable platforms in the hot site for use as remote mirrors.

Figure 4-11   EMC SRDF multihop mirroring using synchronous and adaptive copy modes. (*Source:* EMC Corporation, Hopkinton, MA.)

According to SunGard's Grogan, another reason for the popularity of mirroring generally, and the EMC solution in particular, is product maturity.

> Mirroring products have matured over the past few years. They are proven. Cut and dried. They aren't rocket science anymore. SunGard was a beta customer of SRDF. From a usability perspective, the first generation product was not very friendly. You had no read access. If you wanted to see the data, you would basically have to stop the mirror operation. Today, with features such as [BMC Corporation's] Enterprise SnapShot and [EMC's] TimeFinder, you can see it, work with it and test with it. Again, with the costs of telcom links falling, the cost model is down. We have doubled the number of customers using remote mirroring in just the past couple of months.[20]

Sungard's first remote mirroring customer was the Philadelphia Stock Exchange. The organization set forth with an objective to recover its operations within two hours of a disaster that rendered its trade management applications unusable. In April 1996, the first tests of the configuration were conducted using mirrored EMC Symmetrix arrays, SRDF, and a SONET network ring interconnecting the Exchange and Sungard's disaster recovery hot site. Actual recovery in the test required only 58 minutes, which SunGard claims has since been decreased to 45 minutes.[21]

In addition to EMC's SRDF offering, a number of hardware-based and software-based products are available that provide mirroring functionality for a broad range of disk configurations. ARCserveIT Replication Option, from Computer Associates, can be used as a Windows NT server storage mirroring solution, according to Product Marketing Manager Mohess. He says that the product was used in a test environment by CA itself to provide remote failover of servers in Islandia, NY to peer servers in the United

Kingdom. Storage on the two servers is synchronized in near real time via an IP connection with speeds equivalent to a 28.8 modem.[22]

MIRRORING NOT A PANACEA

Disk mirroring, especially the remote variety, has special appeal to disaster recovery planners because of its time to data characteristics and vendor promises of zero downtime. Zero downtime, however, is an unrealistic expectation even in a properly configured, perfectly operating, remote mirroring arrangement. Several factors mitigate the realization of this disaster recovery *nirvana.*

For one, remote mirroring is subject to data gaps. That is, because some sort of asynchronous mirror process is typically used in a WAN-based remote mirroring configuration, there is always a difference in the state of the data contained on the primary and mirrored arrays. This difference may be minor, or it might constitute a delayed shipment to a customer, a lost contract, or a missed investment. For remote mirroring to be effective, data gaps need to be identified and strategies for their resolution determined.

One approach is to use synchronous mirroring across the WAN, enhanced with a capability known as *Mirrored Write Consistency mode.*[23] This mode, available on some mirroring products, results in the creation of a detailed record of all write requests that have not been completed at both the local and the mirrored array. This record, in turn, can be used as a starting point for reentering older transactions and starting new transactions. A significant performance penalty must be paid for this type of security, however. Use of a synchronous operating mode combined with CPU-intensive transaction journaling can slow production system performance substantially. In general, the tradeoff between parity (synchronous mirroring with Write Consistency) and performance (asynchronous mirroring with data gaps) remains an issue for remote mirroring solutions.

In addition to the asynchronous mirror data gap, the zero downtime goal of many companies that choose remote mirroring is also mitigated by the fact that data restoration is only part of a recovery. In the wake of a disaster, many other activities need to occur before recovery can be accomplished. System hardware may need to be installed and operating system software loaded and configured. Networks may need to be rerouted. End users need to obtain remote access to systems. These and many other tasks may need to be performed before the first transaction begins to be processed in the post disaster environment. From this perspective, remote mirroring is not a panacea for disaster recovery.

In addition to the above, more than one observer has pointed out that mirroring itself is not without risks. In some mirror configurations, improper array maintenance and disk swapping errors can cause the reference points for synchronized data to be lost, rendering the mirror array and the data it contains inaccessible and unusable. Moreover, any logic errors that affect the primary array and corrupt its stored data can also be transferred to the mirrored array, affecting its data efficacy and integrity as well. In short, mirroring can be a multiplier of disaster just as easily as it can be a mitigator.

For these reasons, and many others, tape backup should remain a part of data recovery planning even when remote mirroring is used. This fact is acknowledged by Don Swatik, Vice President of Product Marketing for EMC Corporation. Swatik, while arguing that the same content replication errors that can occur in a mirroring configuration are also the bane of tape backup, notes

> Here's a statistic: For every bit stored on a disk, there are ten bits stored on tape. Most companies that choose to have a mirrored copy of data that is in synch with its production data may well have an older generation of that data on tape. The difference is, if you have data on tape, it's data you hope you'll never have to use. If it's data you believe you will need to use, you ought to have it on disk."[24]

Swatik and others point to the declining price and increasing availability of high-speed telecommunications links as enablers of significant growth in both remote tape vaulting and disk mirroring implementations. Telecommunications providers, including AT&T (with its INC offering) and Sprint (with its ION initiative), are currently rolling out their "next generation networks." These NGN solutions promise to deliver redundant, high-speed (OC3 or OC12), SONET ring connectivity to corporate facilities. Their speed and performance characteristics will provide the quality of service provisioning required to reduce the latency associated with electronic vaulting and remote mirroring and position the telcos to become vendors of data vaulting solutions themselves (see Chapter 7).

OPTIONS FOR RECORDS STORAGE

As of this writing, electronic data vaulting and remote mirroring are not part of the data protection strategies of most companies. This may be a function of the cost of these options or an acknowledgment of the greater tolerance to downtime inherent in their mission-critical applications. Whatever the reason, the preponderance of companies that do tape backups use manual methods for moving the tapes in and out of local and/or off-site storage.

It should also be noted that electronic tape vaulting and remote mirroring offer no solutions for the problems of paper and microform-based records storage. For these media, also, on-site or off-site storage may provide an answer.

Once documents and data files have been identified and classified, special attention must be paid to identifying any current methods that are being used to safeguard data from loss. Disaster recovery coordinators may find that the fear of potential data loss has motivated "owners" to develop their own strategies for safe storage. A host of capabilities may already be present within the company that provide varying degrees of records protection.

In certain areas of the company, auditors may have left their mark. Their comments about the security and recoverability of vital records may have led to the purchase of fireproof cabinets or to "informal" storage arrangements between company records administrators and vendors who prepare microform documents for remote storage of copies or source documents. Any number of "home-grown" strategies to safeguard data may have been devised by concerned departmental personnel.

Ferreting out existing strategies can be a challenging proposition. Migrating these individual strategies into a consolidated off-site storage plan can also be daunting. Not only are home-grown storage strategies often extremely informal and poorly documented, but they are also frequently a source of pride for those persons who formulated them.

The disaster recovery coordinator needs to be cognizant of the personal stake that people sometimes have in the most innocuous things. Applaud the ingenuity of the owner who has perceived the need for security and survivability and stored his or her backups in the safe deposit box at the local bank. Be diplomatic when telling the owner that a new strategy is being developed that will consolidate his or her off-site storage arrangements with those of less conscientious departments. Perhaps the owner can be recruited to assist in identifying and classifying other information assets in the company.

Once these steps have been completed, it is time for the disaster recovery coordinator to begin working toward a corporate solution to safe storage. Off-site storage is a common part of an overall strategy for data protection and survivability. However, off-site storage may be neither required nor appropriate for every data asset. The following options for data storage provide varying degrees of protection. A typical data protection strategy may integrate one or more of these approaches.

Local Storage Using Fire-Related Safes and Cabinets

A variety of fire-resistant cabinets and safes are available to safeguard data at the location where it is produced. Vendors typically reference performance ratings established by Underwriter Laboratories (UL) when describing their products. Table 4–4 summarizes the UL ratings of various fire resistant safes and cabinets.

It should be noted that damage to magnetic tape and diskettes begins to occur at temperatures of 100 to 125 °F and that newer, higher-capacity, hard disk media lose their integrity at temperatures of 145 to 149 °F.[25] Paper and microform are considerably more resilient to heat (350 °F for paper, 225 to 300 °F for microform, depending on the presence of steam) and may derive greater benefit from fire resistant safes and storage cabinets.

As a common sense response to these facts, NFPA Standard 75[26] emphasizes the need to store duplicates of key, expensive-to-replace records in a location where they will not be affected by a disaster affecting the originals. The clear implication is that the practice of storing records in and around the data center or operations area of the business in which they are produced or used is ill-advised. Other options to strictly on-site storage, therefore, need to be considered.

Shell Game Strategy

One option, perhaps the least expensive, can be termed a "shell game." In this option, important data is moved around company offices but remains locally accessible.

If an organization's offices are dispersed around several buildings in an office park development, for example, copies of the records from one building may be stored in another building. This strategy has the advantage of providing ready access by those who would need to access records in an emergency. However, local storage may be vulnerable to the effects of the same disaster that damages the originating facility.

It may also be prohibitively expensive to outfit several sites within the company with the requisite safety and security capabilities to safeguard stored data. Storage rooms used for magnetic media, for example, should have features that approximate those in a data center environment, including temperature control, humidity control, static grounding, fire protection, water detection, environmental maintenance, and physical security. Table 4–5 summarizes NFPA recommendations regarding fire suppression

Table 4–4   Underwriters Laboratories Safe and Safety Cabinet Performance Ratings

Rating	**Meaning**
Construction Ratings	
B Rated	Steel construction, doors less than 1 inch thick, walls less than 1/2 inch thick.
C Rated	Steel construction, doors at least 1 inch thick, walls at least 1/2 inch thick.
E Rated	Steel construction, doors at least 1 1/2 inches thick, walls at least 1 inch thick.
ER Rated	Safe or chest labeled with "UL Inspected Tool Resisting Safe TL 15 Burglary."
F Rated	Safe or chest labeled with "UL Inspected Tool Resisting Safe TL 30 Burglary" or "UL Inspected Explosive Resistant Safe with Relocking Device X 60 Burglary."
G Rated	Safe or chest labeled with "UL Inspected Torch and Explosive Resisting Safe TR 60 Burglary" or "UL Inspected Torch and Tool Resisting Safe TRTL 30 Burglary."
PEFORMANCE RATINGS–BURGLARY CLASSIFICATIONS	
TL-15	Successfully resist entry for a net assault time of 15 minutes when attacked with common hand tools, picking tools, mechanical or portable electric tools, grinders, drills or pressure devices.
TL-30	Successfully resist entry for a net assault time of 30 minutes when attacked with common hand tools, picking tools, mechanical or portable electric tools, grinders, drills or pressure devices.
TRTL-30	Successfully resist entry for a net assault time of 30 minutes when attacked with common hand tools, picking tools, mechanical or portable electric tools, grinders, drills, pressure devices and oxy-fuel cutting or welding torches.
TRTL-60	Successfully resist entry for a net assault time of 60 minutes when attacked with common hand tools, picking tools, mechanical or portable electric tools, grinders, drills, pressure devices and oxy-fuel cutting or welding torches.
TXTL-30	Successfully resist entry for a net assault time of 60 minutes when attacked with common hand tools, picking tools, mechanical or portable electric tools, grinders, drills, pressure devices, explosives and oxy-fuel cutting or welding torches.
PERFORMANCE RATINGS–FIRE CLASSIFICATIONS	
4 Hour	Maintain an interior temperature of less than 150 degrees F and an interior humidity less than 85% when exposed to fire up to 2000 degrees F for 4 hours.

(*continued*)

Table 4–4 *Continued*

Rating	Meaning
PERFORMANCE RATINGS—FIRE CLASSIFICATIONS	
3 Hour	Maintain an interior temperature of less than 150 degrees F and an interior humidity less than 85% when exposed to fire up to 2000 degrees F for 3 hours.
2 Hour	Maintain an interior temperature of less than 150 degrees F and an interior humidity less than 85% when exposed to fire up to 2000 degrees F for 2 hours.
1 Hour	Maintain an interior temperature of less than 150 degrees F and an interior humidity less than 85% when exposed to fire up to 2000 degrees F for 1 hour.

systems and other elements of a protected computing environment and its storage facilities.

Cooperative Shared Storage Arrangements

A variation on the local storage option—one that might reduce some of the expense for redundant, specially equipped storage facilities within the corporate premise—is to share a storage room with another business. This, of course, is replete with issues of security and access control.

Subscribe to a Commercial Off-Site Storage Facility

Commercial records storage facilities remain one of the most often used options for secure, off-site storage. Commercial storage facilities are of two basic types: those offered by banks and moving-and-storage companies, and those offered by companies that specialize in off-site data and records storage.

Banks and moving-and-storage companies often make space available for records storage without knowing the types of records that are to be stored. Thus, their facilities do not generally meet the security and/or environmental requirements of data processing media or microform storage. Other drawbacks of using these facilities are that records are not available at all hours of the day, facilities are shared, access controls are insufficient, and physical storage sizes are limited.

Commercial off-site storage facilities specializing in electronic media storage cost about the same as bank or moving-and-storage company ser-

Table 4–5 Select NFPA Recommendations for Data Center/Records Area Protection

Building construction	Construction in accordance with NFPA 220, *Standard on Types of Building Construction,* preferably a single-story building, with protection provided where subject to damage from external exposure; separated from other occupancies within the building, including atria or other open-space construction, by minimum 1 hour fire-resistant-rated construction. All interior wall and ceiling finishes Class A rated per NFPA 101®, Life Safety Code® (if sprinklered, may be Class B); no exposed cellular plastics. Raised floors should include provisions for drainage from water leakage, sprinkler operation, coolant leakage, or fire-fighting operations. Structural supports and decking for raised floors should be of noncombustible materials. Access sections or panels shall be provided in raised floors and tools for providing access should be located in the room and their locations well marked. Cable openings or other penetrations through fire-related assemblies should be fire stopped. Openings, such as pass-through windows, should be equipped with automatic fire-related shutters. Air ducts should be provided with automatic fire and smoke dampers.
Materials and Equipment Restrictions	Only computer equipment and support equipment should be permitted in the computer room; office furniture in the room should be of metal construction. Records in the computer rooom should be kept to the absolute minimum. Tape libraries and record storage rooms within the computer area should be protected by a separate extinguishing system. Records storage rooms should be used only for storage, not for other activities, such as reproducing, erasing, etc. Paper stock, inks, and other combustibles should be restricted to the absolute minimum necessary for efficient operation. These materials should be kept in completely enclosed metal file cases or cabinets. Raised floor space should not be used for storage.
Fire Protection and Detection	Automatic detection equipment should be installed to provide early warning of a fire: at a ceiling level throughout the computer area; below the raised floor over cable assemblies; and, above suspended ceilings/below raised floors where these spaces are used to recirculate air. Sprinkler systems should be provided if computer room enclosure is constructed of combustible materials, or the operation of the computer room involves a significant quantity of combustible materials, or the building is otherwise required to be sprinkled. Sprinklers for computer areas should be valved separately from other sprinkler systems.

(continued)

Table 4–5   *Continued*

Gaseous Total Flooding Extinguishing Systems may be used when there is a critical need to protect data in process, reduce equipment damage, and facilitate return to service. Design, install, and maintain in accordance with NFPA 12A (for HALON), NFPA 12 (for CO2) or NFPA 2001 (for Clean Agents). Power to electronic equipment should be disconnected automatically upon activation of a gaseous agent total flooding system except where the risk considerations indicate a need for continuous power. Air handling systems that might exhaust the agent supply should be interlocked to shut down upon agent system actuation.

Source: Extracted from "NFPA Standard for the Protection of Electronic Computer/Data Processing Equipment 1999 Edition," National Fire Protection Association, Quincy, MA, 1999.

vices. However, in these facilities, ideal conditions for environment, security, and accessibility are provided.

Commercial off-site storage centers are designed with magnetic and microform media storage requirements in mind. A well-designed facility is similar in all respects to one that a disaster recovery coordinator might wish to construct at his or her own facility, although costs are generally much lower because they are shared among several customers that make use of the same facility.

What makes the commercial facility preferable to a cooperative storage arrangement, however, is the use of trained, single-tasked personnel at the commercial facility to control access to stored data. Rarely are clients allowed to access their storage directly; they must rely instead on storage center staff to pull tapes and storage boxes.

For most medium to large companies, a combination of the preceding options is used to provide safe storage of critical and vital information. For example, companies may set up an in-house records center to facilitate day-to-day information requirements, may utilize a local but off-premise storage area for tape backup storage, and may contract with a commercial off-site storage vendor for longer-term media and records storage.

Some companies have gone even further to ensure backup survival by engaging redundant backup and redundant off-site storage. To wit, the case for redundant backup holds that if original data is lost and damage occurs to backed-up media while in transit to the backup site or during the effort to restore a system, a second backup would be needed to complete the system recovery process.

This may sound excessive, possibly even neurotic, until one considers the accidents that can and do occur in storage centers. In October 1996, for example, a fire at the Brambles Information Management Center in Chicago, IL, consumed 220,000 boxes of stored archival and vital records. The following year, three fires at supposedly impervious Iron Mountain Records Centers in South Brunswick, NJ, consumed over one million boxes of paper records and affected 200 companies. In May of the same year, the Diversified Records Services Center, a football stadium-sized building near Scranton, PA, burned to the ground with all of its paper and microfilm stores.[27] Whether the fires were accidental or deliberate, these events suggest that redundancy has value, even in backup strategies.

Other proponents of redundant backups point to the possibility of disasters that are regional in scope (i.e., hurricanes in coastline states, earthquakes in various parts of North America), which might affect both the subscriber company and its off-site storage facility.

Redundant backups would ideally be stored at separate locations: on-site, off-site locally, and off-site remotely. For many data processing centers, a three-cycle retention program is observed as a matter of standard operating procedure. "Grandparent" and "parent" backups are removed to remote and local off-site storage, respectively, while "child" backups are retained in-house for use in conjunction with day-to-day mishaps.

The point is that most businesses with a backup storage plan utilize a combination of redundant data backup procedures and complementary storage options to lessen their exposure to critical data loss. Most use, as part of their backup storage strategy, a commercial off-site storage vendor.

SELECTING AND OFF-SITE STORAGE VENDOR

One of the more controversial issues in disaster recovery planning revolves around criteria for selecting a vendor of off-site storage services. This, in part, reflects the nature of the data processing industry and the explosion of new companies that have formed to fill this niche over the past five to ten years.

The first commercial off-site storage facilities for magnetic media (and records generally) were designed for archival storage over decades or even centuries. Some were specifically constructed to withstand the anticipated force of an atomic explosion (see Figure 4–12).

Records were rotated in and out of these centers at the relaxed rate of once per month. Today, with an increased awareness of the need for off-site storage in the face of other threats somewhat less devastating than nuclear war, numerous above-ground centers have been built for local and regional users.

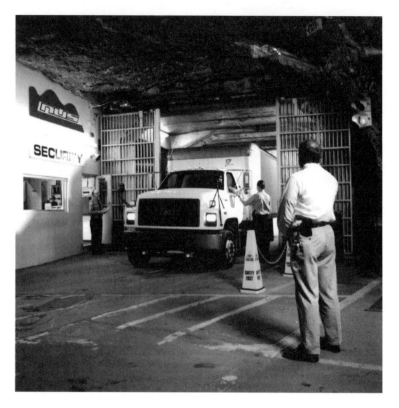

Figure 4–12   An underground commercial records storage facility.
(*Source:* Iron Mountain/National Underground Storage,
Inc., Boyers, PA.)

In fact, one reason that commercial off-site storage facilities have become less expensive is that there are more and more facilities. In most metropolitan areas of the country, information managers now have a choice among several vendors. Added to this number are the dozens of vault-equipped banks, thrifts, and moving-and-storage companies who market their own facilities for media backup. This explosion of facilities has led to increased competition and relatively low prices; it has also had the positive effect of promoting a drive to establish "THE RULES" for identifying what makes one off-site storage facility superior to another.

In the search for distinction, vendors advertise that their facilities comply with any number of authoritative guidelines, including those articulated by the Association of Records Managers and Administrators (ARMA), the National Fire Protection Association (NFPA), American National Standards Institute (ANSI), the U.S. Government's National Bureau of Standards (NBS), the Underwriters Laboratories (UL), and various state and local agencies. Compliances often follow the facility logo in advertising literature like alphabet soup.

Despite all these guidelines, there is not a single set of rules that defines the "best" off-site backup facility. None of the above organizations, in fact, claim to have defined rules for *selecting* anything. Rather, each organization cites environmental or operational characteristics of a well-designed facility. Adherence by vendor facilities to these standards is a plus, but facility design alone is not a sound basis for selecting a vendor.

For example, the fact that a vendor complies with ANSI standard on temperature, humidity, and air purity requirements says little about the safety of the data of the business that uses the vendor. Similarly, vendor adherence to NFPA standards for vault construction or fire protection offers little consolation if the vendor has internal management problems, cannot effectively manage its stored inventory, or fails to answer emergency calls from clients over the holidays.

There is some truth in the arguments of some vendors who do not comply with certain standards in their facilities when they claim that technological advance has outpaced guideline revisions. Managers of storage facilities may decide that complying with outdated standards is less cost-effective than providing appropriate security, fire protection, and other quality services. For this reason, the selection of the right backup storage facility is less a function of counting compliances than evaluating vendor performance and capability.

At a minimum, the following evaluative criteria should be considered, and to the extent possible, validated by an independent third party:

- **Reputation.** How long a facility has been in existence, its association with a larger corporate entity, its financial statement, its record with the Better Business Bureau, and even its reputation within the community of information management professionals are all important factors in selecting an off-site storage vendor.
- **Site security.** Security at the storage site should be no less (and possibly a good deal more) stringent than at one's own facility. Some questions to consider:

  What are the access controls in the facility? Is visitor access restricted?

  Are client names concealed, even from one another?

  What security measures are observed during the transportation of media? (Unmarked vehicles, security in vehicles, employee monitoring, etc.)

  How are employees screened?

Are cameras, videotape, or other devices used to monitor facility traffic?

How are emergency calls handled in terms of authorizations and so on?

- **Media management.** A very important factor, how the facility manages client records, may present the following questions:

  How is media of several clients segregated?

  Is magnetic media stored separately from microform and paper? Are there certain types of media that will not be stored in the facility?

  Is media transported in plastic containers or cardboard boxes?

  Are employees trained in proper media handling?

  Are media maintenance activities, including periodic tape rotation, performed as standard operating procedure?

  What kind of inventory management system is used? If an automated system, is it backed up?

  How often is a physical inventory of media performed?

  What controls exist to monitor the flow of media in and out of the facility?

- **Environmental factors.** Although much abused, there are a number of environmental standards that are important in off-site vendor selection. Vendors should recognize the standards, and if they do not comply with them, have a good case for not doing so. Of course, to determine whether a vendor complies, one must first understand the standards involved. Table 4–6 lists several references with which the disaster recovery coordinator should become familiar prior to meeting with vendors.

  Having become familiar with the standards, the disaster recovery coordinator should seek answers and documentation from the vendor on the following points:

  What capabilities are installed to detect and signal smoke, heat, flame, water, and intrusion?

  What extinguishing capabilities are available?

  Is the alarm system tied directly to fire, police, and security services?

  How are temperature, heat, humidity, and contamination controlled?

  What are the facility's backup power requirements and how are they provided?

  How frequently are environmental protection and backup capabilities checked or tested?

  What is the company smoking policy?

Table 4–6 Selected References for Establishing Off-site Storage Vendor Selection Criteria

Source	Title	Abstract
ARMA International 4200 Somerset Dr., #215 Prairie Village, KS 66208 913/341–3808 • 800/422–2762	*Records Center Operations—A Guideline* ARMA International Standards Records Center Operations Task Force	This guideline will assist an organization or company in designing or selecting an appropriate records center site. It includes information on equipping, staffing, and overall management of the center with sample forms used in records center operations and discusses commercial records storage facilities. A section on computerizing a records center discusses design considerations and operating procedures. With appendices, annotated bibliography, and index, (51 p., 1986).
National Fire Protection Association, Batterymarch Park Quincy, MA 02269	*NFPA 75: Standard for the Protection of Electronic Computer/Data Processing Equipment, 1999 Edition*	NFPA 75 outlines requirements for computer installations needing fire protection and special building construction, building construction, rooms, areas, or operating environments. Application is based on risk considerations such as the business interrruption aspects of the function—as in computers used in the stock market—or the fire to the installation (18 pp., 1999).

(*continued*)

Table 4–6 *Continued*

Source	Title	Abstract
	NFPA 232: Standard for the Protection of Records, 1995 Edition	NFPA 232 outlines requirements for records protection, equipment, including vaults, file rooms, safes, containers, and other devices, and for the management of records (17 pp., 1995).
	NFPA 232A: Guide for Fire Protection for Archives and Record Centers, 1995 Edition	NFPA 232A provides guidelines on fire protection for file rooms exceeding 50,000 cubic feet in volume, as well as all archives and records centers (20 pp., 1995).
National Information Standards Organization (NISO) 4733 Bethesda Avenue Suite 300 Bethesda, MD 20814 Voice: 301/654-2512	*NISO TR01–1995, Technical Report— Environmental Guidelines for the Storage of Paper Records*, by William K. Wilson.	This technical report establishes appropriate environmental guidelines for the storage of records in libraries, archives, and other storage facilities. Recommended requirements for temperature, relative humidity, light, and air pollutants are given. Includes a detailed review of the technical and scientific literature. Suggests environmental parameters that influence the preservation of paper-based records in libraries and archives. Storage parameters addressed include temperature, relative humidity, exposure to light, gaseous contaminants, and particulate (30 pp., 1995).

Source	Title	Abstract
National Technical Information Service Technology Administration U.S. Department of Commerce Springfield, VA 22161 Order Desk: (703) 605–6000 Fax: (703) 605–6900	*Care and Handling of Computer Magnetic Storage Media* PB 83 237 271 (Special Publication 500–101), 1989.	Covers tape management systems, tape maintenance schedules, and environmental conditions for archivals storage computer media.
PRISM International (formerly Association of Commercial Records Centers) 16 E. Rowan Street Suite 400 Raleigh, NC 27609	*Media Vault Guideline*	Suggests operational guidelines for media storage.
	Demand the Best	Suggests evaluative criteria for selecting a storage facility vendor.

- **Transportation.** There are statistics that purport to demonstrate that data is most vulnerable while in transit between the client facility and off-site storage house, and between the off-site storage facility and a data processing backup facility. In short, tapes and records are at higher risk of loss or damage while riding in the back of a van on a well-traveled street or highway or in the luggage compartment of an airplane than when they are sitting in a climate-controlled, fire-protected, contamination-reduced storage room. This underscores the fact that the transportation capabilities of the off-site storage vendor must be examined as part of the evaluation and selection task. The following questions can yield valuable insights:

  Is media transported by vendor employees or by independent courier service?

  Is media subjected to ambient climatic conditions during transport or are vehicles climate-controlled?

  Under what conditions may drivers make stops, route changes, etc.?

  Are vehicles equipped with antitheft devices, two-way radios, etc.?

  How is media stored in the vehicle?

  What is the longest estimated time to make a regular delivery? An emergency delivery?

  Are different vehicles used to make emergency deliveries? Does the vendor provide an airport delivery service?

  Does the vendor provide preparatory services (i.e., special services for readying media for long distance travel, including selection, crating, air or freight carrier contact, scheduling, delivery, destination transportation arrangements, etc.)?

The answers to all of the above questions should be verified, insofar as possible, with an on-site visit. Also, ask the vendor for the names of customers who would be willing to speak about the vendor's performance. Despite the security requirements of many companies, the vendor usually has the permission of several clients to disseminate their telephone numbers to prospective customers for validation and endorsement. Be aware, however, that the vendor will nearly always provide only the names of satisfied customers.

Once all evaluative criteria have been validated to the satisfaction of the disaster recovery coordinator, the next task is negotiating the contract and the schedule for regular pickups and deliveries.

Contracting for off-site storage is essentially a task of assigning a cost to each of the services that the vendor will provide. Contracts may be as straightforward as an initial invoice and a handshake, or they may be multipage documents loaded with fine print that need to be reviewed by a lawyer and/or auditor. Costs vary widely, and some storage facility managers have more latitude to negotiate than others.

Before examining the elements of an off-site storage contract, however, it is important to know what information the vendor will require about the prospective client prior to contract negotiation. Initially, the client will be expected to provide two items of information. The vendor will need to know approximately how much storage (and of what media type) the client will require. If the number of tapes or cartons can be estimated before the negotiation of a contract begins, this will help speed the process of setting a price for the service.

The second item of information concerns the frequency of pickups and deliveries. Are all records and media to be rotated to the facility daily? Are some to be rotated back to the client daily, some monthly, and some stored permanently by the vendor?

Until the disaster recovery plan is fully written, tested, and approved, the exact quantity of off-site storage and frequency of rotation may be difficult to determine. However, it may be possible to develop an interim off-site storage plan (for example, covering the storage of weekly system backups and daily transaction backups, plus the archival storage of critical and vital records) that will serve as the basis for negotiating the contract.

Some of the fees in a typical contract are the following:

- **Regular pickup and delivery fee.** This fee covers only the cost to the client of the courier's trip to the client facility on a regular or routine basis. It should state how often, and at approximately what time of day, the courier will arrive to drop off and/or pick up materials. The fee may be written as a per visit charge, or as a monthly aggregate.

- **Emergency delivery fee.** The contract should identify what "emergency delivery" means, whether all *nonroutine visits* are considered emergencies or only those visits in which an emergency timeframe for delivery is invoked. Some facilities will make unscheduled deliveries on a non-emergency basis by allowing the courier to deviate from his or her route during daily deliveries. If this is the case, it should be included in the contract and the fee stated. If an emergency delivery is defined as a visit made to the client site at a time other than normal vendor operating hours, be sure to have the vendor's working hours and holiday schedule spelled out in the contract.

- **Tape (or container) handling fee.** Delivery fees often cover only courier visits and media transportation. They do not necessarily cover the handling of media in and out of the storage facility. A per-tape or per-container fee for handling is often assessed, especially by vendors who must hire special staff to place, track, log, and maintain stored goods. For archival storage, particularly of tape, there may be a fee in addition to a handling fee to pay for the rotation of archived tapes.

- **Storage fee.** In addition to delivery and handling fees, many facilities charge an additional fee for the actual amount of space occupied by client data. This rent is typically assessed on a monthly basis. If the amount of stored information changes during the month, the charge is usually assessed on the basis of the maximum amount of space occupied by client data at any time in the month.

- **Preparatory service fees.** Some vendors offer disaster recovery services in the form of preparing stored records and media for transportation to a recovery facility in the event of a disaster. These services may include boxing records and media for long distance travel by plane or freight, coordinating transport through freight routing services, moving media to an airport or train station, and arranging for the transportation (at the point of destination) of the records and media to the recovery facility. These services may be charged as a regular monthly fee or charged to the customer after the fact. If a regular fee is assessed, ensure that the vendor will provide one thorough-going test of the capability per year.

- **Other fees.** There are a host of other fees that are becoming increasingly prevalent in the industry. These may include special insurance fees to cover media replacement (if the vendor is not insured or bonded for this eventuality, be sure to find out why), schedule revision fees (charged to customers who revise their regular pickup and delivery schedules), plan maintenance fees (for customers who use the vendor to write the section of the plan pertaining to preparatory services), and special fees for upgrades to facilities (sometimes employed instead of price increases). Some facilities offer media maintenance and cleaning services that are also charged on a fee basis. All fees should be clearly spelled out in the contract.

Besides fees, there are other items of information that the disaster recovery coordinator should secure in writing from the off-site storage vendor. The vendor should indicate the exact steps that will be taken if records or media are misplaced in the vault or warehouse. The vendor should also identify the procedure for requesting and receiving a delivery, including emergency contact numbers, authentication of requests, and emergency delivery timeframes. The contract should also supply a complete definition of the vendor's liability for media in its charge, and identify the details of the vendor's insurance or bonding.

COST-JUSTIFY OFF-SITE STORAGE

Once the disaster recovery coordinator is satisfied that a vendor will provide competent, cost-effective service for the foreseeable future, the next step of the procedure may be to cost-justify the service to senior management. Pointing out a number of factors may help simplify this effort.

1. Off-site storage is not just a data processing-related expense. Every department, even administration, may have records and documents that need to be stored off-site. Most senior managers recognize the value of safe, secure storage when it comes to documents such as contracts, agreements, and accounting data.

2. As off-site storage is a solution to a business's overall vulnerability, it may be possible to divide the cost among all corporate departments. Better yet, off-site storage may be handled as a strictly administrative expense item, and may, in many cases, be tax deductible.

3. Off-site storage is rarely a politically charged issue. If the disaster recovery coordinator couches his or her rationale for storage in terms of protecting corporate assets, few detractors can persuasively argue against it.

4. Because of increased competition among vendors of off-site storage, the expense of the service is rarely prohibitive.

Of course, cost-justifications must reference benefits that accrue to the company from the acquisition of a subject product or service. In the case of off-site storage, cost-justifications devolve from the same risk analysis that was generated to identify corporate exposures. While it is difficult to assign a dollar value to the data that is being stored, it is a relatively common practice to demonstrate the cost to the company of prolonged downtime. Therefore, the coordinator can provide a scenario in which the cost of downtime to the company is attributable to the lack of backup data needed to restore the system.

The disaster recovery coordinator can further demonstrate the cost-effectiveness of the off-site option by developing a prospectus showing the costs and relative risks entailed in developing a comparable capability within company-owned facilities. In addition to the cost of environmental control, fire protection, water detection, furniture, shelving, and security, a "home-grown" shell for storage would also require the hiring of additional personnel.

IMPLEMENTING THE DATA RECOVERY PLAN

Once approval has been granted, the disaster recovery coordinator must finalize a schedule for removal of records to permanent off-site storage. The coordinator may need to coordinate with the IS executive to establish a routine for the preparation and rotation of computer media and other records requiring periodic update.

Special attention should be given to the requirement that users of PCs and user-administrated servers become participants in an off-site storage plan. For the first several weeks, their cooperation may need to be closely monitored. Given the increase in the average amount of disk storage shipped with PCs (10 GB drives are increasingly common in Windows/Intel personal computer configurations), as well as the proliferation of PCs in most organizations, this represents a truly staggering potential for data loss.

Obtaining the cooperation of users and administrators of decentralized systems may be a challenge, but it must be overcome if a company's disaster recovery capability is to be fully developed. There may be a need to involve senior management in forging corporate policy regarding data backup and participation in an off-site storage plan. Even then, it may be necessary to monitor the compliance of PC and LAN server users and administrators for a period of time until their participation becomes automatic.

The coordinator may also find it helpful to disseminate information about the backup program throughout the company so that new storage requirements or requirements that were not originally considered may come to light.

To establish controls, a formal log should be kept to record movement of media and records from the tape library and record center to the vendor site. This log documents when couriers were on site and what they took or delivered. The log may also be useful in billing issues or in assessing vendor compliance with established delivery schedules. The log further provides a backup that may be used to track down media or records that are misplaced at the off-site storage facility. The more detailed the log, the better its use in resolving problems.

Once schedules and controls are in place, the disaster recovery coordinator needs to arrange periodic reviews of the off-sight storage program. Depending on how rapidly company procedures and systems change, this review may have to be conducted quarterly or semiannually in order to identify changes in off-site storage requirements. This review should include an investigation of the following:

- **Vendor performance.** Periodically, the record of the vendor should be checked to ensure that billing is correct, media is being properly handled and stored, promised emergency delivery timeframes are being met, and media is being rotated on schedule and without apparent damage. This check should include an inspection of the vendor facility, a review of vendor financial statements and both financial and functional audit reports, and a sampling of opinions of the information management community regarding vendor performance generally.

- **Adherence to classification criteria.** Determine whether company information is being properly classified according to the scheme set forth in the development of the off-site storage plan. This may be done by sampling some of the records and documents as they are prepared for off-site storage. Trace the origins of the documents identified in the spot check, and ask the individual who classified the data to explain his or her rationale for the classification applied.

- **Changes in disaster recovery requirements.** An inventory of media and forms stored off-site should be discussed at a meeting of data "owners" to assess whether it is obsolete or otherwise irrelevant to company requirements. In some companies, this is done as part of departmental review of their sections of the company disaster recovery plan. If some materials stored off-site are no longer necessary or relevant to business recovery, have them removed. Be sure to have the vendor revise the storage fees if there is a substantial reduction in the volume of data being stored.

- **"Awareness" programs.** Verify that awareness programs established at the outset of the off-site storage program are continuing. This may include revising a handout on key characteristics of the storage program and disseminating it to department managers, application end users, and new employees within the company.

It is especially important that new PC users be indoctrinated in procedures for backup and off-site storage of critical data. Having users read, initial, and return a memo covering their responsibility to participate in off-site storage may facilitate this requirement.

FINAL OBSERVATIONS ABOUT DATA RECOVERY PLANNING

Data recovery planning is not the most glamorous aspect of disaster recovery planning, but it is essential to successful recovery from a disaster. Without backups of critical data, and the capability to restore from those backups efficiently, most companies will never recover from a major disaster, regardless of other preparations they have made.

Some additional technologies that may facilitate effective data recovery capabilities include:

- **Electronic document management systems.** These systems enable more of an organizations nonelectronic information assets to be copied and shared efficiently and also provide an expedient means for creating backups for secure storage.
- **Enterprise backup/restore systems.** These applications enable the policy-based management of electronic data backup and restore functions across a broad range of storage configurations. In an organization has not deployed a standardized enterprise backup/restore system, the task of managing the data recovery plan is magnified in proportion.
- **Standardized desktop configuration.** This is a part-policy/part-architecture solution that has been implemented by a number of large organizations to mitigate desktop management costs. Essentially, the applications that may be installed on an end user desktop are predefined by the organization, often on the basis of a user job classification, and application software itself is maintained on a central "library" server. The result is a common desktop with common directories that are much more readily backed up and restored in the event of an equipment outage.
- **Thin client computing architecture.** The mention of standardized desktops provides a natural segue to another technology that has been gathering momentum in the modern IT world: server-centric or "thin client" computing. Without delving into all of the permutations of this emerging technology, the fundamental premise is that data and application software are more cost-effectively maintained on a server than on a desktop device. The desktop device, a thin client, provides the user with an interface to the application, as well as, local processing capabilities (in most, but not all, architectural definitions). By centralizing user data and applications onto a fewer number of devices, they can be more readily managed (and backed up) by a fewer number of personnel. This architecture, too, holds promise for increasing the efficacy of data recovery planning.

- **WORM media.** Certain types of data have special security, confidentiality or integrity requirements, even when stored as backups. The increasing availability of write once, read many (WORM) media provides a useful backup media for meeting such requirements. Once the exclusive domain of optical media types such as Compact Disk-Recordable (CD-R) and specialized magneto-optical products (MO-WORM), magnetic tape-based WORM was introduced to the market by Storage Technology Corporation in 1998. The VolSafe™ Redwood tape cartridge was the first to deliver the level of data security and integrity required under the Securities and Exchange Commission (SEC) amendment that allows brokers and dealers to store records electronically.[28] Recording to tape media can be accomplished at a significantly greater speed than recording to optical media, enhancing the value of this approach. Competitive products to the StorageTek offering are expected and tape vendors will likely leverage improvements in encryption technology to build out the features of these products over time.

ENDNOTES

1. Jon William Toigo, *The Holy Grail of Data Storage Management* (Prentice Hall: Saddle River, NJ), 1999.
2. Interview with Dale Miller, Vice President, Trilliant Group, Cincinnati, OH, 6/99.
3. Gregory Dalton, "Acceptable Risks," *Information Week*, 8/31/98.
4. Interview with Nora Denzel, Vice President of Product Operations, Legato Systems, Palo Alto, CA, 6/99.
5. Interview with Dale Miller, Trilliant Group, *op. cit.*
6. Interview with Nora Denzel, Legato Systems, *op. cit.*
7. From the web page of Network One, Eugene, OR, *http://www.net1.com*.
8. Laurie Hilsgen, "Document Management Still a Struggle," *InfoTech Weekly*, 2/8/99.
9. "DISASTER RECOVERY Information Assets – The Missing Link," a paper published on the web site of FIRELOCK, Kutztown, PA, http://www.firelock.com/articles.htm.
10. Interview with Matt Fairbanks, Backup Exec Product Manager, Seagate Software, Lake Mary, FL, 3/99.
11. Interview with Jeff Wells, Product Manager, SAMS: Alexandria, Sterling Software, Boulder, CO, 6/99.
12. Interview with Allan Mohess, Product Marketing Manager for ARCserveIT, Computer Associates, Islandia, NY, 6/99.
13. Denzel interview, *op. cit.*

14. *Ibid.*

15. Andrew Gup, "Survival in the Terabyte Age: Cost/Benefits of Safeguarding TB Databases," *Storage Management Solutions,* 7/97. While the dollars estimated in this article are somewhat out of date, the methodology for analyzing costs and benefits remains quite sound and may be particularly useful to DR coordinators.

16. Pelin Wood, "Getting Complete Backups with Open File Technology," *Computer Technology Review,* 4/99.

17. "Object Replication: A Revolutionary Advance in Distributed Data Protection and Recovery," Stac Software White Paper, Stac Software, San Diego, CA, 1999.

18. Jason L. Buffington, "Today's Window of Exposure for Data Loss," *Storage Management Solutions,* 1/98.

19. Interview with Jim Grogan, Vice President of Alliances, SunGard Recovery Services, Wayne, PA, 6/99.

20. *Ibid.*

21. SunGard Recovery Services case study, from the SunGard Recovery Services web site at http://recovery.sungard.com/PHLX.htm.

22. Interview with Allan Mohess, Computer Associates, *op. cit.*

23. Tony Rodriguez, "Wide Area Data Mirroring Protects Business Continuity," *Storage Management Solutions,* 1/98.

24. Interview with Dan Swatik, Vice President of Product Management, EMC Corporation, Hopkinton, MA, 6/99.

25. Gary Herbst, "IBM's Drive Temperature Indicator Processor (Drive-TIP) Helps Ensure High Drive Reliability," IBM White Paper, IBM Storage Systems Division, San Jose, CA, 1997.

26. NFPA 75: *Standard for the Protection of Electronic Computer/Data Processing Equipment,* 1999 Edition, National Fire Protection Association, Quincy, MA, 1999.

27. Pat Moore, "Vital Records Protection Issues," *Disaster Recovery Journal,* Summer 1997.

28. Sets Industry Precedent; Delivers First Tape Technology To Meet Sec Requirements For Electronic Records Storage: StorageTek VolSafe is the Industry's First WORM (Write Once, Read Many) Tape-Based Storage Solution; Provides Cost-Effective, Scalable Alternative to Optical WORM," Press Release, Storage Technology Corporation, Boulder, CO, 07/08/98.

Strategies for Centralized System Recovery

To many people, disaster recovery planning is synonymous with planning for the restoration of mainframe operations following a catastrophe. This should come as no surprise, considering that the traditional focus of disaster recovery planning was the recovery of the corporate computer, almost without exception a mainframe or large minicomputer.

Mainframe-centric disaster recovery plans dealt primarily with the procedures for replacing a damaged or inaccessible mainframe with compatible hardware. Tasks included loading system software and defining resources, starting the processes required for use by application software, loading data to direct access storage devices (DASD) from tape, establishing network connections—including a terminal network, and performing the many other preparatory tasks and tests to bring the corporate *oracle* back to life. Given the complexity of the task and the technical skills required, often disaster recovery planning was conceived as an activity confined entirely to the data processing department of the company.

Today, more and more, disaster recovery planning encompasses a wider set of objectives. It aims at the recovery of critical business processes, rather than the restoration of mainframe operations alone. This, in large part, is a response to changes in the business environment in which disaster recovery plans are developed.

Decentralization of data processing functions, the rise of personal computing, and the emergence of distributed computing architectures that leveraged local area networks are just some of the environmental changes that have forced contextual alterations in the field of disaster recovery planning. During the 1990s, a client/server "revolution" occurred in corporate computing that saw the migration of at least 20% of mission-critical applications off the corporate mainframe and out onto the enterprise network. This trend was acknowledged by IBM with the release of its OS/390 operating system in 1995—the first OS from the mainframe vendor touted explicitly as a player in the "open systems" environment.

However, while decentralization has had the impact of broadening both the scope and the "targets" of disaster recovery planning, it has also created tremendous management burdens for corporate IT organizations. By the end of the 1990s, many companies had initiated projects designed to consolidate distributed servers into a fewer number of physical platforms and to recentralize distributed servers within the glass house of the data center. There, the thinking goes, they could be more effectively managed by a disciplined cadre of IT support personnel.

Even personal computers have not escaped the consolidation/recentralization trend. Many companies are considering new, server-centric, desktop computing paradigms that recentralize applications and data onto "application servers" and replace "fat client" PCs with "thin client" terminals as a means to improve management and reduce costs. To be sure, rumors of the death of the Microsoft Windows/Intel architecture-based ("WINTEL") desktop are greatly exaggerated, as were the rumors of the death of mainframe computing a decade before. However, the increasing availability of applications for thin client devices and the increasingly widespread use of the web browser and Java Virtual Machine, enabling technologies for many thin client desktops, have increased the appeal of this WINTEL desktop alternative.

According to one analyst, the application recentralization trend was inevitable, "When servers get more powerful, it just makes sense for them to get used more—for the server to get fatter."[1] Microsoft seems to have gotten this point when it released a Terminal Server Edition (TSE) of its popular Windows NT server operating system. Like other distributed servers, application servers too are being eyed for recentralization within the safe confines of the corporate data center.

One mitigator of this trend, however, has been the concern over the vulnerability of older, mainframe-based, COBOL applications to Year 2000 date issues. In a few documented cases (although the data here is suspect for a variety of reasons), businesses have actually migrated their mission-critical, mainframe-based applications onto distributed platforms—leveraging Y2K-ready software packages to provide an "end run" around the Year 2000 bug. It remains to be seen, however, whether this phenomenon will become less the exception and more the norm in the future.

To the extent that mission-critical business processes are supported by centralized platforms, older strategies for centralized systems recovery are still somewhat pertinent. These are discussed in this chapter. However, the introduction of three-tier and *n*-tier client/server application architectures pose entirely different challenges to the disaster recovery coordinator. They cannot be addressed effectively by simple hardware replacement strategies and are thus considered separately in the next chapter.

In the final analysis, the disaster recovery coordinator must think in terms of protecting and restoring business processes rather than CPUs. Specifically, the coordinator needs to look at the infrastructure supports for business processes, including hardware, operating systems, application software, and databases, as well as networks, interconnects and end users. Planning only for the replacement of a computer is no longer sufficient, if it ever was.

DEVELOPING CENTRALIZED SYSTEM BACKUP STRATEGIES

As indicated above, centralized system backup means more than hardware replacement and entails more than software or data backup. Centralized system backup strategies are interdependent with data protection strategies and with other disaster recovery plan elements.

For this reason, centralized system backup strategies are best developed *concurrently* with data recovery plans and with plans aimed at recovering business processes supported by distributed systems in which the mainframe plays a role. If mainframe recovery plans are created without careful consideration of the requirements and conditions imposed by these other plan elements, important interdependencies may be overlooked.

For example, even the most mainframe-centric application often has a role to play in other mission-critical applications residing on distributed platforms. The "legacy" transaction processing application that operates on the "back office" mainframe often has an important role to play with respect to the operation of Enterprise Resource Planning (ERP) applications residing on distributed platforms. A similar interdependency often exists between the legacy environment and the distributed e-commerce applications that companies are increasingly fielding to capitalize on the business potential market of the Internet.

Centralized system recovery procedures need to take into consideration important gateways and interfaces required by distributed applications, and process restoration must often be timed to meet distributed application requirements.

Figure 5–1 shows, in a simplified way, some of the relationships among these activities. While centralized system recovery is primarily a technical matter, it also requires the coordinator's complete understanding of the business processes that the system supports. Thus, data acquired during risk analysis is very important.

The risk analysis provides answers to the following questions that will impact directly on the strategies developed for centralized system recovery.

What Applications Are Critical or Vital?

One task of risk analysis was to rank the relative criticality of applications to business recovery following a disaster. Critical and vital applications are defined by the support they provide to critical business processes and also by the lack of ready alternatives (e.g., manual methods) for providing their core functions. In short, these applications need to be restored within a short time following a disaster if business recovery is to be accomplished.

Having identified critical and vital applications, the disaster recovery coordinator can begin defining the infrastructure support requirements for the applications. Infrastructure support, in this context, may include users, input data and forms, output data and forms, processing hardware and necessary peripheral devices, and documentation.

It is important to note that, in addition to the personnel, equipment, networks, and data required to support an application, it may also be dependent upon the processes of another application for key inputs. Application interdependencies need to be clearly identified in order to determine accurately what applications are critical unto themselves and what applications may be critical based on inputs they provide to critical applications. Much of this analysis should have been completed during the initial analysis phase of the project.

What Is the Minimum Acceptable Hardware Configuration?

Once application criticality is defined, the risk analysis goes further to identify the hardware (both CPUs and storage devices) used by the application in performance of the critical or vital business function. From the

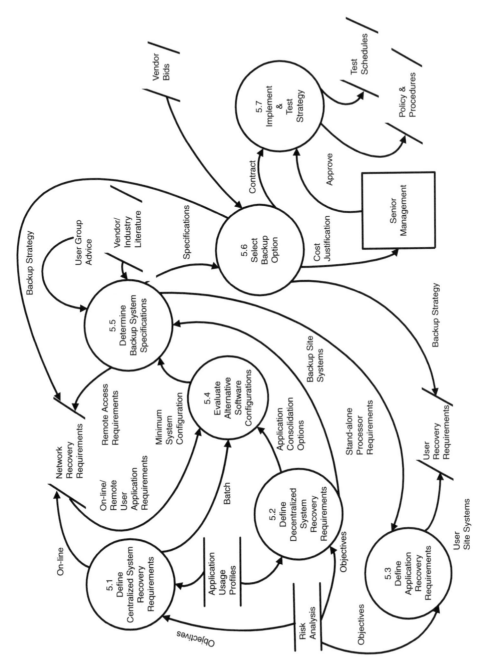

Figure 5–1 Systems Recovery Planning.

perspective of disaster recovery planning, it may be possible to view hardware capabilities utilized by all noncritical and nonvital applications as "spare capacity."

Hence, during its emergency operations, the business may be able to settle for far less processor and storage capacity than it normally utilizes. The ramifications of this view are twofold.

If less capacity is needed to run critical and vital applications, the centralized platform required for recovery need not match the configuration of production system hardware on a one-to-one basis. A high-end model CPU may be adequately backed up with a lower-end processor of adequate capacity.

It also follows that, if critical and vital applications run on several homogeneous (or compatible) processors in normal business operations, it may be possible to replace several low-end servers with a single high-end server. Through the use of the right operating system software, even applications that reside on heterogeneous processors may be able to run successfully on a single processor. Again, the total capacity requirement of the backup server and related storage devices may be substantially less than that of the production environment.

The net result of this analysis is what may be called a *minimum acceptable hardware configuration*. This configuration, which must be implemented quickly in the event of a disaster, may require substantial technical assistance to design. Still more assistance may be required to deploy and test it. However, a workable minimum configuration can drastically reduce the costs of the disaster recovery capability.

How Many Users?

The risk analysis should also have identified the characteristics of application use, including the number of users who would need access to applications to continue business functions at emergency levels. The number of personnel required during emergency operations may be far fewer than the normal complement of personnel who use systems in day-to-day operations. Additional staff might be put to better use supporting business processes that are being continued by manual means, or aiding in other aspects of the recovery effort.

From the size of the "skeleton crew" using restored applications to provide critical and vital business functions, certain other facts may be discerned. For example, the number of users will help to define the recovery network for the application by identifying how many end stations (workstation/terminals) and what type of access and bandwidth will be required. This information, too, must be taken into account by the centralized system recovery strategy that is developed.

The strategy must account for peripheral devices as well as CPUs and mass storage devices. It must also provide for a location where recovery personnel will work, in addition to providing an environment where processors, tape drives, and disk drives, and other equipment will be operated.

CAUTIONS AND CAVEATS

The above description may seem to oversimplify the task of defining the parameters for centralized system recovery. However, the task can be, and often is, just that straightforward. Having identified key business processes and their application supports, the balance of the centralized system recovery planning effort is made substantially easier because of the well-defined operating environment of the mainframe.[2]

According to Tim Humphreys, Chief Architect for Trident Services, assuming that a "floor system" is available for use and backups of data are available, OS/390 mainframe application recovery is typically a by-the-numbers (or by the acronyms!) proposition.

> First, you need to do a software-based Hardware Configuration Data (HCD) activation to dynamically change the configuration of the platform [to identify the network addresses of devices that will be used to interface with the system]. Then, load your initial program load (IPL) volume [which defines resources and parameters], followed by your master catalog pack, and you IPL the system. Next, you initialize the direct access storage devices (DASD) for use with Systems Managed Storage (IBM's DFSMS manages storage volumes), and you begin performing logical restores of your backups. This may be done using IBM's Data Set Services (DFDSS), or IBM's Hierarchical Storage Manager Application Backup and Recovery System (DFHSM ABARS), or third party data dump restore products like Innovation's Fast Dump Restore (FDR). With this done, you're basically ready for business.[3]

Humphreys' description makes centralized system recovery seem almost routine. He points out, however, that running an application on a platform having a different configuration, or in a system that is partitioned or shared with others, can introduce some problems. He notes that products such as Trident Services' Operating System/Environment Manager (OS/EM) may provide an easy to use mechanism for supporting ABARS data set recovery and for dynamically altering region sizes and memory resources available to applications.[4]

Even with environment management tools, however, problems can and do present themselves when defining a minimum system configuration that may require effort and creativity to surmount. First, not all applications have been written in such a way that they can be deployed in alternative configurations. Systems programmers are an important source for information about application resource requirements that might be missed by less technical analysts. Job Control Language (JCL), customized Job Entry System (JES) "exits," and a number of other factors may conspire with poorly written "spaghetti code" to mitigate the ability to move applications readily from one set of environment conditions to another.

In some cases, there is no minimum equipment configuration option for applications without a significant rewrite of application- and system-level code. Few organizations are inclined to modify or rewrite code merely to facilitate the recoverability of an application in a disaster situation. However, identifying such problems and alerting management to their existence might add another argument to an existing business case for rewriting or replacing the old application code.

In any case, minimum equipment configuration goes beyond the definition of the mainframe platform. The analysis of inputs and outputs to the business process, included in risk analysis, defines the equipment requirements to recover the business process overall, not just its application host. Based on the risk analysis, it is possible to formulate a fairly clear picture of how many users (or processes) will use the application, and what the network, end station, and peripheral requirements are for that use.

For example, if printed reports are a necessary output of a given business process, a printer may need to be added to the minimum configuration of the recovery system. Also, if input data needs to be received, via data communications from remote sites (for example, "lock box" transmissions used to update customer payment records), the minimum equipment configuration would need to provide for the network hardware and software for this function.

Business process analysis will also identify any special preprinted forms required for work, as well as voice communications, electronic mail, photocopying, facsimile transmission, and ground mail resources needed to do the job.

From this brief overview, it should be evident that much of what is needed to develop an effective centralized system recovery strategy is available from the risk analysis. Given this information, it is up to the co-ordinator, in conjunction with technical staff, to select the best strategy for the restoration of critical and vital business functions.

MAINFRAME BACKUP STRATEGIES

As observed above, disaster recovery planning techniques were once limited to developing strategies for replacing mainframe computers. While this is not an adequate context for business recovery today, the focus on mainframe backup has yielded some time-tested techniques that can provide useful information for more sophisticated system recovery plans.

The following are typical strategies for backing up the corporate mainframe. The explanation of each strategy identifies the merits and demerits that have come to be associated with it.

"Next Box off the Line"

One strategy used by many companies in the past to backup their data processing mainframe was to absorb the impact of the disaster until a data center could be readied and a comparable or compatible mainframe and peripherals network could be installed to replace the lost facility and equipment. In the interim—until a new mainframe became available—the company would "make do" with manual procedures, locate and prepare a new facility or refurbish the existing facility, and retrieve a current backup of system and application software and data from storage. When the new mainframe was installed, IT personnel would load the software and data backup and users would frantically re-input interim data until files and records were up to date.

The drawbacks of this approach—which stands today as more a straw man than a strategy—are numerous. First, the plan could work only in an environment where there were no critical systems. By definition, if viable, manual alternatives existed to all mainframe-supported business processes, no application would be considered critical to business survival. Only in such an environment could the open-ended timeframes involved in replacing computer equipment with new hardware be tolerated. Certainly, very few companies today would find their automated systems so easily replaced with manual means.

Second, this option does not provide, in advance, for a facility in which the new mainframe can be installed. Locating a suitable facility may not be a very difficult task, but the preparation of such a facility, including the installation of a raised floor, air conditioning, UPS, electrical wiring, security systems, fire protection, etc., would be a major undertaking. In short, even if the "next box off the line" were available in a timely way, the facility might not be.

Cold Site

The cold site (or shell site) strategy is similar to the "next box off the line" option in that the actual restoration of mainframe operations is on hold until replacement hardware can be obtained. By using the cold site strategy, however, the business has already prepared a facility with the requisite physical capabilities to serve as an alternate data processing site.

Company-owned cold sites have the drawback of being expensive to outfit with all of the requisite disaster prevention systems provided in a production data center. However, the facility may be able to be used for other purposes, including off-site storage or new employee training, when not in use for disaster recovery.

Commercial Cold Site

This option is identical to the cold site strategy above except that a commercial cold site is a contracted facility. The facility may be located in the subscriber's vicinity or distant from it. Or, a cold site may be able to be moved to the customer's location. Mobile cold sites have become widely available in the United States and are offered by leading disaster recovery services vendors, including Hewlett Packard Business Recovery Service, IBM Business Continuity and Recovery Service, and SunGard Recovery Services. Figure 5–2 shows a typical mobile shell site offering from SunGard.

Commercial shell sites, whether mobile or not, provide a capability that is cost-effective because expenses for its construction and maintenance are shared by multiple subscribers. Like the preceding strategies, however, this approach to centralized system recovery assumes that the company can absorb the impact of being without a mainframe until one can be obtained from either a leasing company or system vendor. For many companies, this option is unacceptable.

As with the private cold site option, commercial cold sites do not provide a means to test the effectiveness of this recovery strategy until a disaster actually happens. A company cannot verify its estimates for system restoration timeframes without testing restoration procedures on actual hardware.

Given their inherent systems recovery "lag time," the role of shell sites has been substantially recast in recent years. In some cases, the shell

Figure 5–2   Mobile data center offering. (*Source:* SunGard
Recovery Services Inc., Wayne, PA.)

site is positioned as a transitional facility—a location to which company systems that have been supported on a "hot site" platform (see below) in the hours or days following a disaster can be migrated for operation over a substantially longer period of time.

For example, if a data center has been demolished by a disaster, it is sometimes necessary to support mission-critical operations at an alternate site for an extended timeframe while a new facility is being located and equipped. A shell site can be equipped with company replacement hardware while the company's critical applications are being supported at a hot site. When the system is ready at the shell site, the company can migrate applications to the shell site host, freeing the hot site platform for use by other subscribers. Hot site contracts generally require this strategy and limit the period of hot site occupancy. In some cases, the shell site serves as a staging area for replacement systems from the mainframe vendor.

Mobile shell sites, too, have been largely retasked to support transitional operations, or to serve different functions in the recovery environment, such as small systems and/or user recovery. According to Jim Grogan, SunGard Recovery Services Vice President of Alliances, mobile shell sites can and do serve as mobile data centers:

> We can move one of our 11 Mobile Data Centers within 48 hours anywhere in the country. We used them recently in several regional disasters, such as the Red River floods, after the California earthquakes, and so forth. Following a flood in Grand Forks, SD, one of our customers, a bank, operated from the Mobile Data Center and had to move the center two times to stay ahead of the water.... We are able to ship smaller processors with the mobile units, and we have used them for user recovery in many cases, providing workstations and equipment for 20 to 25 users. We are also building two custom mobile MetroCenters® that will provide 1300 square feet of raised floor environment for workgroup and distributed systems recovery.[5]

The forty-eight-hour mean restoration timeframe has emerged as an industry standard for mobile shell sites. Both Hewlett Packard and IBM offer mobile shells, equipped with smaller server hosts, that can provide facilities for workgroup and distributed systems recovery. Cast in this role, vendors can make at least one test per year possible on actual equipment.

Reciprocal Backup Agreement

To address the problem of facilities and hardware outages in companies unable to manage for extended periods of time without their mainframes, one option, less frequently seen today than in the past is the reciprocal backup agreement. Essentially, two companies having spare processing time and compatible hardware capabilities agree formally or informally to back up each other's critical applications. In a simple arrangement, if Company A experienced a disaster, Company B would allow Company B to restore its critical applications on Company B's hardware. The reverse would be the case if Company B had a failure.

The problems with this strategy, even at the time that it was popular, were twofold. First, it was extremely difficult for a company to find a partner who had the right hardware, spare capacity, and the inclination to participate in such an agreement. Location was also a factor: The potential partner could not be co-located to the company seeking the arrangement, since the same disaster that affected Company A might at the same time affect Company B.

Second, if a suitable partner were found, it was difficult to find a mutually agreeable time to test the arrangement. Having an untested strategy is nearly as pointless as having no strategy at all.

Companies that experimented with these arrangements in the 1970s and 1980s found that it was also difficult to maintain the relationship on mutually acceptable terms. Managers chafed at having to notify their partners of changing configurations or new processing requirements. One could not cost-justify to one's own management the need to acquire a new item of hardware on the grounds that it would facilitate the disaster recovery capability of another company.

These arrangements also carried the risk of domino-effect disasters. The relocation of Company A's processing load to Company B's host might also disrupt Company B's operations. Company B would need to activate its emergency plan, requiring that its business operate in disaster recovery mode until Company A was recovered. Needless to say, this was unacceptable to Company B's management.

Today, reciprocal arrangements are rarely seen, except in large companies with numerous subsidiaries. Even in these cases, it is rare that enough spare processing time or equipment capability exists to support a mutual backup arrangement without deliberate planning to support such a scenario. Where there is substantial excess capacity, it has a tendency to be drawn into normal production use over time, making it unavailable for DR.

Service Bureaus

Some companies elect to back up systems against failure by contracting with a service bureau for emergency processing services. For example, the vendor of a loan administration application used by mortgage banking companies may offer a "service bureau" capability for the application.

Software vendors that provide service bureaus typically market the service to customers who prefer not to invest in their own computer systems and software. User terminals are installed in the client offices, and jobs are submitted to CPUs located at the vendor service bureau via data communications. In some cases, printers are also installed at the client office so that reports and other output can be printed locally.

For customers who purchase vendor software but operate independently of the vendor's service bureau, the service bureau offering may still be available in a disaster recovery situation. Service bureau backup may be part of a software sales contract, or may be a separately negotiated arrangement.

What are some of the potential drawbacks of this approach? Vendor service bureaus are typically application-specific. They process customer data all together, then distribute output to individual customers. This may create some difficulties for a company that has several critical applications, including some for which recourse to a software vendor's service bureau is not available. Also, the prospect of dividing numerous applications among several vendor-provided service bureaus is unsettling.

For a service bureau arrangement to be effective, several conditions must be met. First, the disaster-stricken company must have an existing facility where remote access to applications by users can be provided. Second, the customer's data backups must have been saved from the disaster that consumed the originals, and these data backups must be in the proper format for speedy integration with the service bureau storage and systems. If vendor-recommended maintenance procedures have not been observed, if applications have not been updated to the most current software release, or if file formats have been "customized" to better suit the business's needs, there may be incompatibilities with the service bureau application that will be difficult and time-consuming to correct.

It should be mentioned that, despite the caveats expressed above, there is a new spin on service bureau backup that is giving the concept a renaissance of sorts. As the 1990s drew to a close, the emergence of "virtual infrastructure outsourcing" descended. Companies have begun experimenting with remote application hosting via the Internet as a means to reduce internal system support costs.

One vendor that has been quick to see the disaster recovery implications of this trend is Exodus Communications. According to Prabakar Sundarrajan, Vice President of Research and Development, the e-commerce explosion has driven many top-tier companies to the web and made small companies instant players in a bigger world.[6] Exodus provides application hosting services to a significant percentage of the largest concerns on the World Wide Web. Serving as a virtual data center for this clientele requires Exodus to provide service level guarantees exceeding those of non–Internet-based outsourcing service providers.

Exodus has created its own network of redundant Internet Data Centers interconnected by OC3/OC12 backbone. Mission-critical e-business applications are mirrored across these data centers to provide enhanced performance and uptime guarantees. According to Sundarrajan, the company is working with customers to develop Internet disaster recovery (IDR) plans that will enable the application service provider to also play the role of disaster recovery provider.

Application service providers (ASPs) are quickly becoming the modern service bureau processors, not only for e-commerce applications, but also for databases, enterprise resource planning (ERP) applications, and other mission-critical applications.[7] While not technically a "mainframe backup strategy," the potential for the use of the Internet as a mechanism for application backup is intriguing. A new category of backup options, closely related to the service bureau strategy of two decades ago appears to be coalescing on the disaster recovery landscape.

Hot Sites

Hot sites are rather like generic service bureaus. Typically, they are fully equipped IT operations facilities to which a number of companies having compatible hardware subscribe. Machine time is made available to subscribers for the purpose of testing their recovery procedures, and this testing schedule can be quickly interrupted so that facilities can be made available to any customer who declares a disaster.

Once a disaster is declared, the customer sends its backup media (or uses an on-site tape vault or remote mirror) and a team of operations personnel to the hot site. Critical applications are loaded and tested, users are provided with access from their work location, and IT services are restored.

Unlike a service bureau, a hot site is usually equipped to run any application that is compatible with its hardware and operating system. Hot sites are often equipped with technical support personnel to assist the company operations team in its efforts to get systems configured, data transferred, and applications up and running.

In addition to the fixed complement of hardware at the hot site, specialized equipment can be added to satisfy the customer's backup requirement. However, this is often done at the customer's expense, especially if other facility subscribers do not need the required equipment.

Some hot site vendors also offer cold sites that a customer can lease if disaster conditions persist for an extended period of time. Hot site vendors may also provide assistance in obtaining replacement hardware for use in the cold site or for delivery to the customer's own new or refurbished facility.

Hot sites have become the mainframe backup option preferred by medium to large companies. Their reliability and recent notable successes in recovering companies in the throes of a disaster have greatly offset initial concerns about their price. Some considerations and cautions in selecting a hot site are provided later in this chapter.

Recent public announcements of pricing for hot site services by some vendors have contributed to the perception that this type of service offering is becoming a commodity. In January 1999, *Network Computing* magazine built a feature story around a hot site services request for proposal (RFP) issued by hypothetical retailer, Dewey, Cheatham, and Howe.[8] The RFP specified requirements and invited hot site vendors to respond with solutions and pricing. Three vendors, Exodus Communications, IBM, and Comdisco, responded to the RFP, while several declined to participate. Of those who refused, only one vendor (SunGard) did so because, reportedly, it was unwilling to discuss price in an open forum.

In June 1999, Hewlett Packard BRS went public with "a portfolio of services" specifying estimated recovery timeframes, and, in conversations with the press, pricing (see Table 5–1). According to George Ferguson, Marketing Manager for HP BRS, "Our portfolio of services are designed to address the different criticality requirements of companies. Criticality is being determined today at the Chief Financial Officer and Chief Operating Officer level. It is no longer primarily an IT concern."[9]

Table 5–1   Hewlett Packard BRS Portfolio of Services

	BRS Continuous	**BRS Immediate**	**BRS Critical**
Typical end-user availability following disaster invocation (RTO)	Less than 1 hour	2 to 8 hours	8 to 24 hours
Service Level Objective	Less than 1 hour for end-user availability	2 to 8 hours for end-user availability (an exact number of hours will be specified based on the customer's environment)	7 hours for the system to be fully commissioned, operating system loaded, and volumes configured
Currency of data (RPO)	Nearly the same as the moment of the disaster	Nearly the same as the moment of the disaster	Same as the last backup
Customer access to recovery center following disaster invocation	Within 2 hours	Within 2 hours	Within 2 hours
Shared vs. dedicated components	Dedicated system Dedicated storage Dedicated networking	Shared system Dedicated storage Shared networking	Shared system Shared storage Shared networking
Location of recovery system	HP Recovery Center	HP Recovery Center	HP Recovery Center
Disaster rehearsals included	Yes	Yes	Yes

	BRS Core -HP Recovery Center	**BRS Core -Ship-to-Site**	**BRS Core -Mobile Data Center**	**BRS Basic**
Typical end-user availability following disaster invocation (RTO)	24 to 72 hours	24 to 72 hours	24 to 72 hours	Greater than 72 hours (based on no rehearsals)
Service level objective	24 hours for the system to be fully commis-	6 hours for the system to be fully commis-	6 hours for the system to be fully commis-	8 hours for the system to be fully commis-

	BRS Core -HP Recovery Center	BRS Core -Ship-to-Site	BRS Core -Mobile Data Center	BRS Basic
	sioned and operating system loaded	sioned and shipped; operating system will be loaded before or after shipping	sioned and shipped; operating system will be loaded before or after shipping	sioned and shipped
Currency of data (RPO)	Same as the last backup	Same as the last backup	Same as the last backup	Same as the last backup
Customer access to re-covery center following disaster invocation	Within 4 hours	Nonapplicable	Nonapplicable	Nonapplicable
Shared vs. dedicated components	Shared system Shared storage Shared networking	Shared system Shared storage Shared networking	Shared system Shared storage Shared networking	Shared system Shared storage Shared networking
Location of recovery system	HP Recovery Center	Customer-provided data center	HP Mobile Data Center at customer-specified location	Customer-provided data center
Disaster rehearsals in-cluded	Yes	Yes	Yes	Optional

Source: Hewlett Packard Company, Palo Alto, CA.

Ferguson observes that the range of services provided by the vendor cater "to the differing recovery time objectives and differing recovery point objectives of various business processes. These are not linear to cost. For a high availability uptime solution, companies can expect to pay upwards of $750,000 per year. For other business processes, in which recovery timeframes range from eight hours to three days, there is a huge pricing drop—well below $100,000 per year."[10]

Menu-based pricing, unheard of in the industry a decade ago, reinforces the commodity view of hot site services. SunGard's Jim Grogan, however, takes exception to the trend toward price disclosure on several grounds.

> There is little doubt that service pricing is a little more open now. Industry groups have challenged vendors on their pricing policies. But are disaster recovery services commodities now? I have heard it said over the past two years that they are. At SunGard, we have to disagree. There is no one-size-fits-all solution. The technology simply has not matured enough.[11]

Redundant Systems

Of course, the singlemost reliable system backup strategy is to have fully redundant systems. While most companies cannot afford to build and equip two identical data centers, those that can enjoy the comfort of full confidence in their ability to recover from almost any disaster.

In the event of a disaster, redundant systems at a separate facility—which must be far enough distant so as not to have been affected by the same disaster—are brought on-line. Users are either transported to an operations center that is co-located to the backup site or are provided remote access to the backup CPU via some sort of pre-established data communications network.

Besides being the most reliable method of centralized (or decentralized) systems recovery, redundancy also tends to be the most expensive. A commercial hot site, for this reason, is often a more acceptable alternative from a cost perspective, provided that the longer recovery window is acceptable.

This spectrum of alternative mainframe backup strategies are graphed in Figure 5–3 to show the relative measure of confidence afforded to the company whose survival is dependent upon each strategy. The highest measure of confidence is afforded by the redundant systems strategy in which hardware availability is immediate, facilities mirror those that were lost, and backup systems duplicate production systems so closely that only minimal adjustments to normal business processes are required. The least confidence is placed in the "next box off the line," or replacement strategy. Such a strategy provides no timetable for system replacement or restoration of business processes as hardware delivery dates, facility location, and preparation dates, and other factors are unknown. A caveat to

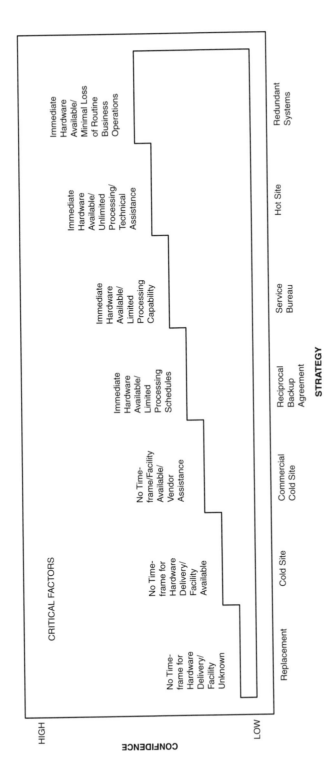

Figure 5-3 Centralized system recovery strategies and confidence levels.

this simple comparison goes without saying: No strategy affords any greater level of confidence than any other unless it is accompanied by a carefully thought out, documented, and tested recovery process. Contracting for a hot site does not absolve the DR coordinator of the responsibility for planning for or testing its use.

WHICH STRATEGY IS PREFERRED?

Considering the large population of companies that have not prepared at all for the disastrous interruption of business processes, some crafty analyst might say that the most popular strategy for centralized system recovery is the "do nothing" strategy. The fact is that the preferred strategy for the recovery of centralized platforms is not known.

IBM Business Continuity and Recovery Service claims to have had 10,000 customers subscribe to its service since its inception in 1989.[12] IBM's original offering consisted of hot site facilities and consulting, but, like most hot site vendors, the company has rolled out additional services over the years, ranging from mobile shell sites to expedited delivery of replacement hardware (a sort of contractual next-box-off-the-line) for its smaller systems.

As of this writing, the company has added two offerings aimed at very specific and vertical markets to its portfolio of services: the recovery of call centers and the recovery of Enterprise Resource Planning (ERP) systems. These, according to IBM BCRS spokespersons, are part of the company's effort to provide "skills-based offerings" that meet specific market demands. In short, while IBM BCRS may have contracts with over 10,000 customers, the actual recovery method preferred by those customers is not public information.

So as not to single out IBM, SunGard Recovery Services also boasts over 5000 customers. According to Vice President of Alliances, Jim Grogan, the average customer comes to the vendor today with at least three different types of system platforms to recover.[13] How many customers are purchasing hot site contracts versus mobile shell sites or versus other recovery or service offerings remains unclear.

Comdisco Continuity Services (CCS), too, exclaims that "well over 2000 customers have over 4500 contracts with CCS to address their continuity and high availability needs."[14] Comdisco's service offerings range from consulting and disaster recovery planning software to hot site, workgroup recovery, Y2K testing, and others. These are presented on their web site in true e-commerce shopping cart form: CCS provides a "Business Continuity Catalog" (sans pricing). No information is provided on the number of contracts that are associated with specific service offerings.

This "information gap" regarding preferred centralized system recovery strategies is unlikely to be resolved in the near future. Industry surveys conducted by trade journals or analysts also do not provide a clear picture of strategy preference, in part because of the comparatively small number of companies surveyed. Disaster recovery–specific publications do offer periodic reader survey results, but capture only the behavior of the small subset of planners who actually subscribe to the publications.

At least three studies are presently underway within academia, but these are hampered by numerous factors. Some use the World Wide Web to collect data, which inevitably skews results (falsified reports are common). Plus, academic surveys, like industry surveys, are subject to the "PBS factor." That is, just as surveyed television viewers overwhelmingly claimed to watch intelligent programming on Public Broadcasting System (rather than the intellectually-mediocre fare on broadcast or cable television channels), companies almost inevitably point to DR plans that are "under development," rather than acknowledging that they have never undertaken any planning whatsoever. The latter would be politically incorrect.

For these reasons and many others, the best evidence regarding the preferred strategy for centralized system recovery is strictly anecdotal. It is derived from press accounts of recovery efforts, consultant tales, DR planner "war stories," and vendor-provided statistics. Added together, this less-than-scientific evidence favors the commercial hot site strategy as the preferred *modus operandi* for centralized system recovery in businesses with critical downtime sensitivities measured 1-to-48 hour range.

While some companies do build redundant data centers or have mutual assistance agreements with the data centers of their subsidiaries, most do not enjoy these luxuries. To them, the commercial hot site provides a less expensive and equally effective option for large system recovery.

Hot sites remove many of the unknowns inherent in strategies that involve the acquisition of replacement hardware in a disaster situation (i.e., replacement, cold site, and commercial cold site). Moreover, the increasing diversity of installed software products and a concurrent increase in the utilization of hardware capacities have rendered service bureaus and cross-firm mutual backup agreements increasingly anachronistic as competent mainframe backup strategies.

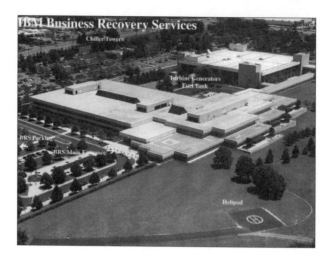

Figure 5-4   A hot site facility. (*Source:* IBM Business
                 Continuity and Recovery Service, Sterling
                 Forest, NY.)

As of this writing, the Internet-based virtual data center strategy em-braced by companies such as Exodus Communications is very new. It is entirely conceivable that these services will come to rival traditional hot sites in the future, especially given the interest of telecommunications providers such as Sprint and AT&T in delivering system hosting services within their Next Generation Networks.

For now, commercial hot sites, such as the facility pictured in Figure 5–4, are available to recover nearly all brands and sizes of large systems and mainframes. Most also offer recovery services for smaller server con-figurations, though the efficacy and price/performance of these solutions remains a debatable issue (see Chapter 6).

SELECTING A HOT SITE

Selecting a hot site is a straightforward process, but one that requires the disaster recovery coordinator to have (1) a detailed understanding of the company's minimum acceptable system configuration and (2) some savvy about the hot site industry and its practices. Armed with this information, the coordinator will be better able to identify the vendor offering that best fulfills a company's mainframe backup requirements.

Since minimum acceptable configurations are company-specific, they cannot be treated here in any detail. Suffice it to say that considerable technical assistance may be required to define a system hardware configuration that is capable of restoring all critical and vital applications. These applications may include both those that are normally resident on a mainframe as well as portable applications that are normally deployed to distributed computers but may be recovered in a centralized system environment. It is obviously advantageous to have completed this analysis and to have a requirements list in hand before going hot site "shopping."

In addition to system hardware specifications, DR coordinators need to understand the data communications requirements of their critical and vital applications. Most of the larger hot site vendors offer recovery networks for use by their customers in re-establishing links between the recovery system and peripherals located at user recovery facilities. While most organizations have moved from 3 to 4 Mb/s channel interfaces to peripheral devices to 18 Mb/s ESCON, 40 Mb/s UltraSCSI, or 100 Mb/s Fibre Channel interconnects for remoting storage, printer, and other types of devices,[15] or have moved to an entirely ethernet-based peripheral attachment strategy,[16] there may continue to be the odd item sorter, controller, or other peripheral at a company branch office that requires special service. Be sure to know what requirements exist for reconnecting the recovered system to its peripheral network before approaching vendors.

Also, if critical or vital applications require the exchange of data between locations other than the user recovery site and the hot site (for example, electronic data interchange between the company's systems and the systems of suppliers, service bureaus, government agencies, etc.), these communications requirements must be specified in as much detail as possible. Information about the location and type of communicator, the communication methods, the access methods, protocols, encryption standards, and even the timing of scheduled communications should be at the DR coordinator's fingertips when he or she sits down to define backup requirements with a vendor marketing representative.

Technical suitability is a primary criterion for selecting a hot site vendor. However, there are several other factors that the coordinator would be well advised to consider. Many of these factors can be derived from the experience of other DR coordinators who have developed effective centralized system recovery strategies through the use of hot site facilities.

In the past, one consideration was the veracity of vendor claims that they could actually deliver promised services. In the 1970s and 1980s, disaster recovery planners confronted the reality of fly-by-night companies who misrepresented their facilities and capabilities. Legitimate vendors struggled to offset the damage caused a few unethical charlatans who collected large monthly fees for nonexistent or phantom hot sites on the gamble that a customer will never have to declare a disaster.

In the 1990s, the DR industry underwent enormous change. The rise of organized associations of disaster recovery planners created a type of informal industry watch. Word spread quickly within these groups regarding any questionable practices by vendors, the adequacy of their offerings, pricing differences, and so forth.

In addition to tighter monitoring, the vendor community itself went through a winnowing-out period in the 1990s. Many smaller vendors either closed their doors or were acquired by larger companies. As a result, most hot site solutions today are provided by established firms with extensive client references and demonstrable records of successful recoveries.

The last point is extremely important. Cases of disaster recovery plan implementation are now front page stories in the computer trade press. In the past, companies that experienced disasters—even those that recovered successfully from them—were very circumspect in disclosing information about the event. The fear was that stockholders, business partners, or customers would respond negatively to the perceived vulnerability of the company and its business processes to unplanned interruptions.

Corporate culture has changed in most (though not all) firms. No longer is the best information about disaster recovery locked away in confidential corporate records: Now, disaster recovery is grist for splash headlines in trade magazines and tabloids. Editors welcome the exciting visuals of wrecked buildings, flooded data centers, and shattered glass houses as a break from stock product photos, software screen shots, and mug shots of IT corporate luminaries.

With more information readily available to DR coordinators about the legitimacy of vendor offerings, attention can be focused on other important components of the system recovery service. These considerations become apparent upon review of the steps typically involved in contracting with a vendor for hot site service.

Meet with the Marketing Representative

One of the first steps in selecting a hot site is to meet with a marketing representative of the vendor. During this meeting, the representative will seek information about company backup requirements, minimum configurations, communications requirements, and even the current status of the company disaster recovery plan.

Obviously, the representative will strive to inform the prospective customer about the merits of his or her facilities, identify some of its more prestigious subscribers, and even recount instances in which the facility rescued a subscriber in distress. Be sure to ask for the names of contacts in several subscriber companies for later use in vendor evaluation.

Do not accept the representative's word for the fact that his or her facility can meet recovery needs. Only in rare cases can a marketing rep make such a determination without input from the hot site technical staff. Even if a technical support person has accompanied the marketing representative, verbal assurances are not sufficient.

Ask the marketing representative to develop, within a specified time, a written proposal responding to the specific recovery requirements that have been explained to him or her. The vendor should clearly define how the hot site facility being offered will fulfill each requirement. Hot site vendors are highly competitive, so legitimate vendors will usually go out of their way to ensure that the prospective customer has all the information needed to make the right choice (presumably, a choice that favors their service).

The proposal should detail costs associated with both subscription to, and actual use of, the facility. It should also provide details of other vendor offerings. Many hot site vendors also maintain cold sites that are available to customers in the event that the recovery period becomes protracted. Some will help the customer locate and install new hardware in the vendor cold site or at some other specified location. Some vendors are subsidiaries of larger concerns involved with disaster recovery consulting, equipment leasing, system manufacturing, or other data processing services. A list of the vendor's other services and interests may be a factor in coordinator's decision.

Inspect the Facility

Once two or more potentially suitable hot site vendors have been identified and their proposals and credentials have been evaluated, the coordinator should go no further until a physical inspection has been made of each candidate's facilities. It is often a good idea to have a systems expert and an auditor accompany the coordinator during the inspection, as their observations and criticisms may go beyond the scope of a purely disaster recovery-oriented focus to identify important vendor inadequacies.

Some hot site vendors will purchase the plane tickets or underwrite lodging for serious prospects. The coordinator should strive to avoid being influenced by these or other perks that the vendor provides. Weighed against the monthly fee that the vendor will charge once the prospect signs a subscriber contract, these perks amount to very little indeed.

One of the purposes of the facility visit is to evaluate the vendor's nonemergency operations and staff. The coordinator should find out how processors are used during nondisaster periods: Are they idle, are they in constant use for customer tests, or are they used to provide other services?

If the vendor's own business applications reside on processors during nonemergency operations, or if the processors are utilized to provide service bureau functions, the coordinator should ask for an explanation of how these processing functions will be handled in the event of a customer emergency.

Be aware that, in many cases, the facility that a vendor shows to its prospective customers may not be the facility that will actually be used if recovery is required. Since the mid-1990s, some disaster recovery service providers have been selling MIPS (processing capability measured in millions of instructions per second) rather than sites. In other words, if a customer declared a disaster, the vendor might recover the customer not at the facility being toured, but on another system offering adequate MIPS located somewhere in the vendor's infrastructure.

While there is no obvious reason why the MIPS, not sites strategy will not work, there are several key issues that need to be addressed by the vendor to the satisfaction of the DR coordinator. For one, if the MIPS will be taken from system platforms that are used by the vendor for other purposes (time sharing with non-DR customers, for example), how will the user be displaced by the vendor and how soon will the MIPS become available for use?

Another important, though subjective, evaluation the DR coordinator needs to make of a MIPS, not sites offering is whether valuable "affinity" is being sacrificed in this strategy. Once a deal is made for a hot site, testing is usually undertaken one or more times per year. Through this process, the vendor's support staff becomes intimately familiar with the recovery requirements of the customer and affinity develops between hot site staff and corporate recovery team personnel that can be of value in an actual disaster recovery situation. This is lost if different vendor personnel from those who tested with the customer implement an actual recovery at a different facility.

IBM's Martinez minimizes the importance of such concerns, noting that recovery processes are "carefully documented and ISO 9001 certified" so "all of our 17 sites serving 62 countries throughout the world have the same look and feel." He credits this fact and the IBM BCRS Network, with the "31 simultaneous recoveries" accomplished by IBM BRS for its customers in the wake of Hurricane Georges (1998). "Some customers," he notes, "based on configuration requirements, require recovery at a specific site. But Georges provided evidence that we could do multiple recoveries at different locations."[17]

SunGard's Grogan agrees that MIPS, not sites is a technically feasible solution and acknowledges that SunGard's recovery agreement does not specify the site where a customer can expect to be recovered. He notes that regional disasters have often resulted in simultaneous disaster declarations that have required some shuffling by vendors to recover multiple customers.

> But just promising MIPS can be deceptive. There are cases in which a customer would need to engineer a recovery solution very differently based on the limitations of different environments. If this needs to be done during a recovery, it introduces some additional risk and usually lengthens the recovery timeframe. Some of our competitor's customers have come to us because they didn't like this strategy. Others are contracting with more than one hot site vendor at a time.[18]

It is also important for the coordinator to ascertain how many subscribers are assigned to the service. An excessive number of users assigned to a fixed set of processing capabilities can be a warning sign. The coordinator should tread cautiously with a vendor that promises that new capabilities are being added to take the overload within X months.

Regardless of whether the number seems high, the coordinator should follow up by asking how multiple, simultaneous disaster declarations would be accommodated. The coordinator should also ask for a list—or at least a count—of hot site customers located in the same geographic region as his or her company. This is extremely important if the region is especially vulnerable to regional hurricanes or earthquakes.

Be sure to ask whether and how the vendor discriminates between customer disaster declarations and proactive alerts issued by customers in advance of a disaster event? Are these types of "declarations" treated equally or is preference given to the company that declares, rather than alerts?

For shared facility offerings, be sure also to obtain an explanation of how security will be provided to limit the access of unauthorized personnel (including recovery teams of other customers) to sensitive company materials and processes.

Contract for Service

Based upon information collected from the marketing representative, research, the vendor proposal, and the on-site visit, a final decision must be reached. In the best of circumstances, the ultimate decision will come down to price differences among two or three equally qualified candidates.

Hot site agreements, like off-site storage agreements, typically contain a number of fees and provisions that the coordinator should understand and examine thoroughly.

- **Subscription fee.** This is the fee (typically expressed as a dollar amount payable to the vendor on a monthly basis) for the base equipment configuration that will be made available to the subscriber. Equipment covered will generally include all CPUs, storage devices, input devices (other than user terminals), output devices, and communications equipment that is held in common with other subscribers. A schedule of the exact equipment covered by the fee should appear in the contract. There is often a discount on the monthly fee for subscribers who contract for service over a period of many years.

- **Extra equipment fee.** This fee (also payable monthly for most facilities) covers special hardware that is not used by a preponderance of subscribers but is made available at the hot site for emergency use by companies that subscribe for it. The fee may also cover additional storage devices, tape drives, and other equipment not part of the base configuration. Extra equipment should be listed on a schedule that appears in the contract.

- **Annual test time allocation and additional test time fee.** The hot site contract should spell out how many hours per year the subscriber will have to test its plan without charge and indicate the hourly fee for test time over and above this amount.

- **Disaster notification fee.** This fee is assessed by some (but not all) hot site vendors to "discourage frivolous use of hot site facilities." Fees may be nominal or quite expensive, depending on the vendor. In addition to stating the fee, the contract should indicate how the customer declares a disaster and when the fee will be collected.

- **Daily usage fee.** This fee is included in the contract to show daily (or hourly) rates for use of the hot site in a disaster situation. Other associated fees may be assessed for technical support, maintenance services, administrative office space rental, and cold site use. The hot site may also provide facilities for local and off-site storage of data and supplies. These charges should be spelled out in the contract.

- **Network services fee.** Some hot site vendors will contract separately for the use of their network services, while others will specify the fees on the hot site services agreement. Fees may be assessed on a monthly basis, or there may be a setup fee and a table for charges on a usage basis. If no fees for network services appear on a proposed agreement, ask for them so they can be added to the bid price. Only in this way can a fair comparison of multiple vendor pricing be accomplished.

- **Plan fees.** The hot site vendor may also contribute to the development of a disaster recovery plan and testing strategies and the documentation of tests. These services may be provided on a fee basis or at no charge to the customer. Be aware that even cost-free planning software tools provided by the hot site vendor may have far-reaching costs in terms of future software maintenance fees, user training, and so on. When in doubt, just say no, thank you.

- **Multiple simultaneous disasters.** The methodology that the hot site will observe in allocating resources among customers that experience concurrent disasters should be spelled out in the contract. In some cases, resources are allocated on a "first come, first served" basis, while vendors with multiple facilities may offer primary and secondary recovery sites. Declaration policy should also be formally stated.

- **Subscriber limitations.** The hot site contract should also formalize its policy, assuming it has one, on the maximum number of subscriptions that will be taken for any extant facility.

- **Prior notice of price increases.** The contract should stipulate how much notice the subscriber will be given of fee increases. Ninety days advance notice seems to be standard.

- **Equipment modifications and additions.** The contract should clearly describe how equipment changes and resultant changes in configuration fees will be handled. Contracts typically provide 60-day prior notice of hardware changes that significantly affect the configurations for which the subscriber has contracted. Longer term (multiyear) contracts expose the customer to contract modification fees that would dramatically outstrip the cost of negotiating contracts on an annual basis.

- **Hot site liability.** The hot site contract should indicate the extent to which the hot site assumes responsibility for providing services at contracted levels. Typical components include a "reasonable care" clause and a *force majeure* clause. The former is the vendor's guarantee that it will exercise reasonable care in the handling and processing of subscriber media and data. The vendor should also provide client confidentiality. *Force majeure* releases the vendor from liability for outages resulting from acts of God, nuclear wars, and so on. These caveats are fairly common to service contracts of any type. They take on particular importance when considering the location of the hot site facility *viz.* the normal business IT data center. If a hot site is selected that is subject to the same regional disaster event that impacts its customer, *force majeure* may release the vendor from supporting the recovery of its customer. This is another reason to select a hot site that is sufficiently distant to prevent it from being included in a regional disaster such as an earthquake or hurricane.

Selecting a hot site vendor is an important step in building a disaster recovery capability for the company. It is a partnership with an outside vendor who is willing to share responsibility for corporate survival in the wake of an unplanned interruption. Some DR coordinators may seek to include intangible, yet important, factors in their selection of a vendor— especially when this will help to identify the best-suited vendor from among a group of more or less equally qualified vendors.

One method is to contact the sales rep for each company and explain that an impasse exists in selecting the winner, that the bids are too close to call, and that the offerings seem about equal to each other. The vendor representatives will probably react in one of three ways:

- **Criticize the competition.** Some sales reps will respond by criticizing their competitors. They may relay "off the record" information about competitor incompetence or competitor failures in supporting customers in actual disaster situations. While this practice is ethically questionable, it may provide a basis for further investigation. It may also say something about the vendor whose representative is doing the criticizing: If criticisms are found to be patently false, how much trust can one vest in the critic?
- **Negotiate the rate.** Like used car salesmen, some vendor representatives enjoy a certain amount of latitude in pricing their services. If they perceive that they are losing a prospective customer because of price, they may seek to decrease the originally quoted price. Since the

proposal solicited at the outset of the selection process was intended to show the vendor's best offer, some valid questions about negotiations and good faith may be raised by this practice of price cutting.

This issue is also brought to the fore by vendors who will not provide pricing until competitive bids have been disclosed to them. Once the best offers of the competition are known, these vendors will proceed to undercut their price.

Costs are as important in disaster recovery planning as in any other business activity. However, the coordinator must weigh pricing against the value of good faith negotiations, realizing that the latter, more than the former, may indicate how conscientiously the vendor will execute its responsibilities under the hot site agreement.

- **Offer presubscription testing.** Faced with the impasse of several qualified candidates, some vendor representatives will seek to reinforce their bid by inviting the prospective customer to conduct a live test at their facility. This "puppy dog sale" technique is intended both to demonstrate that vendor can deliver what has been promised and also to ingratiate the customer to the vendor. The coordinator would be well advised to accept the vendor's offer. The test can provide important information not only about vendor capabilities but also about the solvency of the backup strategy itself.

  The willingness of the vendor to provide precontract testing time may demonstrate sincerity and a willingness to go beyond the stipulations of the contract to aid subscribers that are experiencing disasters. The value of this business ethic cannot be understated.

Any of the above factors can provide the intangible, yet compelling, basis for selecting one vendor from a field of several technically qualified candidates. When the selection has been made, the strategy for centralized system recovery needs to be documented and tested, then maintained in a state that reflects ongoing changes and modifications to business processes and their system supports.

THE BOTTOM LINE ON CENTRALIZED SYSTEM RECOVERY

On the preceding pages, some critical assumptions have been made that merit additional discussion. The first assumption is that the disaster recovery coordinator has selected a hot site vendor whose recovery facilities are not located near the company data center.

The rationale for selecting a "distant" hot site is fairly straightforward. Considering the company's exposure to regional disasters (hurricanes, earthquakes, local exchange carrier (LEC) central office (CO) failures, local long distance carrier point of presence (POP) failures, power company failures, etc.), it makes little sense to select a backup facility that might be affected by the same adverse conditions as the company data center.

This issue is perhaps less critical for large hot site vendors having multiple facilities and guaranteeing MIPS for recovery to their subscribers. Smaller vendors, on the other hand, generally have only one or two facilities. So, the issue of geographical proximity remains.

With hot sites available in numerous locations throughout North America, the one selected by the DR coordinator will probably be as near the company data center as possible (to save on travel expenses) while being sufficiently distant to insulate it from regional disasters.

This assumption leads to another. Since the hot site is located at a distance, chances are that relocating the entire management and staff of the company to the vicinity of the hot site would be cost-prohibitive for most businesses. Hence, the assumption is made that users will need to be restored independently of systems, then connected to remote systems via data communications networks.

The nature and scope of the disaster confronting the company will ultimately determine the requirements for restoring users. If the disaster affects only the data center, but leaves company offices and work areas intact, then user relocation will be unnecessary. Recovering user functions will consist mainly of re-establishing data communications links with operations at the remote processing site. Of course, if only critical and vital systems are restored, user function recovery may also entail the implementation of manual systems for nonvital applications, as well.

On the other hand, if both user work areas and the data center are rendered unusable by the same disaster, some sort of end user recovery plan may be required to complement system and network recovery plans. Users will need to be directed to a work site outside the disaster perimeter, in new quarters equipped with all that is necessary to continue work at emergency levels—telephones, office supplies, desktop computers and peripherals, preprinted forms, typewriters, and a myriad of other essentials.

Each of these scenarios presumes planning. Without advanced planning, not only will employees not know where to go, but they will also have no means for performing work when they get there. Thus, planning for centralized system recovery is not a synonym for disaster recovery planning. It is only a component of a larger plan designed to provide a business continuity capability for the company.

ENDNOTES

1. Greg Blatnik, Vice President, Zona Research, Redwood City, CA, quoted in Jon William Toigo, "Thin Computing: Bustin' Out All Over," *Solutions Integrator*, 9/1/98.

2. For the purposes of this discussion, the term *mainframe* refers to IBM and IBM plug-compatible mainframe platforms. For non-IBM mainframes, readers should consult with their vendors for comparable recovery procedures.

3. Interview with Tim Humphreys, Chief Architect, Trident Services, Sausalito, CA, 8/99.

4. *Ibid.*

5. Interview with Jim Grogan, Vice President of Alliances, SunGard Recovery Services, Wayne, PA, 6/99.

6. Interview with Prabakar Sundarrajan, Vice President of Research and Development, Exodus Communications, Inc., Santa Clara, CA, 6/99.

7. Jennifer Mateyaschuk, "App Alternatives," *Information Week*, 6/28/99.

8. Brian Walsh, "RFP: Heading for Disaster," *Network Computing*, 1/11/99.

9. Interview with George Ferguson, Marketing Manager, Hewlett Packard Business Recovey Service, Wayne, PA, 6/99.

10. *Ibid.*

11. Grogan interview, *op. cit.*

12. Interview with Tony Martinez, General Manager, IBM Business Continuity and Recovery Service, Sterling Forest, NY, 6/99.

13. Grogan interview, *op. cit.*

14. Comdisco web site, Business Continuity, "History and Overview," 1999.

15. Interview with Dan Broadway, Director of ClearPath Storage, Unisys Corporation, Mission Viejo, CA, 7/99.

16. Humphreys interview, *op. cit.*

17. Martinez interview, *op. cit.*

18. Grogan interview, *op. cit.*

CHAPTER 6

Strategies for Decentralized Systems Recovery

As described in the previous chapter, the centralized systems model identified with traditional mainframe computing lends itself readily to disaster recovery planning. Indeed, strategies for centralized systems recovery have evolved over the past twenty years to nearly the point of routine procedure. In the view of some observers, commercial mainframe recovery centers, or hot sites, have become veritable "commodity offerings" from disaster recovery vendors.

In addition to having a high degree of recoverability, centralized data centers avail themselves readily to the disaster avoidance and facility protection techniques discussed in Chapter 3. Data centers are typically raised-floor, environment-controlled, physically secured facilities operated and/or monitored by disciplined IT staff on a 24x7 basis. While the electrification requirements of such facilities can and do lead to facility fires, detection and suppression technologies work well in the positive pressure atmosphere of the "glass house," often enabling the cataclysmic outcomes from fire-related disaster potentials to be avoided completely.

Jim Grogan, Vice President of Alliances for SunGard Recovery Services, has gone on record with an interesting observation about mainframe recovery:

> In recent years, there have been fewer mainframe disasters. Over the past three years or so, our customers have declared only six mainframe disasters, [considerably] fewer than there used to be.[1]

If SunGard's experience is mirrored by other hot site vendors, and the frequency of "smoke and rubble" disasters affecting centralized systems has dropped dramatically, then DR coordinators should be able to rest easier each night. Perhaps they can begin concerning themselves less with the "dark side of corporate computing" and more with regrowing some of the hair they have nervously pulled from their scalps over the past two decades.

Or can they? With apologies to the advertising copywriter for the popular motion picture sequel, *Jaws II*, just when you thought it was safe to go back into the water, another shark has discovered the pleasures of dining *alfresco* at the beach. Like so many Chief Brodys, DR coordinators must return to work—vigilant bordering on paranoid—to develop new ways to keep corporate business processes from becoming box lunches.

DISTRIBUTED CLIENT/SERVER COMPUTING: THE ACHILLES HEEL OF DISASTER RECOVERY PLANNING

From the perspective of disaster recovery planning, everything that centralized data centers are, distributed computing environments are not. In the realm of distributed computing, traditional disaster recovery planning methods and techniques confront a range of challenges that are distinctly different from those designed with the mainframe-based computing infrastructure in mind.

Today, there is a tendency in most DR planning literature to gloss over the special recovery requirements posed by client/server computing. Partly, this is attributable to a lack of understanding of client/server technology itself. However, part of the blame must be assigned to DR methodologists themselves, many of whom "came to maturity" during the bygone days of mainframe-only data processing. Asked about the apparent oversight in their "core methodologies," they will emphasize that at least 80% of mission-critical information processing continues to be handled on mainframes. The statement begs the question: If it is true that 20% (or more) of mission-critical business processes are supported by distributed client/server computing architectures, why don't modern disaster recovery planning methodologies account for them?

Some who maintain a mainframe-centric view of disaster recovery planning disparage distributed servers and PCs as "children's toys," especially when compared to "Big Iron." They continue to emphasize mainframe recovery techniques and ignore or oversimplify the requirements for distributed applications. DR coordinators who are dealing with modern corporate IT environments know better: Distributed servers are not "off-the-shelf products that can simply be replaced at a local computer store in the event of a disaster."

To operate high-performance, mission-critical applications on a distributed computing platform typically requires considerable customization of that platform, including its server, client, and middleware components. It is foolish to believe that such applications and their system, network, and software infrastructure cannot be replaced "on the fly" or without substantial advanced planning following a disaster.

Distributed computing tends to be more vulnerable to disaster than its mainframe counterpart. Some explanations include the following:

- The administrative tools and disciplined management, which are taken almost for granted in the IT data center, frequently do not exist in the realm of distributed computing.

- Operating systems are often heterogeneous, and in the absence of any willingness on the part of operating system vendors to "work and play well together," distributed computing often features a kludge of interfaces, gateways, and bridges to enable cross-platform cooperative computing. In short, there are more parts to break and more complexities involved in fixing or replacing them.

- Distributed computing environments tend to be less physically secure than centralized data centers. Servers may be located in closets, ceilings, or basements, or out on the cubicle farms and shop floors that constitute modern user work areas.

- As suggested in Chapter 4, coordinating data backups for distributed computing environments can be daunting; coordinating data restoration can be nightmarish.

- Disaster prevention systems are certainly more difficult and costly to deploy in a distributed environment.

It is only a small overstatement to compare the world of distributed computing to the Hobbesian "state of nature," where life is nasty, brutish, and short.

For all that is challenging about disaster recovery in distributed computing environments, there is one thing that distributed environments have that centralized computing lacks. In a geographically dispersed distributed computing environment—one designed with a bit of attention to disaster recovery requirements—it is unlikely that all resources will be consumed by the same disaster potential. Case in point is Tokio Marine and Fire Insurance Company, headquartered in Kobe, Japan, and its speedy recovery following the devastating Kobe earthquake in 1995.

Shortly before the earthquake, Tokio Marine had concluded work with Hewlett Packard Company to deploy a Distributed Computing Environment (DCE)-based client/server computing platform. By design, the DCE infrastructure provided for the replication of data and resources at different locations within the insurance company's offices. When disaster struck and demolished part of the company's network, including several key servers, replicated resources were quickly brought on line. Disaster recovery was accomplished in a matter of hours. By comparison, one of Tokio's competitors, a mainframe shop, was down for nearly four weeks.[2]

This example and others point to the potential resilience of distributed computing platforms to disaster. Of course, for such availability-enhancing characteristics to be present, companies have to have designed them into their distributed platforms.

Today, few organizations have gone to the extra expense and effort to deploy high availability architectures. Fewer still have any sort of plan for the recovery of distributed computing if and when an outage occurs.[3] This is the *Achilles heel* of modern disaster recovery planning.

This chapter explores the requirements for disaster recovery planning in distributed environments. It does not include a separate data flow diagram because the broad tasks involved in developing a strategy to recover distributed environments are quite similar to those for recovering centralized systems.

- First, mission-critical business applications and their dependencies must be understood.
- Next, minimum equipment configurations need to be identified.
- Finally, an appropriate recovery option, from among a range of options, must be chosen and implemented.

The differences in planning for centralized and decentralized systems recovery reveal themselves at a finer level of analysis. This, quite possibly, accounts for the paucity of literature on recovery methods for distributed client/server systems. As stated previously, many DR coordinators do not understand enough about client/server to know what to do about recovering these systems. If it is any consolation, most client/server system developers, integrators, and product vendors know even less about disaster recovery.

To approach this subject intelligently, it is necessary to provide some historical background on the evolution of distributed computing and a brief review of client/server components and architecture before launching into a discussion of recovery options. For readers who are already familiar with these subjects, a bit of review won't hurt.

For DR coordinators who are totally unfamiliar with the rarefied world of client/server, numerous resources exist to facilitate a deeper understanding, including courses at local colleges, trade press publications, and informative web sites. DR coordinators are strongly encouraged to develop a deeper understanding of this technology, especially in light of the near total lack of concern for recoverability evidenced by the architecture of most client/server software products.

A BRIEF OVERVIEW OF DISTRIBUTED COMPUTING

As the name implies, distributed computing environments are defined by their lack of centralization. Processors and data are dispersed across the business enterprise—on end user desktops and on minicomputer hosts (servers) located in workgroups, in department offices, and elsewhere. These resources are interconnected by physical networks and, at a higher level, by predefined processes or middleware functions that enable input, processing and output operations to occur as though within a single system.

Distributed computing emerged in the late 1970s and early 1980s in part as a redress for mainframe computing costs, delays, and accuracy problems. If the denizens of the glass house (the mainframe data center) could not meet the service levels that business managers required, the business managers were going to deploy local systems that would do the job.

Vendors contributed to the rebellion. They reassured nontechnical business managers that inexpensive, easy-to-administer systems and software tools were becoming available that would enable them do more than they were ever able to do with mainframes. PCs were secreted into offices without the Data Processing department's approval—sometimes recorded on invoices as typewriters or office machines.

Of course, there was more to the case for distributed computing than a simple rejection of mainframes. Advocates touted it as a means for moving information closer to decision makers who needed it to perform work. It was also a mechanism to enable and empower knowledge workers to do more productive work than ever before. (Though, in many companies, empowering and enabling knowledge workers was actually a code phrase that meant disbanding corporate typing pools and eliminating secretaries.)

The introduction of PCs and minicomputers was a tremendous success, automating departments and end user desktops. However, the phenomenon also introduced a problem of isolated, uncoordinated computing within the organization. In an effort to regain some control over these "islands of automation," networks were implemented to interconnect distributed servers and desktops. Predicated on the assumption that interconnected distributed computers would facilitate cooperative computing between workgroups, as well as improved manageability, local area networks were established and eventually linked to one another via backbone networks.

Thus, within the brief span of less than a decade, distributed computing evolved from a collection of independent processors, to a network with loose interconnections, and finally to a tightly integrated distributed computing platform.

CONTEMPORARY CLIENT/SERVER APPLICATIONS

Quick to capitalize on the increasing integration of networked computers, client/server architecture for distributed computing began to appear in the middle 1980s. *Client/server* remains a confusing concept for many—in part because of the variety of meanings applied to the term by vendor marketing departments. In essence, it is a software partitioning paradigm in which an application is split between one or more server tasks.

In a client/server application, server tasks accept requests for information or action from distributed client tasks. Client tasks communicate their requests to server tasks according to some predefined protocol. Server task components may be centralized or distributed across several computing platforms, enabling clients and servers to be placed independently on any nodes in a network.

Early client/server implementations featured a two-tier architecture (see Figure 6–1). Typically, client tasks were located on intelligent work-stations, or PCs. Server tasks were located on a second tier of processors, called, appropriately, the server tier.

In a simple model, client tasks communicated requests to servers, and servers communicated with each other to process requests. In the end, the requested output (information or action) was returned to the client. This operation was transparent to the end user—that is, the end user had no idea what was going on "under the covers." With a well-defined client/server application, it appeared to the end user that all applications were being executed at his or her client workstation. The server components could be anywhere in the network.

Subsequent implementations of client/server provided for three or more tiers (see Figure 6–2). In effect, client requests were received by a second tier of application server tasks that, in turn, relayed requests to another tier of server tasks (say, database servers), which responded to the request, allowing the second-tier server to complete request processing and to relay the results to the client tier. Specialized message handling

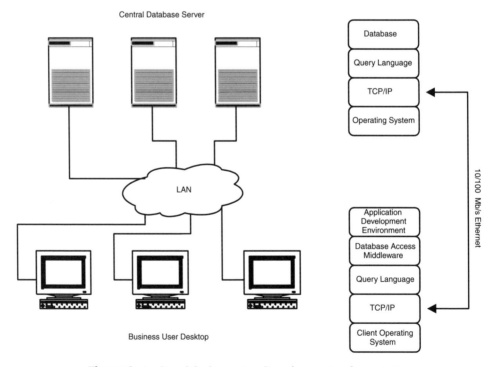

Figure 6–1   Simplified two-tier client/server implementation.

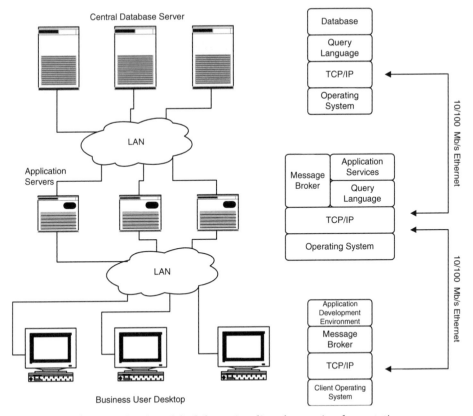

Figure 6–2   Simplified three-tier client/server implementation.

software, called *middleware,* came into use as a mechanism for ensuring that requests and responses were conveyed to their intended destinations.

As the number of server tasks (and tiers) increased, the performance of client/server had a tendency to degrade. Requests would be lost or become corrupted. Server tasks would receive the wrong requests or would simply drop incoming requests when they were already busy processing other requests. Network or server interruptions (resulting from device failures, software failures, etc.) would cause synchronization problems in request processing. The bottom line was that the performance of client/server computing did not encourage companies to entrust the distributed architecture with mission-critical applications. Thus, disaster recovery planners did not need to concern themselves with these applications.

However, throughout the decade of the 1990s, vendors and integrators expended considerable effort to improve the performance and reliability of distributed, client/server applications. While initiatives to establish a common, vendor-agnostic, "open" framework for message exchange, security, fail-over, and other characteristics common in a single system environment (such as Distributed Computing Environment), met with limited acceptance, several proprietary middleware products emerged as market leaders.

By the middle of the decade, multi-tier applications were being deployed using a variety of proprietary message-oriented middleware (such as IBM MQSeries, Microsoft MSMQ, BEA Systems MessageQ, and PeerLogic Pipes), transaction-oriented middleware, and object-oriented middleware. The latter capitalized on Common Object Request Broker Architecture (CORBA) services, which were slowly added to popular server operating systems by the mid-1990s.

Regardless of the differences in approaches embodied in these middleware products, the objective was the same. Vendors and their customers were looking for ways to establish a distributed infrastructure that could deliver the levels of dependability and performance to client/server computing environments that were "givens" in centralized mainframe systems.

Middleware selection, however, was a confusing proposition. Somewhere along the way, vendors of mainframe-based enterprise planning applications decided to address the problem (and, in some cases, to prop up their own sagging mainframe product revenues) by porting their applications to the distributed platform in the form of "packaged" solutions. They introduced client/server application suites with integral middleware components or with pretested application programming interfaces (APIs) enabling quick deployment with third-party middleware product offerings.

Perhaps the ultimate expression of client/server computing today is to be found in the client/server application suites from vendors such as SAP, Baan, PeopleSoft, and Oracle. Companies have been deploying these packaged client/server products—known by acronyms such as Manufacturing Resource Planning (MRP), Enterprise Resource Planning (ERP), and Customer Relationship Management (CRM)—in record numbers throughout the 1990s. This trend portends to continue into the next millennium.

According to the *1999 Information Systems and eBusiness Spending Study*, conducted by Computer Economics, 18.9% of organizations across all industry sectors had ERP software in place. Another 34.1% were researching, piloting, or implementing ERP software (see Table 6–1).[4]

Both "packaged" and "home grown" client/server applications are now in evidence in most corporate environments and are depended upon to support a broad range of mission-critical business processes. For this reason, DR coordinators must include provisions for their recovery in the corporate disaster recovery plan if the plan is to be comprehensive.

Table 6–1   ERP Software Implementation Percentiles

Industry Sector	No Activity	Researching, Piloting, or Implementing	Already in Place
Composite for all sectors	47.0	34.1	18.9
Manufacturing	24.3	35.3	40.5
Distribution	50.0	31.7	18.4
Banking and Finance	38.7	48.4	12.9
Insurance	65.4	26.9	7.7
Healthcare	64.5	25.8	9.7
Trade Services	50.7	37.0	12.3
Professional Services	47.8	26.0	26.2
Utilities	50.0	34.6	15.4
Transportation	57.2	33.3	9.5
State and Local Government	62.5	25.0	12.5
Federal Government	76.0	20.0	4.0

Source: Computer Economics, Carlsbad, CA www.computereconomics.com.

The requirement to consider client/server recovery becomes even more critical within the context of e-businesses—businesses that depend on the Internet and World Wide Web for their sales and marketing, supply chain management, or other mission-critical business processes. With the advent of e-commerce and the Internet, many companies added still more tiers to their client/server applications in order to enable data sharing, or actual application interaction, via the World Wide Web. Figure 6–3 depicts an *n*-tier client/server configuration designed to facilitate web access to internal corporate applications.

What is important to recognize is that most (if not all) of the n-tier client/server applications that are in use today within companies have been deployed through a *cumulative process* over a number of years. This basically means that a certain set of application functions were implemented at one time, then additional application functions (server and client tasks) were added later, and still others later, over the course of several years. (Client/server applications are rarely delivered as a single "turnkey" solution.)

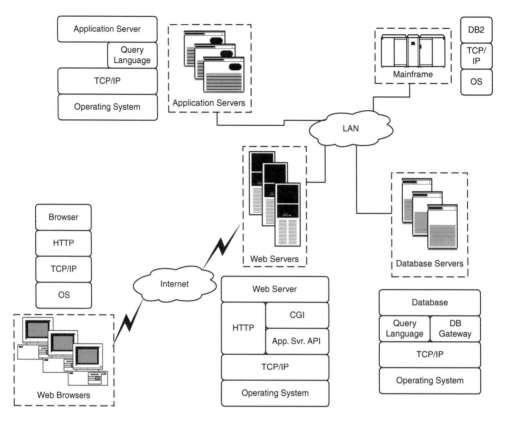

Figure 6–3　Simplified *n*-tier client/server configuration for web-enablement.

The result of this application delivery process, in many cases, is that mission-critical business processes are supported by client/server application platform that includes a mixture of different technologies. As in most software markets, client/server and middleware software products have a tendency to be changed or upgraded by their manufacturers every few months. Thus, client/server applications that have grown their functionality over a period of years are typically a conglomeration of server task components that communicate with each other via a hodge-podge of different, proprietary, middleware products. The resulting application is a *kludge* of software and middleware that makes mainframe COBOL spaghetti code look like fine dining.

Among the first to identify the difficulties associated with this situation were integrators tasked with "web-enabling" internal business applications. Seeking to capitalize on the growing popularity of the Internet and the growing prevalence of the web browser as a "universal client," companies engaged integrators to add a web interface to their applications.

Delivering a robust solution (beyond that of simple "screen scraping") to the problem proved a significant challenge to integrators. They quickly realized that they were dealing with multiple client/server applications, each with its own mixture of software and middleware technologies. In a white paper from Bluestone Software, the problem is summarized at a fairly high level,

> Information deployment is the most fundamental challenge facing the modern enterprise. To meet this challenge, corporations must overcome the difficulties of information sharing on a large scale. Over the years, various hardware and software technologies have been employed. The result? In most enterprise environments, you'll find a complicated patchwork of domain-specific solutions.[5]

Bluestone's web-enabling solution approaches the problem by "nesting" the existing client/server environment inside its own "Enterprise Interaction Management" framework (see Figure 6–4). The vendor's development tools, Sapphire/Web™, capitalize on existing application programming interfaces (APIs) in server task components and service interfaces offered by some middleware component vendors. To complement these, the vendor adds custom-developed interface modules. In

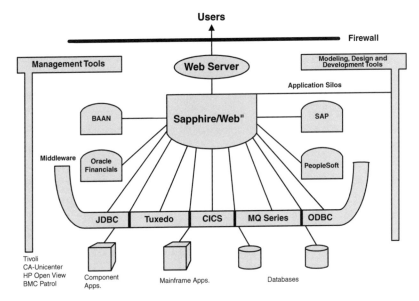

Figure 6–4 Nesting existing client/server applications in an Enterprise Interaction Management Framework. (*Source:* Alternative Technologies, Boulder Creek, CA. Sapphire/Web is a registered trademark of Bluestone Software, Mt. Laurel, NJ.)

short, Bluestone endeavors to deliver a mechanism for adding a web interface "non-obtrusively"—that is, without requiring client/server applications to be rewritten or existing architectures to be reengineered.

The experience of vendors like Bluestone is offered as a reference point for thinking about the disaster recovery challenges posed by n-tier applications. From a disaster recovery planning perspective, the challenge is to recover the functionality of mission-critical client/server application quickly and cost-effectively—and also unobtrusively. Few companies would be willing, strictly on the basis of disaster recovery requirements, to rewrite their client/server applications or to re-engineer them for recoverability.

PREVENTIVE MEASURES

Existing client/server applications pose a challenge for disaster recovery planning because of the investment that companies have already made in developing and deploying these applications into production. For existing applications, coordinators may have little option but to plan for a one-for-one replacement of the entire hardware and software infrastructure in order to guarantee the business process continuation in the wake of a disaster. (This is discussed in greater detail below.)

With new or planned client/server applications, however, there may be an opportunity for DR coordinators to take more proactive posture. If the DR coordinator can influence the design of new client/server applications, there is a chance that less expensive and more efficient strategies for recovery can be found.

To address the Achilles heel of modern disaster recovery, DR coordinators need to become involved, in a consulting role at least, with the development of new client/server applications. Considerable diplomatic skills and a firm grasp of technical concepts are important prerequisites to earning the respect and attention of client/server application architects. It is critical that a relationship be established, however, since, in the words of Larry Finch, Vice President of Prolifics, Inc., "application design elements favoring recovery will not be included in client/server applications unless they are put there deliberately."[6]

According to Finch, there are many design choices that can be made to enhance the recoverability of client/server systems. As evidenced by the experience of Tokio Marine, one strategy is resource replication.

There are various methods for recovering databases [and other resources] within a client/server application. Providing for the replication of resources in real-time at different locations within the enterprise is one approach. It is expensive to do and you must explicitly plan for it in your design, but it can be done. Among other things, you need to provide the means for clients to know where servers are once a failure has occurred and resources failover to other servers. That will require configuration files in the server or other code-level approaches, but it can be designed to work. The nice thing is that replication can enhance performance in non-disaster operations, so it isn't like "you are just wasting money on disaster recovery."[7]

The selection of middleware components is also an important step to ensuring high availability and recoverability. According to Finch, some messaging middleware products can provide failover capabilities with less design effort than others can.

Some messaging middleware products don't require addresses or identifiers for server components. If a block of servers fail that are replicated elsewhere in the network, the messaging [broker] broadcasts to all servers in the network and automatically updates itself with the locations of the available [failover] servers. In a disaster recovery situation, you may be able to use this feature to move the client/server configuration to a different platform. Just tell the [middleware broker] the location of a database resource, for example, and it will automatically update application servers and begin processing.[8]

Finch is quick to point out that this capability is only available if the right middleware components are selected and the design of the application facilitates this recovery mechanism. Some middleware, he notes, is highly address-dependent.

Some of the componentware, the COM middleware, is not designed with recovery in mind at all. The design goal of the product vendor is to replicate an object model in the multi-tier environment, not to provide support for disaster recovery. In a COM middleware environment, when a client needs a service, it initiates an object that addresses a server by name. [To recover a client/server application that uses this type of middleware], you would need to update all of the clients with new server addresses. In such a case, failover would not be transparent—mainly because reliability was not a design goal of the middleware or the designer who chose it.[9]

Finch's views are echoed by other client/server application developers and integrators, most of who confess that they have never given disaster recovery a thought when designing and deploying client/server solutions. One, who works closely with one major ERP package vendor, communicated his concerns about the vulnerability of these applications. Asking not to be identified, he noted that the disaster recovery concerns manifested in custom-developed client/server applications are not mitigated through the use of packaged application suites.

> The fact is that the ERP application suite vendors are in a fiercely competitive business. They are constantly challenged to add features and functions to their integrated suites in order to compete with the functions and features that exist in competitor products. They often do this by acquiring another software house, adding its software components to their package. I know for a fact that, in the case of one major ERP product vendor, many functions in the current release are not fully tested or integrated and that a great number of problems exist that could bring the application down at any time. Disaster recovery isn't just a problem with home-grown client/server software that you can fix by buying a packaged product. The quality of the packaged products falls prey to the requirement to add functions in order to compete.

Beyond application design choices, another concern to some observers are the host platforms that are being used to operate client/server applications. Graham Thompson, Vice President of Marketing for InCert Software, notes that approximately 60% of client/server package products are being deployed on Windows NT platforms "without any benchmarking prior to deployment, or scalability testing."[10]

> The availability specification for the Windows NT server is about 99.5 percent. UNIX has something like 99.7 percent availability and OS/390 has 99.999. When you think about it, that means your unplanned downtime on an NT server will average about 50 hours per year. With UNIX, the number is around 26 hours per year. And, with OS/390, you are looking at five minutes of unplanned downtime per year. Considering the cost to companies for an hour of unplanned downtime—$100,000 for a retail operation, $6 million or more for a brokerage—you can see that the drive to client/server is a costly one.[11]

Thompson believes that if a company is committed to deploying mission-critical applications on distributed platforms, both design and deployment methodologies need to have a strong disaster recovery focus.

This point of view derives from InCert Software's product focus. InCert is a vendor of mainframe-centered tools used in COBOL code execution tracing and debugging. The tool has proven useful in resolving Y2K code failures expeditiously and offers capabilities for software failure analysis that are now being ported into the client/server world to facilitate NT-based application fault detection and repair.

PROACTIVE MEASURES

What specific steps can disaster recovery coordinators take to ensure the speedy (and cost-effective) recoverability of mission-critical client/server applications following a disaster? These fall into two categories: proactive and reactive measures.

The goal of disaster recovery planning is to deliver capabilities for recovering business processes following unplanned interruptions within an appropriate timeframe and at an acceptable level of business risk. Since disaster recovery planning exists in the real-world environment of a functioning business, it is also important that planning take into account the cost of recovery strategies relative to the business revenue losses accrued to protracted outages.

That is a fancy way of saying that DR planners should never spend more money to recover from an outage than the outage itself would cost. In most companies, budgets for disaster recovery restrict spending to levels far below outage costs. DR coordinators can optimize their scarce resources by planning to avoid preventable disasters, while selecting the best strategy they can for coping with disasters that cannot be predicted or avoided.

Proactive and preventive measures are particularly important in client/server application recovery. While planners may need to "play the hand they are dealt" with regard to existing client/server apps, if they can become involved in new application development, they may be able to influence developers to construct applications in a manner that facilitates disaster recovery.

Emphasize Middleware Standards

Given the opportunity to influence client/server application design, DR coordinators should press for the adoption of middleware standards for present and future development. They should research middleware products to obtain an operational understanding of each product being considered for use by application designers and be prepared to advise designers and architects regarding the limitations of the product from a recoverability standpoint.

A middleware product that uses a "hard" resource naming scheme (specific names must be assigned to server and/or client tasks and each component must be "hard coded" or configured with these names) poses greater difficulties for recovery than does a product using a flexible or adaptive resource naming scheme (e.g., tasks are identified "on the fly" through broker broadcast messages). This is not to say that the DR coordinator can tell the designer which middleware product to use. There may be performance reasons for using a less flexible product. But, it is the DR coordinator's job, at least, to sensitize the designer to the importance of such considerations as recovery.

In addition, the DR coordinator should emphasize the importance of building applications around a single middleware product, rather introducing new middleware products with each application upgrade. The use of multiple products has a tendency to reduce options for disaster recovery to a one-for-one replacement of client/server platform components.

Encourage Partitioned Design

DR coordinators should know from experience with non–client/server applications that the most expeditious recovery is accomplished when the data used by an application is clearly delineated and defined. In an ideal world, the data for a specific application can be backed up and maintained in a well-defined way and restored readily when needed. With deliberate effort, according to Prolifics' Finch, "the overall [client/server] work can be partitioned into discrete applications and data can be partitioned [to correspond with these applications]."[12] If this is done, it would be possible to enable processes and their related data sets to be restored and restarted individually.

Emphasize Resource Replication

Redundancy is expensive in large systems, but substantially less so in distributed computing environments where processor and storage hardware costs, as well as network bandwidth costs, are constantly dropping. DR coordinators can avoid some disaster potentials, such as hardware failures, by emphasizing redundancy and resource replication as an aspect of client/server application design. Where possible, the case for replication should be based on application performance improvements rather than disaster recovery advantages alone.

Unlike other redundancy strategies, where it is best to maintain redundant components as "hot standbys" that are unused except in the event of an outage, replicated client/server resources can play an active, ongoing role in day-to-day processing. They can be used to eliminate network congestion or to speed throughput or to provide extra capacity when primary resources are being utilized at near maximum capacity levels.

Lobby for High-availability Components

The failure rates of server operating systems are well known in the industry (as discussed above), even if they are debated by operating system vendors. Additional disaster avoidance capability can be obtained by acknowledging the reality that client/server host platforms can and do fail and recommending the acquisition of fault-tolerant hardware configurations.

Fault tolerance can be added at many levels of hardware. Servers can be clustered for failover. Disk can be mirrored through the application of various RAID configurations. Array controllers can be obtained that deliver failover and failback capabilities. Drives can be dual ported to facilitate hot swapping. Redundant power supplies, network interface cards, and even motherboards are available. DR coordinators need to research fault tolerance technologies and be prepared to recommend additional, and often low-cost, enhancements to client/server platforms that will enable them to withstand equipment failures that could become disasters for the company.

Lobby for Application Web-enablement

Many companies have come to the conclusion—without considering its potential disaster recovery benefits—that the web-enablement of legacy and client/server applications has definite business advantages. For the "dot.com" companies (businesses that execute primary business processes via the Internet and World Wide Web), providing a browser-based client interface to applications is a given. Other companies have seen advantages in web-enabling applications for use in internal intranets or in business-to-business extranets established with suppliers, business partners, and other external entities. Web-enablement provides opportunities for enhanced disaster recovery as well.

There are many approaches to web-enabling applications, but the net result is the delivery of secure access to necessary application functions via a browser software client. This capability can be harnessed to facilitate flexible end user application access in a post-disaster situation. From a disaster recovery perspective, flexibility has two meanings: If applications are web-enabled, end users may be able to access applications via an intranet at a user recovery site using virtually any client device capable of supporting a browser. If web-enabled applications are accessible via the Internet, end users can access applications from virtually any location, including their homes. The bottom line is that, if an organization has web-enabled its applications, the range of user recovery options may be increased dramatically.

Of course, web enabling applications is not without its down side. DR coordinators also need to ensure that proper attention is paid to protecting web-enabled applications from security threats and that the applications themselves are accessible in the face of Internet disruptions and outages (see Chapter 7 on network recovery for more details).

PLANNING FOR RECOVERY

Fault-tolerance capabilities and resource replication designs do not substitute for disaster recovery planning, but they can help avoid some of the most commonly cited disaster potentials associated with client/server computing. According to SunGard's Grogan, while the number of mainframe disaster declarations has decreased substantially, the number of "component failure" disasters supported by his company has increased significantly.[13] He attributes this to the increasing importance of client/server applications and the vulnerabilities of their host platforms.

In addition to component failures, distributed computing platforms are as vulnerable as centralized computing platforms to regional power failures, weather events, seismic disturbances, cataclysmic fires, riots and civil unrest, telecommunications outages, and a number of other disaster potentials that deny access to corporate facilities generally. Unplanned interruptions can and do happen in the client/server environment, regardless of fault-tolerance capabilities. To prevent the interruption event from resulting in a full-blown disaster for the business, decentralized systems recovery strategies must be developed and tested.

Through the late 1990s, there were only two decentralized system recovery strategies available to DR coordinators.

- **Next Box off the Line.** As in the case of mainframe recovery options, one alternative is to take copious data backups of client/server systems and to make arrangements with equipment vendors or distributors to provide replacement hardware on a priority basis following a disaster. This procedure was actually recommended in the past by some consultants and analysts because of the expense of the alternative: the redundancy option.[14]

- **Redundancy/Hot Site Option.** This option involves the establishment of a fully redundant distributed computing platform at an alternate facility, either business-owned or provided as a subscription service from a commercial hot site vendor. According to SunGard's Grogan, this expensive option is sometimes the only way to safeguard mission-critical client/server applications—especially when they have not been designed with disaster recovery in mind.

> Client/server is a challenge, especially when the pieces of an application have been purchased *à la carte*. Even packaged applications such as SAP need to be integrated to back-end and front-end processors. It can be very convoluted. You literally have to restore each piece of equipment by itself. There is a high degree of risk involved in getting it correct. The time requirements for these restorals can be much greater than [mainframe application] recovery.[15]

Spokespersons for other leading disaster recovery service providers agree with SunGard that the increasing mission-criticality of client/server applications is raising the bar for recovery timeframes and practically mandating that recoveries be performed on redundant hardware configurations. Hewlett Packard BRS Marketing Manager George Ferguson notes,

> As ERP applications move to full supply chain management, companies are dependent upon those applications as well. About 35 percent of the customer base is recovering [their client/server] applications with our service. We can bring their recovery times down to a modest 8 to 24 hours depending on the last backup. We also offer full replication via our network. Rather than copying database changes, the customer can just transmit Special Query Language (SQL) updates and the replicated server performs an identical change on a replicated database. That avoids the difficulties [associated with] pushing physical data across the wide area network. The trend is that higher-end services such as these require us to take on more responsibility for the recovery.[16]

More responsibility translates to increased expense, which vendors nearly universally agree is the price paid for fielding mission-critical applications on distributed platforms. However, two additional strategies for client/server recovery are becoming available that promise to deliver expeditious recovery at a lower cost.

- **ASP Service Bureau.** In 1998, Application Service Providers (ASPs) began to appear on the corporate computing scene. These modern Internet-based service bureaus provide remote hosting of applications, including client/server applications, on behalf of corporate customers. Some, like Exodus Communications, feature extensive Internet expertise and multiple data centers interconnected by high-speed OC3/OC12 networks, while others, such as Qwest Cyber.Solutions LLC (a joint venture of Qwest Communications International and management consulting firm, KPMG), combine telecommunications network services with business automation management expertise. Even database giant, Oracle, has an ASP service, Oracle Business Online, that offers remote implementation and hosting of Oracle enterprise client/server applications. The value proposition of the ASP is cost-of-ownership reduction and many smaller and medium-sized companies are already leveraging these web-based outsourcing companies to obtain the benefits of client/server packages without the hassle. A growing number of ASPs, spearheaded by Exodus Communications, are placing disaster recovery capabilities high on their list of service benefits.

    Service bureau-based disaster recovery has been an alternative strategy for centralized systems recovery for some time. However, the diversity of applications in the typical corporate data center and the limitations of service bureaus to supporting only a set number of hosted software applications, has limited the strategy to a niche market.

    The current generation of ASPs presents similar limitations. Most ASPs offer support for only a short list of packaged client/server application suites. For some companies, this is sufficient. For others, especially those with "home-grown" client/server apps that support mission-critical business processes, ASPs, like their service bureau predecessors do not provide a complete solution.

    However, the ASP industry is growing. On the horizon, analysts expect a more diverse set of "infrastructure outsourcing" services to be provided. Of particular interest is the expressed intention of telecommunications giants such as Sprint and AT&T to enter this market. Given their multiple data centers and core network access capabilities, application outsourcing with disaster recovery provisions is a very real prospect early in the first decade of 2000.

- **Application Consolidation.** Another strategy for client/server application recovery will be possible only when applications themselves incorporate the design characteristics addressed above. If the middleware interconnecting application components is standardized, applications and their data are properly partitioned, and attention is paid to the selection of message brokers based on their adaptability to platform changes, it is possible to recover even the most distributed client/server application on a more centralized hardware platform. That is a much less expensive and configuration-intensive proposition to recovering platforms on a one-for-one basis.

  It should be kept in mind that the rationale for distributing client/server application components in a production environment does not necessarily apply in a recovery environment where fewer end users and "emergency" (reduced) levels of performance are expected. If such a strategy is selected, the DR coordinator should work out the details of the alternative application configuration in advance and test the configuration on target hardware platforms and under actual conditions of load.

Server Recentralization versus Consolidation

Some observers point to the current trend toward server recentralization as a boon for client/server recoverability. Recentralization refers to the physical relocation of server hosts, once deployed throughout the work environment of the business organization, back into the data center environment. Enabling server recentralization are concurrent trends in local area networks toward increased bandwidth and decreased network equipment prices.

A snapshot of a business network in the late 1990s would likely find a high-speed network interconnect, such as switched Gigabit Ethernet (1 Gb/s), deployed as the "corporate backbone network"; medium speed networks, such as Fast Ethernet (100 Mb/s), deployed to connect departmental LANs and "power" workgroups to the backbone; and slower speed networks, such as 10BaseT Ethernet (10 Mb/s), used as a general-purpose LAN interconnect for desktops (see Figure 6–5).

While the recentralization of servers in the controlled environment of the corporate data center may reduce certain disaster exposures and provide for better monitoring and management of equipment by trained IT

Figure 6–5   Typical Ethernet network, c. 1999.

personnel, the physical location of servers does nothing to enhance the re-coverability of client/server applications themselves.

Server consolidation, too, does nothing to enhance the survivability of client/server applications, though the process of consolidating the applications residing on many smaller servers onto a fewer number of larger platforms can provide a fertile testing ground for client/server application consolidation strategies.

Of course, there are other types of applications in the decentralized computing environment besides client/server applications. The consolidation of these onto fewer platforms can benefit the organization directly from a disaster recovery standpoint, in part by providing a centralized location for backup and improved restoral speed.

One consolidation trend that received considerable press as the 1990s drew to a close was "thin client computing." Essentially, this is a desktop computing architecture aimed at the replacement of "fat client" personal computers (e.g., those running Microsoft's Windows operating system) with terminal-like devices running "thin" operating systems. One approach to server-centric architecture, promulgated by Citrix Systems, provides for client desktops to be connected to "application servers," which serve as central repositories for the software and data that previously

Figure 6–6 Server-centric computing. (*Source:* Citrix Systems, Inc., Ft. Lauderdale, FL.)

resided on PCs. In operation, the client desktop receives only interface information from the application, which executes on the applications server (see Figure 6–6).

After an initial false start, the "fat server/thin client" architecture (not to be confused with client/server application architecture) shows

Figure 6–7 Delivering application interfaces to diverse client computing devices. (*Source:* Citrix Systems, Inc., Ft. Lauderdale, FL.)

signs of becoming an increasingly prevalent architecture for desktop computing in the new millennium.[17] From a disaster recovery perspective, consolidating desktop applications on fewer application servers provides numerous advantages. Such an architecture enables the umbrella of data protection and physical security that is closely associated with centralized data center operations to be extended around the most decentralized of corporate information assets: the hard disks of PCs.

Also, as shown in Figure 6–7, if the server-centric desktop computing architecture is deployed in a corporate environment, it can be used to restore desktop device configurations rapidly, regardless of the type of desktop device being used.

This server-centric desktop computing strategy, and others, will be discussed in greater detail in the following chapter on end user recovery. For now, it may be useful to close on a positive note.

Decentralized computing has multiplied the targets for consideration by modern disaster recovery planning and made the job of the disaster recovery coordinator more complex than ever before. However, it has also provided an opportunity for the disaster recovery coordinator to play a more active role in shaping the enterprise that he or she is assigned to protect.

Client/server applications, because of their underlying distributed paradigm, represent an unprecedented challenge to traditional disaster recovery methodology. However, by acquiring the necessary background knowledge, and by cultivating good working relations with application designers, developing frugal and effective recovery strategies for these mission critical applications is not beyond the capability of the DR coordinator.

For other decentralized applications, the disaster recovery coordinator needs to champion the implementation of consolidation strategies where they make business sense. Each success will simplify the requirements for putting the business back in business quickly following an unplanned interruption.

ENDNOTES

1. Interview with Jim Grogan, Vice President of Alliances, SunGard Recovery Services, Wayne, PA, 6/99.
2. Jon William Toigo, "Mission: Impossible? Disaster Recovery and Distributed Environments," *HP Professional*, 6/98.
3. Thomas Hoffman, "Risk Mounts for Mission-Critical Data," *Computerworld*, 3/27/95, quotes Tari Schreider of Contingency Planning Research, who ob-

serves that fewer than 3% of the consultancy's 400 Fortune 1000 clients have contingency plans that incorporate client/server networks.

4. "Nearly 20 Percent of Businesses Have Implemented ERP," *Business Wire*, 6/11/99.

5. "The Heart of Sapphire/Web™: The Sapphire/Universal Business Server," white paper, Blue Stone Software, Mount Laurel, NJ, 1999.

6. Interview with Larry Finch, Vice President, Technology Division, Prolifics, Inc., New York, NY, 6/99.

7. *Ibid.*

8. *Ibid.*

9. *Ibid.*

10. Interview with Graham Thompson, Vice President of Marketing, InCert Software Corporation, Cambridge, MA, 6/99.

11. *Ibid.*

12. Interview with Larry Finch, *op. cit.*

13. Interview with Jim Grogan, *op. cit.*

14. Jaikumar Vijayan, "Client/Server Disaster Plans Fall Short," *Computerworld*, 11/3/97.

15. Grogan interview, *op. cit.*

16. Interview with George Ferguson, Hewlett Packard Business Recovery Service, Wayne, PA, 6/99.

17. International Data Corporation (Framingham, MA) is projecting a dramatic increase in the deployment of thin-client technology as the millennium begins, according to a press release dated 4/29/99, "Worldwide shipments of enterprise thin clients will jump 87% from 369,000 in 1998 to 1.2 million in 1999. By 2003, they will top 6 million." This projection is also supported by Zona Research, an IntelliQuest Company (Redwood City, CA), which issued its findings on 4/27/99 that predited the "growth of the worldwide commercial market to over 2,250,000 thin-client units by 2001, with factory revenues exceeding $1 billion."

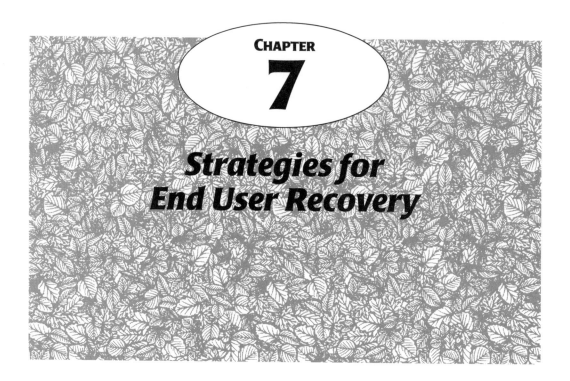

Strategies for End User Recovery

In the past, disaster recovery plans focused rather narrowly on the recovery of technology platforms: mission-critical applications, their data, and their server and network infrastructure components. The advent of "business continuity planning" in the mid-1990s refocused traditional disaster recovery planning on business processes rather than solely on IT platforms.

From the perspective of business continuity planning, company personnel (sometimes referred to as "end users" of information systems) and their work processes were elevated onto an equal plane with IT infrastructure as targets for recovery planning. Business continuity planners perceived that it was only the end user's interaction with systems and networks to provide critical business functions that made the recovery of IT infrastructure worthwhile. Without end user recovery in the wake of a disaster event, all other recovery strategies were rather pointless.

Why had traditional DR missed so obvious a point as the need for end user recovery planning? One explanation might be that the focus of early DR planning mirrored the interests of most corporations and the predominant information systems architecture of the day. Companies that undertook disaster recovery planning tended to focus their efforts on the mainframe data center, the primary source of processed information for roughly three decades. Since end users were typically restricted from entering mainframe data centers, and since end user access to mainframe applications was a fairly straightforward proposition (typically accomplished via a "dumb terminal" and communications controller), end user recovery requirements were often taken for granted in the data processing recovery plan.

A frequent, though unstated, planning assumption held that end users would continue to work in their business offices even if the systems and networks they were using needed to be relocated to an alternate facility. Indeed, a goal of DR planning was to make the transition between primary and backup computer centers transparent to the user—an admirable objective, though not always practical.

Recent history is replete with examples of disasters that compromised entire corporate facilities—data centers and business offices. Regional disasters—whether the result of hurricanes or fires within telecommunication company central offices, tornadoes or terrorist bombings—can take out sprawling corporate campuses and high-rise headquarter buildings in a single blow. These disasters demonstrated the inadequacy of plans that focused on data center recovery while ignoring end user recovery.

Moreover, unplanned business process interruptions can and do result from events that do not affect corporate computing infrastructures at all. The break of a sewer pipe in a ceiling or wall may require the evacuation of end users from their offices, as may the overturning of a tanker truck transporting a noxious gas on a highway some miles away from the company site. While health hazards may require the evacuation of end users, systems and networks may continue operating undisturbed by such events.

Additionally, user work areas are often not as effectively protected as data centers and communications equipment rooms against fires and other avoidable disaster potentials. Lacking these prevention capabilities, which have contributed greatly to risk reduction in data centers, the statistical likelihood is actually greater that certain types of disasters will originate in user work areas, rather than corporate data centers.

With everything that we have learned about disasters over the past three decades, the failure to include a user recovery strategy in a modern-day disaster recovery plan must be regarded as a violation of one of the basic tenets of modern DR: Plan for the worst case scenario. To be comprehensive, disaster recovery plans need to include documented and tested procedures that may include:

- The location and provisioning of backup end user work facilities
- The notification of employees who will staff the recovery site
- The transportation of employees to the recovery site
- The redirection of ground mails, telecommunications, and data networks to the recovery site
- The acquisition of supplies at the recovery site
- The application of remote access technologies for operating mission-critical applications from the user recovery site

In addition to the above, and as a matter of the highest priority, all disaster recovery plans should provide for emergency evacuation of personnel from the corporate premises in the event of a hazardous or life-threatening disaster event.

DEVELOPING AN END USER RECOVERY STRATEGY

Figure 7–1 provides an overview of the activities involved in end user recovery planning. As depicted in the data flow diagram, the definition of end user recovery requirements draws upon the analysis and objectives-setting processes that were undertaken at the outset of the project and also the details of centralized and decentralized systems recovery strategies discussed in chapters 5 and 6. Case studies providing the practical experience of other companies in the area of end user recovery can also provide valuable insights.

Based on this analysis, facility requirements, supply and logistics requirements, and application, system, and network requirements will emerge. These become inputs for activities aimed at delivering properly equipped facilities for use by end users when and if they are required.

The term *user recovery facility* can be interpreted in a variety of ways. In many disaster recovery plans, the user recovery facility consists of a temporary working location, such as conference facilities rented from a local hotel in the hours following a disaster event. In other cases, end user recovery may be accomplished using a permanent, company-owned facility put to a secondary use. In still other cases, mobile shell facilities from commercial vendors may be deployed as temporary work areas, or employees may be able to work from home using dial-up connections to private networks or the Internet. These options are discussed in greater detail below.

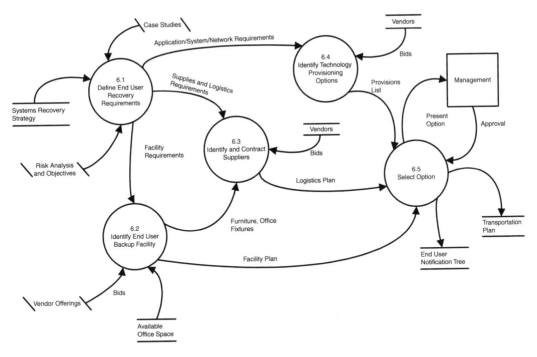

Figure 7–1 End user recovery plan development.

The end user recovery option that is selected by the DR coordinator needs to address all of the requirements users have for performing purposeful work. In addition to providing access to mission-critical applications, the fully developed option will consider everything from workspace ergonomics to preprinted forms; from telephones, fax machines, workstations, and email access to the personal hygiene, lodging, and transportation requirements of the users themselves.

Information security and disaster prevention provisions in the alternate worksite setting are also extremely important considerations in any user recovery plan. Among other things, planners need to become familiar with the ramifications of emergency work arrangements on corporate liability and insurance.

As with every other disaster recovery strategy, the timeframe for end user recovery is an important consideration. Options must be evaluated in part on the basis of the amount of time they would take to implement. Evaluating the "time to implement" criteria presumes the ability to test the strategy in advance of its actual use. Thus, it follows that the best strategy will be one that avails itself of testing and validation.

OPTIONS FOR END USER RECOVERY

With the recovery requirements defined by earlier processes in the planning project, and with the criteria cited above clearly in mind, options for end user recovery may be evaluated. The DR coordinator should note that the strengths and weaknesses of the fairly typical options discussed in the following pages are relative. Companies differ greatly in terms of their assessment of outage costs and their recovery priorities, as well as their existing infrastructure and technology preferences. Thus, the assessment of advantages and disadvantages of any given strategy will be a matter of perspective, which differs from one company to the next.

End User Recovery "On the Fly"

This approach involves locating a user recovery facility only after a disaster occurs. Advocates argue that this approach is valid because of the large amount of unoccupied office space in most metropolitan areas that is generally available for lease on short notice. Even a conference facility at a hotel, advocates argue, could be turned into a temporary operations center within a short time. The option has the additional advantage of presenting little or no cost to the company until (and unless) a disaster actually occurs.

   The potential drawbacks of this *laissez-faire* strategy are numerous however. Although it may be possible to locate a warehouse, hotel conference center, or office space within a short time following a localized disaster—such as a building fire, this approach offers little confidence in the case of a regional disaster. If a recovery team must look for new user quarters in "unfamiliar territory" (that is, areas outlying the disaster region), a significant amount of recovery time could be lost.

   Time would also be lost while preparing the recovery facility for telephones and network interconnections and provisioning the facility with the necessary workstations, communications devices, disaster prevention systems, security systems, and power distribution and protection capabilities once it has been located.

   Considerable coordination would be required with vendors of technology products and services, with off-site storage vendors, and with others who need to direct products to the temporary facility. Additionally, because advanced arrangements could not be made for redirecting long distance and local telecommunications traffic, data networks, and ground mails to the new facility, these activities would need to be accomplished at the time of recovery. So, too, would the notification of employees regarding where and when to report for work.

With so much planning left up to the post-disaster timeframe, a laissez-faire strategy introduces substantial risk and numerous opportunities for delay into the recovery process. However, its suitability to the requirements of a particular company is entirely contingent upon the sensitivity of the company to longer duration outages.

The Either/Or Approach

A second approach to user recovery planning—one that imparts only a slightly higher confidence level than the laissez-faire approach—is to implement a dual or "either/or" strategy. With such a strategy, if the disaster is localized, user recovery facilities are located "on the fly." If the disaster is regional in scope, employees are relocated to a predefined company-built user recovery facility at a remote location.

Advocates of this type of strategy observe that a "localized" disaster scenario does not manifest the same obstacles to a laissez-faire strategy that may be present in a regional disaster. For example, with a local disaster, such as a fire at a company's office building, company facilities may be lost, but local utilities and telecommunications infrastructure will probably be intact. Given the limited geographical scope of the disaster, finding and equipping replacement facilities on the fly might be accomplished more readily. Telecommunications providers may be able to respond to requests to reroute networks more promptly. Sources of supply for necessary provisions may be quite accessible. Notifications of employees regarding new work schedules and office locations could be made in an efficient manner.

By contrast, in a regional disaster, the expeditious completion of all of the activities outlined above may be compromised by the scope of the disaster itself. Following an earthquake, hurricane, or other disaster with geographically widespread impact, the integrity of the public infrastructure cannot be assumed. Vendors and providers may be fielding large numbers of emergency requests for services and products in the wake of such a disaster. Thus, to safeguard against the difficulties inherent in a regional disaster, a "hard" site is designated for user recovery.

This either/or approach has the merit of building flexible response into a disaster recovery plan. It embraces the worst-case scenario of a regional outage, but acknowledges that different circumstances might obtain that enable a scaled response.

Unfortunately, the laissez-faire strategy that is to be used in the event of a local disaster is still very amorphous. Any disaster recovery element must avail itself to testing and validation. Laissez-faire strategies do not.

Another potential problem with the either/or strategy is its designation of a company-owned "hard site" at a remote location that is to be used in the event of a regional disaster. Many companies would be hard pressed to cost-justify the construction and maintenance of duplicate user work areas at an alternate remote location to be used only in the event of a regional disaster.

An alternative to constructing a stand-by operations center may be to use a large remote branch office or other company-owned facility, such as a remote training or customer education center, as a backup site. The benefits of dual use of an existing facility are both compelling and deceptive. Dual-use facility strategies can present other problems that require close attention by the DR coordinator, including the following:

- Equipment and furnishings that will be used in a user recovery situation must be securely stored and routinely inventoried at or near the recovery site. If the designated recovery site is publicly accessible (for example, a customer education facility), providing the security of recovery supplies storage can be a difficult and costly proposition.

- Secondary network interconnects, WAN and telecommunications services, power and water utilities, and other infrastructure components, must be preinstalled. Whatever the primary purpose of the designated facility, its use as a user recovery center will likely place an enormous strain on available power, telecommunications, network infrastructure, and even plumbing. Secondary capabilities may need to be added, often at substantial expense, to augment those resources used during normal operations of the facility.

- Other logistical requirements such as proximity to highways, airports, lodging, and restaurants, must be considered to ensure that users who will be working from the remote site will be able to access the site and obtain suitable living quarters during the recovery period.

- Tests of the user recovery strategy must be conducted periodically and this may interfere with the primary operations of the dual-use facility. The requirements for testing the recovery option and for actually activating the strategy must not constrain, impair, or inhibit the normal operations of the dual-use facility. For example, DR coordinators should consider how testing will be coordinated with the scheduling of the training facility for normal use, or how normal branch operations will be impacted by the sudden influx of unfamiliar recovery personnel into the branch facility if a disaster occurs.

As the above suggests, while this either/or approach goes part of the way toward preplanning facilities for user recovery, it still leaves room for delays and problems. Other potential problems with the strategy may include the reluctance of employees, given a regionalized disaster scenario, to leave friends and families behind while they travel to a remote location for work.

Moreover, the costs of maintaining such a facility in a ready state may be high, including costs of leased communications facilities that terminate in the backup operations center, storage space rental, wiring and cabling, and so on. These factors, plus the costs for transporting a cadre of personnel to a remote site and sustaining them while there, must be carefully evaluated to determine the solvency of such a strategy for expeditious end user recovery.

The benefits of having a "hard" relocation site are several. Such a strategy facilitates testing and logistical planning. Knowing a site location and capabilities in advance can ease the transition of critical and vital operations in an emergency as well as provide a location for storing emergency supplies of preprinted forms, office supplies, hardware, and others. An alternative to developing a company-owned facility is to contract for the services of a user recovery vendor.

The Commercial Work Area Recovery Center Option

A number of vendors, both of off-site storage and of hot site facilities, are now providing a "user work area" recovery offering. For a monthly fee, companies can subscribe to the facility, much in the way they do for a systems recovery hot site, that will be used for end user recovery. Presumably, this fee would be substantially lower than the cost to the company of renting, preparing, and maintaining a private user relocation site.

As a variation on this theme, some hot site service vendors offer mobile shell facilities (see Figure 7–2) specially configured for rapid deployment as user work facilities at or near normal operating facilities. Assuming that public infrastructure (power and water) is available, the end user recovery facility can be positioned within 48 hours in the parking lot of the disaster-stricken facility. Some localities also require building permits and other formalities before a shell facility can be positioned

Figure 7–2   Mobile user facility. (*Source:* Hewlett Packard Company Business Recovery Services, Palo Alto, CA.)

on a site. Coordinators will need to check the requirements of local government when considering this option.

Subscription service-based user recovery plans, while expensive, can be tested and validated—increasing the DR coordinator's confidence in their success. Moreover, mobile end user recovery facilities provide tremendous flexibility in deployment in response to a wide range of disaster scenarios.

In addition to these benefits, coordinators also need to consider the potential drawbacks of mobile shells. In the event of a regional disruption, travel to a mobile facility site may be disrupted. Moreover, such sites may fall prey to post-disaster cataclysms such as aftershocks following earthquakes, post-hurricane floods or mudslides, or looting following building fires. One vendor reports that mobile sites enjoy a singular characteristic that may mitigate some of these drawbacks. Says Jim Grogan, Vice President of Alliances for SunGard Recovery Services, his company's mobile offering was used frequently during regional disasters in the late 1990s. In one case, a Grand Forks, South Dakota-based bank set up operations in a SunGard mobile site, then moved the site a few miles from its original location in response to rising flood waters, then moved it once more when Red River flooding exceeded all anticipated levels.[1]

EMERGING TECHNOLOGY: HARNESSING REMOTE ACCESS CAPABILITIES

In a growing number of cases, end user recovery may be possible without relocating users at all. In 1999, according to International Data Corporation, 35.7 million workers in the United States routinely worked from home—"telecommuted" to their company offices using direct dial-up or Internet-based remote access methods. This number is expected to increase to 47.1 million by 2003.[2]

The telecommuting trend has been around for nearly a decade but has experienced a surge of growth in recent years for a number of reasons. In some cases, telecommuting has been implemented by companies to provide employees with flexible work schedules—a job perk designed to retain employees in the face of knowledge worker shortages. In other cases, remote access capabilities have been deployed to meet the needs of "road warriors"—staff that routinely travel and need to remain connected to corporate networks and applications. Within certain metropolitan areas, telecommuting programs have been developed as a means to offset long employee commute times or as an automobile pollution reduction measure encouraged by federal, state, and local government. Regardless of the company motives for enabling telecommuting, where remote access capabilities have already been deployed, these may be leveraged for the purposes of end user recovery planning.

TYPES OF REMOTE ACCESS

There are numerous variations of remote access computing. Some companies utilize client-side remote access methods such as remote node or remote control.

Remote control typically utilizes a software package running on an office desktop and a remote desktop. The end user working from home or some other remote site, uses a dial-up modem connection or other communications method to access and take control of a desktop system that is already attached to corporate networks. In effect, the end user operates the office desktop remotely, running applications on the remote desktop as though sitting in his or her office chair. Products in this category feature such capabilities as encryption and password protection to safeguard links from being misused or tapped. Figure 7–3 depicts a remote control scenario.

With *remote node* methods, the end user dials into the company network and identifies itself as another member of the LAN. There are numerous techniques for accomplishing this feat, including direct dial-up to a remote access server (RAS), as depicted in Figure 7–4. Dial-up connections may utilize slower-speed 56K analog modems, Integrated Switched Digital Network (ISDN) services, cable modem services, or even emerging Digital Subscriber Line (xDSL) technologies increasingly available from public telecommunications carriers.

Figure 7–3   Remote control of a corporate desktop from a remote location.

As the number of external nodes increases, substantial investments in remote access configurations are made by companies in order to enhance performance and security. Remote access servers (RAS) are available in a wider range of configurations to meet varying connectivity requirements. At the high end, RAS devices enable the consolidation of hundreds of dial-up ports, handle communications from a mixture of link services (analog, ISDN, Frame Relay, etc.), and provide high-speed switching and routing functions to facilitate the smoothest possible operation and highest possible performance of applications. Figure 7–5 is an example of one vendor's product offering in this space.

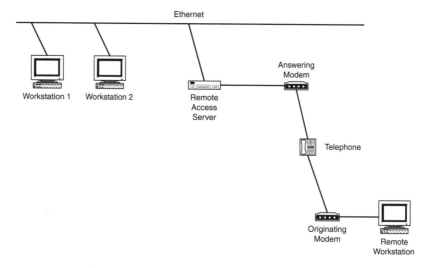

Figure 7–4   A simple remote node configuration.

Figure 7–5   A consolidated remote access configuration. (*Source:* Copyright © 1998 Ascend Communications, Inc., a wholly-owned subsidiary of Lucent Technologies. All rights reserved.)

Another method for achieving remote node access is via the Internet and virtual private networking (VPN). With a VPN, the end user uses a desktop system and browser software, usually augmented with VPN client software, and connects to a corporate web address or Universal Resource Locator (URL). A secure session, or tunnel, is established between the VPN server and the end user workstation, and the end user gains access to internal corporate networks and systems (see Figure 7–6).

Establishing a VPN through the Internet is a comparatively new scheme with several competing standards for tunneling under review by the Internet Engineering Task Force. Some of the areas of difference between techniques involve the manner in which security will be handled and how quality of service will be guaranteed across the Internet back-

Figure 7–6   Simplified VPN tunneled through the Internet. (*Source:* Indus River Networks, Inc., Acton, MA.)

bone network. While universal standards have not been formalized, this has not prevented some companies from pursuing VPN technology to establish convenient remote access for end users, smaller branch offices and suppliers, especially in situations where high-speed private network interconnects would be costly.

Especially keen to see an increase in VPN popularity are network service providers, including Internet Service Providers (ISPs) and telecommunications carriers, who are endeavoring to provide VPNs as a managed service to corporate subscribers. Figure 7–7 depicts a communications flow proposed by Lucent InterNetworking (formerly Ascend Communications), which is used to establish a secure tunnel for virtual private networking through the Internet.

Such a tunneling method as described in the cited RFC can be implemented using equipment installed on premise at company locations. Remote access devices that comply with the underlying protocol could be deployed in conjunction with RADIUS servers (RADIUS is a security technology) and management software to provide a secure, manageable, company-owned and operated solution.

Alternatively, as depicted in Figure 7–8, carriers (called Network Service Providers in Lucent's parlance) can implement this equipment into their own points-of-presence (POPs) readily. By so doing, the carrier or ISP can provide a VPN gateway function and sell managed VPN services on a subscriber basis to companies that do not want to shoulder the costs or management burdens internally.

VPN outsourcing shows signs of catching on as a service offering of telecommunications companies and ISPs with national or international network presence. iPass, an Internet services company, as well as CompuServe, IBM, and AT&T, are already offering VPNs on a subscription basis. As depicted in Figure 7–9, iPass advertising literature describes several of the advantages of subscription VPN services generally:

- Remote access with a local call from all over the world
- Reliable, redundant connectivity through top-tier networks
- Comprehensive security and the VPN solution of your choice
- Simplified administration and complete administrative control
- 70 to 80% cost savings compared to modem bank solutions
- A simple point-and-click interface, easy for novice users
- Improved convenience with one consolidated account[3]

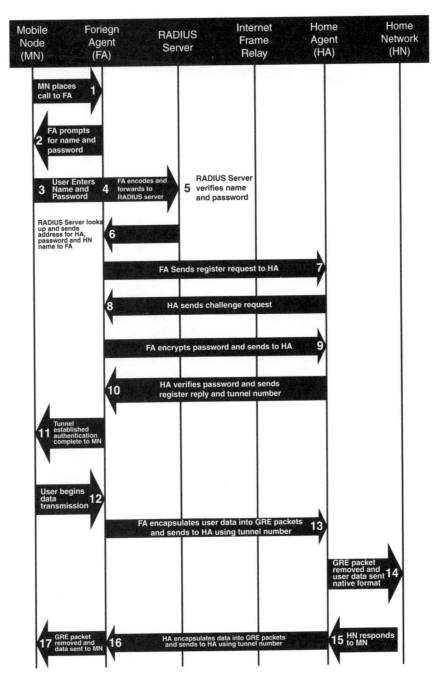

Figure 7–7 Ascend Tunnel Management Protocol (ATMP) (RFC 2107) communications flow diagram. (*Source:* Copyright © 1998 Ascend Communications, Inc., a wholly-owned subsidiary of Lucent Technologies. All rights reserved.)

Figure 7–8 Outscored virtual private networking services. (*Source:* Copyright © 1998 Ascend Communications, Inc., a wholly-owned subsidiary of Lucent Technologies. All rights reserved.)

Figure 7–9 iPass VPN Service. (*Source:* iPass Inc., Mountain View, CA. www.ipass.com)

CONSIDERATIONS REGARDING THE USE
OF REMOTE ACCESS FOR END USER RECOVERY

The selection of which remote access method a company uses to facilitate the requirements of mobile workers, telecommuters, or small branch offices is not within the scope of this discussion. What is important about remote access technology is (1) that existing remote access capabilities may provide an alternative to user relocation in the event of a disaster that affects company facilities; and (2) that, generally speaking, some sort of remote access solution will need to be used in a recovery situation regardless of what strategy is selected to restore user operations following an unplanned interruption.

On the first point, it should be noted that existing remote access solutions, whether dial-up or Internet-based, need to be evaluated for their capacity to handle increased loads placed on them from end users who would normally conduct work at office locations. DR coordinators should obtain information from network management personnel about the feasibility of utilizing remote access services for critical personnel during a disaster. Moreover, coordinators should ascertain the viability of such a strategy from the standpoint of application requirements. Not all applications perform well across a low-speed dial-up connection or an Internet connection. As demonstrated in Table 7–1, transmission speeds of communications links have a great deal to do with application performance

Table 7–1   File Transfer Speeds at Different Link Rates

File Type	File Size	33.6 Kb/s	56 Kb/s	64 Kb/s	128 Kb/s	512 Kb/s
Word Processing (20 pages)	40 KB	9.5 secs	5.7 secs	5 secs	2.5 secs	.625 secs
Spreadsheet	100 KB	23.8 secs	14.3 secs	12.5 secs	6.25 secs	1.6 secs
B&W Presentation	1 MB	4 min	2.4 min	2 min	1 min	15 secs
CAD/CAM	2 MB	8 min	4.8 min	4 min	2 min	30 secs
Digitized Photograph	4 MB	16 min	9.6 min	8 min	4 min	1 min
Color Presentation	10 MB	40 min	24 min	21 min	10 min	2.5 min
X-Ray File	100 MB	6.6 hrs	4 hrs	3.5 hrs	1.7 hrs	26 min

and response times. While newer high-speed line options are becoming increasingly available, they represent a substantial cost and may not be readily activated by telecommunications providers to meet the needs of a company confronting a disaster.

Simple file transfer speeds may not be the only indicator of the potential efficacy of a remote access solution for end user recovery, however. As touched upon in the preceding chapter, thin computing technology is increasingly coming to the fore in many organizations. Thin computing solutions from companies such as Citrix Systems and Microsoft provide demonstrated high-performance characteristics even across "thin pipes" (low bandwidth network connections).

Citrix Winframe technology, which is also used by Microsoft in its NT Terminal Server Edition operating system, is a server-based computing technology in which applications execute entirely on a server application host system. Rather than passing all data to the remote client device (a PC, terminal, or other device), only interface data is transmitted. In turn, the client passes only keyboard keystrokes and mouse clicks back to the server. The bandwidth required for such interaction is minimal, reflecting the heritage of the Citrix presentation services protocol in the days when slow modem technologies prevailed. Citrix's technology is optimized for Microsoft Windows and delivers specified performance for all native Windows applications.

Used in conjunction with remote access technology, server-based thin computing architectures have the potential to provide tremendous flexibility in application access. The same may be said of applications specifically enabled for use via the Internet and a web browser.

If end users require access to additional capabilities besides applications themselves (for example, if they need to print copies of forms, send faxes, etc.) or must perform other manual tasks to sustain a business-critical process, the notion of at-home recovery may be moot. However, the presence of a preexisting telecommuting capability at a company implies that the end users who routinely use it can and do support critical corporate functions while at off-site locations.

Of course, basing a user recovery strategy on a telecommuting premise must also account for how remote access will be accomplished if local communications services are impaired. For companies using Internet-based VPNs, it may be possible for end users to connect to alternate ISP access numbers as a simple workaround if primary ISPs are unavailable. This is one of the advantages touted by the growing cadre of VPN service providers: Their services feature multiple access numbers, including an 800 number, so that access is assured wherever the end user travels.

Assuming that a disaster is not so widespread as to have disabled the telecommunications infrastructure of a given region, access constraints may not be a factor. Once servers are recovered and applications are restored at a hot site or other systems recovery facility, connecting to the remote systems recovery center from home-based client systems will require only the restoration of the remote access system and any necessary private network or Internet access links. These activities are logically part of any systems recovery and network recovery strategy.

If a regional disaster does occur that renders all telecommunications services unavailable, user relocation to a remote recovery center (or provisions for an exotic replacement of local telecommunications service, such as satellite communications, see Chapter 8) may provide the only solution.

The second point made above, that remote access is almost always part of a disaster recovery plan, should also be discussed here. End user recovery, whether accomplished via some home-based strategy, at a remote location, or even in normal offices following a disaster that affects only the corporate data center, will require the restoration of access to mission-critical systems, wherever they are being recovered. To this end, remote access technology of some type will be part of the network recovery strategy for a company.

OTHER ISSUES IN END USER RECOVERY

The determination of which of these remote access approach will best meet the needs of a specific company must be made by the disaster recovery coordinator after reviewing all relevant options. Coordinators will need to have identified and prioritized in advance which business functions, resources, process, and employees need to have these capabilities. In addition to selecting a recovery option, other end user recovery requirements also need to be considered and accounted for in the end user recovery strategy.

Employee Notification Procedures

Depending on the selected approach to facility replacement, special procedures will need to be developed to ensure that employees who are vital to the recovery are notified in the event of a disaster. Recovery teams and operations staff will need to know when and where to report for work. (This topic is treated in greater detail in Chapter 9.)

Employee Transportation Arrangements

The disaster recovery coordinator also needs to make provisions for the relocation of users to the user recovery site. Preparations may be as extensive as establishing a provisional service contract for private air transportation or as limited as designating a recovery team to hire buses at the time a disaster occurs. Here, as in any dimension of disaster preparedness, the coordinator may face tradeoffs between the certainty of advance preparation and the cost savings of a more open-ended approach.

Redirection of Voice Telecommunications Traffic

For many businesses, the loss of voice telecommunications for any period of time is tantamount to the loss of business functions. For this reason, user recovery strategies must account for the recovery of voice telephony capabilities as well. Another factor making restoration of voice telephony at the user facility extremely important is that this often provides the means for coordinating the work of the various recovery teams involved with systems restoration, network restoration, and user recovery. Chapter 8 treats network recovery strategies (including both voice and data communication networks) in detail.

Supply Logistics

Once a facility is designated for user recovery and provisions have been made for notifying and transporting users to the location, the disaster recovery coordinator must determine what supplies users must have to perform productive work. Some supplies, identified in the risk analysis, may have been stored off-site as part of the off-site backup plan. Arrangements have to be made to ensure that they are retrieved and delivered to the user recovery site.

If some supplies (i.e., office supplies) are expected to be acquired from regular sources, the disaster recovery coordinator should so state in the recovery plan. Sources and alternates for needed supplies should be specified together with procedures for obtaining them (purchase orders, corporate accounts, etc.).

For items that may be somewhat more difficult to obtain due to size, cost, order processing intervals, and so forth—including computer terminals, PCs, peripheral devices, portable photocopiers, FAX machines, printer paper, diskettes, ribbons, and other computer-related supplies— advance planning may help minimize recovery time delays. The coordinator should compile a list of all necessary items and then identify possible sources for them in the general vicinity of the recovery site (if known in advance).

For electronic equipment, the coordinator may be able to make an arrangement with the vendor, a value-added reseller (VAR), or retailer to deliver replacement hardware within 24 hours. If this timeframe is unacceptable, either to the company or to the supplier, the coordinator should explore the possibility of purchasing needed hardware and storing it off-site with other critical supply items.

At least two suppliers should be identified for any critical item. Redundant supply arrangements can safeguard against the possibility that a critical item or a supplier will be unavailable when needed.

Where possible, emergency purchase orders should be completed so that only a signature is needed to activate them. Suppliers may require this and may wish to have copies of the purchase orders in their possession as a part of an emergency supply agreement.

Of course, all suppliers and the items they will provide must be listed, together with office and emergency contact telephone numbers. These contact lists will be included in the disaster recovery plan, kept up-to-date through regular plan maintenance, and included in the notification procedures set forth in Chapter 9.

Employee Accommodations

If a "hard" user recovery site is specified in the plan, it may be possible to make advance arrangements with a hotel or motel in the site's vicinity to accommodate recovery personnel in an emergency. At a minimum, an inventory of lodging facilities should be made prior to selecting a recovery site if the site is located too remotely for users to commute from their own homes.

FINAL THOUGHTS ON END USER RECOVERY STRATEGIES

As with all aspects of disaster recovery planning, end user recovery requires creativity and imagination. In addition to striving to minimize costs by leveraging existing capabilities and providing a flexible response to different disaster potentials, coordinators need to consider in this aspect of planning the very real human factors involved.

Depending on the nature of the disaster, end users may be confused, terrified, or in a state of shock in the hours following the event. Their foremost concern may be with the safety and well being of their families and friends rather than with the survival of the business. Some may have experienced personal losses or even injuries. It is important to plan for the worst case and to discuss with management the possibility of including provisions in the plan for crisis counseling and family assistance.

Carol Dorris Andersen summarizes the situation succinctly:

> During disasters, employees sometime become dysfunctional. They are worried about families, have thoughts of inadequacy, or react to seeing an injured co-worker...On a typical workday, under normal work conditions, a company will have approximately 10–20% of its labor force under enough work related stress to result in decreased performance, safety hazards, or poor work habits. After a crisis, performance is decreased from 30–75% for a period of time. 6 to 12 weeks is considered average. However, individual needs may increase or decrease the time required.[4]

To address the problem of human factors in a disaster, Andersen recommends a two-phased approach. She suggests that certain activities conducted in advance of disasters by DR coordinators, such as disaster awareness programs and plan tests, that help to familiarize employees with disaster potentials and their roles in responding to emergencies provide important psychological benefits to the employees as well. Secondly, she recommends that "debriefings" be conducted with employees in the hours following the disaster event. Allowing personnel to talk about their experience typically provides a catharsis for pent-up stress, bringing "closure to the crisis."

> The memories of the event may last, but the impact is significantly reduced with an appropriate debriefing that includes large group meetings, small group support programs, and individual counseling for those who require it. These programs will get your workforce back to work quickly.[5]

This view is echoed by Dan Paulk, PhD, who serves as a Senior Consultant with Crisis Management International in Atlanta, GA. Plan provisions for post-disaster user recovery recommended by Paulk are summarized in Table 7–2.

While post-event counseling may be mandated in some situations, many DR coordinators who have activated plans in the wake of hurricanes and other cataclysmic events have discovered that, once the human needs of employees and their families were attended to, the employees became veritable zealots in corporate recovery activities. In some cases, companies have actually reported a surge in productivity during post-disaster peri-

Table 7–2   Structured Response Checklist for Post-Crisis Human Factors

Provide "psychological first aid"	Identify and assist those who are deeply affected by traumatic stress. These people need to be separated from the disaster scene, but not isolated. Move them to a safe place, under the care of counselors or caring friends. Get appropriate help.
Provide management-led deescalation meetings	It may seem kinder to simply let them go home, but people suffering from traumatic stress do not need isolation. They need structure, peer support, facts, and information. If these immediate concerns are well met, recovery will be greatly aided. The deescalation meetings should be provided before allowing employees to leave the worksite for their homes.
Contact family members of casualty victims	Death and serious injury notification (also known as next-of-kin notification) is a very difficult and stressful duty. It is best if two management representatives make the initial visit—quickly—before the message is delivered by the media or other less caring messengers.
Protect your employees from the media	Guard affected employees and family members from media contact. All employees are to be instructed not to comment if approached by the media. They are stressed, stunned, dazed, and confused following a traumatic incident—a poor time to make any public statements.
Plan your communications to the media	An Emergency Communications Team should handle all media interaction per a preestablished plan.
Telephone operators	Receptionists and others who must confront the public need careful instructions in what to say and do. These employees may be under particularly heavy stress. Consider short shifts, or relief from duty. Have them log all calls.
Assess the need for professional traumatic stress intervention	Having made prior arrangements with experienced professionals, determine the need for intervention. Traumatized individuals may need intervention services, such as group debriefings or private interviews. These sessions provide for emotional venting—to share and normalize reactions.

(continued)

Table 7–2   *Continued*

"At-risk" employees	Identify persons who may be at potential risk of continuing or escalating traumatic stress reactions. At-risk persons may be identified by the group debriefing leader, by local management and supervisors, by co-workers, or by self-referrals.
Provide management briefings for employees returning to work	Management briefings should be offered as the initial processing step for employees when they return to work.
Maintain communication with your employees	Employees have a great need for information and facts following a critical incident. They need this directly from management. It is important to give truthful, accurate, and complete information.

Source: Extracted from Daniel Paulk, "Human Factor in Disaster Recovery," *Disaster Resource Guide,* 1998.

ods. Disasters can create a common bond and mission among staff and management if provisions are made to attend to human needs first.

Like all other aspects of the disaster recovery capability, the user recovery plan will need to be tested and refined over time. Coordinators should make every effort as they assess the solvency of remote access strategies, the efficacy of recovery facilities, and the intricacies of logistics and supplies, not to lose sight of the human factor.

ENDNOTES

1. Interview with Jim Grogan, Vice President of Alliances, SunGard Recovery Services, Wayne, PA, 07/99.
2. "Working Outside the Office Spurs Demand for Remote and Mobile IT Products," *Recent News,* International Data Corporation, Framingham, MA, 08/99.
3. iPass Inc. marketing materials, from www.ipass.com, iPass Inc., Mountain View, CA, 1999.
4. Carol Dorris Andersen, "Critical Incident Stress Management," *Disaster Resource Guide,* 1998.
5. *Ibid.*

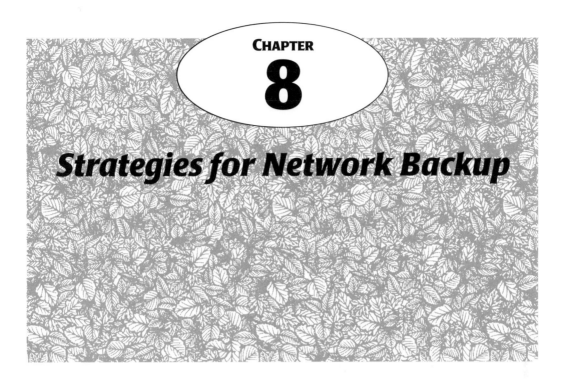

CHAPTER

8

Strategies for Network Backup

Planning for business recovery entails more than developing strategies for the backup of computer hardware, critical applications, and data. As discussed in the previous chapter, DR planning must also consider the recovery of those who produce and use information assets to provide critical and vital business functions.

This community of users may be quite vast. It typically includes employees and managers of the company (the classic definition of the end user community), but it may also include a host of others who trade with the company, invest in its growth, monitor or regulate its activities, or consume its products and services.

In the late 1990s, concern with the Year 2000 "bug"—a date-change error embedded in many applications and chips—forced many companies to redefine the concept of "user community" in disaster recovery planning. Given the dependencies that existed between internal business processes and the business processes of key suppliers, many firms "discovered" that defining disaster recovery and business continuity requirements solely in terms of company-owned facilities was inadequate. Key suppliers also needed to have adequate disaster recovery plans.

Of course, ensuring the preparedness of other companies is usually beyond the purview of corporate DR coordinators. As companies concerned about Y2K discovered, the only "stick" they possessed to encourage the preparedness of business partners was a threat. Assuming that other potential suppliers of some needed good or service were available, a company could threaten to change partner/suppliers if a current partner could not demonstrate requisite levels of disaster preparedness.

In the case of Y2K issues, however, these threats rarely translated into action.[1] One problem was the lack of any effective means to verify partner preparedness. Some companies did perform joint Y2K testing with their key suppliers, while others contented themselves with partner-supplied results of Y2K preparedness audits conducted by trusted third parties. All in all, these were the exception rather than the rule. The fact was that companies were often tied to their suppliers by business realities, including the expense of change, difficulties in acquiring customized goods or services from alternate suppliers within a short time, or contractual obligations that bound companies to their partners. Discontinuing a supplier relationship was often perceived as potentially more costly than a temporary Y2K-related supply interruption.

What this brief flirtation with "supply chain DR planning" did accomplish, however, was to demonstrate how interdependencies between external organizations and the company might also create exposure to corporate disasters. Moreover, for those who did not clearly understand up to this point the business criticality of communications networks—used to interconnect a company and its geographically dispersed user community—supply chain DR planning was a wake up call.

Awareness of the business interruption risks posed by networks has also grown with the expansion of the Internet. Business use of the public data network, which had long served the Department of Defense and the international university community as an information-sharing medium, exploded in the mid-1990s. Ubiquitous browser technology, email, and searchable directories established the public Internet and World Wide Web as a gateway to a vast user community. Sensing opportunity to access a global customer base, older businesses established a "presence" on the web, while newer "dot coms"—businesses built literally out of Hypertext Markup Language (HTML) running on a web server (.com is a domain name extension signifying a business site address on the World Wide Web)—proliferated.

Today, business use of the Internet is varied, and applications run the gamut from simple presentations of corporate brochure information to electronic catalog displays and on-line order-taking and customer service systems. Many companies use Internet-centered electronic mail to extend corporate communications networks to remote offices and telecommuter sites. As security and performance improve, the Internet is becoming an increasingly viable alternative to expensive private line networks, an alternative vehicle for remote access to internal corporate applications, an alternative voice telephony service, and a platform for outsourcing applications and entire data center operations.

As the business use of the Internet grows, even traditional companies are recognizing what the "dot coms" already know: E-business is synonymous with dependency upon the smooth functioning of the Internet. Unplanned interruptions of Internet-based business processes can impact corporate revenues negatively and cause other significant damages to the company.

For many other companies, the growing importance of networks—both within company premises and between corporate offices—was perceived long before Y2K or the Internet underscored the value of data communications. The acquisitions and mergers of the late 1980s, particularly within the financial industry, saw the formation of large conglomerates whose operations often spanned vast geographical areas. Following an acquisition, it was usually desirable to consolidate information processing assets under a single point of management and control. This often translated to closing the data centers of acquired companies and relocating applications and data to a central data center supervised by a corporate IT organization.

In the case of banks, this effort was often paralleled by a drive to substitute data communications networks for local data processing assets. High-speed data communications links enabled personnel in the branch offices of acquired banks to access remotely hosted applications and data and to continue to deliver the same levels of customer service and support despite the consolidation of the IT architecture. The reliability of these wide area networks (WANs) was understood to be as critical to business success as the operation of automated teller machine (ATM) networks.

Within company offices themselves, local area networks (LANs) took hold throughout the 1980s as well. LANs were initially introduced as a technology for interconnecting "islands of automation" created by the PC revolution and later provided the "plumbing" for client/server computing. The evolution of LANs from a simple conduit for data transport and file exchange into a strategic framework for distributed business-critical applications is a subject of computing lore. Business dependency on LANs, interconnected by enterprise backbone networks, grew over time. Based upon experience with network interruptions and outages, companies quickly discovered that network availability was as much a determinant of business success as application integrity and system uptime.

One network that has always been recognized as critical by modern business is the public telephone network. In recognition of this fact, most disaster recovery plans, whether developed in the 1970s or the 2000s, provide procedures for the restoration of voice telephony services following a disaster. The dependency of business processes upon voice telecommunications during normal operations is a given. During a disaster, telecommunications becomes even more vital as a vehicle for coordinating recovery activities and communicating with shareholders, customers, suppliers, and corporate end users.

The public telephone network has undergone (and is undergoing) significant changes over the years. From its roots in analog switchboards and relays and copper transmission lines, the telephone system has evolved into a complex, fully meshed network of high-speed digital switches transporting data through fiber optic and copper cabling. Note the use of the term *data:* whether voice, computer signal transmission, or video, everything is data.

As of this writing, modern interexchange carriers (IXCs) provide "long distance network core switching services"—that is, long distance calls—using redundant, high-speed (mostly) fiber optic networks interconnected via digital switch equipment. Access to the IXC network is made at points of presence (POPs) located throughout the network. IXC POPs may be co-located with the central offices (COs) of local exchange carriers (LECs), which, in turn, maintain their own switched fiber optic or copper line networks to meet the local calling requirements of business and private consumers. Local Exchange Carriers generally provide "last mile services"—that is, switching and cabling from the LEC Central Office to the "demarc" or physical termination point at the customer premises— as well as "gateway service" interconnections to the IXC POP and into the long distance network (see Figure 8–1).

Also as of this writing, the telephone network provides the bulk of resources used for corporate WANs and for the Internet. Some companies utilize private network facilities that include a mixture of lines leased from the public telephone network, satellite communications links, and even digital radio. However, the preponderance of medium and smaller companies use the Plain Old Telephone System (POTS), enhanced with some specialty networking services and facilities, to meet their business WAN and voice telephony requirements.

By 1999, there were 13.3 million fiber circuits in North America and some 123 million copper lines that had been in service for approximately

Figure 8-1   Simplified diagram of the public telephone network.

twenty years. The system was showing significant indications of strain as demands for performance, access, and availability increased. By the millennium, most analysts agreed that an entirely new public network infrastructure was required. Vendors are steadily working toward a next generation network, the New Public Network (NPN), "overhauling most of the equipment hanging off [the old Public Switched Telephone Network]—upgrading everything from the POPs and COs to the core infrastructure."[2]

As a result of both the current strain and upgrade activities (as well as the occasional line cut, CO fire, CO power outage, or switch equipment failure), many significant interruptions of POTS services occurred in the final years of the 1990s. These outages have impacted virtually every company in North America at one time or another within a given year, alerting everyone to the need for recovery plans that address public network outages.

WHAT IS INVOLVED IN FORMULATING A NETWORK RECOVERY STRATEGY?

Network recovery planning often eludes DR planners because, on the surface at least, it seems far removed from the central issue of business continuity: the recovery of mission-critical business processes. The plethora of terms and acronyms used by network specialists obfuscates matters further, as does the fact that a strategy must encompass three very different networks: LANs, WANs, and telephony.

The watchword of modern networking is *convergence.* Just as the public telephone network now carries voice, computer data, and video—all digitized and packaged into data packets or cells—so too, eventually, will a single network infrastructure within a company premises serve as a common carrier for different data types. That is the holy grail of enterprise network convergence. Opinions vary widely as to when the transition will occur. Until it does, network recovery strategies will need to contain several subordinate strategies.

As depicted in Figure 8–2, network recovery plan formulation involves the development of at least three discrete recovery strategies to cover:

- Internal enterprise networks (loosely defined as departmental or workgroup LANs interconnected via a switched or routed backbone network, as well as separate or converged telephony networks used to provide dial tone at the desktop for company employees)
- "Local loop" (Local Exchange Carrier services connecting the company facility to the LEC Central Office) and wide area networks (connecting the company to IXC network-based services), including voice and data networks
- Network relocation—providing a means to rebuild mission-critical internal network services and to reroute WANs and telephony services to alternate end user and/or systems recovery sites in the wake of a disaster.

Of course, the three-strategy approach is only one method that may be used to tackle the problem of network recovery strategy building. Depending on company configurations and requirements, there may be a need for other subordinate strategies to cover the restoration of cellular, satellite, or digital radio networks. Some coordinators may elect to develop a separate network recovery plan for telephony-intensive call centers or for Internet operations or for video broadcast systems. The above approach is adequate for the preponderance of companies that have based internal networks on Ethernet, Token Ring, or other standard networks using common protocols such as Netbios, Novell Netware, ATM, SNA, or TCP/IP, as well as those that utilize public telephone network services for WANs and telephony.

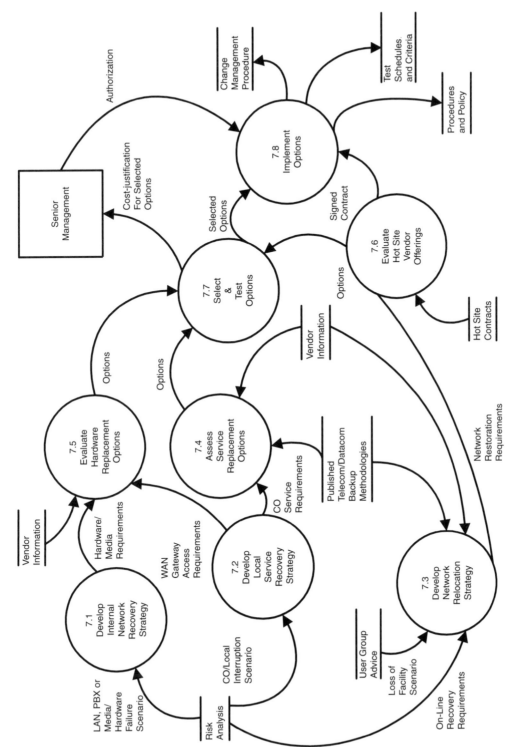

Figure 8–2 Building a network recovery capability.

The strategy formulation effort does not occur in a vacuum. Networks, in and of themselves, are not appropriate objects for disaster recovery unless they enable mission-critical business functions. Thus, network recovery objectives should be determined, preliminarily at least, by risk analysis and business process analysis activities conducted earlier in the planning process.

As with system platforms and applications, it may not be necessary to recover production networks in their entirety in the wake of a disaster. Network recovery requirements are determined in part by the requirements of mission-critical applications and by the details of system and end user recovery strategies formulated in prior processes.

To assist in formulating effective strategies, it may be useful to define a loss scenario that will guide planning. To assist in the development of internal network recovery strategy, for example, DR coordinators may wish to use a scenario of equipment or media failure. To facilitate the development of a local loop/WAN recovery strategy, a scenario envisioning the disruption of normal access to CO services may be used. The third strategy, for network relocation, is based on a scenario of user and data center facility loss, though it may be implemented in response to a wide range of actual disaster scenarios that force the relocation of end users, systems, or both.

This scenario-based approach has the benefit of enabling flexible response to network interruptions of different kinds. It also provides a basis for analyzing and implementing preventive measures to protect against certain types of outages.

As shown in Figure 8–2, the requirements generated by strategy-building activities serve as inputs to other activities aimed at evaluating options for hardware and service replacement. Once options have been evaluated, selections can be made, senior management approvals can be solicited, and capabilities can be implemented and tested.

ANALYZING NETWORKS: A LAYERED APPROACH

As Figure 8–3 suggests, network recovery planning can be thought of as an effort to address the disaster avoidance and recovery issues associated with three distinct layers or domains of networks. In the diagram, these domains are represented as a series of concentric circles. Each layer contains a functionally related set of technologies, transmission facilities, and components that enable data to be propagated over greater and greater distances. At the hub of these circles are the mission-critical business applications themselves.

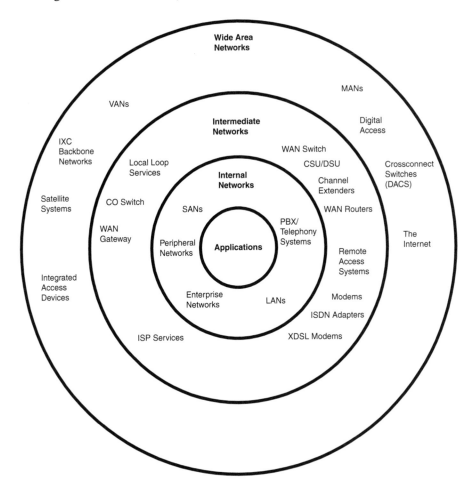

Figure 8–3   A conceptual model of networks grouped by functionality.

The innermost layer surrounding the application hub consists of internal networks—networks that exist within the physical boundaries of the business itself. Included in this layer are:

- Peripheral device networks, connecting terminals, printers, etc., to large processors
- I/O device networks, such as Storage Area Networks, connecting disk arrays and storage pools by means of a high-speed serial network fabric directly to a server or set of servers

- Enterprise and local area networks (LANs) that may be used to provide shared access to Network Attached Storage (NAS) devices, server-based applications, and databases and intranet web sites, and to facilitate network mail and file exchange
- A voice communications network, often consisting of a separate cable infrastructure interconnecting a Private Branch Exchange (PBX) switch and numerous communications devices, including telephones, modems, facsimile machines, and various network management and troubleshooting devices

Taken together, the internal network layer (generically depicted in Figure 8–4) provides telephony services and business-critical application access to end users situated within the company premises. In most businesses, dual networks—one for telephony and another for data—persist.

Figure 8–4   A generic enterprise network.

The two are frequently managed by separate organizations within the company. Thus, DR coordinators may need to develop separate recovery strategies for coping with voice and data network outages resulting from internal causes, such as equipment failures or cable cuts. In the future, the development of convergence technologies (including as IP telephony—a technology for combining voice traffic on IP data networks) may see the consolidation of voice and data within the corporate premise, thereby consolidating recovery plans.

The second, or intermediate, layer of corporate networking encompasses technologies for extending internal networks from the company "demarc" across the local loop to the Central Offices of Local Exchange Carrier. (By the way, coordinators are likely to find LECs referred to as "ILECs" and "CLECs." This contribution to the alphabet soup of telephony was introduced in the wake of local phone service deregulation. ILECs are Incumbent Local Exchange Carriers—service providers who used to own all telephone services within a specific local exchange. CLECs are Competitive Local Exchange Carriers, new service providers who compete with the incumbents to provide services to a local exchange area.)

From the ILEC/CLEC Central Office, voice and data traffic can be passed to the IXC-controlled network, or it can be switched to local Internet Service Providers that provide Internet access (sometimes called "on-ramp services") and/or to telecommuters located in the local region covered by the ILEC/CLEC.

Simply put, functional components of this layer include customer premise equipment and demarc facilities (switch and router WAN ports, MODEMs, etc.) that provide interfaces to local area transmission facilities (groups of lines or "trunks" provided by the local carrier), the physical trunks themselves, and CO-based switches that receive and route voice and data communications traffic. (Figure 8–5 provides a high-level diagram of how connections are typically made between a company premise and a CO currently.) Typical components of this layer include:

- Enterprise network equipment such as WAN switch "ports" (hardware connections that bridge internal network switch to telco transmission facilities), WAN router ports, and similar data networking interface devices such as Channel Service Unit/Digital Service Units (CSU/DSUs), mainframe channel extenders, modems, etc.
- Remote access systems facilitating dial-up access to internal networks for off-site users equipped with analog modems or ISDN and DSL connection devices

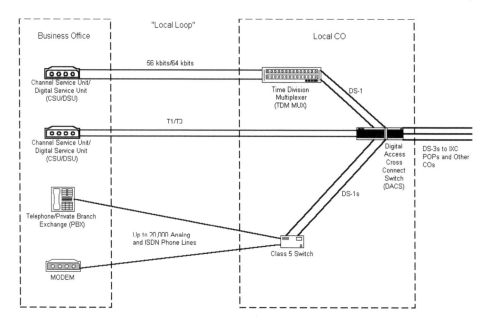

Figure 8–5   Company-to-central office connections.

- Connections, often made via CO-provisioned or CO-switched facilities, to Internet Service Providers that provide on-ramps to the Public Internet
- Trunk connection points on PBX systems interfacing the internal telephony network to the local telco provider (CLEC/ILEC)
- Transmission facilities themselves—the physical media for connecting the company voice and data networks to CO switches
- CO switches and multiplexers that provide the gateway to the third layer of wide area or long distance networks (although there are now a number of options for circumventing the local CO in accessing the third network layer)

The third network layer consists of wide area network services that handle the movement of voice and data traffic between COs in different local exchanges whether via the IXC network, value-added networks (VANs), or satellite networks. At present, most connections to the IXC occur via digital access cross-connect switches (DACS) located in CLEC/ILEC COs. The DACS aggregate data and voice traffic from customers onto high capacity links and forward it to larger switches located in IXC POPs on the boundaries of the IXC network.

In some cases, it is possible to direct traffic from the company premises directly to switches located in an IXC point of presence, though the cabling involved usually remains the property of the ILEC/CLEC that controls the "last mile"—as fiber and copper cabling to the CO or POP is sometimes called.

It is worth noting that in many metropolitan areas of the United States, IXCs are beginning to roll out broadband metropolitan area networks (BMANs) that interface corporate sites directly to the high speed IXC backbone networks. AT&T's Integrated Network Connection Service (INC) and Sprint's Integrated On-Demand Network (ION™) are two examples of such services.

In the case of the Sprint offering (see Figure 8–6), an Integrated Access Device (IAD) installed at the customer site combines company data and voice traffic onto a high-speed transmission facility (such as xDSL) that connects the company to an ATM edge switch at the Sprint ION POP.

The Sprint ION BMAN consists of a redundant, fiber optic, SONET dual-ring network that integrates with Sprint's core IXC network. The redundant dual-ring topology provides a guarantee against interruption.

IAD = Integrated Access Device
POP = Point Of Presence
FRAD = Frame Relay Access Device
BMAN = Broadband Metropolitan-area Network
CIR = Committed Information Rate
DSL = Digital Subscriber Line

Figure 8–6   Sprint ION™ metropolitan area network ring.

Sprint spokespersons claim that the topology of the ION BMAN (see Figure 8–7)—especially, its self-healing characteristics in the event of a POP failure or ring cut—negates much of the planning and provisioning that companies must undertake to recover from interruptions in last mile facilities and CO problems. Potentially, it will eliminate the expenditure of company resources on technologies for ensuring WAN-access survivability, while delivering a several-orders-of-magnitude improvement in production WAN operations. (This claim is addressed in greater detail below.)

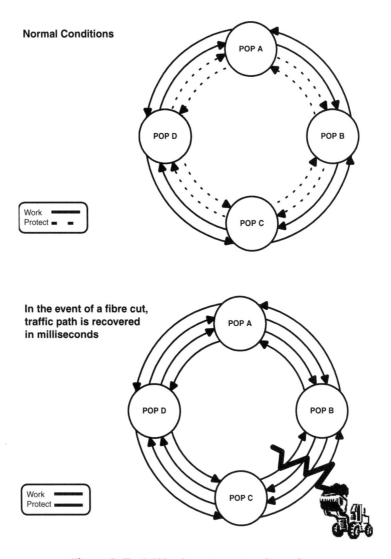

Figure 8–7   Self-healing ring network topology.

Convergent voice and data traffic delivered directly to the IXC network is one of many innovations expected to characterize the New Public Network (NPN) over the next decade. Additional use of wireless networking and cable modem-based technologies is also anticipated throughout the early 2000s. These last-mile technologies, combined with new fiber optic signaling and switching technologies, promise to increase the performance and capacity of the IXC infrastructure for the foreseeable future.

Viewed from the perspective of multiple network layers, DR coordinators may be able to see more readily the threats to mission-critical networks and the disaster avoidance and disaster recovery capabilities that are required to address them. The primary objective of network recovery planning is to prevent avoidable interruptions of network services that might impact critical business processes and to minimize the consequences of interruptions that cannot be prevented. A second, though equally important, goal is to develop a capability to transition vital networks to meet the needs of system and end user recovery strategies.

PRELIMINARY ACTIVITIES IN NETWORK RECOVERY PLANNING

It is the disaster recovery coordinator's job to identify the dependency of business functions on the proper operation and the availability of each layer of network services as summarized above and to evaluate the impact of a loss of a service. Some activities that may be part of this undertaking include the following.

Review Risk Analysis and Business Process Analysis Documents

These documents, created at the outset of the disaster recovery planning project, contain information about critical business functions and the automated systems and networks that support them. Analyses should be reviewed to identify dependencies on networks, the criticality of network services, and the minimum network service levels that will be required for business continuation.

Obtain Network Configuration Documentation

In addition to the insights obtained through analysis, the coordinator may need to solicit the assistance of a company telecommunications manager, network administrator, and/or network security manager to develop an understanding of network configurations used to support business processes under normal operating conditions. For companies that have implemented network management systems (NMS), configuration information may be readily available, together with network traffic data, and even hypothetical outage impact projections. A number of NMS vendors are following the lead of Micromuse, Inc. to deliver impact analysis tools "designed to help corporations and service providers rapidly assess the business impact of IT service outages and accelerate service restoral by following procedures that are closely aligned with business objectives."[3] (See Figure 8–8.)

Figure 8–8   Micromuse Netcool/Impact depicts what-if outage impact scenarios. (*Source:* Micromuse, Inc., San Francisco, CA.)

Subordinate diagrams may also have to be compiled showing specific characteristics of specific LANs or subnetworks, including topologies and protocols, characteristics of transmission media between network nodes, and traffic patterns, loads, and transmission rates.

Good network documentation is prerequisite to the task of relating critical business functions and applications to specific communications services. It provides a framework that the disaster recovery coordinator can use to analyze what effect the loss of a particular network service will have on the company. This, in turn, can guide the disaster recovery coordinator in planning measures to safeguard against network failures that threaten critical functions.

Build Disaster Scenarios

Once network configuration documentation has been prepared, the disaster recovery coordinator may find it useful to develop scenarios to account for failures within networks that could lead to unacceptable network service levels for critical business functions.

Often scenario building begins with an examination of internal networks for single points of failure. The disaster recovery coordinator looks at the topology of voice and data networks and subnetworks with an eye toward identifying the impact of device or network media failure. The coordinator then develops recommendations for network enhancements that will eliminate single points of failure where possible and strategies for recovering network operations in the event of failures that cannot be prevented.

A similar approach is then taken to develop a scenario for intermediate network interruptions. Device or media failures within company premise equipment, within the local loop, or at CLEC/ILEC COs can compromise such key corporate networking requirements as access to WANs, local and long distance telephone services, remote access services for telecommuters, virtual private network access, frame relay network access, and the Internet, just to name a few.

According to a first quarter 1999 Macro-Analysis Report of the Alliance for Telecommunications Industry Solutions (ATIS) Network Reliability Steering Committee, which correlates network outage information accumulated by the U.S. Federal Communications Commission, there were forty-one outages in the opening months of 1999 that fit FCC reporting criteria (at least 30 minutes in duration and affecting a minimum of 30,000 lines).[4] Significant increases were seen in certain root causes for the outages, such as procedural errors, while the frequency of outages attributed to other root causes—including CO power failures, facilities (mainly cable cuts), and non-procedural error-based CO switch failures—remained in-line with previous reporting periods or declined slightly (see Figure 8–9).

While NRSC numbers cover only a subset of intermediate network outages (those that meet FCC reporting requirements), DR coordinators may be able to leverage the organization's causal hierarchy to identify threats and build a scenario to guide recovery planning. (See Table 8–1.)

In addition to Central Office and Local Loop interruption potentials, outage scenarios in the IXC network should also be considered as a prelude to planning. In the first edition of this book, as well as in other writings by the author on the subject of disaster recovery, remarks regarding the potential vulnerability of Frame Relay services provided by IXCs elicited a barrage of criticisms from carriers themselves. Critics responded that Frame Relay service failures were highly improbable given the safeguards and redundancies inherent in IXC network itself.

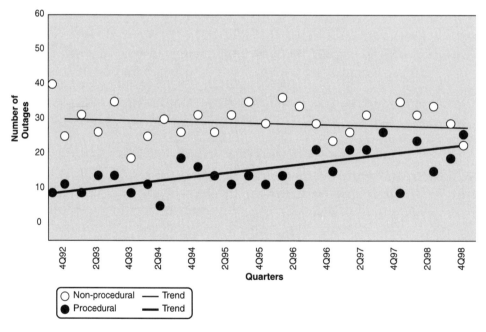

Figure 8–9   Procedure error and nonprocedure error outage frequency by quarter. (*Source: Procedural Outage Reduction: Addressing the Human Part,* Alliance for Telecommunications Industry Solutions (ATIS) sponsored Network Reliability Steering Committee (NRSC), Washington, DC, May 1999. Reproduced with permission of ATIS.)

Table 8-1 Causal Classification of Telco Outages Used by ATIS NSRC

Cause	Subcategory	Explanation
Procedural—Service Provider	**Failure to follow standard procedures/documentation.**	Work error by telco personnel; correct procedures exist and were generally available, but correct procedures/documentation were not used or were used incorrectly.
	Followed procedures/documentation that were incorrect.	Flawed documentation or procedures used by telco personnel.
Procedural—System Vendor	**Failure to follow standard procedures/documentation.**	Work error by system vendor personnel; correct procedures exist and were generally available, but correct procedures/documentation were not used or were used incorrectly.
	Followed procedures/documentation that were incorrect.	Flawed documentation or procedures used by system vendor personnel.
Procedural—Other Vendor	**Failure to follow standard procedures/documentation.**	Work error by other vendor personnel; correct procedures exist and were generally available, but correct procedures/documentation were not used or were used incorrectly.
	Followed procedures/documentation that were incorrect.	Flawed documentation or procedures used by other vendor personnel.
Design—Software	**Faulty or defective software design.**	Includes inadequate fault recovery strategies or failures; ineffective software fault isolation performance that triggers system reinitializations, or requires manual system recovery action for resolution; and insufficient software/memory capacity allocation problems.
Design—Firmware	**Faulty or defective firmware design.**	Includes inadequate fault recovery strategies or failures and ineffective fault isolation performance that require manual recovery action for resolution. Includes problems associated with incomplete firmware restoral (with or without accurate state indicators) following re-initialization.

(continued)

Table 8–1 *Continued*

Cause	Subcategory	Explanation
Design—Hardware	**Faulty or defective system hardware design.**	Includes problems with component independence and single-point-of-failure problems between otherwise duplex components, as well as physical hardware design problems (i.e., bad connectors, inadequate grounding techniques).
Hardware Failure	**Random hardware failure not related to design but due to the inherent unreliability of the system components.**	If (single) hardware failure causes loss of duplicated critical systems, consider procedural or design fault. If system outage resulted from hardware failure occurring during simplex operation, consider root cause procedural fault if simplex mode resulted from inappropriate deferral of normal maintenance.
External Environment	**Natural (storms, lightning).**	External environmental conditions that exceed limitations documented in the vendor's technical specifications; includes direct effects of flooding, freezing, excessive temperature or rate of temperature changes; includes outages resulting from lightning or external high voltage transients introduced into the system. If bonding and grounding violations caused the entry of lightning into the system, consider root cause procedural or design fault. If water damage was the result of cable pressurization failure, consider root cause procedural fault.
	Man-made (vandalism, accidents).	External man-made conditions that exceed documented (or reasonable) technical specifications; includes direct effects of water system ruptures, fires, vehicular accidents, vandalism, and explosions. If incident was the result of inadequate security precautions, consider root cause procedural fault.

Cause	Subcategory	Explanation
	Cable damage.	Cable damage caused by dig-ups, (fiber) micro-bending, rodent damage, falling trees, etc.; includes underground and aerial cable failures associated with natural and man-made external environments. If incident was the result of faulty cable installation, or of cable locating activities, consider root cause procedural fault.
Internal Environment	**Water.**	Entry of water into the system, including roof leaks, air conditioning leaks, excessive humidity, fire suppression activities, flooding, etc. If failure was the result of environmental systems failure (e.g., AC leaks, pressurization failures), or inadequate property management (e.g., unreasonable delay in repair or roof leak, predictable flooding), consider root cause procedural fault.
	Temperature.	Excessive ambient temperatures, excessive rate of temperature changes. If failure was the result of environmental systems failure and a more effective response to the failure would have prevented/minimized impact of incident, consider root cause procedural fault.
	Corrosion/ contamination.	Corrosive contamination that enters the system from surrounding environment; includes dust, airborne dirt, and smoke and/or fire suppression chemicals. If failure was the result of inadequate air filtration strategies or maintenance, consider root cause procedural or design fault.

(continued)

Table 8–1 *Continued*

Cause	Subcategory	Explanation
	Fire.	Fires within the telecommunications facility environment; includes fires in test sets, peripheral equipment, power equipment, and building systems. If incident was the result of telco/others' activities, consider root cause procedural fault.
Traffic/System Overload	**Reduced capacity due to system trouble.**	System overload or congestion associated with decreased system throughput or trouble-caused resource limitation; does not include system congestion associated with simple high-volume traffic conditions. If failure was the result of excessive out-of-service conditions, consider root cause procedural fault. If failure was a result of overload triggered by moderate increase in traffic/attempts, or recovery-associated activities, consider root cause design fault.
	High call volume.	System overload or congestion associated with high traffic or load conditions that exceed the engineered capacity of the system; includes unexpected traffic that was the result of media-stimulated calling, natural disasters, political or social activities, or other external conditions. If failure was the result of poor event notification and planning, or network management response to media-stimulated call-in, or a result of inadequate capacity engineering, consider root cause procedural fault.

Cause	Subcategory	Explanation
Commercial and/or Back-up Power Failure	**Instances of outage directly related to failure of the external power system, or failures of telco back-up power systems.**	Includes failures associated with commercial power, standby generators, building electrical systems, Direct Current (DC) power plants, DC distribution systems, and alarms/monitoring systems. Does not include failures of dc/dc converters or fuses embedded in switches and transmission equipment, unless the problem was caused by the power plant. If the failure was the result of inadequate/no response to (alarmed/unalarmed) failures, consider root power alarm fault. If the failure was the result of overloaded or under-sized power equipment, consider root cause procedural or design fault.
Other/Unknown	**The cause of the outage cannot be determined, or the cause does not match any of the classifications above.**	Does not include cases where outage data was insufficient or missing or where direct cause is still under investigation. When direct cause cannot be proven, it is usually still possible to determine probable cause, which is preferred to the use of "unknown." When classifications provided do not match direct cause, approximate match is preferred to the use of "other."

Source: Procedural Outage Reduction: Addressing the Human Part, Alliance for Telecommunications Industry Solutions (ATIS) sponsored Network Reliability Steering Committee (NRSC), Washington, DC, May 1999, Reproduced with permission of ATIS.

Short of a complete failure of the network, the loss of a specific service such as the Public Frame Relay Network was inconceivable. AT&T's April 1998 Frame Relay Network outage, followed by MCI WorldCom's August 1999 Frame Relay Service failure, demonstrated that the inconceivable was entirely possible.

In the case of AT&T, the 20-hour outage affecting 6,600 customers started on a Monday at 3 PM EST and ended at approximately 1 PM the next day. During that period, only customers with backup networking provisions were able to conduct business using their WANs. Wells Fargo Bank in San Francisco lost one-half of its Automated Teller Machine network during the period, while Unisys, the American Red Cross, TRW, and a host of other organizations were unable to provide normal customer services and other operations.

MCI WorldCom's outage (in fact, a succession of several outages of varying duration over a week-long period) resulted from a software upgrade being conducted by the IXC to its legacy network switches. Instead of backing out the destabilizing software, which had already been deployed across 30% of the network switches, when outages first began to occur, the company made a controversial decision to forge ahead after temporarily stabilizing the network during the first affected weekend. By the following weekend, several short-term outages and various system measurements confirmed that it was time to take action and the new software was backed out. In the process, the vendor earned the public wrath of thousands of its customers, including the Chicago Board of Trade, which was unable to use the network to conduct trades for nearly five days.[5]

As these events demonstrate, the paths through the IXC network created by special switch services (Frame Relay, ISDN, etc.) can and do fail, requiring DR coordinators to consider alternatives for providing mission-critical network functions.

The same logic applies to the Internet, which is increasingly used by companies to provide virtual private networks (VPNs) and other business-critical services. Like Frame Relay Network services, Internet services, which use the IXC network as a transport, can also be interrupted without the complete failure of the public network. DR coordinators whose companies use these special services may wish to develop specific interruption scenarios that can then be used to create recovery strategies.

Depending on the company, additional scenarios may need to be developed to address specific network vulnerabilities. For example, companies that have adopted integrated access strategies (i.e., Sprint ION or AT&T INC) or are early adopters of voice/data network convergence may need to make special plans to recover these types of network technologies. Also, companies that use value-added networks (VANs) from third-party providers may need to make special provisions for the replacement of these services in the event of a failure. In many cases, VANs are simply companies that lease lines from the IXCs and pay to colocate their own switch equipment in IXC POPs. They operate their own applications across these "private network services"—such as enhanced financial market ticker tape feeds, for example—and sell subscriptions to the service to customers. If these services are important to business-critical processes, plans must be made for their replacement in the event of a service failure.

Finally, DR coordinators need to leverage the scenarios that have guided the development of system and end user recovery strategies to define a set of network recovery capabilities to "reconnect the dots" if a disaster forces the relocation of either data centers or user work facilities or both.

FORMULATING STRATEGIES
FOR INTERNAL NETWORK RECOVERY

Once the preliminary steps outlined above are completed, the disaster recovery coordinator will be able to address specific network recovery issues. At first glance, the multiplicity of scenarios might seem overwhelming. Fortunately, the principles of redundancy and replacement can be successfully applied to creating strategies to cope with most network failures. By making plans for less-than-worst-case scenarios, the coordinator may also find that a pattern of problem escalation emerges that will support emergency management decision making.

Several generic options for recovering failed networks are presented in the following sections.

Internal Voice Communications Systems

Planning for the recovery of internal communications networks must consider two aspects of the network: station failures and PBX failures. In most modern PBX-based voice communications networks, the failure of a station or group of stations will not cause the PBX to fail (though a facility power failure will affect a switch that does not have a backup power supply such as a UPS). Indeed, station failures, due to media faults or hardware malfunctions, are often treated as maintenance issues rather than disaster recovery issues. It is conceivable, however, that the loss of network wiring integrity could create an emergency for the affected operational area of the company. Thus, line redundancy may be a valid measure to insure network integrity for critical business functions. It is also important to acquire appropriate network diagnostic and troubleshooting software and to train technicians in its use so that sources of trouble within the network can be rapidly localized, identified, and repaired.

In the event of a PBX failure, two alternatives may speed recovery. First, sufficient dedicated lines (i.e., analog or digital lines that do not have to operate through the switch itself) may be installed for critical, telecommunications-dependent business functions. These lines can be used to handle critical traffic until the PBX malfunction can be resolved or the unit replaced.

For some companies, however, leasing sufficient private lines to sustain critical functions may be more costly than purchasing and installing second switch as a backup to the primary unit. In such cases, purchasing or leasing a backup PBX may provide a cost-effective recovery option. If a second PBX is obtained, common sense dictates that it be installed in a different location than the primary unit. In this way, the second unit may be insulated from disaster conditions that may affect the primary switch. Both the primary and secondary PBX installations should also be backed up for power (via UPS), have appropriate environmental controls, and be equipped with a suitable fire detection/suppression capability.

Most modern PBXs are programmable. Station services and capabilities (i.e., call pickup, call forwarding) may be defined in a series of program statements or "translations." It is important to ensure that these programmed instructions are backed up regularly to portable media, and that a copy of the backup is stored off-site, together with documentation, for recovery purposes.

Computer Peripheral and Terminal Networks

Computer input and output devices, together with the servers to which they are attached, comprise a straightforward (though often complex) data communications network. Once the mainstay of the centralized mainframe computing environment, device networks have recently returned into vogue with the increasing interest in server-centric and thin client computing architectures.

Provided that systems management software—either delivered with the server operating system or purchased from a third-party provider—is used, peripheral device failures and access interruptions can usually be detected promptly. Redundant hardware should be stocked for use in the immediate replacement of failed critical devices.

Cabling can be another vulnerable aspect of these networks, but exposures to severe loss due to cable cuts or other problems can often be predicted and limited. Proper upfront planning for long cable runs will help ensure that obvious hazards are avoided. Careful attention to proper grounding and surge protection can prevent lightning and other power variations from being conducted back to the server or attached device—resulting in damage. If cable cuts occur, it may be possible to utilize alternative media to handle data traffic while repairs are made. Balun™ adapters, for example, may be employed with some systems to convert coaxial cables for use with PBX station wiring.

Storage Area Networks

Another peripheral network, the storage area network (SAN), is rapidly gaining presence in modern IT architectures. SANs derive their heritage from the ESCON-managed Direct Access Storage Device (DASD) "farms" of a decade ago, and while still evolving, comprise a network of storage devices shared among servers and accessed by means of a SAN switch or hub. Because of the sensitivity of applications and server operating systems to storage latency, the interconnect technology for a SAN is typically a high-speed serial interface such as Fibre Channel.

As of this writing, SANs lack any sort of "in-band management" mechanism (*in-band management* refers to a mechanism for managing and monitoring the operation of connected devices via some technology that operates over the link connecting the devices themselves). Instead, the monitoring SANs for proper operation is a function of Simple Network Management Protocol (SNMP) agents operating over a separate Ethernet network that interconnects SAN networking and storage devices via management ports.

This is not to say that early SANs are disasters waiting to happen. First-generation SANs feature homogeneous storage components combined with data networking products that have been selected by vendors based on demonstrated interoperability. These proprietary SANs, while not the "open storage nirvana" ultimately sought from the architecture, do capitalize on proprietary storage management and resiliency capabilities provided by their vendors and deliver high-availability performance in some configurations. Switch fabrics can and are constructed with link redundancy and failover in mind, and fault tolerance is considered a key design criteria considering the critical nature of the SAN: It is the repository for a significant percentage of corporate data.

DR coordinators within companies that have adopted SAN technology should understand how SAN availability is being provided. They may also wish to find out how SANs can be leveraged to support the timely mirroring or tape backup of mission-critical datasets.

LANs

Local Area Networks (LANs) pose a challenge for disaster recovery planning because of the diversity of types, functions, transmission media, equipment, and topologies currently in use. In many cases, LANs enable mission-critical client/server applications by providing a medium though which distributed servers and workstations can participate in the processing of data.

Some types of LANs can be readily protected against catastrophic loss due to the failure of a node (an individual workstation), loss of media integrity, or software-related factors. The solution resides in the software used to create and control the LAN as well as the topology of the LAN itself.

At a generic level, LAN communication may be viewed as a multi-faceted programming problem. It is depicted as such by the International Standards Organization (ISO) in its open systems interconnection (OSI) model of data communications. Figure 8–10 illustrates the OSI model as it applies to peer communications within a LAN.

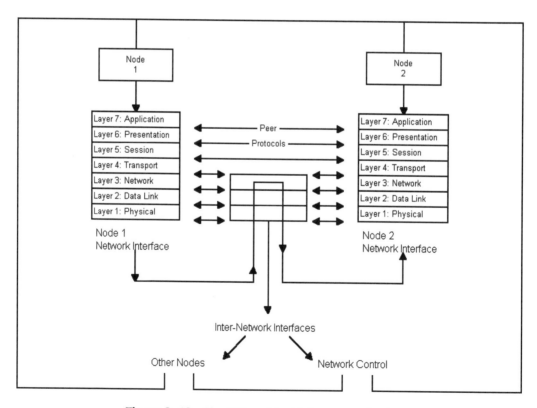

Figure 8–10   The OSI model of data communication.

As the model suggests, there are seven levels, or layers, of data communications between nodes attached in a LAN. These layers correspond to software components imbedded in the node device operating system (or the network operating system). The following summary describes the layer functions within the OSI model.

- **Layer 7: Application.** The application layer provides the commands or functions, such as file transfer, document printing, or electronic mail, by which the node communicates with other available or open nodes on the network. The command will not result in the actual performance of the function, however, until it has been interpreted by other protocol layers. Common application service elements defined in the application layer allow application programs to find each other and exchange information without requiring special user intervention and guidance.

- **Layer 6: Presentation.** This layer provides translation, and sometimes encryption and compression, functions in intranetwork communications. The presentation layer thus provides communication between nodes with disparate internal codes as well as security in network communications.

- **Layer 5: Session.** The session layer is responsible for handling conversations between network nodes. In addition to managing node interaction, the session layer oversees network operating conditions and can reestablish communications after temporary disruption of network connections. The session layer also provides a means for mapping network node addresses to names, thus minimizing the impact to application programs of hardware changes within the network.

- **Layer 4: Transport.** The transport layer provides error checking between nodes during communication. In the event of an erred transmission, layer 4 may generate error messages and requests for retransmission of data.

- **Layer 3: Network.** This layer provides internetwork communications as well as the translation of logical addresses (node names) into physical addresses. It also serves as a traffic controller, selecting the best route on the network for communications between two nodes.

- **Layer 2: Data Link.** The data link layer handles the packaging of data to be communicated and its successful entry onto the network. Data may be packaged as frames or packets and, depending on the network software, may conform to certain packaging standards such as those articulated by the Institute of Electrical and Electronic Engineers (IEEE). If packets arrive at their destination in a corrupt or improper form, layer 2 may notify layer 4 to signal an error and request retransmission.

- **Layer 1: Physical.** This layer consists of the hardwired instructions of the network—cabling and physical circuitry. Depending on the media, this layer defines the signaling method that is to be used to represent on and off bits.

It is important to understand clearly that the OSI layer functions are provided by the network software and hardware used in a company LAN that is to be safeguarded against disaster. DR coordinators also need to familiarize themselves with the specific network products deployed by the company, as vendors differ widely in their adherence to the OSI model, with some software packages and hardware products providing the functions of several layers in a single layer. Generally, the functions of layers 1 and 2 are provided by network interface cards (NICs) and cabling. The functions of layers 3 through 5 are usually provided through a combination of network software and switch, router, and hub firmware. The functions of layers 6 and 7 may be provided by nodal operating systems, application software, or both.

The OSI Network Model can provide a useful analytical tool for approaching the subject of LAN disaster recovery. However, the flexibility of LAN technology facilitates highly customized deployments that mitigate efforts to develop a "boilerplate" methodology for protecting and recovering LANs.

For example, knowing how the OSI model functions are provided with respect to company LANs may help the disaster recovery coordinator to set important parameters on recovery procedures. The coordinator can use the information collected about the LAN to determine how network nodes are identified (i.e., by name or physical address). If nodes are identified by name, node hardware may be able to be changed readily in the event that a node fails or if new workstations need to be used to restore the LAN at a recovery site. If hard-coded addresses are used to identify nodes (i.e., firmware associated with specific network interface cards), replacement of node hardware and restoration of network operations may be more complicated and time consuming.

Depending on the OSI layer 1 through 4 characteristics of a LAN, which describe the physical, data link, network, and transport parameters for normal LAN operation, it may be possible to specify a wireless LAN interconnect as a temporary substitute for a cabled interconnect in the event of a cable infrastructure problem. Wireless LAN products (see Figure 8–11) have been growing in capability and corporate presence since the adoption of a wireless Ethernet standard (IEEE 802.11) in 1997. While companies have largely deployed these slower-speed network interconnects in locations where conventional cabling is difficult, the technology has merit both as a short-term workaround for network cabling breaks and as a quick deployment solution for emergency LAN restoral with certain applications.[6]

Security-related factors are also of importance in network software. Generally, layers 6, 4, 3, and 2 in the OSI model are utilized to provide security for data and applications on the LAN. The disaster recovery coordinator needs to understand the security measures being employed to determine the extent to which they might interfere with node or network recovery.

Depending on how OSI layer functions are provided, the recovery of LAN-based applications may not need to be accomplished on a LAN at all. In certain cases, the applications and data that are being shared across the LAN are portable to alternative processing platforms. If LAN applications are critical, it may be possible to plan to move them onto a centralized host system for emergency operation. There, the programs and data can be accessed, in a dial-up mode, by users from a recovery site.

As the above examples suggest, understanding how a LAN is physically interconnected is only one part of the equation for defining recovery strategies. An understanding of topology enables the identification of sin-

Figure 8–11   A wireless LAN topology. (*Source:* Breezecom, Inc., Carlsbad, CA.)

gle points of failure, either in cabling or hardware, that can be addressed through configuration enhancements or additional, redundant hardware. However, LANs also need to be understood at the level of internodal communications to identify both impediments to recovery and opportunities for disaster prevention. In these efforts, DR coordinators may be well served by an understanding of the OSI model and the development of a good working relationship with corporate network administrators.

The importance of establishing an effective dialog with corporate network management cannot be understated. The fact is that network administrators work to leverage the capabilities of network equipment and infrastructure to provide quality of service guarantees for mission-critical applications on a day-to-day basis. In most modern networks, this activity involves a combination of application review and policy setting on the one hand and ongoing network monitoring on the other. Network managers understand the service level requirements of applications and endeavor to meet them through a combination of network design and policy-based traffic switching. This knowledge extends to disaster recovery planning in several important ways.

First, network managers can usually identify what service levels will be required for restored LAN-based applications in an emergency operations mode. They can identify the bandwidth requirements and traffic patterns of applications from which hardware and cabling infrastructure requirements can be gleaned. They are also familiar with the security requirements that must be upheld in a recovery setting and can work with DR coordinators to ensure that appropriate security is applied even in alternative recovery network configurations. Network managers may also have access to Network Management Systems that can provide "views" of the IT infrastructure that pertain to specific applications. Products such as Computer Associates UnicenterTNG and others are often used by corporate network managers to provide selected information about complex networks and systems on an application or business function level for presentation to less technical business managers (see Figure 8–12). This type of utility can aid DR coordinators in focusing recovery planning efforts on specific business processes rather than becoming overwhelmed by the complexities of the entire enterprise network.

The resources and insights of the network manager extend beyond the internal LANs of the company. DR coordinators can leverage the relationships they cultivate with corporate network professionals to obtain a clearer understanding of the service-level requirements for applications distributed beyond the corporate boundaries as well, as discussed in the following section.

Figure 8-12   Computer Associates UnicenterTNG business process views can describe IT and network infrastructure components associated with a specific business process. (*Source:* Computer Associates International, Inc., Islandia, NY.)

BACKUP STRATEGIES FOR THE LOCAL LOOP AND WIDE AREA NETWORK SERVICES

In addition to an internal network failure scenarios, the disaster recovery coordinator also needs to consider how the company will replace mission-critical local loop and wide area network services in the event of interruptions. Despite the assurances of IXCs with respect to the resiliency of their new SONET ring services (one, who shall not be named, went so far as to claim in an interview that DR planners for businesses using her company's service no longer need to plan for the recovery of local loop facilities), the fact remains that these offerings are (1) not available on a widespread basis, (2) meeting challenges from ILECs and CLECs who will not surrender last mile services without a fight, or (3) still require some kind of local loop interconnect technology such as xDSL to connect the company Integrated Access Device with the IXC-provided metropolitan area network.

Thus, ensuring the solvency of connections between the corporate premises and the outside world remains within the scope of DR planning. Coordinators need to address the issues involved with an eye toward avoiding interruptions.

Local Loop Protection Through Link Duplication

The last mile—shorthand for the cable connections between the LEC Central Office (CO) or IXC point of presence (POP) and the company premise—is vulnerable to a broad range of disaster potentials. Conduits containing thousands of voice and data lines can be cut, deliberately or accidentally, or can fall prey to natural hazards (gophers that chew on casings, for example, or natural cataclysms such as earthquakes, lightning strikes, hurricanes, etc.). It is beyond the purview of the DR coordinator to protect telco-owned facilities, but it is within the coordinator's power to develop backup schemes for critical links.

One strategy for coping with line cuts is to secure lines from two different COs or POPs. With full line redundancy, supplied through different conduits from different sources, line dig-up resiliency may be guaranteed. Typically, an automatic switch or PBX cutover is made from one set of trunks to a redundant set if a failure is detected, though additional details for switching trunk identities may need to be worked out with the telecommunications service provider.

Coordinators opting for a replacement strategy need to work together with service providers to ensure that redundant lines are not provided through the same physical conduits or the presumed resiliency of the solution is defeated before it is implemented. It is also important to note that different carriers often lease circuits from each other and share the same fiber, conduits, and/or rights-of-way. Thus, obtaining backup services from different carriers does not of necessity ensure that primary and backup services are physically separate from one another. Coordinators need to get the facts before settling on a solution.

In some cases, it is possible to replace land-based links with satellite or wireless transmission options available from third-party providers such as Value Added Network (VAN) companies. These options are worth investigation, especially if geographic distances or right-of-way issues prohibit link duplication through land-based COs or POPs.

Properly implemented, a strategy of link redundancy has the additional merit of safeguarding mission-critical communications against a number of disaster potentials linked to CO or POP operations, including switch port failures, power outages, fires, and other internal problems.

Local Loop Protection with Unlike Link Substitution

Of course, duplicating all communications services, from voice-grade lines to T-3 links, with fully redundant backup facilities that are to be used only in an emergency may be beyond the DR budget of a company. Jeff Davis, Director of Service Level Management Products with Paradyne Corporation observes that

> [Like kind or one-for-one] link backup is not always economical for "always-on" services [like T-1 or xDSL]. Analog lines and Integrated Switched Digital Network (ISDN) lines may be better suited for transient use. With these you have a minimal fee, then a toll charge assessed on a per use basis. [Suggesting that you replace high-speed facilities with slower links may seem questionable,] but not when you consider that most T-1 connections to business offices are actually running at a fraction of the available link rate. They are often configured at 56k or below.[7]

According to Davis and others, consolidation and creativity are usually required to come up with the most effective link replacement solution at the right price. Network managers can be of enormous assistance, given their knowledge of application bandwidth demands and typical traffic patterns, to identify link substitution strategies that might be adequate to handle application traffic loads during an emergency operations period.

Service Failure Circumvention with Unlike Link Substitution

In addition to replacing last mile links, DR coordinators also need to consider how companies will circumvent IXC or VAN-provided networking services in the event that these services become unavailable. One obvious example is Frame Relay. Most IXCs offer some sort of Frame Relay Network services as a replacement for expensive private point-to-point networks. With these services, company offices establish connections to the IXC's Frame Relay Network "cloud," which handles all necessary switching functions to establish secure, private network sessions between communicators. These services are vulnerable to interruptions due to any number of problems and alternatives need to be found for reestablishing point-to-point connectivity in the event of an outage—in effect, to circumvent the service when needed.

For the last five years, many companies have replaced high-speed connections to Public Frame Relay Network services with a fewer number of less capable ISDN facilities. This ISDN "safety net" was credited with seeing many firms through the infamous AT&T Frame Relay network outage in April 1998 as well as the MCI Frame Relay network failures of August 1999.[8]

The ISDN safety net strategy offers a number of valuable considerations that can be applied in other service circumvention scenarios. For one, it is important to test and evaluate any non-like replacement strategy for its impact on applications. If normal link bandwidth is 256 kbit/s (fairly standard for Frame Relay links), replacing the normal link with an ISDN basic-rate interface (BRI) backup link, which offers 64 kbit/s, will have a noticeable impact on application performance.

A company may be able to get by despite the diminished bandwidth if fewer end users utilize applications during the period of interruption in primary link services. Another fix may be to quiesce less essential applications for the duration of the primary link outage, saving all available BRI bandwidth for the mission critical application(s).

Another consideration that can be derived from the ISDN backup strategy and applied in other circumvention strategies involves the implementation of such an alternative service. DR coordinators need to look closely at how the replacement strategy is provisioned. In the case of ISDN backup, many companies have discovered that some service providers take circuits out of service when they are not being used regularly—even when the customer keeps subscription payments up to date.[9] This can create havoc if primary link services fail and recovery teams must spend hours with backup service providers trying to get backup link services restored.

This is one reason, according to Paradyne Corporation's Davis, why some vendors of ISDN backup devices (including Paradyne) are building in "background test features that check to ensure that the ISDN link is up and running."[10]

In addition to capacity and provisioning, another important consideration when defining a service backup strategy is configuration. As the diversity of ISDN backup products demonstrate, there are often several competing hardware and/or software solutions to address any given link replacement/service circumvention requirement. For example, one method,

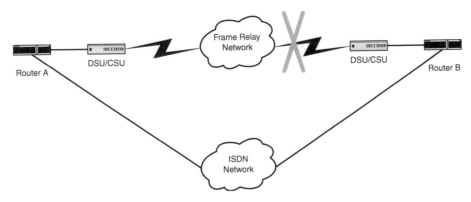

Figure 8–13   Router-based backup. (*Source:* © Paradyne Corporation, Largo, FL.)

encouraged by router vendors, for responding to a Frame Relay service outage is to reprogram routers to utilize an ISDN backup link if a primary link or service fails (see Figure 8–13).

On the surface, this strategy has the advantage of requiring a minimum of additional equipment to be provided at the customer premise. Assuming that ISDN interfaces are provided in the router WAN ports directly, no additional hardware is necessary to make a connection to the replacement network. If interface support is not provided, an ISDN interface device will need to be connected to a router port at each communicating site.

Paradyne Corporation, as well as ISDN backup equipment providers such as Controlware Communications Systems, argue that the router-based ISDN backup solutions are inherently inefficient and flawed. Consolidating both normal operations and backup capabilities in the same router introduces a potential single point of failure, critics contend. Moreover, programming a router to use an ISDN link as a substitute for a Frame Relay link is a complex and time-consuming undertaking—so much so, observes Davis, that router vendors teach it as part of their advanced router programming course.[11] The performance of consolidated router-based offerings also suffers, he contends:

> The speed of the [implementation of the backup] is slower using Layer 3 routers. It may take more time for the router to sense that the Frame Relay net is down. When alternative ISDN backup lines are implemented, the routers can take several minutes to exchange protocols

and routing tables across the network [before the network connection is reestablished]. With an [ISDN backup device placed between the router and the WAN], the device quickly senses that the Frame Relay network is down and cuts over [immediately and transparently] to ISDN backup links (see Figure 8–14).[12]

Router-based implementations of ISDN backup are also short on specialty features, according to vendors of the devices. One vendor touts the advantage of its product in being able to combine multiple ISDN B-channels into one large virtual channel, or to package data for transport via satellite.[13] These operating modes, not available with generic ISDN dial backup capabilities in general purpose routers, may be more or less important within the context of corporate network backup strategy.

Another vendor offers "Time of Day backup" settings that enable network managers to indicate certain times of the normal workday when, if a network outage occurs, the backup network (ISDN links) will NOT be activated. Says the vendor, there may be certain times during the day when Frame Relay networks are not being used and outages do not represent a cost to the company. Time of Day settings avoid the costs associated with turning on backup links unnecessarily.[14]

Yet another special feature of some ISDN backup devices is a toll charge savings algorithm. According to Jeff Davis, Paradyne's "Dial Nearest Neighbor" capability enables the ISDN backup device to identify and connect to the closest node, avoiding long distance fees (see Figure 8–15).

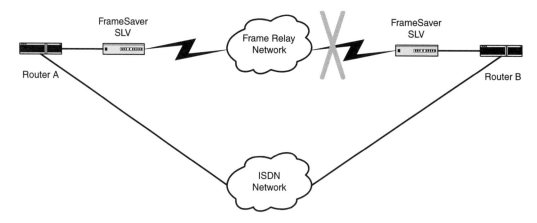

Figure 8–14 ISDN backup device implementation. (*Source:* © Paradyne corporation, Largo, FL.)

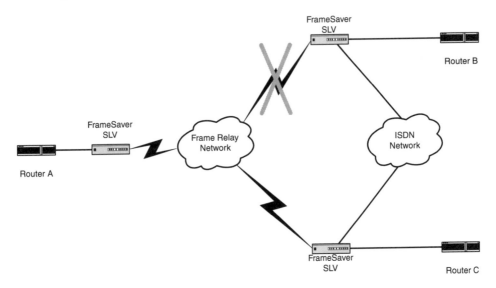

Figure 8–15   Dial Nearest Neighbor implementation. (*Source:* © Paradyne Corporation, Largo, FL.)

Davis also adds that vendors of ISDN backup units typically add capabilities for collecting statistics on latency, availability, and throughput that can be used to evaluate the adequacy of the link.

In addition to discriminating their products from router-based solutions, ISDN backup device vendors also strive to discriminate their products from one another. DR coordinators need to work with knowledgeable network specialists to wade through the features and functions of each product offering to determine the best fit, given recovery requirements.

Frame Relay services are not the only services that may require circumvention in the event of an outage. Similar strategies may be required to circumvent carrier or VAN-provided Virtual Private Networks (VPNs) in the event of a service outage. It should be noted that leading disaster recovery systems backup vendors such as Hewlett Packard Company, IBM, and SunGard Recovery Services offer value-added networks as a feature of their total recovery solutions. In some cases, these services may be available to subscribers who are confronting IXC service failures. However, they may come into greater use when companies experience disasters in their data centers and/or user work areas, and relocation to hot sites or other vendor-supplied facilities is required.

PLANNING FOR THE RESTORAL OF WIDE AREA VOICE AND DATA NETWORK LINKS FOLLOWING A USER OR SYSTEMS RELOCATION

The previous discussion of network recovery strategies has focused on the recovery of critical network operations in the face of a LAN- or WAN-specific outage. A mixture of proactive (preventive) and reactive (recovery) techniques were discussed. A third strategy that must be developed by the DR coordinator considers the network recovery dimension of a systems and/or end user relocation. Following a fire, earthquake, or other disaster event that forces the relocation of the data center and/or end user work areas to an offsite location, it is necessary to reestablish a LAN/WAN infrastructure that will accommodate the resumption of business-critical operations.

A good place to begin this analysis is with a simple assertion: If a disaster leaves company offices intact but without necessary local loop or WAN connectivity, activation of system and end user recovery plans will likely be mandatory. Just as a company without power to its offices cannot continue productive business, so too communications are part of the vital business support infrastructure. If telecommunications outages occur that promise to exceed in duration the maximum acceptable thresholds established in DR risk analysis, it stands to reason that the relocation and recovery strategies developed for IT and end user operations will need to be invoked.

To the above assertion must be added a corollary. Even if network infrastructure is intact, the relocation of end users or data center operations in response to a disaster will necessitate the activation of network recovery strategies that support the relocation. Note that network recovery will be necessary whether data center relocation, end user operations relocation, or both are necessitated in response to a disaster.

Recovering critical networks expeditiously following a relocation requires advanced planning. From the perspective of local area networks, a suitable LAN infrastructure will be needed to ensure that applications and other resources are available to end users at prescribed service levels. From the perspective of WAN links and services, adequate capabilities must be provided to meet the voice and data communications networking requirements of business critical processes. WAN links must connect the end user community—including suppliers, partners, and other external entities with which the company must interact—to recovered systems and the applications they support.

The general objective of this type of network recovery strategy is to enable the restoration of network services at acceptable service levels in the shortest possible timeframe. This can only be achieved through up-front planning.

Acceptable service levels are determined in a number of ways. Depending on the type of application, the speed of a transaction may be an determinant of an acceptable service level. In other cases, service levels may be dictated by the number of end user sessions that can be supported concurrently over a link. In still other cases, service levels may be evaluated in terms of queue lengths (how many operations await processing at a given time, or how many customers are placed on hold awaiting an operator or service response). Appropriate service levels are generally determined at the time that a business impact analysis is conducted. Information gathered from end users identifies the numbers of personnel who must have access to applications and the response times required of those applications. DR coordinators must consider these requirements as performance baselines for recovery strategies when selecting between options.

Achieving network restoration to acceptable service levels within the shortest possible time implies that plans must be formulated and tested to ensure that recovered networks are deployed in as automatic a fashion as possible. This assertion has several components:

1. Expeditious network recovery is dependent, in part, on the extent to which system and end user recovery strategies have been "concretized." This essentially means that the greater the number of unknowns in the end user and systems recovery strategies, the more difficulty DR coordinators will face in endeavoring to field an efficient network recovery capability. Ideally, end user recovery facilities and systems recovery facilities are known in advance of a disaster. If this is the case, DR coordinators can leverage IXC and CLEC/ILEC services for on-demand rerouting of communications links to the alternate work locations and WAN links can be reestablished rapidly from new operating locations.

2. Expeditious recovery is possible only when underlying assumptions are carefully considered. Network recovery strategies should not depend upon conditions that may or may not exist in the wake of a disaster (i.e., that local CO services will continue to be available following a hurricane that demolishes corporate data centers or user work areas). Network recovery plans have frequently run afoul of

"unpredictable post-disaster conditions"—translated simply to mean the failure of the DR coordinator to plan for the worst-case scenario. Even simple assumptions about the availability of cell phone and pager services must be questioned to prevent erroneous expectations from creeping into plans.

3. Expeditious recovery is enabled by cautious generalization. Network recovery strategies are arguably the most difficult components of DR planning to keep current. Ask any network administrator in any company: Most changes, no matter how small, to applications or end user responsibilities have consequences for network resources and consume most of the administrator's time. Security settings, disk and resource allocations, telecommunications station identifiers, and a host of other details are adjusted on a daily basis. Network recovery, therefore, should be based where possible on general, rather than specific, environmental parameters. That is, individual user accounts should not be recovered unless absolutely necessary. Instead, plan for recovery by role, or by function—according resources, access, and security on a group, rather than an individual, basis where practical.

4. Consolidation is key to efficient recovery. Where possible, network recovery planning should seek to capitalize on consolidation opportunities. Not all applications require immediate restoration in the hours following a disaster, nor will networks necessarily be required to support the full traffic loads that characterize normal operations. The same may be said of support for end users: The number of staff who must work with applications in a post-disaster environment to maintain minimally acceptable service levels may be dramatically fewer than the number of staff using network resources during normal operations. These two facts provide the basis for estimating network resource requirements and providing them in a consolidated fashion.

5. Network recovery can be efficient only when recovery technologies are thoroughly tested and proven. Innovate but don't recreate. Network recovery can be innovative in support of new computing paradigms, such as rehosted applications and server-centric computing. With proper planning, entirely new network technologies can be introduced to augment existing methods (e.g., wireless networking or virtual private networks tunnelled through the Internet). However, any and all strategies implemented to facilitate recovery should have a specific justifying rationale and must be thoroughly tested. The purpose of network recovery planning is not to test out technology,

but to identify appropriate techniques for meeting service level requirements quickly.

The above considerations go to the efficiency of a network relocation strategy and its capability to deliver acceptable service levels throughout the period of a corporate emergency. In addition to the general considerations enumerated above, it may be useful to discuss a few specific points before concluding this discussion.

Restoring End User Access to Networks

As stated in a previous chapter, end user restoral may no longer require a remote facility equipped in advance with office furnishings, desktop workstations, and telecommunications switch hardware. The rise of the Internet and advancements in dial-up remote access technology provide alternatives for enabling productive end user operation of remote applications. Such an end user recovery strategy is typically only realistic for companies that have already instituted a program of telecommuting within day-to-day operations. From a network recovery standpoint, technologies for web-based or dial-up telecommuting should already be in place; they should not be tried for the first time in a disaster situation.

If telecommuting is a component of normal operations, it may still be inappropriate for end user recovery from a network recovery perspective. A scenario of total loss requires planners to think in regional terms. If a CO serving the company is lost in a cataclysm that also forces the company to relocate its operations to another venue (a total loss scenario would embrace this view), then end users who must also access the same CO for Internet or dial-up access services would also be without the ability to connect. The work-at-home strategy for end user recovery is practical only if a sufficient number of key end users are located outside of the area served by the business office's primary LEC CO so that their communications access is handled by a different CO or POP.

Assuming that at-home end user recovery is practicable, network recovery planning requires that access methods be examined for potential cost and efficacy. If planning assumes that fifty end users will need to dial-up to a distant data center remote access system, a certain cost is associated with this approach. Coordinators may wish to check with hot site providers to determine whether toll-free access can be provided, and at what cost. To determine the efficacy of such an approach, prospective end users need to be polled to determine how many have (1) telephone service provided by a CO located outside of the anticipated disaster zone and (2) two or more incoming lines to the CO. Doubtless one line would be required for network access, while the other would be needed for voice communications.

Connections Through Value Added Services

These connections, including IXC broadband metropolitan area networks and hot site provided WANs, need to be carefully assessed. Despite vendor claims regarding the internal resilience of these services, value added networks are usually still at the mercy of CLEC/ILEC-provided last mile services, which are already at risk in a regional disaster. If a local CO or POP is devastated, the "on-ramp" provided to the company by the local exchange carrier for access these services may also be lost. Once again, network recovery planning must consider alternative methods for restoring access to critical voice and data WAN services. This may include an examination of alternative CO or remote POP access utilizing either special ground lines or more exotic methods such as satellite and/or digital radio services. Be aware that these alternatives can introduce new issues to networks, including new security requirements and even operational issues related to propagation delay in signalling.

Security and Integrity in the New Network

Special consideration should be given to the security and integrity of data communications in the new network. Data that is deemed sensitive in normal operations remains sensitive in a recovery operations mode. All levels of program and database security should be rigorously tested both at the systems recovery site and at the user recovery site to ensure that one disaster does not lead to another. Integrity in data communications refers to the susceptibility of the data being transmitted to corruption due to a hostile communications environment. If data is being transmitted over new routes, there may be new environmental factors that can corrupt it. It is therefore important to obtain the "cleanest" media possible to handle communications between the user recovery facility and systems backup facility. Coordinators may also wish to consider installing new error-checking software to facilitate detection and correction of data communications errors due to link noise and other environmental factors.

While the parameters of the network relocation strategy may be largely determined by end user and systems recovery strategies, DR coordinators will still have much to do to formulate, test and select component options. For the network relocation strategy to deliver timely communications restoral at acceptable service levels, careful attention will need to be paid not only to technology, but also to the realities of the recovery environment. Simply put, it is not enough to recover applications, provide end user work arrangements, and restore network connections. The successful implementation of a disaster recovery capability also depends on the quality of decision making that governs its execution. The meaning of this assertion is the subject of the next chapter.

ENDNOTES

1. Tim Wilson, "Severed Chains," *Information Week*, 07/19/99, reported that only 15% of 250 surveyed companies had suspended contracts or replaced non-Y2K suppliers. Some had requested written information about Y2K compliance, a lesser number had conducted joint tests or requested third party certification, and most had taken no action or had determined that non-Y2K compliant suppliers could not be replaced in any case.

2. Andrew Cray, Peter Heywood, with additional reporting by Joanna Makris, "New Public Network: Building the Brave New World," *Data Communications*, 10/98.

3. "Micromuse Unveils Netcool/Impact™," Micomuse Press Release, 08/16/99, Micromuse Inc., New York, NY.

4. Raymond F. Albers, "Macro-Analysis: 1st Quarter 1999," Alliance For Telecommunications Industry Solutions (ATIS), Network Reliability Steering Committee, Arlington, Virginia. ATIS is responsible for analyzing telecommunications outage reports submitted by telco providers to the Federal Communications Commission. Mr. Albers chairs the NRSC and oversees the production of quarterly analyses of outage data. Visit www.atis.org to view documents of NRSC on line.

5. Carol Sliwa, David Orenstein and Kathleen Ohlson, "MCI Network Outage Hits Chicago Trading Board Hard," *Computerworld*, 08/13/99.

6. Jon Toigo, "Wireless Wends Its Way," *Solutions Integrator*, 05/01/99.

7. Interview with Jeff Davis, Director of Service Level Management Products, Paradyne Corporation, Largo, FL, 08/99.

8. Many accounts of the impact of AT&T's Frame Relay outage are available in the trade press. Some good reportage included: Ben Heskett, "Nationwide Breaks in AT&T Service," CNET News.com, 04/14/98. Robin Gareiss, "Frame Relay," *Data Communications*, 06/98. Kate Gerwig, "AT&T Network Outage: Disaster for Customers without Backup Systems," *Internet Week*, 04/15/98. Kate Gerwig, "Companies Tap Contingency Plans as AT&T's Frame Network Crashes," *Internet Week*, 04/20/98. John Rendleman, "AT&T Users Regroup," *PC Week*, 04/17/98. Rebecca Sykes, "AT&T Outage Points Up Network Weaknesses," *Computerworld*, 04/15/98.

9. Andrew Cray, "Leased Line Backup: The ISDN Safety Net," *Data Communications*, 10/96.

10. Interview with Jeff Davis, Paradyne Corporation, *op. cit.*

11. *Ibid.* See also, Vince Ciletti, Theresa McGuire, and Jeff Davis, "Improved Frame Relay Quality of Service Using ISDN Dial Backup Solutions," Paradyne Corporation White Paper, 01/14/99, Paradyne Corporation, Largo, FL.

12. *Ibid.*

13. "A Guide to the TAXI-System," Controlware Communications Systems, Neptune, NJ, 01/98.

14. Davis interview, *op. cit.*

Emergency Decision Making

One aspect of disaster recovery that is particularly elusive and difficult for many disaster recovery coordinators to treat adequately in their plans is emergency management. Emergency management planning aims at the management of three projects that are intrinsic to disaster recovery: evacuation, recovery, and relocation or reentry.

An emergency management plan provides the skeleton of a disaster recovery capability implementation. It is the organizational and policy structure that will be referenced to determine whether and by whom the disaster recovery plan will be invoked and who will do what when. Development of the emergency management plan (see Figure 9–1) requires the disaster recovery coordinator to

1. Define recovery teams and their missions.
2. Work with business and technology managers to staff the teams and to develop mechanisms for their notification and activation in an emergency.

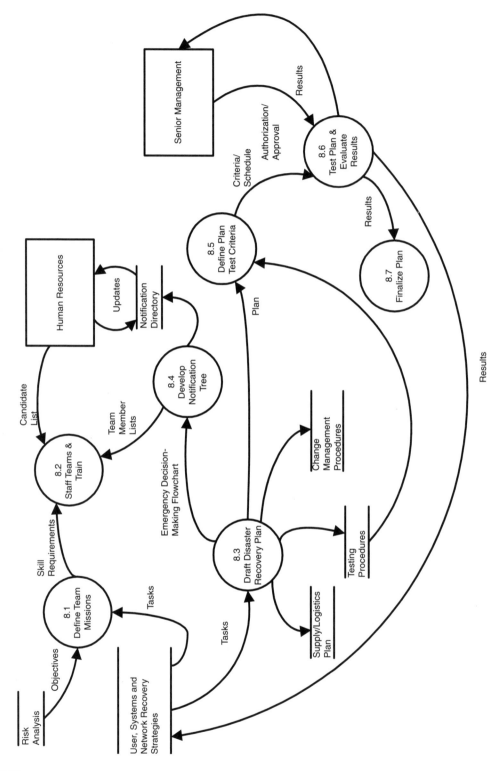

Figure 9–1 Developing an emergency management plan.

3. Develop timelines and flowcharts identifying the sequence of and interrelationships between various disaster recovery tasks—in short, draft the disaster recovery plan document itself.

The third activity, developing procedural flowcharts, often poses the greatest problem to novice DR coordinators for a number of reasons. First, most coordinators have never directly experienced a company disaster. Many endeavor to compensate for this lack of direct experience through detailed description. They try to predict and chart every conceivable decision point and write procedures that spell out too rigidly what each recovery team member will do.

An overly detailed approach ignores the realities of plan implementation. In an actual crisis, flowcharts purporting to map crisis decision making on a step-by-step, thought-by-thought basis are often set to one side. This fact underscores the point that there is no script for the frantic, urgent, and imperfect world of disaster recovery.

In other cases, novice planners may seek to compensate for a lack of direct experience by understating emergency management requirements. The flowcharts they develop embrace a view of crisis management as a mere extension of normal management practices. Little thought is given to how the extraordinary impact of a disaster will affect managers as they perform their recovery duties.

Between these extremes of excess and defect, there is a workable medium: a plan that is sufficiently detailed to guide decision making without dictating it—a plan that provides, at a glance, a holistic appreciation of what is to be done and where efforts stand at any given point in the recovery process. Experience dictates that, in the absence of such a plan, the coordination of strategies for systems, network, and end user recovery can be an even more difficult task.

Without an emergency management plan that provides for top-down direction and coordination of recovery tasks, inefficiencies can result that will extend the length of downtime following a disruption of normal business processes. If the business is out of operation for too long, regardless of the integrity of plan components, the plan itself may be ineffective in supporting business recovery.

Thus, coordinators need to develop an emergency management plan that will formalize certain aspects of the management process and provide guidance for managing situations that cannot be anticipated prior to a disaster. Such a plan is less than a script for emergency management from which actors dare not stray, but it is also more than a collection of platitudes.

The following discussion aims to clarify emergency management planning by detailing its several dimensions and providing simplified examples of some of its typical components. Note that the flowcharts offered here are for illustration only. The decision-making processes developed by a DR coordinator will need to fit the specific strategies that have been developed for corporate business processes and their IT infrastructure supports.

As depicted in Figure 9–1, the activities comprising this effort include the development of test criteria and the performance of plan testing. A more detailed discussion of testing is reserved for a later chapter.

One final point deserves mention before proceeding with this discussion. Both practical and philosophical, it is simply this: Too much of the writing surrounding DR planning concerns itself with the plan document. DR planning projects often, and incorrectly, take as their primary objective the creation of a paper or electronic document. Among business people and IT professionals alike, the DR planning effort is often reduced to a simple objective of creating a paper volume that will pass muster with auditors and examiners.

While documentation is important and good organization is always a plus when addressing any complex subject, DR planning is less about building a paper document than creating a demonstrable capability for ensuring business continuity in the face of unplanned interruptions. Clearly, strategies need to be documented together with the options that were evaluated and the rationale for their selection, in order to satisfy auditors and others who are interested in the planning process. The emergency management plan is a particularly important component of the plan document because it provides a high-level roadmap for the implementation of the DR capability. However, the primary purpose of DR planning is ultimately the preparation of corporate personnel to respond rationally to the great irrationality of a disaster.

DESIGNATING TEAMS

One of the first steps in emergency management planning is to identify where personnel resources will be needed in order to implement the strategies that have been developed for business recovery. At this stage, the task is not to assign specific individuals to specific teams. Team assignments will be discussed in greater detail later this chapter. For now, the objective is to identify the roles and missions of teams themselves.

Teams should be created to support a critical recovery process—defined as a set of tasks for achieving a plan objective. With well-organized plans, an overview of recovery processes, organized as a time line or consolidated flowchart, should be the first item of information presented to the reader. The rationale for this is simple: Such a diagram provides a snapshot of the recovery process as a whole, which then provides links to the compilations of procedures associated with specific system, user, and network recovery strategies.

In a typical user-friendly plan document there is usually a section devoted to each of the following processes.

SECTION 1. Emergency Action Processes—procedures for reacting to crises, ranging from fire suppression activation procedures to emergency evacuation procedures.

SECTION 2. Notification Processes—procedures for notifying relevant managers in the event of a disaster. A contact list of home and emergency telephone numbers is typically provided. This section may also include processes for setting up an emergency operations center (EOC) that will subsequently be used to coordinate additional recovery activities.

SECTION 3. Disaster Declaration Processes—instructions pertaining to the assessment of damage following a disaster, criteria for determining whether the situation is a disaster, and procedures for declaring a disaster and invoking the plan.

SECTION 4. Systems Recovery Processes—procedures to be followed to restore critical and vital applications at emergency service levels within a specified timeframe in accordance with the systems recovery strategy defined in the plan. Separate procedures may be established for centralized and distributed systems-based application recovery.

SECTION 5. Network Recovery Processes—procedures to reinstate voice and data communications at emergency service levels within a specified timeframe in accordance with the network recovery strategy defined in the plan.

SECTION 6. User Recovery Processes—procedures for recovering critical and vital user functions within a specified timeframe in accordance with planned strategy.

SECTION 7. Salvage Operations Processes—procedures for salvaging facilities, records and hardware, often including the filing of insurance claims and the determination of the feasibility of reoccupying the disaster site.

SECTION 8. Relocation Processes—procedures for relocating emergency operations (system, network, and user) to the original or a new facility, and the restoration of normal service levels.

The above is a generic example. Plan sectioning may vary substantially from one company to the next. For example, a company may have a set of processes designed to bring Internet-based e-business operations back on line, or it may have a separate set of processes for activating an emergency operations center. In some cases, companies assign different names to the processes shown here or adopt recovery strategies other than those described here (for example, end user recovery via work-at-home telecommuting rather than a new end user hard site). The point of this illustration is to provide a stepping-off point for readers of this book who will be developing their own plans.

When viewed from the perspective above, one begins to see that the disaster recovery project actually consists of three distinct projects. The procedures in sections 1–3 pertain to an evacuation project; sections 4–7, to a business recovery or business resumption project; and section 8 to a relocation or reentry project. Teams are designated to fulfill the functional requirements of each project.

COMMON EVACUATION PROJECT FUNCTIONS AND TEAMS

What are the functional requirements of the evacuation project? Basically, there are three. First, the emergency must be met with an appropriate response. Responses range from use of an extinguisher to suppress a small fire, to performing last-minute backups and evacuating hardware in the hours before a hurricane, to evacuating personnel in a bomb threat.

Another function of the evacuation project involves the preliminary assessment of damage caused by the interruption event and the determination of whether disaster declaration criteria have been met. If DR planning has determined that 24 hours is the maximum length of time that the company can be without critical or vital business operations, this may serve as the primary criterion for declaring a disaster. If the critical business functions will likely be unavailable for more than 24 hours, it may be necessary to declare a disaster and activate the plan. However, to make this determination, event impact will need to be accurately assessed and realistic recovery timeframes estimated.

A third function in the evacuation project is to declare a disaster and invoke the plan. The plan may need to be activated in whole or in part, since a data center disaster may not affect user facilities, or a telecommunications switchroom fire may leave both key servers and user work areas intact.

Activating the disaster recovery plan also entails certain risks from a public relations standpoint. Al Czarnecki, APR, who helms a Canadian PR firm specializing in crisis communications, recommends that the items identified in Table 9-1 be part of any organization's crisis communications readiness checklist.

Some companies designate "crisis communications center activation"—establishing a central point for handling communications with the media and other interested parties—as a separate function of the evacuation project. Experience has shown that implementing an effective vehicle for crisis communications as early as possible in a disaster can make the difference between a hostile or a supportive response from corporate shareholders, business partners, and customers.

As a rule, however, a crisis communications center should be established away from a company's emergency operations center (EOC), which is often used to control actual recovery activities, and from other recovery sites. EOCs, hot sites, end user recovery centers, and the like are not appropriate venues for the media—particularly in the early stages of recovery. Their operations are sensitive to disruption. Plus, observation of recovery efforts by untrained media personnel may result in a misapprehension of the progress of the recovery effort. The object is to avoid the communication of erroneous information to those who might have an interest in the company.

This above list of functions associated with evacuation is not exhaustive and there may be others that are specific to a given company. However, to fulfill the three basic requirements for evacuation, the following teams may be developed.

Emergency Action Teams

Sudden emergencies rarely lend themselves to team efforts. However, in some companies, there are designated "fire wardens" and "bucket crews" whose function is to deal with fires. Emergency action teams are trained in their functions and drill regularly. They may handle the evacuation of personnel or provide informational support to local fire fighting officials, explaining security systems or structural features of the facility.

Table 9-1   Crisis Communications Checklist

These ten items should be in place PRIOR to a crisis situation. This is of great help in maintaining poise and being able to concentrate on your top priority, the crisis response plan.

Public relations policy and procedures	A statement of mandate, values, program, leadership.
Crisis communications action plan	Key people, roles, action sequences, scenarios.
"Big Picture" information piece on your organization	This could be your annual report.
"Window" information piece on every major program	Content and being up-to-date is most important. Can be kept as text files and printed on special masthead.
Reference files on potential crisis situations	Minutes, reports, clippings—indexed and portable.
Key person list	Work and home phone numbers, one-page job summary and one-page bio—board, senior management, senior person at every physical location—indexed and portable.
Designated spokesperson(s)	Establish default assignments prior to a crisis. Arrange for everyone to have some public speaking experience. These people and your public relations counsel should know each other.
Designated media coordination	This function should be established as credible and helpful with BOTH your staff and the media prior to a crisis. Trust is an outstanding asset in the midst of mayhem.
Media directory or detailed list	[Commercial Media Contact Database] or your own contact database. You should have a concise list of the major media and your public relations counsel at home with your key spokespeople.
Media contact log	You can have a dozen or more newspapers and radio and television stations on the go at one time. Keep a separate tracking sheet for every journalist/story. Know who contacted you, when, about what, how to contact them, what their deadline is, what you promised, who you've delegated to, when they're due to get back to you, whether you need to follow up.

Source: Al Czarnecki Communications, Toronto, Ontario, Canada. http://www.alczarnecki.com.

In most cases, the emergency response function is provided by individuals rather than teams. A night operator may report a fire, then evacuate himself or herself from the danger area. A late-working employee, confronting a water leakage alarm, might perform emergency program shutdowns, power down electrical equipment, and notify management. Detection of a computer virus might originate in an end user work area, with the desktop operator reporting the situation per a standard operating procedure to a department head or help desk.

These individual responses can be expected only if reaction procedures are developed and employees are trained to perform them.

The point is that response may be a function that does not require a team (except in the sense that every employee is a member of the team). Effective response may be provided by an individual, or it may be automatic, as with a fire suppression system. Indeed, in some cases, there may be no immediate action or response available for a sudden emergency.

Besides sudden emergencies, companies are also subject to phased disasters. Phased disasters are disaster potentials that are known well enough in advance to allow for the implementation of planned response procedures.

One example of a phased disaster scenario, familiar to businesses near the coastlines of North America, is the hurricane or typhoon. Early warnings of a potential storm landfall (or associated tidal surges, tornadoes, etc.) may be issued well in advance of an actual disaster. Procedures can be developed as part of the disaster recovery plan to make the best use of this advance warning.

Reaction to a phased-disaster scenario may include such tasks as the evacuation of backup hardware and supplies, last-minute data backup, notification of hot site and off-site storage vendors, and advance notification of personnel about recovery site relocation. Emergency action teams can be formed to provide these functions, or the functions can be performed at the direction of company managers without the formal designation of teams.

Damage Assessment Team

The second function of the evacuation project is to estimate the extent of damage following the disaster. The team providing this function should be comprised of individuals who are qualified to assess damage and estimate the time required to recover operations at the affected site. Their reports will likely trigger the decision to activate the recovery plan.

This team should include persons who are skilled in the use of testing equipment, knowledgeable about systems and networks, and trained in applicable safety regulations and procedures. The team's product is a report identifying possible causes of the disaster and, more importantly, its impact in damage and predictable downtime.

Emergency Management Team

One team that is common to nearly all disaster recovery plans is an Emergency Management Team. This is the group that will coordinate the activities of all other recovery teams and that will provide a key decision-making role. In the context of the evacuation project, the Emergency Management Team receives the report of the damage assessment team and makes the decision to activate the plan, in part or in toto.

Other functions of the Emergency Management Team in the evacuation project may include arranging the finance of the recovery, documenting losses and damages for insurance purposes, handling health and legal matters evolving from the disaster, and activating a crisis communications mechanism tasked with handling public relations and media inquiries.

If system recovery or end user recovery facilities have not been defined in the plan, the Emergency Management Team may also need to undertake the mission of finding facilities on the fly from which to operate. An additional set of teams would then need to work in a coordinated way to ensure that the sites are equipped and ready for work within the shortest possible amount of time.

In short, the roles of the Emergency Management Team need to be defined in the plan. In some cases, the plan must go so far as to assign specific functions to specific members of the team.

COMMON RECOVERY PROJECT FUNCTIONS AND TEAMS

The functions of the evacuation project define the missions, skill requirements, authority requirements, and activities of the teams that will be active in performing project tasks. The same is true of the recovery project whose basic functions may include the following:

- *Retrieving critical and vital data from off-site storage.* Off-site backups may have to be obtained from off-site storage, if the company has contracted for this service, and shipped to the systems, network, and user recovery facilities.
- *Installing and testing host operating systems software and environmental configurations at the systems recovery site (hot site, cold site, service bureau, etc.).* Depending on the recovery strategy that has been de-

veloped, a number of tasks will have to be performed in order to recover critical system operations. Restoration of host environments—including their security and management components—is usually a component of any strategy. This must be done before applications can be recovered.

- *Application restoration and testing.* This must be undertaken to ensure that applications required by mission-critical business processes are available to end users once network connections are reestablished. Performance service levels should be baselined and monitored on an ongoing basis once applications begin to be used in emergency mode.

- *Identifying, purchasing, and installing hardware at the system recovery site.* If a system recovery option has been selected that does not provide access to installed hardware, another recovery function may be to locate a supply of equipment, lease or purchase that supply, arrange its delivery to the systems recovery site, and install it.

- *Operating from the system recovery site.* System operations tasks, including host administration, job management and accounting, data transfers, storage management, help desk operations, and other system tasks need to be provided on an ongoing basis once systems, networks, and end users are reconnected. The objective of system recovery, after all, is not simply to restore systems, but to operate them over the duration of the disaster to support critical business processes.

- *Rerouting network communications traffic.* Network recovery is another typical function of a disaster recovery plan. Rerouting voice and data communications links to the user recovery site and system recovery site may be more or less complicated depending on the strategies selected. As with systems recovery, additional functions may include the acquisition and installation of new hardware as well as communications device programming and software installation. Security and quality of service (QOS) must also be implemented and baselined, then monitored throughout the recovery period.

- *Reestablishing network links to external entities.* Related to the rerouting function above is the reestablishment of data communications between the user recovery site and system recovery site and external entities such as branch offices, suppliers, and others. This function should be provided as a strategy within the recovery plan and may include the lease or purchase of communications devices and public or private network services.

- *Transporting users to recovery facility.* Depending on the user recovery strategy that has been developed, it may be necessary to provide transportation and housing for employees at the user recovery facility. If prior arrangements have not been made for a user facility, a preliminary function may be to locate a suitable workplace and equip it with the basic furniture, communications capabilities, workstations, and so on required. Another preliminary step may be to notify all employees of the new work location, transportation schedules, and emergency accommodations that will be provided.

- *Reconstructing databases.* If data is lost in the disaster, it may be necessary to restore or reconstruct production databases prior to application use. Typically, this is done by an end user team using available documents. In addition to company personnel, outside contractors may be brought in to aid in the data entry effort. The training and oversight of these personnel may also be viewed as a recovery function.

- *Sourcing supplies.* Yet another function of the recovery project involves the requisition, delivery, and distribution of office supplies and other items, such as computer paper and printed forms, needed to perform useful work. Vendors must be contacted, logistics coordinated, costs and inventory monitored, reorder points established, and so on.

- *Coordinating systems use and employee work schedules.* To utilize minimum system configurations efficiently, it may be necessary to schedule system use rather tightly. The scheduling of user input, processing, and output periods may be necessary, and implementing a regimen of shift work is not uncommon.

It is self-evident that sustaining operations under emergency operating conditions requires considerable supervisory skill. Moreover, preventing and resolving technical and operational problems before they reach disastrous proportions are vital for business recovery.

The above list, which is partial at best, suggests the multiplicity of functions that may be undertaken during the recovery project. In addition, the emergency management team has a continuing role to play—coordinating team efforts, financing the recovery project, and maintaining a focal point for business planning and public information. However, to provide the functions required for the recovery of critical operations the following teams may also be created.

Off-site Storage Team

This team obtains, packages, and ships media and records required for recovery to the end user and system recovery facilities. It may also have an ongoing role of establishing and overseeing an off-site storage schedule for information created during operations at the recovery sites. The off-site storage team may also assist in records salvage and storage efforts as described below.

Software Team

Some companies designate a special team whose mission is to restore host systems, load and test operating system software, and monitor and resolve system-level problems when they arise.

Applications Team

The applications team, together with the software team and emergency operations team (see following section), travels to the system (and end user) recovery site and restores applications programs on backup host systems. The complexities in restoring n-tier client/server and consolidated mainframe applications should be reduced by advanced testing of new configurations. As the recovery progresses, this team may have the responsibility for monitoring application performance, security, and integrity.

Emergency Operations Team

The Emergency Operations Team may consist of shift operators and a shift supervisor who will reside at the systems recovery site and manage system operations during the entirety of the disaster and recovery projects. It may also be called upon to coordinate hardware installation if a hot site or other equipment-ready facility has not been designated as the recovery center.

Network Recovery Team

This team is responsible for rerouting wide area voice and data communications traffic and reestablishing host network control and access at the system and end user recovery sites. This team provides ongoing support for data communications and oversees security and communications integrity as well as network performance and quality of service.

Communications Team

This team travels to the user recovery site where it works in conjunction with the remote network recovery team to establish a user/system internetwork. The Communications Team may also be responsible for soliciting and installing communications hardware at the user recovery site and working with LEC COs, Internet Service Providers (ISPs), and carriers or value-added network providers to ensure last-mile services and remote access. The team may also have responsibility for reestablishing local area network (LAN) services within the user recovery facility itself.

Transportation Team

This team, which may also serve as a Facilities Team to locate a user recovery site if one has not been predetermined, is responsible for coordinating the transport of company employees to a distant user recovery site. Transportation may also assist in contacting employees to inform them of new work locations and schedules and arranging employee lodgings.

User Hardware Team

In addition to locating and coordinating the delivery and installation of user workstations, printers, photocopiers, and other necessary equipment, this team may also support the communications team, and ultimately the hardware salvage team in their functions.

Data Preparation and Records Team

This team updates the applications database, using workstations installed at the user recovery site or at some vendor facility. The team may oversee contract operators and support records salvage teams in acquiring primary documents and other input information sources.

Administrative Support

This team may provide clerical support to the other teams and serve as a message center for the user recovery site. Administrative support personnel may also be tasked with rerouting ground mail and overnight delivery services to new work locations. Accounting and payroll functions as well as ongoing facility management issues may also be controlled by this team.

Supplies Team

The supplies team supports the efforts of the user hardware team and coordinates logistics for an ongoing supply of necessary office and computer supplies.

Some of the teams identified above may, in actuality, perform functions that can be handled by one person. Again, the complexity of the disaster recovery plan for a specific business will determine whether functions require a team, or a single properly trained individual. Conversely, coordinators may find that additional teams are needed or that some of the listed teams need to be combined into a larger conglomerate. Business recovery needs will dictate these adjustments.

Teams are not static entities and they may dissolve after performing their function. Teams may also change and their members may be shifted to other responsibilities as the recovery project gives way to the relocation or reentry project.

RELOCATION AND REENTRY PROJECT FUNCTIONS

Relocation or reentry refers to the two options that may confront a business following a disaster. If the original facility is salvageable, it may be possible to reenter it once cleanup and refit activities are completed. If the facilities are uninhabitable, or prohibitively expensive to reconstruct, the business may choose to relocate to new quarters. In either case, there is usually an interest in salvaging whatever corporate assets can be salvaged, especially when expensive hardware, critical documents not off-site, and other company assets are involved.

Functions commonly associated with the relocation or reentry project include:

- *Facility and hardware salvage.* This function of the relocation and reentry project is to make a more detailed assessment of the damage to facilities and equipment than was performed immediately after the interruption event. The purpose of this assessment is twofold. First, it will provide the emergency management team with the information it requires to determine whether planning should be directed toward reconstruction or relocation; second, it will provide a basis for certain insurance claims that may provide an important funding component for recovery activities.

  If salvage is determined to be economically desirable, salvage operations may be undertaken concurrently with recovery project activities. As teams complete recovery tasks, they may be reassigned to aid in salvage operations.

If facilities are not salvageable, teams may be directed to the task of identifying comparable facilities and preparing them for company occupancy.

- *Records salvage.* Important paper records and documents, damaged by smoke and water, require immediate attention if they are to be salvaged. They need to be cleaned of visible debris, logged and packed, and then moved to a cold storage environment to forestall loss to fungi and mold. Following pack-out and cold storage, they may be recovered through a vacuum freeze-drying process available through records reclamation vendors. Excellent publications are available from federal and private sources describing all facets of this process that can produce amazing results. More discussion follows in this topic later in this chapter.

- *Relocation.* Many of the same activities that were involved in the recovery of systems, networks, and users immediately following a disaster may be repeated for the purposes of relocating systems, communications traffic, and user operations to the new or restored business facility.

- *Transition to normal service levels.* The final function of disaster recovery is to provide a smooth transition from emergency service levels to normal service levels. Although important to full recovery, this function is not generally documented in detail within a disaster recovery plan. It is typically a function of planning undertaken following successful recovery and while salvage or site preparation activities are underway.

To provide these functions, many of the teams previously defined are reassigned to relocation or reentry project duties. However, there are a few specially trained teams, such as a facilities salvage team, hardware salvage team, and records salvage team, that may perform critical tasks depending on the nature and impact of the disaster and the consequent decisions reached by the emergency management team.

STAFFING TEAMS

Once teams are defined by the disaster recovery coordinator, it is important that their tasks be clearly documented in written procedures. If teams are organized by recovery functions, they need to understand in detail only those procedures that pertain to their functions. Thus, they will be trained to perform only the procedures in one section of the well-written plan.

However, someone in the team, such as a team leader, must know how the team's work affects and is affected by other teams. A team leader may also be given the responsibility of reporting on the progress of tasks that his or her team has been assigned and maintaining records of costs associated with team activities.

Staffing teams, then, requires the identification of personnel who have the prerequisite skills and knowledge to perform the technical tasks that are assigned them. Moreover, it is vital to select one person—a team leader (and an alternate)—who has the supervisory and communications skills required to manage team activities effectively.

Staffing efficient teams is a challenge for the disaster recovery coordinator. The coordinator can develop a fairly comprehensive list of skills and knowledge needed for each team. However, the fact that team members possess the listed requirements may offer little indication of how the team will perform in an emergency. The skills and knowledge possessed by a team member cannot guarantee that the person will remain calm in an emergency, think creatively, or handle stress. In the end, team selection may come down to judgment calls rendered with the support of business unit/departmental managers and human resources personnel.

The experience of several companies that have recovered from disasters offers little guidance about the best method of selecting team members and team leaders. For this reason, the following points should be considered in establishing evaluative criteria rather than blueprints for selecting individuals.

Worker Performance

An employee's performance record may not be the best criterion on which to judge suitability for team membership or leadership. That the employee is not punctual, or, conversely, that he or she always comes to work early and stays late may be meaningless in the context of recovery. The same is true of a worker's motivation and attitude. Disasters can reveal surprises about personal mettle.

There are, however, some important dimensions to work performance that should not be ignored. A worker who requires a considerable amount of structure and supervision is probably not the best candidate for a leadership position where some creativity and self-direction are desirable. Also, a worker who is technically astute, but who cannot communicate ideas, is probably a poor choice for leadership in a functional area requiring these characteristics. Similarly, the optimal team leader is seldom an employee who has great difficulty in reaching decisions or reasoning to conclusion in normal operational environments.

The difference between the ideal team leader and the marginal candidate is the difference between a troubleshooter and a technician. The troubleshooter has added analytical thinking to technical skills. Teams need both technicians and troubleshooters, but the troubleshooter is the person who should lead the team.

Worker Tenure

Tenure is another factor that may be considered in staffing teams. Tenured workers may understand the business better than novices. They may have a greater stake in business survival (higher salary, well-developed pension, etc.). They may also command greater respect from fellow, less-senior employees.

On the other hand, tenured workers may lack the exposure to alternatives that would be the forte of a worker who may be new to the company, but not the workplace generally.

Since some team leaders will necessarily be privy to security information (passwords, filenames, etc.), tenure may also be a consideration in this regard. While there is no correlation between tenure and trustworthiness, a more senior employee is often perceived as a better security risk than a new hire.

Worker Marital Status

Despite studies performed by the Defense Department, there is little data to establish that a married worker will handle responsibilities in an emergency any better or worse than an unmarried one. However, many coordinators still assert that married persons are less reliable due to a distraction factor. In the event of a regional disaster, so the argument goes, the married employee is going to be more worried about the well-being of his/her family than about the company. This distraction could affect performance.

This argument has little merit as even unmarried persons can have parents, siblings, or significant others to distract them. In acknowledgment of this fact, some companies have gone so far as to have their facilities approved for use as evacuation shelters. In the event of a regional cataclysm such as a hurricane or earthquake, employees and their families and friends are urged to utilize the shelter. Thus, recovery team personnel will know that their relatives and friends (though not necessarily their property) are safe as they proceed in their recovery tasks.

Residence of Recovery Personnel

One factor that may be important in the consideration of candidates for recovery teams is the location of their homes in relation to the company offices. Employees who must travel two hours (in good traffic) to reach the workplace may be less suitable for critical disaster recovery roles than those who reside in nearer proximity to the company.

Even when travel time is not an issue, there may be compelling reasons to select employees who are located in the general vicinity of the facility. In some disaster scenarios, including natural disasters and civil disturbances, there may be restrictions imposed on movement into and out of the affected region or area. The author's personal experience provides one example, which has been repeated many times in many locations since.

Following the passage of Hurricane Elena in September 1985, along the shores of southwestern Florida, the police cordoned off Pinellas County. Until damage could be assessed, no one from neighboring Hillsborough County was allowed in or out of Pinellas County. Following cessation of disaster conditions, many hours passed during which only those who could *prove residence* in the county to which they wished to travel were allowed into that county. Thus, employees who resided in one county were not permitted to travel to their workplace in the neighboring country for a protracted period of time. Had significant storm damage been sustained by companies in the Tampa Bay area, it is doubtful that many could have activated their disaster recovery plans very effectively.[1]

The above considerations illustrate that there is a lack of hard, experiential data available to disaster recovery coordinators to guide them in team staffing. Coordinators may find themselves completely dependent upon the judgment of the business unit/departmental managers whose aegis extends over the teams and functions in question. Since there are no objective grounds for challenging department management decisions, the only hedge that the coordinator may have against seemingly poor choices is a procedural one.

Coordinators should strive to portray the role of team leader or member as nonglamorous, even clerical. This may be accomplished by requiring team leaders to be responsible for maintaining the integrity of "their" section of the disaster recovery plan according to a plan maintenance schedule. It should also be made clear that plan testing may interfere with off-work activities of those who are designated to play recovery roles. For some, the added responsibility and interference in their personal lives will dissuade them from lobbying for the position of team leader.

If a seemingly inappropriate selection of team leader is made, regardless of the above procedural checks, another hedge against incompetence is to train an alternate person to lead the team if the primary candidate is unavailable. The selection of an alternate may be up to the coordinator if the department manager is appeased by his or her selection of the primary team leader. Where this is not the case, and the coordinator's confidence in both primary and alternate team leaders is low, all team members may need to be cross-trained in recovery team operation and management.

This is not intended to imply that business managers will always make bad choices about team leaders and members. In most cases, not only will the managers identify appropriate candidates, but their insights will be of considerable value to the coordinator, who is not in a position to evaluate the personal qualifications of each and every company employee. As a control against team incompetence, teams can be trained and tested in detailed procedures until the procedures become routine.

DEVELOPING A NOTIFICATION DIRECTORY

Once recovery teams have been staffed, the coordinator will have most of the information needed to develop a notification directory of persons to be notified in the event of a disaster. Besides team members and company employees, phone lists may include the numbers for representatives of equipment and software vendors, contacts within companies that have been designated to provide supplies and equipment, contact persons at recovery facilities (including hot site representatives, representatives of predefined network communications rerouting services, etc.), and insurance company agents.

Primary and emergency telephone numbers for each critical contact person should be compiled and kept in the back matter of the disaster recovery plan. In the case of company employees who will be called on to staff the user recovery facility (other than teams), the human resources or personnel department is often a good resource for compiling a telephone directory and keeping it up-to-date and off-site.

In conjunction with the directory, many disaster recovery planners develop a notification schema or "tree" to indicate who will be responsible for contacting whom. Sometimes the responsibility for contacting team members is vested in the team leader (and alternate). The team leader or his or her designee may also have responsibility for notifying vendor representatives whose roles relate directly to the team's area of recovery responsibility.

Other branches of the notification tree may provide for the notification of company personnel by a team designated to provide this function. Employees will need to know where and when to report for work once a user recovery facility has been prepared and systems and networks have been restored.

Notification trees may also indicate *triggers,* or chronological points, at which a branch of the notification tree is to be activated and contacts on the branch notified of some impending activity or event. A trigger in a notification tree may be the declaration of a "voluntary evacuation order" in a hurricane scenario. Such orders are usually issued one to three hours in advance of a mandatory evacuation order and may be used as a trigger not only for notification trees, but also for activation of other plan components (emergency system and data backups, safe power down of hardware, evacuation of redundant hardware, etc.).

The notification tree, with its carefully defined branches and triggers, is one of several tools that may help emergency managers make order out of chaos following a disaster. Communication is essential for command and control in a disaster situation. Communication of impending disaster conditions can help reduce the impact of the disaster when it occurs, and communication about the extent of damage can be used to determine whether the disaster recovery plan must be invoked and whether to activate it in whole or in part. Finally, communication between recovery teams and emergency managers—regarding the progress of recovery activity, new strategies and directions, decisions and plans, and so on—will determine how effectively business resumption may be realized. Table 9–2 summarizes command, control, and communications factors as they relate to the management of the three projects within disaster recovery: evacuation, recovery, and relocation or reentry.

Table 9–2   Command, Control, and Communications in Emergency Management

Phase I Evacuation	Phase II Recovery	Phase III Relocation/Re-entry
Command	*Command*	*Command*
Emergency Response: On-site personnel react to situation in accorance with emergency action procedures. Emergency Management Team assesses impact, invokes plan. **Phased Emergency Response** Emergency Management Team decides when to take action. Emergency Management Team asesses diaster impact; invokes plan.	Command of Recovery Phase activities vested in Emergency Management Team supported by subordinate recovery team leaders.	Relocation to the evacuated or new permanent operating site will require management oversight and coordination; lines of reporting established by the disaster recovery plan will continue until systems and networks are stabilized and normal service levels are reestablished.
Control	*Control*	*Control*
Emergency Response: Minimal control over employee reaction to crisis; routine drills in emergency action procedures will help to ensure adherence to procedures. **Phased Emergency Response:** Emergency Management Team exercises direct control over last-minute preparations and evacuation of personnel, equipment, and supplies. Management controls disaster declaration.	Control of Recovery achieved through management of teams performing tested procedures. Service level monitoring will be used to aid the Emergency Management Team in managing emergency operations.	Control of relocation/reentry activities accomplished through management channels established by the disaster recovery plan; the Emergency Management Team will control the acquisition and preparation of the salvaged/new facility, direct facility preparation teams, and oversee the relocation of systems and networks; the transition from emergency to normal service levels will be controlled in accordance with a management plan.

(continued)

Phase I Evacuation	Phase II Recovery	Phase III Relocation/Re-entry
Communication	*Communication*	*Communication*

Communication

Emergency Response:

Initial communications conditions uncertain; possible difficulties in locating authorized Emergency Management Team member; possible difficulties in accessing site to perform evaluation; potential for miscommunication of damage assessment if Emergency Management Team unavailable for site inspection.

Disaster definition and inspection criteria may aid in prevention of unwarranted disaster declarations.

Phased Emergency Response:

Generally favorable communcations conditions may exist at outset of disaster. However, damage assessment may be delayed.

Evaluation of damage and communication of situation reports enhanced if Emergency Management Team is present.

Communications with media regarding details of disaster controlled through Crisis Communications function.

Communication

Voice and data network restoration is a priority; until networks are restored, communication between Emergency Management Team and other operational teams may be impaired. Recovery activities are thus conducted according to tested procedures and accomplished within agreed-upon timeframes.

Following network recovery, communications will be normalized, beginning with channels for Emergency Management Team reporting.

Communication with external entities and the media controlled by Crisis Communications functionaries.

Communication

Communication of management plans for preparation and relocation to the salvaged or new operating site are likely to occur within a stabilized communications environment.

Communications with external entities and the media controlled by Crisis Communications functionaries.

CREATING THE EMERGENCY MANAGEMENT FLOWCHART

As stated at the outset, most disaster recovery plans contain an emergency management flowchart that graphically depicts the sequence in which recovery tasks will be undertaken. This flowchart can be of substantial value in helping disaster recovery teams and emergency managers understand the disaster recovery plan as a whole.

The following sample flowcharts are segments of the detailed master flowchart, which can be downloaded from the companion website for this book at HTTP://WWW.DRPLANNING.ORG. To enhance their usefulness to teams, flowchart segments, such as these, may be placed at the front of the sections of the plan to which they pertain.

The diagrams provided here may be less detailed than those that would be developed for an actual recovery plan, but the coordinator should strive in every case to keep the charts he or she develops clear and straightforward. If possible, the coordinator should relate chart symbols to specific plan procedures using a numbering scheme common to both.

EMERGENCY RESPONSE

Figures 9–2 and 9–3 are simplified examples of decision-making flowcharts that may be placed at the front of a plan section treating emergency response.

Figure 9–2 deals with a sudden crisis in which on-site employees may be called upon to take immediate action procedures as outlined in the plan. Since personnel may not have the luxury of time (or presence of mind) to refer to the manual and perform a written procedure, they should be thoroughly trained and drilled in procedures such as interpreting alarms, powering down equipment, initiating security or safety systems, and, of course, evacuating the facility quickly and safely. While these procedures will probably be conducted without reference to a plan document, it is a good idea to document them in a section of the plan both for use as a training aid and as evidence to the auditors that response procedures have been developed and tested.

Following emergency actions, the flowchart indicates that the Emergency Management Team is to be notified. Again, the plan document may not be accessible to the evacuated worker, but all personnel should be provided with contact numbers, possibly on a wallet-sized card, that can be referenced in an emergency. The existence of the card and the

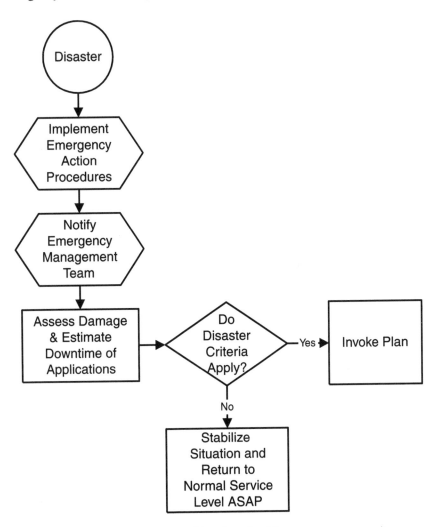

Figure 9–2   Decision-making flowchart (emergency response).

telephone numbers listed on it should be documented in the written plan as well.

The next activity denoted on the chart calls for an assessment of the damage caused by the disaster and an estimate of anticipated downtime or inaccessibility to business-critical applications or their system/network infrastructure. If the facility has to be evacuated, it may not be possible to reenter immediately to assess damage. However, even the "best guess" of fire officials or other emergency officials may be sufficient to determine whether a prolonged business interruption is probable.

Thus, the next symbol indicates that a decision needs to be made whether to activate the disaster recovery plan. If disaster recovery criteria, which should be spelled out in the plan document but are usually common sense considerations (i.e., will downtime exceed 24 hours?), are met, a decision is made to invoke the plan.

If the event does not meet disaster criteria, the situation will be stabilized as soon as possible and operations returned to normal service levels. For example, if the crisis is a power blackout, but power company representatives assure the company emergency management team that power will be restored within eight hours, and this timeframe is acceptable, the emergency management team may decide to ride out the situation and work to restore operations to normal as soon as power is restored.

Figure 9–3 portrays a different type of emergency response: response to a phased emergency. In a phased disaster scenario, the company has advance notification of an imminent crisis. The plan document may contain procedures for bracing for such an event—a hurricane, a labor strike, or even a possible civil disturbance. These emergency procedures may be activated by a "trigger" event such as a warning issued by the National Hurricane Center in Miami, FL, or the Storm Prediction Center in Norman, OK, or on the basis of reports from local TV or radio, police bulletins, or civil voluntary evacuation orders.

Once triggered, planned procedures may include performing last-minute system backups to reduce the amount of "catch up" work that will be required later to restore databases to a current form. Redundant hardware may also be deactivated and evacuated to a designated safe location. The system recovery facility may be placed on alert. Off-site storage facilities may be contacted and teams sent to retrieve stored backups and prepare them for transportation to recovery destinations. Finally, personnel will be evacuated if the threat exceeds safe levels.

If the disaster then occurs, these prophylactic measures should speed the recovery of the company. However, before a disaster is declared, damage will need to be assessed, disaster criteria will need to be applied, and a decision will need to be reached as to whether the plan should be invoked.

Given the variety of possible disasters that can confront a company, the assumption that one or two simplified decision-making flowcharts can cover every contingency is foolish. Whether the disaster is phased or sudden, the decision to invoke the plan rests on human judgment and is subject to all of its foibles. For example, in recent history, a major metals distributor in the Chicago area sustained more than $10 million in hard-

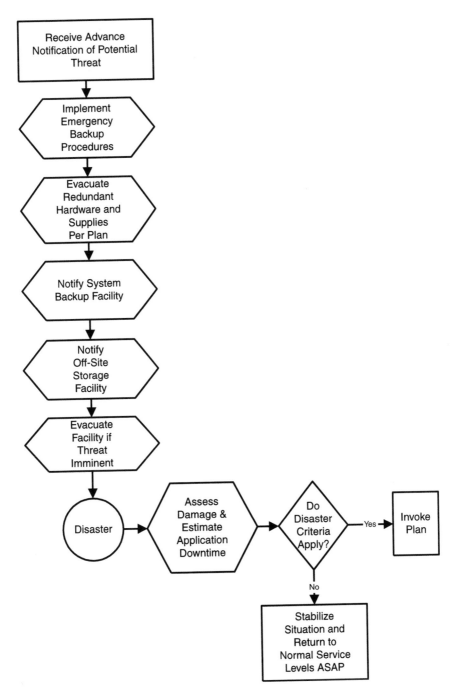

Figure 9–3 Decision-making flowchart (phased disaster scenario).

ware and facility damage (and an incalculable amount in lost revenue) due to flooding. The MIS director reported that he held off on declaring a disaster in the early hours of a torrential downpour, expecting the rain to stop and the water level to fall. Twelve hours (and 10 inches of rain) later the plan was finally invoked. Systems went off-line on Friday and were not restored at a hot site until the following Monday. The company's extensive data communications network was out until Tuesday. Despite his fully tested disaster recovery plan, the director conceded, critical on-line order processing and inventory systems were out of commission for a protracted period—because the plan had not been invoked at the first sign of trouble. On the other hand, added the director proudly, without the plan—although implemented late—the company would never have survived.[2]

The story, one of many with a common theme that have taken place in the last decade, illustrates one of the major flaws with the expectation that emergency management flowcharts will be implemented without delay or modification in an actual disaster. It doesn't fit the facts. However, these charts do provide the means—for testing purposes at least—to "black box" the disaster and superimpose rationality upon a complex, multifaceted, and irrational phenomenon.

SITUATION ASSESSMENT

Once the initial response to a disaster has been made, Figure 9–4 begins the project of recovery from the disaster.

Once the plan is invoked, a number of plan components come into play automatically. As seen in Figure 9–4, recovery teams are notified by the Emergency Management Team. Two teams—responsible for damage assessment and salvage—go directly to the disaster site, if this is possible, to make a more comprehensive evaluation of the situation. Meanwhile, an Emergency Operations Center (EOC) is set up (see below for more information) for use by the Emergency Management Team throughout the duration of the recovery project. The Emergency Management Team—often headed by a senior corporate officer—reviews reports of the Damage Assessment and Salvage teams, determines which parts of the disaster recovery plan must be implemented. If the data center has been rendered unusable, but user work areas and the communications are intact, the decision may be made to implement only the systems recovery section of the plan. If user work areas are untenable, but data centers and networks are

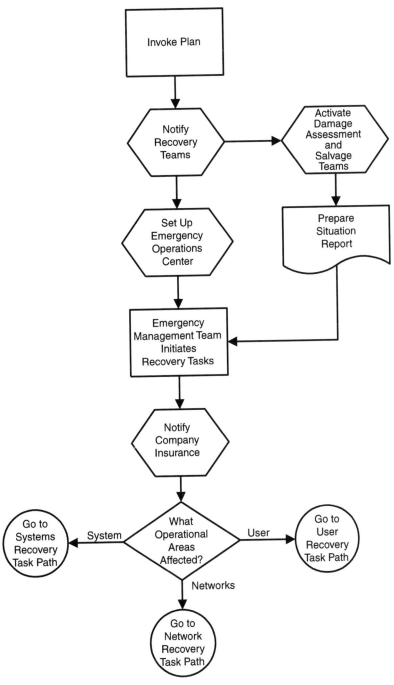

Figure 9–4 Situation assessment and response.

intact, user recovery plans are activated. Plan and team activation are contingent upon the nature and scope of the emergency.

It should be noted that Damage Assessment and Salvage Teams may have some critical tasks to perform. They may tour the facility with electrical contractors and construction vendors to obtain cost and time estimates for repair work. If damage has been done to user areas, there may still be working hardware that can be salvaged, tested, and relocated to the user recovery site. They may also obtain eyewitness accounts from persons who were in or near the facility when the disaster occurred. Finally, an insurance claims adjuster may also need to be part of the Damage Assessment Team in order to facilitate the claims adjustment process.

The disaster recovery plan should indicate, generally, what tasks are to be performed by the recovery teams at the disaster site. Videotape or photographic records may need to be made. If eyewitness accounts are to be gathered, the plan may provide a standard form, possibly developed with the assistance of an attorney, for gathering this information. In addition, hardware testing routines may be summarized in the plan, although it would be wise to have someone on the Salvage team who is thoroughly conversant with the procedures for testing hardware. The plan should also contain safety guidelines to instruct teams in avoiding personal risks.

EMERGENCY OPERATIONS CENTER ACTIVATION

Based on the best information available, the Emergency Management Team decides to activate the disaster recovery plan may be activated in whole or in part. As suggested above, many plans call for the gathering of management personnel at an Emergency Operations Center (EOC), a facility from which they will operate to receive updates and status reports and provide ongoing command, control, and communications functions throughout the emergency operations period.

EOCs are sometimes construed as the equivalent of a NASA command center, the stuff of motion pictures, consisting of a hardened site or bunker equipped with the latest communications and computer technologies used to monitor every aspect of an event from mass media descriptions to stock market ticker tapes to the display screens of network and system monitoring applications. While certain organizations, such as government emergency management organizations, may construct such facilities to provide management capabilities in a disaster, most do not. A number of alternatives exist, including:

- *Facilities Retasked as EOCs.* Some companies select a facility used for other purposes during an normal operations to serve as an EOC in an emergency. They place communications and computer devices in storage at the site that are accessed when needed for an actual recovery or for plan testing. This strategy has the obvious advantages of reduced facilities cost, but may present other problems, including the disruption of normal operations and/or the displacement of end users whenever plan tests need to be conducted. Security issues may also arise if publicly accessible facilities are designated for use as EOCs. Such sites are also of questionable utility in the event that they cannot be accessed by team members in an emergency due to regional disaster impact (roads destroyed, etc.) or to police cordons.

- *Hot-site-based EOCs.* Some vendors of commercial systems recovery facilities are more than happy to provide workspace for corporate executives and Emergency Management Teams for the purpose of managing disaster recovery plan implementations. These sites may be part of the hot site contract and provide an appropriate location for work if management is comfortable with managing the disaster from a remote location (hot sites that are in close geographical proximity to normal work locations are usually regarded as poor choices in systems recovery planning). Should such an EOC option be selected, coordinators need to provide for the relocation of management and Emergency Operations Team members to the remote facility.

- *Mobile EOCs.* An alternative to the facility retasking and hot site-based options is the Mobile EOC—an EOC facility staged on a trailer or other mobile vehicle that can be positioned wherever it is needed. Lynch Diversified Vehicles, self-styled as "the nation's premiere supplier of mobile command/communications vehicles," is one of several vendors offering "special service vehicles" that can be customized to meet the budget and features requirements of a customer (see Figure 9–5). These vehicles have come into common use by civil emergency management organizations including police, fire, and hazard materials management as a means to place command, control, and communications functions at or near the location where they are necessary. A vehicle-based approach has the merits of flexible deployment and nondisruptive testing. It may also serve the needs of an organization whose management prefers to remain around the disaster site during recovery. However, this option can also be expensive and may have limited utility in the event that transportation is constrained by disaster impact or local civil emergency management activity.

Figure 9–5   Special service vehicle used as EOC. (*Source:* LDV/Lynch Diversified Vehicles, Burlington, WI.)

- *Commercial Mobile Facility.* As with end user recovery, many hot site vendors offer mobile trailers that can be tasked for use as Emergency Operations Centers. These offerings have many of the same advantages and constraints of company-owned mobile EOCs but without the acquisition costs. The drawback of this strategy is the timeframe for deployment. Most mobile shell facility vendors promise delivery within 48 hours of notification. DR coordinators need to ascertain whether this timeframe is acceptable or if a more immediate response capability is required.

All of the above options share a common assumption: that Emergency Management Team members will wish to gather in a single location to oversee the response, recovery, and relocation/re-entry phases of the disaster recovery project. This assumption must be questioned rigorously by DR coordinators because it is highly dependent upon corporate culture. In some cases, business managers will defer all recovery tasks to an IT manager or CIO, preferring to focus on their own higher-level tasks at some remote location. In other cases, senior management will wish to have the ability to be on-site as a show of support to workers or to communicate an impression of stability and normalcy to business partners, investors, and others. These factors need to be taken into account when planning the EOC.

An alternative to deploying an EOC hard site is to use a virtual EOC (VEOC). Leveraging the ubiquitous web browser and the public Internet, a secure, Web-based mechanism can be fielded to facilitate command, control, and communications during a recovery effort. The author has deployed similar solutions in the past on behalf of clients and is currently developing a generic version of a virtual EOC for adoption by web-based service providers and vendors of web server appliance products. The value proposition of such a solution is summarized in the paragraphs below, which are abstracted from the author's prospectus for a VEOC:

> The VEOC is essentially a private web site that is activated when a disaster occurs. The domain for the site is preestablished with Internet domain name registration services such as the INTERNIC and is "parked" until its activation is required.
>
> The VEOC can be hosted on a web-server appliance, retrieved from secure off-site storage as a function of plan activation, or it can be an Application Service Provider service customized in advance of use, then stored on a fee-paid basis, until its activation is required.
>
> When activated, the VEOC provides a central point of information about the disaster for company personnel and DR teams. The site is used to disseminate reliable information about the recovery effort, to communicate recovery process status and issues requiring resolution, and to maintain contact with and between recovery teams. The web browser interface provides ubiquitous access for company employees, and features such as chat and email enable near-real-time interaction between management, recovery teams, and corporate personnel as necessary. This approach eliminates the need for predesignated and preequipped EOC facilities, since it can provide a virtual conference facility for all involved in the disaster recovery effort.
>
> As a module of [a larger package of web-based DR planning tools], the VEOC can convert the electronic DR plan into a recovery flowchart and procedural checklist that can be referenced at any time to understand the status of the recovery effort. The VEOC can also be used to capture data on plan tests and to prepare test reports (or reports on actual disaster recovery plan implementations) that capture information about plan efficiency and guide the refinement of the plan. Reports can be appended to the plan document to meet the needs of auditors.
>
> Potential enhancements for this product over time include support for IP telephony and video conferencing.[3]

The decision to deploy an EOC in a building, vehicle, or via the web must be based on an assessment of how management will actually be provided in a disaster situation. Those who will play a role in emergency management need to be personally involved in plan testing so they are familiar with the scope of the recovery effort, the strategies involved, and the decisions they will be required to make.

THE RECOVERY PHASE

Systems

Figures 9–6 and 9–7 depict events in the recovery of systems. In these flowcharts, systems recovery will involve the use of a remotely located commercial hot site. Be aware that the systems recovery strategy will probably already have been initiated if a decision has been made to activate the plan. If, after further examination the original center is found to be inhabitable, the systems recovery plan may advance quickly to the reentry phase.

System Recovery Task Path

In Figure 9–6, the need to activate the systems recovery plan has been acknowledged by the Emergency Management Team, which issues a formal disaster declaration to the hot site. The Systems Recovery Team leader assembles/notifies the teams whose activities must be coordinated to restore both centralized and distributed server hosts that provide mission-critical applications required by key business processes.

An Off-Site Storage Team retrieves backups from the storage facility, crates or otherwise prepares them for transportation, and transports them to the hot site. (This may already have been done in the event of a phased disaster, or it may be unnecessary if the company has chosen a remote tape vaulting or remote mirroring that places the data at the remote recovery facility on an ongoing basis.) The team may also arrange for the pickup of backup media at the remote recovery facility destination and their transportation to the hot site. Once these tasks are completed, the Off-Site Storage Team so reports to the Systems Recovery Team leader.

The Off-Site Storage Team then inventories remaining storage and, if necessary, prepares stored documents, preprinted forms, and other user supplies for transport to the user recovery site. The team will then coordinate new storage arrangements for vital and critical records generated during recovery operations. An off-page connector indicates that the reader should go to the user recovery task path in Figure 9–9 to see additional Off-Site Storage Team tasks.

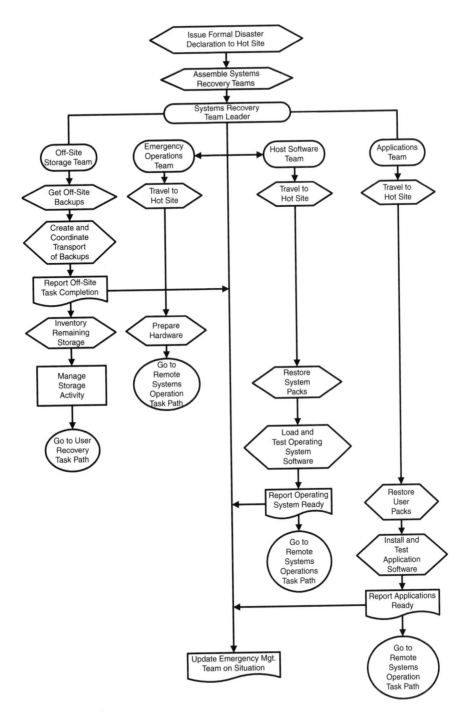

Figure 9–6 Systems recovery task path.

Meanwhile, the Emergency Operations, Software, and Applications Teams travel to the hot site. Once there, the Emergency Operations Team prepares system hardware and the Software Team restores system core datasets (or "packs") from tape, loads host operating system software, and reports task completion to the Systems Recovery Team leader. The Applications Team restores user data, installs and tests application software, reports task completion to the team leader. Off-page connectors direct the reader to go to the remote systems operations task path in Figure 9–7. With systems prepared for operation, the Systems Recovery Team leader so reports to the Emergency Management Team.

The above is a simplification intended to show the manner in which an emergency management flowchart depicts the interrelationships between tasks and provides reporting procedures. In actuality, a number of additional steps may be required.

For example, the complexity of a client/server platform restoral may be much greater than what is depicted here. Client/server platforms that must be recovered on a one-to-one basis (with respect to platforms used in the production environment) often entail more than host operating system and application software installation from backups. Middleware must also be installed in many cases. Dynamic directories that identify and link messaging nodes in the multi-tier platform may need to be updated with new nodal identifiers. Security, performance measurement, and system/application monitoring resources need to be deployed and configured. It is also a good idea to perform workload simulations and to measure outputs to ensure that client/server configurations produce predictable results and acceptable service levels.

In general, a combination of the restoral requirements for an application and the advanced provisions made in DR planning will dictate the number and complexity of tasks involved in any restoral. Indeed, as noted previously, team designations are generally linked to such considerations as task complexity and recovery timeframe requirements.

Regardless of the complexity and number of tasks involved, each task should be thoroughly documented in the disaster recovery plan, linked by some sort of numbering scheme to the emergency management flowchart, and regularly tested at the hot site. Also, in point of fact, systems are not restored until databases are current, communications have been reestablished with users and data communicators, and users are on the system performing work. Network and user recovery tasks occur concurrently with systems recovery, as shown in the master flowchart available on the companion website to this book. (See HTTP://WWW.DR PLANNING.ORG.)

Remote Systems Operation Task Path

In some disaster recovery plans, procedures for operating applications from a remote hot site are documented only in broad sweeping strokes. However, a better approach is to detail the tasks and responsibilities for application and host performance management and to implement a program of service level accounting that will keep the Emergency Management Team apprised of how well business process needs are being met. Specific attention should also be paid to cost accounting and reporting. In Figure 9–7, the ongoing responsibilities of systems recovery teams during operations at the hot site are set forth.

As depicted in Figure 9–7, the Emergency Operations Team is responsible for operating systems and applications at emergency service levels. This may include scheduling jobs, performing backups, and maintaining System Recovery Team time and expense records, as well as records of other accrued expenses. Expenses are reported on a regular basis to the Systems Recovery Team leader, who includes them in his or her regular reports to the Emergency Management Team.

The Host Software and Applications Teams monitor system performance, work to resolve problems, maintain applications security and data integrity, and report performance and utilization measurements to the Systems Recovery Team leader. Presumably, the team leader will advise the teams of changing requirements and the decisions of the Emergency Management Team that pertain to their activities.

These tasks are ongoing until the recovery phase gives way to the relocation of systems to the original or newly constructed facility. Relocation may need to happen more than once in a recovery. As mentioned in a previous chapter, with some commercial systems recovery vendors, facility use in excess of a set number of days is prohibited. The hot site may be used only until a cold site at or near the vendor location can be fitted with necessary hardware. Then, the customer is moved to the cold site. This allows the hot site to be used by other subscribers wishing to test their plans or needing a recovery facility in a disaster.

Networks

Network recovery consists of a set of tasks, such as those depicted in Figure 9–8, which may be undertaken concurrently with system recovery and remote system operation tasks. In this flowchart, it is assumed that the company has contracted with a wide-area network service vendor for rerouting WAN services and voice communications along a preplanned alternate path. Such services can be used effectively if systems and end

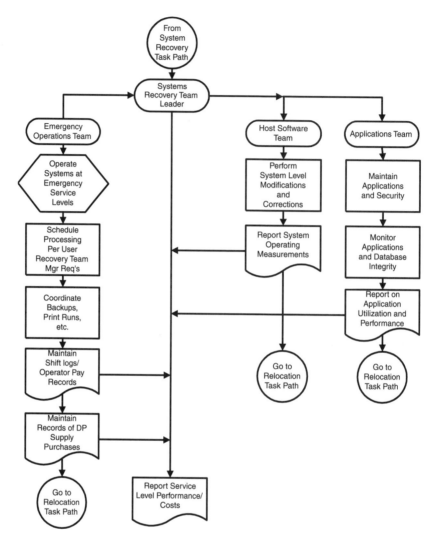

Figure 9–7 Remote systems operations management (remote systems operations task path).

user recovery facilities are designated in advance of any disaster. In situations where this is not the case, additional procedures may be needed to accommodate the on-the-fly rerouting strategies (for example, the solicitation of services from IXCs or Value Added Network service providers, the acquisition of requisite hardware, testing of new facilities, etc.)

In addition, the flowchart shown in Figure 9–8 describes a response to a total loss of both user work areas and systems facilities. Hence, a Net-

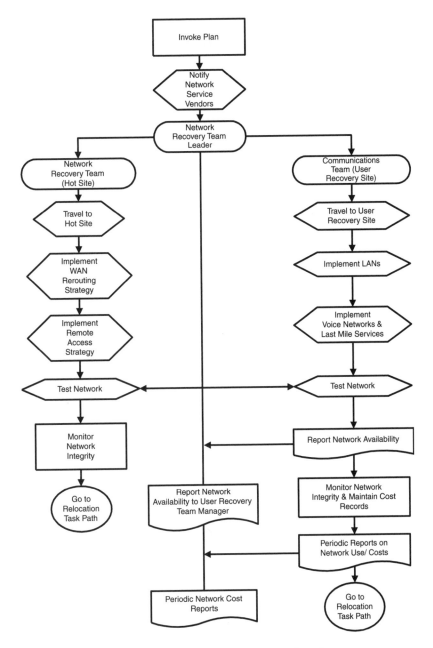

Figure 9–8 Network recovery task path.

work Recovery Team located at the systems recovery site and a Communications Team located at the user recovery site work cooperatively to facilitate full recovery of corporate voice and data communications networks. Other flowcharts may need to be developed to reflect a partial disaster scenario in which only a part of the corporate voice and data networking capability needs to be restored or rerouted.

Network Recovery Task Path

As depicted in the flowchart, once the network recovery section of the disaster recovery plan is invoked, the network rerouting service vendor is contacted and communications are rerouted along predefined paths. The Network Recovery Team leader activates teams responsible for restoring voice and data interconnects at the systems recovery and end user recovery site respectively. Each team travels to its intended destination. The Network Recovery Team leader proceeds to one location or the other per plan specifications.

The Network Recovery Team is responsible for implementing the WAN rerouting strategy and for deploying remote access technology that will be used by end users to access and operate hot-site-based applications. Other tasks may include the installation and preparation of communications hardware at the hot site for use in the network, the deployment of network management software, the implementation of network security hardware and software and the notification of remote communicators about changes to network configuration and anticipated service levels. Thorough testing of the new systems recovery site-user recovery site network can only be accomplished after tasks have been completed at the end user recovery site by the Communications Team.

Following successful completion of the above tasks, the Network Recovery Team will monitor network traffic for performance, utilization, and integrity throughout the recovery period and will report on network costs and service levels to the Network Recovery Team leader. The team leader will provide these reports to the Emergency Management Team. This will persist until systems and end users are relocated to their original or to new company facilities.

At the user recovery site, the Communications Team works with User Recovery Teams to install and make operational local area networks used to support local end user business processes. The Communications Team installs telecommunications hardware received from backup inventory or from prearranged vendor sources. This team also works with ILECs/CLECs and other last-mile service providers to implement both local communications circuits and any WAN or Internet gateway services designated in the disaster recovery plan.

Tests of wide area network and remote access services between the systems recovery site and end user recovery site are conducted and performance levels baselined according to a planned testing strategy. When network tests are completed, the availability of the network for use is reported to the team leader who in turn reports this to the Emergency Management Team.

Until systems and networks are relocated to original or new company facilities, the Communications Team monitors network performance at the end user recovery facility and maintains cost records that are periodically summarized and reported to the Network Recovery Team leader for inclusion in management reports.

End Users

Figures 9–9 and 9–10 refer to user recovery tasks, which are undertaken concurrently with system and network recovery tasks. These flowcharts assume that a user recovery site has been preplanned and designated in the recovery plan. Were this not the case, advanced planning for the automatic rerouting of communications networks would be impossible and recovery would be delayed by the need to locate and outfit a recovery site, then to notify end users of the new address.

As telecommuting-based end user recovery becomes more viable, the recovery tasks involved will be very different from those depicted here. As of this writing, however, the preferred strategy for end user recovery is to relocate end users to an alternate facility that is either company-owned or leased from a vendor.

User Recovery Task Path

As depicted in Figure 9–9, once the decision has been made to activate the user recovery section of the plan, the Emergency Management Team notifies the company insurer so that extra expense coverages for user relocation and extraordinary operating costs can be activated. The User Recovery Team leader activates an Off-Site Storage Team, Transportation Team, Replacement Hardware Team, Administrative Support Team, Supplies Team, and Data Preparation and Records Team to begin the work detailed in the DR plan.

The Off-Site Storage Team is responsible for retrieving stored materials required by the user recovery site and delivering them to the site. They also assist in preparing off-site stores, particularly magnetic media backups and restoral software, for use.

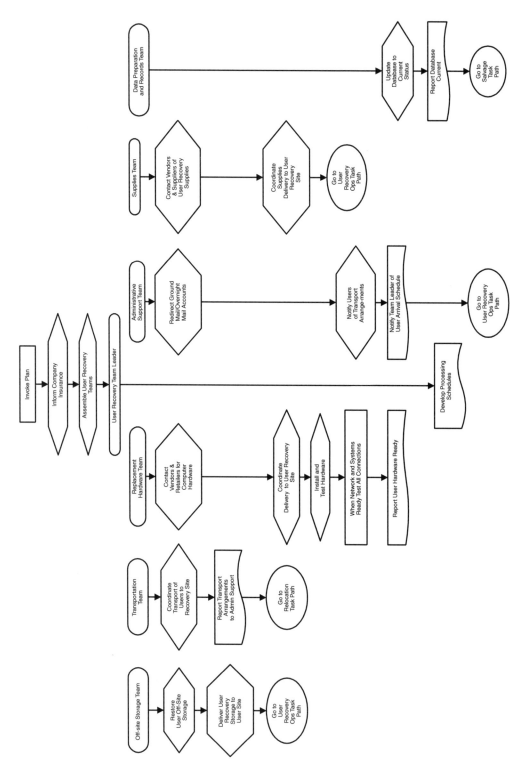

Figure 9–9 User recovery task path.

The Transportation Team coordinates the transportation of end users to the recovery site, although this is not done until other aspects of site preparation are completed. Transportation arrangements are reported to the Administrative Support Team.

A Replacement Hardware Team contacts vendors and retailers, identified in the plan, to coordinate shipments of workstations and peripherals, photocopying equipment, fax, and other office equipment to the user recovery site. This team is then responsible for installing and testing hardware in cooperation with the Communications Team, which will be working on the restoral of office LANs and voice communications capabilities at the user recovery site. Following LAN and communications tests, the Replacement Hardware Team reports readiness to the User Recovery Team leader.

While systems and LANs are being readied, the Administrative Support Team contacts ground mail and overnight delivery services and arranges for the redirection of services to the new end user recovery facility. Upon receipt of the details of transportation arrangements from the Transportation Team, and at the direction of the User Recovery Team leader, Administrative Support advises end users to report to work. Administrative Support staffs work shifts and coordinates end user arrivals, meals and lodging.

Meanwhile, a Supplies Team coordinates the acquisition and delivery of office supplies from vendors identified in the plan. Supplies are delivered to the recovery site, shipments are verified, and records are maintained of costs and deliveries.

Once systems and networks are ready, a Data Preparation and Records Team uses salvaged records as well as documents stored off-site to bring databases to as current a state as possible. Once databases are current, this is reported to the User Recovery Team leader and the user recovery site is ready for operation.

The user recovery task path depicted above assumes that certain capabilities already exist and will not need to be hastily developed. This may not be the case for every business. Additional teams, such as a Facility Location Team, may need to be commissioned and staffed to handle additional functional requirements of user recovery.

Note also that the Data Preparation and Records Team, unlike the other teams in this task path, may have responsibilities in the salvage task path, as they will assist in records reclamation and other salvage activities. With application access restored, operations in the end user recovery site may commence. The ongoing activities of the user recovery teams during this period are depicted in Figure 9–10.

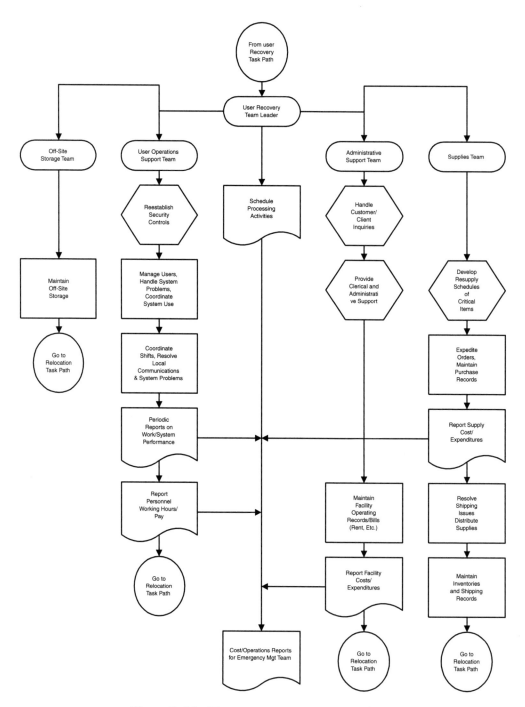

Figure 9–10 User recovery operations task path.

User Recovery Operations Task Path

As illustrated in Figure 9–10, this task path comprises the ongoing procedures for managing day-to-day operations at the user recovery site. The Off-Site Storage Team maintains a storage schedule for records and data generated at the site. The User Operations Support Team oversees premise security, manages users, handles system problems, provides help desk functions, coordinates shifts, and supervises work, making routine reports of work and system performance, personnel time, and payroll to the User Recovery Team leader. Administrative Support handles customer and client inquiries, provides clerical and administrative support for the other teams, and maintains operations cost records. Reports of facility costs and expenditures are made by the team to the User Recovery Team leader on a regular basis. Finally, the Supplies Team coordinates the resupply of critical office and computer supplies. This team escalates orders, maintains purchase and inventory records, resolves shipping issues, and distributes supplies upon arrival.

The activities described above may or may not have corresponding procedures in the disaster recovery plan document. However, special forms and report formats may be developed and included in the plan with instructions for their use.

Salvage

The User Recovery Team continues its operations until a plan is developed to relocate the users to the original or a new facility. Decisions regarding where and when to relocate are made by the Emergency Management Team, based in part upon the findings and progress of the salvage effort.

Salvage Task Path

Salvage activities may begin the moment that entry is permitted to the disaster-stricken facility. These efforts continue concurrently with response and recovery activities undertaken by other disaster recovery teams. Figure 9–11 provides an overview of some of the activities that may be a part of a salvage effort.

As indicated above, once the plan is invoked, a Damage Assessment Team—possibly comprised of the Salvage Team leader, a qualified member of the Emergency Management Team, and others familiar with source records and computer hardware—enter the facility. A photographic record is made of facility damage by a team member (or a professional photographer on retainer to the company for this purpose). Witness accounts may also be collected at this point.

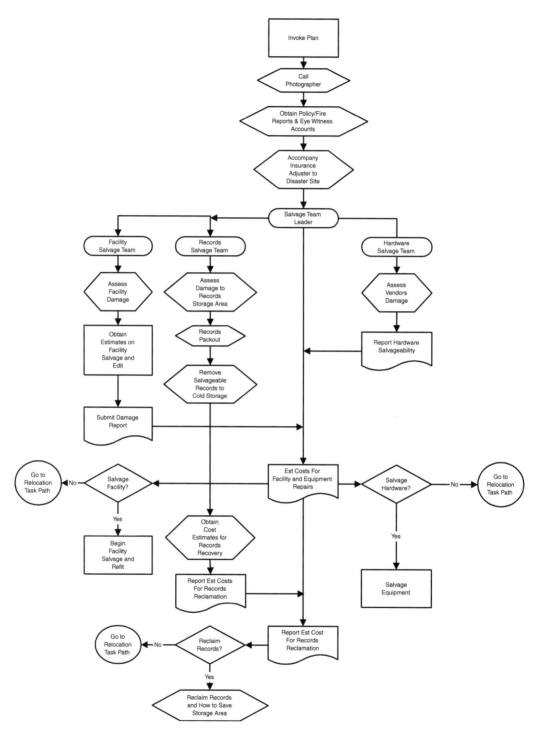

Figure 9–11 Salvage task path.

Some plans provide for a claims adjuster from the company's business interruption insurer to accompany the Damage Assessment and Salvage Teams to the disaster site. Since payment on insurance claims may provide part of the financing for the recovery, the quicker that claims can be filed and adjudicated, the better.

Following this initial visit, formal salvage operations commence under the auspices of a Salvage Team leader. A Facility Salvage Team determines whether the data center and user operations area environments can be restored, and at what cost. An itemized report of team findings is provided to the Salvage Team leader. Similar reports are filed by the Hardware Salvage Team, whose task it is to determine how much computer and networking hardware can be restored reliably to service.

Concurrently, the Records Salvage Team sets to work. The job of the team is to determine what magnetic media, paper-based, and microform records can be rescued at the disaster site; to clean, pack, and inventory these records; and to remove them to cold storage. Generally, this must be done within 24 to 48 hours, before mold and fungi begin to corrupt salvageable documents, though some documents may be vital to database restoration activity and may require faster action.

The procedure for packout should be set forth in the disaster recovery plan, as should a list of cold storage facilities in the vicinity of the company.[4] Alternatively, DR coordinators may wish to place a data recovery vendor and a records reclamation vendor on retainer and utilize their services to recover magnetic media and records, respectively. Table 9–3 summarizes some of the media-specific procedures that may be performed by the Records Salvage Team.

Following packout, and once the extent and quantity of damaged records are known, the Records Salvage Team should obtain a salvage work cost estimate from a records reclamation vendor (also noted in the disaster plan) detailing the expenses for restoring the volume of records salvaged from company facilities. This cost estimate should be reported to the Salvage Team leader.

In the case of magnetic media, firms such as Ontrack Data Recovery Services offer cleanrooms and laboratories distributed around the world, as well as on-site engineering support, to facilitate data reclamation from damaged disk media. Typical recovery of data takes about three days on average, though special services are available in a post-disaster context that can cut restoral time by half.[5] Recovering data from client workstations may be necessary to facilitate database restoration or to access special workstation-based information that has been added since the last backup. However, the Records Salvage Team should work with other re-

Table 9–3 Salvage Priority by Media Type

TYPE OF MEDIA	Color films and photographs	Silver or emulsion films and photographs	Diazo or vesicular (duplicate) films	Bond, rag, or duplication paper	Magnetic media (including tape, disk, floppy disk, audio and video-tape)
PRIORITY	Immediate.	Immediate.	Last.	Within 48 hours (depending on temperature and humidity levels at the disaster site, and upon the extent of damage).	Immediate.
IMMEDIATE ACTION	Once wet, keep wet.	Immerse totally in water.	If time and staff available, rinse off and lay out flat on clean surface to dry; otherwise, leave until last.	Air dry in well-ventilated area. If volume of wet records is large, consider freeze or vacuum drying.	Contact vendor.
PURPOSE OF ACTION	To avoid further damage and loss of image.	To avoid further damage.	To prevent water spotting and curling of films or fiche.	To prevent further deterioration of paper materials and eruption of mold and fungus.	To obtain professional advice and service.
FOLLOWUP ACTION	Within 48 hours, obtain professional advice and/or assistance with cleaning, drying and restoring. Freeze if professional help is delayed longer than 48 hours.	Seek professional assistance with cleaning and drying. Freezing may cause image damage. If freezing will be delayed more than 48 hours, immerse films in 1 percent solution of formaldehyde in cool water.	Wash with liquid detergent and rinse. Dry on flat, absorbent paper towels.	May include freeze- or vacuum-drying. If mold erupts, treat with an approved fungicide.	May include special cleaning techniques and professional assistance in retrieving data.

334

covery teams to ensure that only the most important data is submitted for fast-turnaround recovery services to minimize expense.

The Salvage Team leader is responsible for reporting cost estimates for facility, equipment, and records salvage to the Emergency Management Team. The Emergency Management Team will decide whether to undertake salvage or to write off the loss and look for new hardware and new quarters for the company.

If the decision is made to salvage and reenter the original facility, the Facility Salvage Team initiates contract work and provides a completion schedule to the Salvage Team leader. The other salvage teams move forward with salvage activities, identifying task progress and anticipated completion schedules as work proceeds.

THE RELOCATION/REENTRY PHASE

Whatever decision is reached by the Emergency Management Team, it is followed up by the development of a relocation or re-entry plan. The components of the relocation plan cannot be determined in advance by the disaster recovery coordinator. However, if the relocation plan capitalizes on the same team structures that were defined in the disaster recovery plan, this may facilitate efficient relocation of systems, networks, and users to the original or new company facility.

In addition, the relocation or reentry plan should provide a scheme for the gradual transition back to normal service levels from the emergency service levels in effect during recovery operations. Presumably, this transition will be scheduled following the successful relocation of critical and vital systems to the company site.

Figure 9–12 summarizes the tasks that may be involved in the relocation of emergency operations to the original (salvaged) facility. The task path mirrors recovery task paths in many respects, except that emergency service levels are gradually replaced by normal service levels per a plan developed by the Emergency Management Team during recovery operations.

FINAL THOUGHTS ON EMERGENCY MANAGEMENT DECISION MAKING

The above is only one example of an emergency management flowchart. The team descriptions and roles depicted, the specific tasks described, and the recovery procedures enacted will, by necessity, differ from one

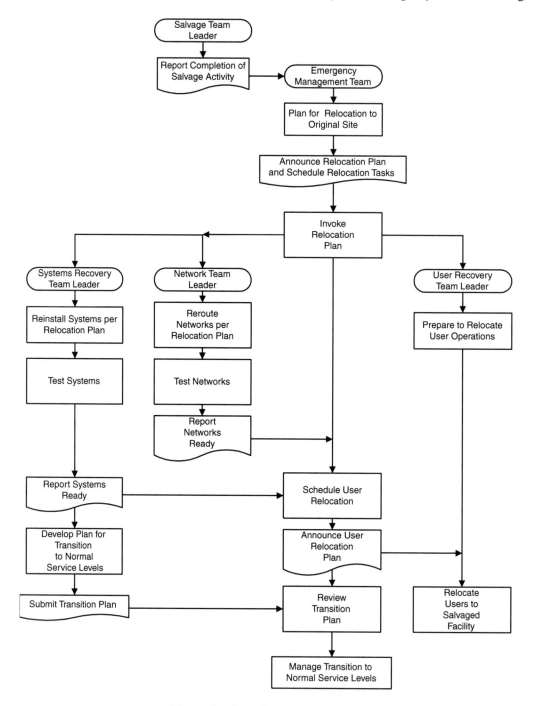

Figure 9–12   Relocation task path.

company to the next. The purpose of designing an emergency decision-making flowchart is to help readers (including those who must implement the plan and those who merely want to understand plan provisions) to see the interrelationships between the strategies developed for systems, network, and end user recovery.

Emergency management remains as much art as science. In an actual emergency, senior managers and technical managers together need to use the emergency management flowchart as a jumping-off point for the innovation and creativity that is always required to surmount the hurdles of critical business process restoration.

ENDNOTES

1. Jon William Toigo, "Storm Warnings Sound," *The Databus*, 07/86.
2. Richard Sandhofer, "Chicago Not Prepared for a New River," *Disaster Recovery Journal*, 01/88.
3. Jon William Toigo, "The Disaster Recovery Planning Assistant and Virtual Emergency Operations Center: A Brief Prospectus," 01/99. The VEOC and Disaster Recovery Planning Assistant described in the document are copyright to the author. However, beta test versions of the solution are expected to be provided on the companion web-site to this book, www.drplanning.org.
4. Some excellent background reading on records salvage include Richard Harms, et al., *A Program for Disaster Response in Michigan*, Michigan Archival Association, East Lansing, MI, 1981. See also *A Primer on Disaster Preparedness, Management and Response: Paper-Based Materials Selected Reprints*, issued by Smithsonian Institution, National Archives and Records Administration, Library of Congress, and National Park Service. A Collaborative Publication Sponsored by the Conservation Analytical Laboratory and the Office of Risk Management, SI; the Preservation Policy and Services Division, NARA; the Preservation Directorate, LC; and the Curatorial Services Division, NPS, October 1993, available on the World Wide Web at the National Archives and Records Administrators site: www.nara.gov/nara.
5. See "Data Recovery Services," on Ontrack Data Recovery's (Eden Prairie, MN) web site at www.ontrack.com. This site provides a wealth of information on the causes of magnetic media failures and restoration techniques.

CHAPTER

10

The Recovery Management Environment

As discussed in Chapter 9, the emergency decision-making plan provides the framework of the disaster recovery plan. Its flowcharts and notification directory depict the interrelationships between all of the strategies, tasks, and procedures that have been developed to recover critical business processes in the event of a disaster.

However, flowcharts—and the scenarios on which they are built—are only theoretical constructs. Disaster recovery teams and emergency managers may have to deviate from preplanned paths in order to respond effectively to the demands of an actual event and its recovery requirements.

There is no way to predict or to develop suitable responses to every recovery scenario in advance. However, there are ways to identify potential obstacles to plan implementation, educate team leaders about them, and, in some cases, develop the means for surmounting them.

To better understand the recovery management environment, disaster recovery coordinators need to research the experience of other companies that have implemented plans. Research entails more than reading this book or disaster-related articles in back issues of popular business computing journals. An important part of the research involves conducting interviews with those who have led or served on recovery teams in a business disaster. Research also entails interviewing local and state civil emergency management authorities and representatives of local utility companies, telephone companies, and others who will help define the milieu in which corporate disaster recovery will take place. Disaster recovery coordinators can perform this research themselves, or they may be assisted by team leaders who will profit from direct participation in the endeavor.

The purpose of this research is twofold: to learn about external factors that may impact the implementation of a plan and also to obtain a greater understanding of the impact of disaster on the behavior and psyche of company personnel, recovery teams, and the community at large. Some of what is discovered may not be useful in writing the disaster recovery plan. However, it may help those who will implement the plan to see their roles more clearly and perceive the parameters within which improvisation (in the face of obstacles to recovery) may be successful.

RESEARCHING LITERATURE

There is an old saying that best information about disaster recovery is locked away in company filing cabinets—often in the exit interviews of business and IT managers who have been fired in the wake of a disaster! While this may be a bit of an exaggeration, it is true that businesses often wish to suppress any information that might indicate instability or vulnerability to investors, customers, stockholders, and auditors.

Despite this desire, accounts of successful (and, to a lesser extent, unsuccessful) recovery projects are increasingly finding their way into the press. Part of the reason, of course, is that some disasters are highly visible events, spectacles for the media or significant in terms of human tragedy. However, even a software malfunction can achieve prominent media attention when it causes a federal reserve bank to borrow billions at the discount window, destabilizing the securities market, or when it prompts the customers of an online brokerage to complain *en masse* to the Securities and Exchange Commission and makes front page news in the Wall Street Journal.

The point is that more and more information about the problems and pitfalls of disaster recovery is available in the public media. This information can be helpful in identifying potential obstacles to the implementation of disaster plans.

In some cases, lessons are preeminently practical. For example, companies located in Canada with hot sites in the United States learned significant lessons from published accounts of the 1986 Steinberg disaster in Montreal. As reported in the trade press, the evening after a fire demolished company headquarters, 25 employees gathered together 10,000 reels of tape containing payroll systems data and other necessities, such as blank check stock, and formed a caravan headed for a hot site in New Jersey. They were prevented from crossing the border into the United States of America, however, by customs agents concerned that the software and checks could be used for illegal purposes.[1] It took the company CEO, working in conjunction with the U.S. Consulate, to straighten out the matter.

More recently, the press has offered a broad range of practical lessons concerning the efficacy of plans. A small sampling:

- After Hurricane Hugo in 1989, an automotive parts manufacturer impacted by the storm discovered that its plans to coordinate the activities of recovery teams using cellular phones ran afoul of local civil emergency management mandates.[2] Cellular communications were reserved for use by emergency services and the IT manager was told to cease using the phones.
- Following Hurricane Fran in 1996, a Bank in North Carolina learned the vicissitudes of counting on the availability of certain key personnel to facilitate recovery. The MIS director had to dodge power lines to drive to the home of a key systems programmer whose car had been demolished by a tree felled by the storm.[3]
- During Hurricane Floyd in 1999, many planners discovered their error in counting on both ground and air transportation to move personnel and supplies to recovery sites at the same time that massive civilian evacuations were taking place. The flood of requests stimulated by the event overwhelmed the reservation systems for airlines and travel agencies and the millions of people seeking shelter inland in advance of the storm turned interstate highways into parking lots.[4]

In addition to print media accounts of disaster recovery efforts, coordinators may profit by spending time reviewing tapes of "on-the-scene" coverage of disaster events made by television media. The advent of all-news television networks (CNN, MSNBC, and others) has made the "dynamic" media (i.e., television, as opposed to "static" or print media) a factor in disaster recovery—in ways that are both positive and negative. On the plus side, television and radio provide a means for disseminating information about the recovery milieu quickly and efficiently. Weather-related warnings, information about earthquake damage areas, locations of civilian disturbances or emergency shelters, and so on, can be communicated quickly via electronic reporting. Accurate reports enable business managers to identify alternative transportation routes, obtain appropriate infrastructure assistance, determine appropriate plan implementation strategies, and even disseminate information to employees regarding alternate schedules or work locations.

On the down side, however, dynamic media accounts can protract emergency timeframes by exaggerating the extent of damage accrued to an event (see below). They can also portray recovery efforts in a less-than-flattering light. For example, following the 1993 bombing of the World Trade Center in New York, CNN covered the efforts of some businesses to recover key operations. Video broadcasts showed the emergency operations center of a "Big Five" accounting and consulting firm impacted by the event, capturing images of frantic employees and recovery personnel engaged in heated arguments and, worse yet, a clearly visible white board on which was scrawled numerous instructions to recovery team members, including what appeared to be IDs and passwords and emergency phone numbers. If nothing else, the coverage communicated a potentially damaging impression of the firm's disaster preparedness (ironically, the firm also provides disaster recovery planning services!) to clients and shareholders watching the broadcast. It further demonstrated the importance of maintaining EOC operations at a different location from crisis communications.

Of course, it would be impractical for coordinators to gather all of the publications covering all of the subjects that might offer insights into disaster recovery planning. However, vendors of products and services used by the DR coordinator often survey this literature and forward relevant articles to the coordinator's attention. Many vendor sales representatives cite their practice of forwarding news clips to customers as part of an ongoing effort to inform and educate clientele.

In addition to subscription publications and vendor clips, many hardware and software companies generate their own disaster recovery guidelines. Coordinators can obtain these through marketing represen-

tatives for the various companies. While this literature rarely provides a comprehensive treatment of disaster recovery, it may provide useful information about a specific application or platform used by the
company.

INTERVIEWS AND TOURS

Other DR Coordinators

Another way to learn about the milieu in which a company disaster recovery plan will be implemented is to conduct interviews with DR coordinators in other companies, as well as providers of public infrastructure
services and government officials concerned with public safety and emergency management. From these discussions, coordinators can identify
what measures similar or neighboring companies are taking to facilitate
disaster recovery, and how the coordinator's plan will be affected by the
plans of those whose plans shape the recovery environment.

In some instances, vendors of disaster recovery products and services can provide the names of contacts in neighboring companies or
arrange introductions between coordinators. By discussing everything
from how the coordinator for another company cost-justified his or her
plan to management, to the technical details of how a certain type of local
area network can be backed up, to the other coordinator's evaluation of
the performance of various vendors, a great deal of useful information
can be gathered.

Public Services and Utilities

Coordinators would also be well-advised to interview representatives of
public services and utilities and local government officials tasked with
emergency management. It would be useful to gather information on the
following:

- **The Power Company's Policy on Repairs and Service Restoration.**
  Most power companies are willing to allow disaster recovery coordinators to tour their facilities. The coordinator should ask questions
  and develop a thorough understanding of how the provider goes
  about localizing and repairing the causes of outages. In addition, the
  coordinator should identify how a "trouble report" is handled: What
  is the emergency telephone number for reporting an outage? Is more

than a single report required to initiate corrective action? What is the typical length of a power outage? What has been the maximum length of an outage in the past two years? Is there a policy regarding priority of service restoration (who is turned on first, second, third, etc.)?

The answers to these questions can lead into a detailed discussion of the coordinator's company power requirements. Ask the representative to show how the company is supplied and what redundancies exist in the system to supply power should system outages occur.

Power company representatives can also provide information that may guide further research. For example, an office park or high-rise building may be supplied power by the public utility at a central service entry point. Power is then distributed from this service entry to offices within the complex or building using secondary lines, transformers, and other hardware that is owned and maintained by the building management company. The power company can point out where its responsibility (and ability to correct problems) ends, and where the building manager's responsibilities begin. This may lead to a subsequent interview of the building manager to understand problem reporting procedures, job order methods, and power restoration timeframes from the management company's perspective.

The coordinator may also wish to identify what hardware the management company is using and whether redundant hardware is available to replace malfunctioning equipment. If the management company is using obsolete or hard-to-find hardware, some tenant pressure may persuade the management company to upgrade to newer, more readily obtained equipment.

- **How Local Telephone COs Are Configured and How They Will Handle Service Restoration in an Outage.** Coordinators will find that many of the same questions asked of the power company also need to be discussed with a local telephone company representative: where to report trouble, how to escalate response, what are the restoration priorities in the event of a regional outage, and how long an outage may persist. It would be useful to coordinators to tour the facility containing local exchange and IXC gateway switches. Find out what redundancies exist and where other COs are located in proximity to the company. This information may be used to determine whether it is necessary, or possible, to obtain local area and gateway services from a second CO.

Find out also what services the CO offers in the areas of line grading and automatic rerouting of local traffic. If the coordinator is able to speak with a CO engineer who has helped other companies with their network planning or disaster recovery projects, he or she may be able to obtain useful information about the techniques and strategies others have applied with success.

Similar visits may need to be made to IXC POP sites used by the company, to local Internet Service Provider facilities, and to cellular carrier offices. In every case, efforts should be made to identify outage scenarios, understand disaster recovery procedures of vendors themselves, and to learn about the recovery practices of other customers of vendor-provided services.

- **Local Civil Emergency Management Plans.** Due to the threats posed to entire communities by natural and man-made disasters, many state and local governments (as well as the federal government) have developed emergency management plans. These plans provide for the evacuation and relocation of the public in the event of hurricanes, typhoons, floods, earthquakes, or nuclear, biological, or chemical disasters.

  While not every disaster experienced by a company will entail government intervention, businesses located in "high-risk" areas (i.e., those located on the coastlines of North America, or near chemical or nuclear plants) need to be aware of the impact that civil plans will have on the implementation of their own plan.

  A local administrator is usually responsible for the maintenance of a civil emergency management plan. In some localities, the administrative function is given to a local law enforcement or fire protection agency. It may take some time to sift through the bureaucracy to locate the individual or group responsible for emergency planning, but the coordinator should make the effort and meet with the responsible party.

  Some coordinators may view this recommendation as superfluous. The concept of civil defense conjures up images of 1950's planning for bomb shelters, air raid sirens, and emergency broadcasts. This perception aside, residents of disaster-prone regions of the United States are aware of the ongoing need and true benefit of emergency management agencies in local and state governments. In the event of a natural or man-made threat such as a hurricane, city, county, and state governments have developed strategies for notifying the people and safely evacuating them.

Following cessation of disaster conditions, governmental emergency management plans often provide for controlled reentry into the evacuated areas. These plans have proven their worth time after time and have probably accounted for saving more lives than the polio vaccine. However, such plans are not without their cost to a business if disaster recovery coordinators have not anticipated how they will impact on their company disaster recovery plans. The following brief story from the author's own experience illustrates the point.

In 1985, Hurricane Elena forced the evacuation of metropolitan areas up and down the Florida Gulf Coast. (Later that same season, Gloria forced civil governments to relocate populations away from coastal areas all along the Atlantic seaboard.) The Tampa Bay Metropolitan Area was evacuated while the hurricane was still more than 21 hours distant and had less than a 30 percent chance of making landfall anywhere near the area. Officials called for the early evacuation because they added a 15-hour period of "prelandfall hazard" to the 9 to 15 hours they calculated it would take to evacuate the residential populations of all flood-prone areas, including the Gulf Beaches and low-lying areas. Local and state emergency managers had to take into account the period of sustained gale force winds (40+ miles per hour) preceding the storm's landfall during which travel would be extremely hazardous. (The length of this period is determined by the size of the hurricane and its rate of movement.) Because of these factors, civil planners anticipated that up to 15 additional hours should be added to the time requirement for safe evacuation. This, in turn, affected the timing of the evacuation order.

While many business planners expected evacuation orders to be inconvenient whenever they were issued, most did not anticipate being ordered out so long before the storm even appeared on local TV radar. Local law enforcement officials ordered the disaster recovery teams of many Bay Area businesses out with last minute backups only partially completed and other planned procedures implemented haphazardly or not at all.

Responding to post-Elena criticisms of their evacuation policy from area businesses, local officials noted that at the time that the mandatory evacuation for Elena was ordered, the storm had been sustaining a 10 mile per hour speed toward Tampa Bay for everal minutes. Applying the government formulas for calculating the prelandfall hazard, there were actually only about six hours in which to safely evacuate flood-prone areas. To provide for the safety of all of the people, there could be no deviation in the evacuation schedule.

As the story suggests, in order to plan effectively for a disaster such as a hurricane, coordinators must develop a firm understanding of governmental emergency management plans. The government will place the safety and well-being of the citizenry before the interests of the business and, in so doing, may create a recovery environment in which business recovery plans will flourish or flounder. When there is a threat, governments will evacuate too often and too early. They will also be unsympathetic to the objectives of business planners if they are perceived as coming into conflict with civil plans aimed at preserving the lives of the population.

Evacuation is the first phase of the two-phase plan employed by most civil emergency management officials. The second phase is reentry. As noted previously, the Elena experience demonstrated that coordinators must consider where their recovery personnel reside when planning for facility reentry and damage assessment. If arrangements cannot be made to utilize only personnel who reside in the same area where business offices are located, coordinators may wish to pursue one of the following alternatives with civil defense professionals.

1. Determine whether an evacuation shelter exists or can be set up near the company facility for use by employees and their families. Not only will this reduce the distraction factor, but it will also reduce the likelihood that recovery will be delayed by prohibitions on travel in and out of the disaster area.
2. Discuss with emergency management officials the possibility of approving company ID cards as valid passes into disaster areas. In efforts to avoid looting, reentry into evacuated areas is often controlled by law enforcement officials who seek proof of *residence* (rather than employment) as the criterion for admission. As in the case of Hurricane Elena, company recovery personnel who cannot prove residence in the area of the business they want to access may be turned away, stalling damage assessment and disaster recovery. Preapproval of company ID with civil defense officials may expedite reentry into evacuated businesses once safety hazards have been cleared.

Coordinators from all types of businesses might find it useful to explore some of the generic issues, raised by the experience of Elena (and more recent storms such as Floyd in 1999), with local government authorities. Depending on the business and its geographical location, there may be other issues that a coordinator may wish to explore in detail to bring business disaster recovery plans into agreement with civil emergency management plans.

For example, local law enforcement and fire department officials may be consulted to determine the manner in which bomb threats or arson investigations will be handled, or to explore the roles that public safety officials will play in approving the reoccupation of salvaged facilities following a fire, flood, earthquake, storm, or other event. The results of these and other investigations will aid in finalizing a plan that can coexist with other emergency management plans that comprise the recovery environment.

PROFESSIONAL DR ORGANIZATIONS

Information about the recovery management environment is available from a variety of sources besides publications and one-on-one interviews with infrastructure providers and civil emergency management officials. Many professional organizations, such as those organized for risk managers, internal auditors, IT and records management professionals, and other industry specific fields, occasionally offer special programs related to various dimensions of disaster recovery planning that the disaster recovery coordinator may wish to attend.

In addition to these educational forums, an increasing number of disaster recovery planning specific associations are available to coordinators. These organizations focus on the disaster recovery issues facing the business communities they serve rather than treating the subject as a peripheral issue. Members can compress a great deal of time-consuming research into several hours of concentrated discussion at a group meeting.

Through participation in a group, members can quickly develop an extensive network of contacts, including other users (and vendors) of disaster recovery plans, products, and services. In addition, members are kept up to date with the latest advancements in disaster recovery techniques and technology and can profit collectively from shared information on vendor or product performance, or from member discounts on expensive services.

Table 10–1 contains contact information for disaster recovery groups and emergency management organizations in the United States that existed at the time of this book's publication. Contact names, telephone

Table 10–1   U.S. Disaster Recovery Groups and Emergency
Management Organizations by State

State	Group or Agency
ALABAMA	State of Alabama Emergency Management Tel: (205) 280-2200
ALASKA	State of Alaska Emergency Services Tel: (907) 428-7000
ARIZONA	Central Arizona Chapter of the Association of Contingency Planners Barbara Martinez Tel: (602) 587-3810 Fax: (502) 587-3999 E-mail: jim_groark@apsc.com
	State of Arizona Emergency Services Tel: (806) 411-2336, or (800) 411-2336
ARKANSAS	State of Arkansas, Office of Emergency Services W.R. "Bud" Harper Tel: (501) 730-9750 Fax: (501)730-9754 E-mail: wharper@state.ar.us
CALIFORNIA	Association of Contingency Planners (ACP) Los Angeles Chapter Deborah Serina Tel: (310) 456-1040 Fax: (310) 456-1040 E-mail: disasterhelp@email.msn.com
	Association of Contingency Planners (ACP) Orange County Chapter Patti Scanlan Tel: (310) 335-4501 Fax: (310) 322-0130 E-mail: pati_scanlan@infonet.com
	Association of Contingency Planners (ACP) San Diego Chapter Marti Lee Tel: (618) 651-1478 E-mail: mlee@qualcomm.com
	Association of Sacramento Area Planners (ASAP) Darrell Baxter Tel: (916) 845-6911 Fax: (916) 845-0525 www.zetsite.com/asap.htm E-mail: darell_baxter@ftb.ca.gov

State	Group or Agency
	Business and Industry Council for Emergency Planning and Preparedness (BICEPP) Los Angeles Chris Wright Tel: (213) 386-4524 Fax: (805) 499-8804 www.kfwb.com/bicepp/bicepp.html
	Business Recovery Managers Assoc (BRMA) Northern California Tel: (925) 355-8660 www.brma.com
	California Emergency Services Assoc (CESA) Southern Chapter Laura Hernandez Tel: (805) 644-0899
	California Emergency Services Assoc (CESA) Coastal Chapter Ray Riordan Tel: (510) 287-1327
	California Emergency Services Assoc (CESA) Inland Chapter Nellie Lee Barber Tel: (530) 224-4113
	City of Los Angeles Emergency Preparedness Division Ellis Stanley Tel: (213) 485-5231 Fax: (213) 847-7143 E-mail: eooweb@cao.ci.la.ca.us
	Southern CA Emergency Services Association Wendy Milligan Tel: (805) 644-0899 Fax: (805) 642-2883 http://scesa.com
	State of California Office of Emergency Services Tel: (916) 262-1800
COLORADO	Association of Contingency Planners Rocky Mountain Chapter Bob Niehoff Tel: (303) 768-2857 Fax: (303) 768-3019 www.acp-crmc-colorado.com E-mail: rniehoff@oppenheimerfunds.com or 103473.1215@compuserve.com

(continued)

Table 10–1 *Continued*

State	Group or Agency
	State of Colorado Emergency Management Tel: (303) 273-1622
CONNECTICUT	Connecticut Disaster Recovery Information Exchange Robert Urion Tel: (203) 925-3900 Fax: (203) 944-9008
	State of Connecticut Emergency Management Tel: (860) 566-8517
DELAWARE	Delaware Emergency Management Agency John P. (Sean) Mulhern, Director P.O. Box 527 Delaware City, DE 19706 Phone: (302) 659-3362 Contact: Jane Gooding, jgooding@state.de.us
	Delaware Valley Business Resumption Information Exchange Group (DVBRIEG) Patricia Bennett Tel: (609) 635-9770 Fax: (609) 635-9766
DISTRICT OF COLUMBIA	Association of Contingency Planners Capital Area Chapter Greg Brown Tel: (301) 803-6168 Fax: (301) 803-6168 E-mail: gsbrown@us.ibm.com
	DC Emergency Preparedness Tel: (202) 727-6161
FLORIDA	Association of Contingency Planners North-East Florida Chapter Brian Vigue Tel: (904) 464-5671 Fax: (904) 464-4264 E-mail: brian.vigue@nationsbank.com or bvigue@aol.com
	Association of Contingency Planners Mid-Florida Chapter Marsha Bacsko Tel: (407) 805-5441 or Fax: (407) 858-8876 E-mail: marshalb@sms.att.com
	Disaster Prevention & Recovery Alliance Lee Keller Tel: (813) 969-3614
	State of Florida Emergency Management Tel: (850) 413-9886

State	Group or Agency
GEORGIA	Association of Contingency Planners Atlanta Chapter Tel: (800) 445-4227 State of Georgia Emergency Management Tel: (404) 635-7000
HAWAII	Hawaii Association of Contingency Planners Ray Trombley Tel: (808) 526-7125 State of Hawaii Civil Defense Tel: (808) 733-4300
IDAHO	State of Idaho Disaster Services Tel: (208) 334-3460
ILLINOIS	Business Resumption Planners Assoc (BRPA) William Lundquist Tel: (312) 540-3717 E-mail: William.Lundquist@US.PwCGlobal.com Illinois Emergency Services Management Assocation (IESMA) Bill Keller Tel: (217) 384-3826 www.iesma.org State of Illinois Emergency Management Association Tel: (217) 782-7860 www.state.il.us/iema/
INDIANA	Midwest Contingency Planners Gary Wyne Tel: (317) 276-6632 State of Indiana Emergency Management Tel: (317) 232-3984
IOWA	Iowa Contingency Planners Roberta Holmes Tel: (515) 225-5489 State of Iowa Disaster Services Tel: (515) 281-3231
KANSAS	Association of Contingency Planners Kansas Chapter Don Martens Tel: (316) 523-6820 Fax: (316) 523-6815 E-mail: don.martens@boeing.com or dmart10299@aol.com

(continued)

Table 10–1 *Continued*

State	Group or Agency
	Business Contingency Planning Forum of Northeast Kansas Dan Swearingen Tel: (785) 296-7422 Fax: (785) 296-8932 E-mail: dansw@dadisc1.wpo.state.ks.us
	Kansas Emergency Management Association Gary Rogers, President Tel: (785) 332-2560
	State of Kansas Emergency Management Tel: (785)274-1409
KENTUCKY	State of Kentucky Disaster & Emergency Services Tel: (502) 564-8630
LOUISIANA	State of Louisiana Emergency Preparedness Tel: (504) 342-1588
MAINE	Maine Business Continuity Information Exchange Linda Norden Tel: (781) 398-8062
	State of Maine Emergency Management Tel: (207) 287-4080
MARYLAND	Mid Atlantic Disaster Recovery Assoc (MADRA) Mike Slingluff Tel: (703) 450-3232
	State of Maryland Emergency Mgt. Agency David McMillion Tel: (410) 486-4422 Fax: (410) 486-1867 www.mema.state.md.us
MASSACHUSETTS	Northeast States Emergency Consortium Tel: (781) 224-9876
	Northern New England Disaster Recovery Information Exchange Bill Bruce Tel: (603) 437-2179
	State of Massachusetts Emergency Management Tel: (508) 820-2000
MICHIGAN	Great Lakes Business and Recovery Group Gwen Pfaff Tel: (248) 265-5724
	Michigan Emergency Management Association Charles Seehase Tel: (810) 469-5270

State	Group or Agency
	State of Michigan, Police: Emergency Management Division Capt. Edward G. Buikema Tel: (517) 333-5042 Fax: (517) 333-4987 E-mail: buikemae@state.mi.us
MINNESOTA	Business Continuity Planners Association Tel: (612) 223-9801
	State of Minnesota Emergency Management Tel: (651) 296-2233
MISSISSIPPI	State of Mississippi Emergency Management Tel: (601) 352-9100
MISSOURI	Mid America Contingency Planning Forum St. Louis Tom Roseler Tel: (314) 466-6662 Fax: (314) 466-4731
	Partnership for Emergency Planning (PEP) Kansas City Barb Ortmeier Tel: (913) 928-6862
	State of Missouri Emergency Management Agency Cathy Zumwalt Tel: (573) 526-9146 Fax: (573) 634-7966 E-mail: czumwalt@mail.state.mo.us
MONTANA	Association of Disaster & Emergency Services Jim King Tel: (406) 873-2084
	State of Montana Disaster & Emergency Services Tel: (406) 841-3911
NEBRASKA	Great Plains Contingency Planners Jerry Tritz, President Tel: (402) 351-3178
	State of Nebraska Emergency Management Tel: (402) 471-7410
NEVADA	County of Clark, Local Emergency Planning Committee Robert Andrews Tel: (702) 455-5710 Fax: (702) 455-5718
	State of Nevada Emergency Management Agency Tel: (702) 687-4240

(continued)

Table 10–1   *Continued*

State	Group or Agency
NEW HAMPSHIRE	State of New Hampshire Emergency Management Tel: (603) 271-2231
NEW JERSEY	Society for Computer and Information Protection (SCIP) Richard Critchley Tel: (973) 430-6725
	State of New Jersey Emergency Management Lt. Eric Sorchik Tel: (609) 882-2000 Fax: (609) 538-0345
NEW MEXICO	New Mexico Office of Emergency Management Emergency Management Center Tel: (505) 476-9600 Preparedness/Mitigation/Training Bureau Chief Tel: (505) 476-9640 Response & Recovery Bureau Chief Tel: (505) 476-9611 Hazardous Materials Bureau Chief Tel: (505) 476-9620 Information Systems Bureau Chief Tel: (505) 476-9692 http://www.dps.nm.org
NEW YORK	Contingency Planning Exchange James Certoma Tel: (212) 983-8644 www.cpeworld.org
	State of New York Emergency Management Tel: (518) 457-2222
NORTH CAROLINA	Contingency Planning Association of the Carolinas (CPAC) Al Wallis Tel: (704) 271-4650 www.cpaccarolinas.org E-mail: awallis@ncdc.noaa.gov
	State of North Carolina Emergency Management Tel: (919) 733-3825
NORTH DAKOTA	North Dakota Emergency Management Association Tim Heisler Tel: (701) 662-7001
	State of North Dakota Emergency Management Tel: (701) 328-3300

State	**Group or Agency**
OHIO	Contingency Planners of Ohio Dr. Calvin L. Taylor, President Tel: (614) 799-3688 Fax: (614) 799-3678 E-mail: ctaylor@dps.state.oh.us
	State of Ohio Emergency Management Agency James Williams, Acting Deputy Director Tel: (889) 880-7150 Fax: (614) 889-7183 www.state.oh.us/odps/division/ema
OKLAHOMA	Association of Contingency Planners Oklahoma Chapter Mick Myscofski Tel: (918) 595-4389 Fax: (918) 595-4374 E-mail: rmyscofski@tulsa-health.org
	State of Oklahoma Emergency Management Tel: (405) 521-2481
OREGON	Oregon Emergency Management Association Kelly Jo Jensen Tel: (503) 378-1329 Fax: (503) 391-9152 www.navicom.com/~oema
	State of Oregon Emergency Management Tel: (503) 378-4124
PENNSYLVANIA	Delaware Valley Business Resumption Information Exchange Group (DVBRIEG) Patricia Bennett Tel: (609) 635-9770 Fax: (609) 635-9766
	Northwestern Pennsylvania's Disaster Preparedness Committee Rick Robie, Committee Chairman Tel: (814) 835-1199 Fax: (814) 835-9203
	State of Pennsylvania Emergency Management Agency Tel: (717) 651-2001
	Three Rivers Contingency Planning Association Kathleen Criss Tel: (412) 641-4860
RHODE ISLAND	State of Rhode Island Emergency Management Agency Tel: (401) 946-9996

(continued)

Table 10–1   *Continued*

State	Group or Agency
SOUTH CAROLINA	Contingency Planning Assoc of the Carolinas (CPAC) Al Wallis Tel: (704) 271-4650 E-mail: awallis@ncdc.noaa.gov
	State of South Carolina Emergency Preparedness Tel: (803) 734-8020
SOUTH DAKOTA	State of South Dakota Office of Emergency Management Tel: (605) 773-3231
TENNESSEE	Association of Contingency Planners Middle Tennessee Chapter Mark Brewer Tel: (615) 781-7257 Fax: (615) 365-5550 E-mail: mark.brewer@fanb.com
	Business Emergency Preparedness Council (BEPC) Rex Holloway Tel: (901) 756-5103 Fax: (901) 756-5190 www.bepc.net
	Emergency Management Association of Tennessee Libbi Rucker-Reed, CEMP EMAT Secretary/Treasurer 1220 W. College St. Murfreesboro, TN 37129-1720 Tel: (615) 898-7764 Fax: (615) 898-7840 www.emat.org E-mail: ematweb@aol.com
	State of Tennessee, Emergency Management Tel: (615) 741-0001
TEXAS	Association of Contingency Planners North Texas Chapter John Small Tel: (214) 515-1226 Fax: (214) 515-1201 E-mail: jsmail@swst.com
	Association of Contingency Planners South Texas Chapter John Link Tel: (713) 216-2524 Fax: (713) 216-2524 E-mail: john.link@chase.com

State	Group or Agency
	Association of Contingency Planners Capital of Texas Chapter Joan Light Tel: (512) 463-4218 Fax: (512) 305-9785 E-mail: joan.light@cpa.state.tx.us
	County of Jasper, Emergency Management Billy Ted Smith Tel: (409) 423-4200 Fax: (409) 994-2543 www.ih2000.net/jasperem E-mail: btsmith@ih2000.net
	State of Texas, Emergency Management Michelle Johnson Tel: (512) 424-2430 Fax: (512) 424-2444
UTAH	Association of Contingency Planners Utah Chapter Michael Stever Tel: (801) 535-6030 Fax: (801) 535-6190 E-mail: mike.stever@ci.slc.ut.us
	State of Utah Emergency Management Tel: (801) 538-3400
	Utah Emergency Management Association Steve Layton Tel: (801) 774-7217
VERMONT	State of Vermont Emergency Management Tel: (800) 347-0488
VIRGINIA	Business Recovery Association of Virginia (BRAV) Clarence Elliott Tel: (804) 272-1549
	Mid Atlantic Disaster Recovery Association (MADRA) Mike Slingluff Tel: (703) 450-3232
	State of Virginia Emergency Services Tel: (804) 897-6500
WASHINGTON	Association of Contingency Planners Washington State Chapter Rick Roller Tel: (425) 865-3639 Fax: (425) 865-3327 E-mail: richard.l.roller@boeing.com

(continued)

Table 10–1   *Continued*

State	Group or Agency
	Western Washington Emergency Network (WWEN) Shad Burcham King County Office of Emergency Management 7300 Perimeter Rd. South, Room 128 Seattle, WA 98108-3848 Tel: (206) 205-8106 Fax: (206) 296-3938 http://hrs.crgnet.com/wwen E-mail: Shad.Burcham@METROKC.GOV
WEST VIRGINIA	State of West Virginia Office of Emergency Services John W. Pack, Jr. Tel: (304)558-5380 Fax: (304) 344-4538 E-mail: dirwvoes@mail.wvnet.edu
WISCONSIN	Business Recovery Planners Association of Wisconsin Paul Bergee Tel: (608) 231-7502
	State of Wisconsin Emergency Management Tel: (608) 242-3232
	Wisconsin Emergency Management Association Wayne Baetsen Tel: (715) 478-3430
WYOMING	State of Wyoming Emergency Management Agency Bob Bezek, Coordinator Tel: (307) 777-4900 Fax: (307) 635-6017 http://132.133.10.9 E-mail: wema@wy-iso.army.mil
	Wyoming Emergency Management Association Chuck Young Tel: (307) 877-9835

numbers, Web URLs, and, in some cases, addresses are provided for further information. With the assistance of the organizations involved, it is hoped that this list will be maintained in an up-to-date form on the website that serves as the companion to this book at HTTP://WWW.DR-PLANNING.ORG.

It is worth noting that the number of disaster recovery information groups has proliferated since the first edition of this book. In 1990, there were approximately ten such grassroots groups located mainly in the Eastern United States and in Canada—the oldest of these being the Delaware Valley Disaster Recovery Information Exchange Group. Each group comprised a mixture of IT and records professionals who perceived the need for DR and acknowledged the dearth of reliable information on the subject. Vendors were pleased to sponsor these organizations and to provide "expert" speakers for their meetings and conventions. Where else could vendors gain such direct access to such a cadre of potential customers?

Over time, these groups wittingly or unwittingly distinguished themselves as reliable DR information brokers and as a "quasi-police force" for an otherwise largely unregulated industry as IT and records managers swapped stories about the performance and cost of vendor products and services. As members exchanged their experiences with plan strategies and testing techniques, a consciousness about DR best practices began to coalesce. Organizations have since sought to replicate this experience on a national and international basis. Today, in the United States, the Association of Contingency Planners (ACP) boasts numerous regional chapters, while in Canada, the Disaster Recovery Information Exchange (DRIE) has grown to more than 450 members in six chapters across the country.[5] While some have complained of the bureaucratic infighting that has characterized some of the newer national and international organizations, DR information groups remain the best venue for learning about disaster recovery technologies and techniques and for gleaning an understanding of the actual disaster recovery milieu.

PROFESSIONAL ASSOCIATIONS

Over the course of this discussion, a number of professional associations in fields not specifically related to disaster recovery planning have been cited for the insights they offer to business preparedness and recovery. Table 10–2 provides a list of some of these associations for further reference by planners.

THE "FRICTION" OF DISASTER

In addition to DR planner/emergency management groups and non-DR-specific professional associations, a number of resources exist for coordinators seeking information that will aid them in planning efforts. From

Table 10–2   Partial Listing of Non-DRP Professional Associations
with DR-Related Focus

Association of Records Managers and Administrators	ARMA International 4200 Somerset Dr., #215 Prairie Village, KS 66208 Phone: 913-341-3808 800-422-2762 (U.S. and Canada) FAX: 913-341-3742 (fax) hq@arma.org URL: www.arma.org	ARMA International is a not-for-profit association serving more than 10,000 information management professionals in the United States, Canada, and over 30 other nations. ARMA International members include records and information managers, MIS and ADP professionals, imaging specialists, archivists, hospital administrators, legal administrators, librarians, and educators. The mission of ARMA International is to provide education, research, and networking opportunities to information professionals, to enable them to use their skills and experience to leverage the value of records, information, and knowledge as corporate assets and as contributors to organizational success.
National Fire Protection Association	NFPA 1 Batterymarch Park PO Box 9101 Quincy, MA 02269-9101 Phone: 617-770-3000 URL: www.nfpa.org	The National Fire Protection Association (NFPA), headquartered in Quincy, Massachusetts, USA, is an international, nonprofit, membership organization founded in 1896 to protect people, their property, and the environment from destructive fire. In more than 100 years of advocacy, NFPA has established its role as the leading worldwide advisor on the topics of fire safety and protection. More than 65,000 strong, NFPA's membership represents nearly 100 nations and is open to all individuals interested in promoting a safer world.

Association of Information Technology Professionals	AITP 315 South Northwest Highway Suite 200 Park Ridge, IL 60068-4278 Phone: 847-825-8124 800-224-9371 FAX: 847-825-1693 URL: www.aitp.org	AITP is the professional association comprised of career-minded individuals who seek to expand their potential—employers, employees, managers, programmers, and many others. The organization seeks to provide avenues for all their members to be teachers as well as students and to make contact with other members in the IS field, all in an effort to become more marketable in rapidly changing, technological careers.
Information Systems Security Association	ISSA 7044 South 13th Street Oak Creek, WI 53154 Phone: 414-768-8000 FAX: 414-768-8001 URL: www.issa-intl.org	The primary goal of the Information Systems Security Association, Inc. (ISSA) is to promote management practices that will ensure the confidentiality, integrity, and availability of organizational information resources. To achieve this goal, members of the Association must reflect the highest standards of ethical conduct and technical competence. Therefore, ISSA has established Code of Ethics and requires its observance as a prerequisite and continuation of membership and affiliation with the Assocation.
Information Systems Audit and Control Association	Information Systems Audit and Control Association/Foundation 3701 Algonquin Road, Suite 1010 Rolling Meadows, IL 60008 Telephone: 847-253-1545 FAX: 847-253-1443 URL: www.isaca.org	With more than 20,000 members in more than 100 countries, the Information Systems Audit and Control Association (ISACA) is well on its way to achieving its vision of being the recognized global leader in IT governance, control, and assurance. Founded in 1969, ISACA sponsors international conferences, administers the globally respected CISA® (Certified Information Systems Auditor) designation held by more than 12,000 professionals worldwide, and develops globally applicable Information Systems (IS) Auditing and Control Standards. An affiliated Foundation undertakes leading-edge research in support of the profession.

(continued)

Table 10–2   *Continued*

International Association of Emergency Managers	IAEM 111 Park Place Falls Church, VA 22046-4513 Telephone: 703-538-1795 FAX: 703-241-5603 URL: www.iaem.com	The International Association of Emergency Managers (IAEM) is a nonprofit educational organization dedicated to promoting the goals of saving lives and protecting property during emergencies and disasters.
National Emergency Management Association	National Emergency Management Association C/O Council of State Governments P.O. Box 11910 Lexington, KY 40578 Telephone: 606-244-8000 606-244-8239 URL: www.nemaweb.org	NEMA is the professional association of State and Pacific Caribbean insular state emergency management directors committed to providing national leadership and expertise in comprehensive emergency management; serving as a vital information and assistance resource for state and territorial directors and their governors; and forging strategic partnerships to advance continuous improvements in emergency management.
Network Professionals Association	NPA 710 East Ogden Avenue, Suite 600 Naperville, IL 60563 Telephone: 630-579-3282 FAX: 630-369-2488 npa@npa.org URL: www.npa.org	NPA endeavors to unite network computing professionals in a worldwide association; determine member needs and interests; deliver programs and services to meet those needs and interests.
Risk and Insurance Management Society ——	RIMS 655 Third Avenue New York, NY 10017-5367 Phone: 212-286-9292 FAX: 212-986-9716	The Risk and Insurance Management Society, Inc. (RIMS) serves its member entities by proactively providing the highest quality products, services and information to manage all forms of business risk.

severe weather tracking to virus alerts to emergency assistance (both financial and personal), the World Wide Web provides a wealth of resources. Table 10–3 summarizes information resources that may be useful in understanding the milieu in which disaster recovery may take place, and in seeking assistance and information, before, during and immediately following a disaster event.

Participating in DR organizations, reading the case studies, and talking to infrastructure service vendors and emergency managers are all part of an ongoing "sanity check" in DR planning. They are as important as any other plan development activity because they help to "condition" the coordinator and his or her DR teams to the world in which their plans will execute.

In some respects, disaster recovery planning can be likened to the preparations for a battle during war. The classic military thinker, von Clausewitz, expresses the difference between planning and execution as the "friction" of battle.

> Everything is very simple in war, but the simplest thing is difficult. These difficulties accumulate and produce a friction that no man can imagine exactly who has not seen war...Friction is the only conception, which in a general way corresponds to that which distinguishes real war from war on paper. The military machine, the army and all belonging to it, is in fact simple, and appears on this account easy to manage. But let us reflect that no part of it is in one piece, that it is composed entirely of individuals, each of which keeps up its own friction in all directions.[6]

Without bending the metaphor too far, von Clausewitz's description of friction in battle can also be applied to the implementation of disaster recovery plans. Many factors—from human to milieu—can and do impact the execution of most plans. Regardless of the theoretical soundness of the paper plan, it is at best a jumping off point for disaster response.

The DR coordinator and his or her lieutenants need to understand and rehearse the strategies and procedures detailed in the plan until they have honed their ability to perform their assigned roles within acceptable timeframes. Plan testing, discussed in the next chapter, helps to build this type of ability.

However, in the absence of actual experience with disaster, coordinators and teams need to exploit every possible avenue for understanding

Table 10–3 Milieu Information Resources on the Web

Books and Magazines	The Rothstein Catalog on Disaster Recovery URL: www.rothstein.com	Since 1989, one of the most comprehensive resources for books, DR software tools, videos and research reports related to disaster recovery.
	The Disaster Resource Guide URL: www.disaster-resource.com	An excellent guide to the latest articles on DR-related topics, and up-to-date lists of product/service vendors, disaster recovery-related web resources, and forthcoming conferences and tradeshows.
	Summit Online URL: www.summitonline.com/white.html	The latest industry white papers on systems and network management issues, including DR
	Prove-IT Initiative URL: www2.dlttape.com/proveit/index.htm	Quantum's DLT tape contextualized as a disaster recovery solution. However, good generic information and whitepapers on DR planning.
Alerts and Emergency Information	Federal Emergency Management Administration Tropical Storm Watch URL: www.fema.gov/fema/trop.htm	Latest FEMA information on tropical storms and disaster relief activities.
	U.S. Geological Survey Water Data URL: h20.usgs.gov/public/realtime.html	Latest data from USGS on drought, floods, and other water-related issues.
	National Oceanic and Atmospheric Administration URL: www.noaa.gov/	Portal provides links to the National Hurricane Center, National Weather Service, and Weather Satellite Imaging Information.
	National Earthquake Information Center URL: www.neic.cr.usgs.gov/	Another USGS site with up-to-date earthquake information.
	Symantec Antivirus Research Center URL: www.symantec.com/avcenter/	Two websites from anti-virus software makers providing alerts about computer viruses and tools for removing them from systems.

	Trend Micro AntiVirus Alerts URL: www.antivirus.com/ vinfo/	
Emergency Response	CERT Coordination Center URL: www.cert.org/	The CERT Coordination Center is part of the Survivable Systems Initiative at the Software Engineering Institute, a federally funded research and development center at Carnegie Mellon University. CERT was started by DARPA (the Defense Applied Research Projects Agency, part of the U.S. Department of Defense) in December 1988 after the Morris Worm incident crippled approximately 10% of all computers connected to the Internet. Originally, the work of CERT was almost exclusively incident response. Since then, the organization has worked to help start other incident response teams, coordinate the efforts of teams when responding to larg-scale incidents, provide training to incident response professionals, and research the causes of security vulnerabilities, prevention of vulnerabilities, system security improvement, and survivability of large-scale networks.
	Forum of Incident Response and Security Teams (FIRST) URL: www.first.org	Since November 1988, an almost continuous stream of security-related incidents has affected thousands of computer systems and networks throughout the world. To address this threat, a growing number of government and private sector organizations around the globe have established a coalition to exchange information and coordinate response activities.

(continued)

365

This coalition, the Forum of Incident Response and Security Teams (FIRST), brings together a variety of computer security incident response teams from government, commercial, and academic organizations. FIRST aims to foster cooperation and coordination in incident prevention, to prompt rapid reaction to incidents, and to promote information sharing among members and the community at large. Currently FIRST has nearly 70 members.

American National Red Cross
URL: www.redcross.org

The American Red Cross, a humanitarian organization led by volunteers and guided by its Congressional Charter and the Fundamental Principles of the International Red Cross Movement, will provide relief to victims of disasters and help people prevent, prepare for, and respond to emergencies.

National Infrastructure Protection Center
URL: www.nipc.gov

The mission of the NIPC is both a national security and law enforcement effort to detect, deter, assess, warn of, respond to, and investigate computer intrusions and unlawful acts, both physical and "cyber," that threaten or target critical infrastructures, including telecommunications, energy, banking and finance, water systems, government operations, and emergency services. The NIPC's job is not simply to investigate and respond to attacks after they occur, but to learn about preventing them. The site lists current advisories and warnings the "friction of recovery," albeit, secondhand. They need to listen to the accounts of those who have actually experienced disasters (the only true "gurus" in this field) and attempt to define better the milieu in which their plans will be executed. This milieu focus is critical to the translation of capability into recovery.

ENDNOTES

1. Wendy Goldman Rohm, "That's All That's Left!" *InfoSystems*, 02/87.
2. Jon William Toigo, "Bosch Overcomes Hurricane Hugo," *Contingency Journal*, 03/90.
3. Carol Silwa and Julia King, "Storm Tests IT Plans," *Computerworld*, 09/20/99.
4. Carol Silwa, "Plans Being Laid for Next Time," *Computerworld*, 09/20/99.
5. The DISASTER RECOVERY INFORMATION EXCHANGE (DRIE) can be contacted via telephone at (416) 491-2420 or on the web at *www.drie.org*. According to the DRIE website, the six chapter organizations include:

DRIE Toronto
Graeme Jannaway
2175 Sheppard Avenue East, Suite 310
Willowdale, Ontario, Canada M2J 1W8
(416) 359-6218 Fax: (416) 491-1670
E-mail: Graeme.Jannaway@NesbittBurns.com

DRIE Ottawa
Brian Miller
(613) 238-2909 Fax: (613) 238-2902
E-mail: bp.miller@sympatico.ca

DRIE Montreal
Andre Gagnon
(450) 466-4911
E-mail: agagnon@zercom.net

DRIE West (serving Calgary, Edmonton & Vancouver)
Cheryl Bieson
(403) 543-4699
E-mail: cbieson@telusplanet.net

DRIE SW Ontario
Rod Mabley
(519) 895-1213 x 795 Fax: (519) 895-1215
E-mail: mableyr@recall.com

DRIE Central (serving Manitoba, Saskatchewan, & NW Ontario)
(204) 985-4854

Another organization endeavoring to establish an international presence for disaster recovery planning is SURVIVE! INTERNATIONAL, Tel: 011-800 SURVIVE 5, Fax: +44 181 874 6446, with a web presence at www.survive.com.

6. Carl von Clausewitz, *On War*, translated and edited by Michael Howard and Peter Paret (Princeton, NJ: Princeton University Press, 1976 and 1984).

CHAPTER

11

Plan Maintenance and Testing

The plan is finished at last! Strategies for system, network, and user recovery have been meticulously honed into straightforward, step-by-step procedures, tied together by a solid-but-flexible emergency decision-making flowchart. To the extent possible, a documented capability has been put into place that will safeguard the company against the vicissitudes of nature and man.

Coordinators who reach this point in the disaster recovery planning project often sense a special moment of exhilaration. Too many, however, end their efforts here.

The disaster recovery document for a large company with numerous critical functions can be voluminous and impressive in appearance. Perched atop a shelf in the office of the coordinator or information manager, it may be a source of pride, evoking praise from senior management and auditors alike. However, there on the shelf, gathering dust, the document is also useless.

Disaster recovery plans are living documents that must grow and change as the businesses they are to safeguard grow and change. In short, plans must be tested frequently and maintained in a state that is consistent with the requirements of changing business processes.

As previously cited, plans must exist not only on paper or electronic media, but in the minds of those who will enact them. This presumes training and education.

These points are more than philosophical. Given the increasing pressure of federal regulation and state legislation, the increasing scrutiny of the media and of shareholders, and the decreasing tolerance of companies to even short-term interruptions of critical applications, auditors are less inclined to pass untested plans without comment. They want to see proof that the plan will work and that the company's money has not been invested in anything less than the best capability their money can buy.

Unlike science fiction television dramas, in which desperate last-minute repairs made to critical systems are tested in mortal combat, disaster recovery plan testing should occur in advance of disaster itself. Clearly, it is the wrong time to discover erroneous conclusions and errant strategies when the company is in the throes of an unplanned interruption of mission critical business processes. At that point, the plan's disaster is the company's as well. Plan components need to be tested in a context of rationality, not crisis, so that lessons learned are not learned at the expense of business survival.

Some of the elements of plan maintenance and some approaches to testing planned strategies and procedures are discussed in the following sections. Many coordinators, including those who owe their expertise to having recovered from smoke-and-rubble-type disasters, argue that testing is the most important element of disaster recovery planning. For all of the reasons cited above, they are probably correct.

TEAM EDUCATION

Before a disaster recovery plan can be implemented, whether in a test situation or in an actual crisis, those who will be called upon to implement the plan must understand their roles. Educating recovery teams may require a mixture of classroom, distance learning, and hands-on instructional methods. Getting all team members to become committed to and conversant in the plan is sometimes as great a challenge as developing the plan itself.

The coordinator needs to keep in mind that those who attend DR training may not be terribly enthusiastic participants. Some may have been compelled to attend and may view the training as an unwelcome interference with their important work. Conversely, to others, training may be viewed as a vacation, an escape from day-to-day work schedules. Generally, the majority of trainees do not share the coordinator's zeal for disaster recovery planning. Being cognizant of this will help prevent misunderstandings on the part of the coordinator and dissuade him or her from seeking or expecting the appreciation of the planning effort undertaken up to this point.

The coordinator should focus team training as narrowly as possible on the specific components of the plan that pertain to the team being trained. (Teams, by the way, should be trained separately, then team leaders and alternates should be given special education in the "bigger picture"—the ways in which the activities for which they are responsible interact with other activities documented in the plan.) Teach trainees what they need to know, not how well the plan is organized.

There are a number of guidelines that coordinators need to keep in mind when presenting the plan in a training environment. Knowing what they are can aid in training even the most reluctant student.

1. Be brief and to the point. Especially when training technical teams, it is important to package the information in short, digestible amounts, appropriate to the skill level of the trainees. Unless asked, avoid lengthy digressions into the rationale behind the selection of a particular strategy.

2. Target the audience for level of presentation. Coordinators need not explain the differences between multi-drop and point-to-point circuits to a network team. Where possible (i.e., where the coordinator clearly understands the concepts and jargon), use terms and language familiar to the trainee.

3. Use multimedia teaching methods. Coordinators should try to mix their methods for communicating information. Provide text handouts. Use overhead projectors, video, slides, flip charts—whatever is available and appropriate. Nothing is duller than an hour of lecture.

4. Make the presentation formal. Prepare an agenda. Rehearse. Designate start and stop times. Set objectives for the group and meet them. This demonstrates respect for trainees and earns their respect.

5. Address all questions to the extent possible. If the coordinator cannot answer a question competently, he or she should make a note and follow up at a later time. Encourage constructive participation and make notes of serious questions or concerns the trainees offer. They may be valuable considerations that will improve the plan.

6. Finish on time. If there is more material to cover, plan another session.

7. Advise the trainees that there is no test at the conclusion of the training, but that their performance in a forthcoming plan test may be evaluated by their managers.

8. Give the team members copies of the plan sections that pertain to them. Ask them to review the procedures, submit any comments or corrections that they feel may be needed, and designate a date. If the next test date is known, announce it so they are prepared.

Team leaders and their alternates require extra training to familiarize them with the "big picture"—the interdependencies of the activities of their teams and how they combine to provide the business recovery capability. Here, some informality is recommended in order to create a sense of self-confidence and team unity. Team leaders are generally assigned several time-consuming tasks, such as maintaining their sections of the plan and ensuring that staff turnover does not leave a team position vacant. To facilitate their cooperation, coordinators should strive to develop a good personal rapport with team leaders.

Often the most difficult training problem exists at the senior management level. The Emergency Management Team is typically comprised of senior managers. If possible, the coordinator may be able to offload the task of "training" senior management to his or her manager (usually an IT director or CIO). If this is not the case, the coordinator needs to be prepared to provide senior managers with a high-level overview of the plan, emphasizing the emergency decision-making flowchart.

Most decision-making flowcharts are rather vague when it comes to the emergency management task path. The idea is that the team will coordinate the activities of other teams and make key decisions along the way, as well as arranging the financing of the recovery effort. Thus, "procedures" for the Emergency Management Team plan section often consist of lists of issues that the team will need to address as recovery proceeds. Criteria or guidelines for addressing the issues within the context of planned recovery strategies may also be offered.

Because of these characteristics, the emergency management section of the plan requires little maintenance. Thus, training senior managers in their recovery role may take the form of a presentation rather than a formal training session, often combining a tour of emergency operations center facilities.

PLAN MAINTENANCE

One of the more challenging aspects of the disaster recovery coordinator's job is maintenance of the plan over time. Changes to the business processes that the plan seeks to protect (or changes in the technology infrastructure that supports these processes) come to the coordinator's attention in one of three ways. The first (and preferred way) is through the change management procedure. This procedure should be outlined in the plan to provide a means for regularly auditing plan procedures for their continued adequacy.

The second way in which changes reach the coordinator's attention is through tests. Tests are conducted for a variety of reasons, such as acclimatizing teams to their roles, verifying new strategies, establishing or validating restoration timeframes or other plan assumptions, appeasing auditors, and so on. However, a test can also identify where deficits exist within the plan in the recovery of a given business process.

The third way in which changes affecting the plan are discovered is through audit reports. This is the least desirable method since it may call into question the adequacy or effectiveness of the overall plan or the competence of the plan coordinator. With adequate testing, however, problems can be detected before an audit notes their existence. This is one reason why auditors should be involved in testing: They tend not to criticize test results, even if deficits are discovered, inasmuch as testing is a sign of intent to correct. There is no such thing as a failure in testing. Tests are used to gain knowledge, not to disparage plans.

Of course, there is one other way that problems in the plan can reveal themselves: in actual implementation. However, this is the least desirable way to discover plan inadequacies.

CHANGE MANAGEMENT

Suffice it to say that change management procedures, combined with periodic testing, comprise the preferred approach to plan maintenance. The question remains: Is there an approach to change management that can streamline and make the plan maintenance function less burdensome?

The answer to this question is yes. An important first step is to examine the business processes and their IT infrastructure supports in order to identify elements that are likely to change over time. These elements probably include data, programs, documentation, supplies and forms, hardware, and personnel. Of these items, changes in the size and shape of company databases are probably the most expected and self-evident.

Changes in data have two ramifications for disaster recovery planning. First, the disaster recovery coordinator needs to be familiar with the procedures for purging old data and archiving data that needs to be preserved. The coordinator needs to ensure that backup and off-site storage procedures remain adequate to safeguard data against loss.

Also in the realm of data change management issues is the creation of specialized databases on servers and workstations within the company. As new PCs and servers are acquired, their purpose and use need to be documented and provisions need to be made to securing and backing up their data. This task requires vigilance on the part of the coordinator and may be greatly facilitated through a combination of corporate policy and data discovery and classification tools discussed in Chapter 4. In the absence of these mechanisms, tracking data recovery requirements alone may pose as great a challenge as the entire disaster recovery planning process.

If IT acquisitions (including PCs) are controlled through a company IT department, the coordinator only needs to develop an interface to the acquisition process to remain informed about new installations. Controlled server and workstation acquisition can yield other benefits as well. For example, users requesting workstations may be required to schedule time for disaster recovery and security awareness training in conjunction with their acquisitions.

However, it is still the case in many companies that workstations are not acquired through conventional IT channels. As prices decline and user knowledge increases, the disaster recovery coordinator may find that PCs are acquired in the same manner as office supplies and that the number of company "data centers" increases from week to week. In this case, the coordinator may need to solicit a senior management policy to be kept apprised of acquisitions. Even if management cannot be convinced to place control over the purchase of computer technology in the hands of corporate IT professionals, few would disagree with efforts to track distributed computing assets and most would agree to implement policies aimed at safeguarding assets from loss. With management support, the coordinator may be able to arrange with departmental managers to be informed of technology purchases.

The second ramification of data change is its impact on hardware. As data grows, it may be necessary to acquire additional mass storage devices, including hard disks, arrays, network attached storage (NAS) devices, or storage area network (SAN) peripherals. These acquisitions need to be documented in the equipment inventory included to the plan and will need to become part of a hot site agreement if their replacement is expected as part of the vendor's services.

In addition to changes in data and its storage, coordinators also need to remain vigilant to the introduction of new applications as well as changes, enhancements, and modifications to existing applications that may impact the plan. Such additions and changes may also be an indicator of changing business processes that must be accounted for in the plan.

While some application changes do not affect the procedures for restoring critical systems in the event of a disaster, each change should be documented—usually as a function of IT development operations. At a minimum, the DR coordinator should ensure that copies of the documentation are removed to off-site storage for use in recovery efforts.

By contrast, major modifications or additions to the software inventory of the company must be investigated for their impact on recovery requirements and strategies. New applications may introduce significant new demands on processors, memory, and storage, altering the recovery systems configuration envisioned in the plan and provided for in a systems recovery service agreement. New applications may also impact network requirements and end user recovery.

Of even greater significance, enhancements or additions to the software inventory may also reflect changing business processes and associated criticalities. Company business plans may offer insights into these changes, but more often the managers of end user departments can provide information about new directions for their operational areas. Thus, periodic questionnaires, accompanied by a copy of the original responses, should be circulated to end user managers with the request that managers update their information.

In the case of software changes and enhancements prompted by technical rationales (that is, changes required by operating system or applications software upgrades, etc.), recovery team leaders, who are generally members of IT department staff, should be directed to update their sections of the plan at periodic intervals. It is worth noting that the term "software changes" may include changes to telecommunications switch or data networking device programming as well as computer software.

Documentation changes associated with software additions, modifications, and changes nearly always entail a review of the disaster recovery plan's provisions for off-site storage. Coordinators, or their off-site storage team leaders, should regularly inventory documentation that is off-site to ensure that only the most current documentation is stored and outdated or obsolete documentation is destroyed. This includes the disaster recovery plan itself.

As business processes change, support requirements such as pre-printed forms and other supplies are also likely to change. If stores of these materials are kept off-site or at a user recovery facility, they need to be inventoried periodically and outdated materials culled from useful supplies. The emergency supplier list (persons to be contacted to obtain replacement supplies and materials in the event of a disaster) also needs to be reviewed to ensure that changing supply requirements can be met by listed suppliers. This review should reveal whether a designated supplier has gone out of business. Where this is the case, any open purchase orders with the former supplier should be closed out and new suppliers should be identified.

Hardware changes require that plan inventories be updated and that hot sites be notified of these changes. Major system conversions may invalidate the existing hot site capability by creating backup requirements that the hot site vendor cannot meet. Thus, a major hardware change may necessitate evaluating new hot site vendors and negotiating a new contract.

Hardware change is a broad category that includes changes to communications as well as computer configurations. It is also important to review network configurations for line changes and additions, communications hardware changes and upgrades, and other network modifications that threaten to invalidate traffic rerouting plans or network backup strategies.

Personnel turnover poses a major challenge to disaster recovery change management. New personnel must be trained in the roles they will play in disaster recovery. Emergency contact directories also need to be updated to reflect new personnel and changed home and emergency telephone numbers. For the company as a whole, the maintenance of a general employee contact directory might best be delegated to the human resources or personnel department; while for teams, team leaders should be responsible for keeping contact lists up to date.

Tools for Change Management—No Easy Fix

As of this writing, no commercially available DR planning tool exists that can reasonably claim to improve the efficiency of disaster recovery plan maintenance. Some vendors claim to provide ease of maintenance features as a function of their "canned plan" product. In other words, if the coordinator uses the template provided by the vendor to develop the plan, data elements inserted by the coordinator into the planning tool boilerplate will be neatly organized in a table or database for ease of editing.

While there is value to collecting changing data elements in a discrete table, the proposition that this simplifies change management assumes several things. First, the vendor is implying that the boilerplate plan tool is compatible with the specific requirements of each and every company that uses it. As previously suggested, the disaster recovery requirements of any two companies are often highly dissimilar, mitigating the efficacy of such boilerplate planning tools generally. This limitation extends to the "ease of maintenance" features as well.

Second, simple changes to data elements, as noted above, are rarely all that is needed to maintain a plan in its current state. For example, it is rarely an adequate response to a change in application software to simply note the new application filename in a table. The impact of an application change may be, and often is, much more far reaching.

In some cases, an application change may require the reengineering of the recovery hardware platform, the creation of a new team, changes to supplies lists, new data storage requirements, and so forth. The "change management features" of boilerplate plan tools offer little to streamline the review that must accompany each and every data element change; they simply make the easiest task—editing an element list—a bit easier.

To facilitate the change management task requires several things. First is good communications traversing over well-defined processes.

The coordinator needs to define routine intervals for gathering change data and standard reporting mechanisms for collecting change data. Intervals may be based on calendar periods (that is, team leaders will make a quarterly report of business process and IT infrastructure changes and their impact on the disaster recovery capability) or events (that is, changes will be undertaken following plan tests or significant corporate events such as the implementation/reorganization of new/existing business units, deployment, upgrade or migration to new host systems, and so forth). However reporting intervals are defined, they need to be articulated as a matter of policy, and team leaders and business unit managers need to be made responsible for adherence to established change management policy and procedures.

Modern email and collaborative computing software provide powerful resources for coordinating the collection of change management information. Based on the input from reporting sources, the DR coordinator needs to review existing tasks and provisions, solicit additional input as needed, and make the necessary modifications to the existing plan. Teams

need to be trained in new requirements and tasks and testing and validation activities need to be scheduled.

By organizing the plan document on some rational basis—sectioning
recovery plan procedures by business process, for example—change management may be somewhat simplified. However, no amount of upfront
organization can substitute for the application of careful analytical reasoning to the evaluation of change and its impact on plan elements. Were it
otherwise, the DR coordinator could hand off the maintenance of the plan
to a tech writer once it was first implemented and tested.

TESTING TO MAINTAIN THE PLAN

Plan testing is an important component of plan maintenance activity as
tests are the crucibles in which the plan's validity is demonstrated. The
central purpose of testing is to ensure that plans can be successfully applied to recover the business processes that they have been developed to
safeguard. However, there are other purposes for testing the plan.

- *Testing as an audit tool.* Plan tests are often used to evaluate the efficiency of the plan and to reveal its shortcomings. If the criteria
  for evaluating test results are properly defined, tests can provide
  useful information about deficiencies in the plan so that they can be
  corrected.

- *Testing as benchmarking.* Plan tests may also reveal useful information
  about performance of the recovery capability. Certain tests can
  benchmark how quickly, under optimal conditions, recovery can be
  reasonably expected to occur following plan activation. Live tests (involving the actual implementation of plan provisions) can also provide information on the service levels that are likely to be provided
  from remote system and network configurations during a period of
  emergency operations. This data can be used to fine tune plan provisions and to evaluate the adequacy of business interruption insurance coverage.

- *Testing as rehearsal.* Tests are a valuable training experience for team
  members. They provide an opportunity for teams to become familiar
  with their roles in disaster recovery as well as how their activities relate to the activities of the other teams. Moreover, post-test debriefings
  of test participants can provide insights into implementation factors
  that the disaster recovery coordinator may not have considered.

Testing also provides a psychological benefit to participants. They become better prepared to function in a crisis due to the familiarity they acquire with procedures and tasks in a test situation. Furthermore, testing can help to build team unity by demonstrating the interdependence of team members upon each other.

Testing methods are numerous and the ones employed should be customized to the needs of a given business. Disaster recovery coordinators differ in their approaches to testing. Some prefer to test without prior notification of test participants in order to simulate the shock and crisis of an actual disaster. Others believe this approach has little merit, claiming that tests should be routine exercises that provide a basis for calm, rational implementation of plan procedures in an actual emergency. Some companies test sections of the plan separately (i.e., they perform a hot site test on one occasion and test various other plan components, one at a time, on other occasions). Other coordinators prefer a dry run of the total recovery process.

The approach taken by a specific company will generally be determined by the tolerance of the company to interruption of normal work for testing. Few companies are willing to allow a coordinator to "pull the plug" on their computer systems in order to see how efficiently teams will react to a mock disaster. Not many more are willing to shut down normal operations for an evacuation drill. However, it may be argued that effective testing does not require these approaches. The following procedures are some of the basic requirements for effective testing of the disaster recovery plan.

- *Establish a scenario in advance.* Before undertaking a test, a test strategy needs to be developed. The strategy, often set forth in a document, should identify the scope of the disaster scenario (total loss of facility, loss of CO services, fire in the user working area, flooding of the data center, etc.). The document should also indicate any assumptions that are being made, such as the anticipated duration of the outage, the availability (or unavailability) of key recovery personnel, or the opportunity to perform a last minute backup of critical data.

  In addition to these stage-setting directions, the coordinator may wish to provide details on specific production files that will be recovered, special security requirements, or other factors that will define the elements that are to be tested. In other words, although the disaster may encompass all systems, the coordinator may wish to test only the part of the system recovery plan that pertains to distributed systems application recovery or accounting system recovery. This will limit the actual procedures that are executed in the test.

- *Set test objectives.* Tests should be performed only after formal objectives have been set. Objectives should state clearly what the exercise is to test. For example, the test may seek to determine, under certain conditions, how quickly system and applications software can be brought up on hot site hardware. Or, the test may seek to determine how long data reconstruction will take if a disaster occurs at 3:00 PM on a working day and transactions entered since 9:00 AM have been lost. The test may also seek to measure the performance of a concentrator used in conjunction with a set of user workstations thought to have low activity profiles.

  Whatever the objectives, they should be clearly stated prior to the test exercise to aid in the interpretation of test results at the conclusion of the exercise. Generally, the narrower the objectives, the more useful the information derived from the test will be.

- *Define the rules.* The rules in a test may be to perform the required recovery operation in strict adherence to planned procedures. Where deviation from the plan is required to accomplish the task, this reveals something about the adequacy of plan procedures, and participants may be required to make careful notes of what undocumented steps they must take to accomplish the objective.

  In rare cases, the rules for the test may be open-ended. Traditionally, this type of test rule is used to evaluate how well a team participant can improvise or develop procedures where none previously existed.

- *Identify participants and observers.* A list should be made of the team members and observers (often internal audit, IT management, and others) who will participate in the test. Each should be made fully aware of his or her role *before* the test occurs (unless the test is a surprise). Observers should be told what to look for and what to do (i.e., take notes, ask questions). Team members should be told the rules and given any other directions that will help them to collect valuable information during the test.

- *Document the test results.* Depending on the objectives of the test, output may be printed in the form of system performance measurements, transaction logs, or other reports containing data sought from the test. This data will be analyzed, and both the original documents and the conclusions drawn from them retained with the plan. Test conclusions and source documentation are an important part of the documentation an auditor will require when auditing the disaster recovery plan.

In addition to machine-generated data, test objectives may require written reports from test participants. Specific performance measurements, such as elapsed time to perform a given task or delays in recovering systems, may be included in post-test documentation. In addition, subjective assessments of plan performance may be sought from participants. These subjective assessments may be balanced by obtaining more than a single viewpoint on a given subject. Conflicting views or interpretations necessitate a group discussion with the results summarized in a final test report. Written reports, like the machine output, should be kept with the plan document for review by auditors.

There is no guideline for how often plans should be tested, but tests should be conducted as often as necessary. In stable, evolutionary data processing environments, system recovery plans should be tested quarterly or semiannually. However, in shops where system configurations and applications change often, more frequent testing may be required.

In addition to what is presented here, much more detailed information on testing methods is available from a number of sources:

- *Consultants and vendors:* Many DR planning and business continuity planning consultants specialize in developing and overseeing tests. They offer experience and a "fresh perspective" that may be of use to DR coordinators in ensuring that tests are performed efficiently and yield productive results. Vendors of disaster recovery services, such as hot sites, can also provide assistance on test definition and management. Coordinators should consider using the resources, especially if they have never tested a DR plan before.

- *Books and other educational resources:* The number of books on disaster recovery and business continuity have increased almost exponentially since the publication of the first edition of *Disaster Recovery Planning* in 1990. One book in particular, *Disaster Recovery Testing* (1995), edited by consultant Philip Jan Rothstein, provides the views and techniques of numerous practitioners. This book and a host of others on related subjects can be acquired via the web-based Rothstein Catalog on Disaster Recovery (http://www.rothstein.com), arguably the most complete repository of information about books, software tools, videos, and research reports in the disaster recovery field.

- *Consult fellow planners:* The disaster recovery groups listed in the previous chapter provide yet another opportunity to learn about the testing methods used by disaster recovery planners. The meetings, conventions, and other forums offered by DR groups typically include educational presentations geared to a practical business environment. Additionally, some junior colleges, colleges, and universities offer short courses (and a few degree programs) on disaster recovery and emergency management. Program administrators may be able to recommend a particular class that treats testing methods and issues in detail.

MANAGING THE RESULTS

Given the massive amounts of information that will often be generated by maintenance and testing, it is possible for the disaster recovery coordinator to lose sight of the purpose of plan testing itself. Testing provides more than back matter to the paper plan. While good test documentation will satisfy auditors and others that the plan is not simply gathering dust on a bookshelf, this is not the central objective of testing any more than producing a paper plan is the primary objective of DR planning.

Testing provides the means to cultivate understanding and preparedness among those who will need to behave rationally in the face of the great irrationality of disaster. For this reason, the old saw—that there are no failed tests—continues to have merit. Testing provides a period of time during which participants focus on the difficult "what ifs." Through testing, participants may find that strategies and procedures have missed important requirements and these insights will yield important improvements to the corporate recovery capability. A test cannot fail. Regardless of the outcome, testing always achieves its two primary objectives: (1) rehearsing teams who will be responsible for coping with a disaster and (2) identifying ways to improve the coping capability that has been established in advance of a disaster.

A final thought on plan maintenance and testing is this: It is important to have a copy of the plan stored on magnetic media to facilitate edits and changes. If this approach is adopted, however, it is essential that both hard copy and magnetic media backups be made of the plan. Every effort needs to be made to ensure the accessibility of the plan to decision makers and implementers if and when an unplanned interruption occurs.

Beyond this, to quote Shakespeare, "All things are ready if our minds be so."

CHAPTER 12

Conclusion

When originally released in 1990, this book was conceived as a practical guide for information managers. In fact, it was a compilation of all of the information that I wished I had known when, as a technical staff member within the MIS Division at a medium-sized financial services company, I was first handed the task of disaster recovery planning. At that time, when asked how long I thought the project would take to complete, I estimated confidently, "About two weeks." Little did I know!

Two months and one hurricane later, I found myself still wrestling with the myriad details of a thousand what-if scenarios. Not one procedure had been written. Not one strategy had been developed. No testing had occurred. Yet, somehow, the document had grown to exceed the page count of the *New York Times* Sunday Edition.

Assistance came in the form of two persons: a marketing representative for an off-site storage vendor, who possessed a wry sense of humor and a disdain for unmerited self-aggrandizement, and a contingency planner-turned-consultant, who gave away more valuable advice than he should have—a practice that ultimately required his return to the secure embrace of corporate employment. Through these persons, I was introduced to a

383

network of fellow DR coordinators struggling to improve their skills in the disaster recovery craft—now, as then, as much an art as a science.

One thing led to another, and my associates and I co-founded one of the first DRP user groups in the United States—a not-for-profit, Florida-based, professional association called the Disaster Avoidance and Recovery Information Group (DARING). During the next two years, both as a planner and as the president of DARING, I became conversant in the practices and jargon of the disaster recovery trade—and developed and tested several DR plans in the process.

Of particular importance, I learned to discriminate the charlatans of the unpoliced DR industry from the earnest souls who continue to populate this shadowy world of corporate continuity planning. Through ongoing interactions with industry peers and continuing efforts to develop disaster recovery capabilities both for employers and clients, I developed most of what I now know about DR planning.

Disaster recovery planning is, in essence, a pragmatic undertaking. Despite the Byzantine mystique that is perpetuated around the endeavor by some consultants and vendors, DR planning is an undertaking that is well within the grasp of common sense individuals possessing good analytical and communications skills. It also helps to have some political sense and a willingness to keep apprised of new business information technologies.

In 1990, I took it as a personal mission to dispel the myths and mysticism surrounding this activity—hence, the first book. Its publication coincided, purely by accident, with the decision by IBM to enter the disaster recovery field. The vendor was closing several regional facilities in the late 1980s when some bright soul came up with the idea of converting them into a new systems protection service offering. Leveraging its tremendous position within the IT industry in those days, IBM transformed disaster recovery planning almost overnight from back-burner concern to a systems management priority for many companies.

The significance of this transformation can be expressed this way: As late as 1988, IBM systems engineers assigned to our corporate account were still assuring us that mainframes were invulnerable to all but the most cataclysmic disaster potentials (building fires, building explosions, etc.) Data backup was important, to be sure, and IBM had a number of tape products and software to meet this need, but the resilience of "Big Iron" was a given.

The announcement of IBM's Business Recovery Service was a profound departure from this line and a wake-up call for those who had been lulled into complacency about DR. For the first time, the vendor was sending a message to its customers that even Big Blue systems were vulnerable and that some sort of contingency response capability was intrinsic to what IBM defined as "good systems management." While this piece of information may strike many as intuitively obvious ("a duh moment," as my teenage daughter might say), it sent hundreds of IT professionals in hundreds of companies on a quest for current information about DR planning. My book, one of the few in print at that moment, was the beneficiary of this newfound concern. Thanks, IBM.

In the years that followed, *Disaster Recovery Planning* was both celebrated as "an industry standard" by those who used it to guide their own planning endeavors and assailed by others, mainly a few high-priced consultants, as a terrible encroachment upon their daily bread. Imagine, portraying the "black art known only to a privileged few" as a straightforward application of common sense accessible to virtually anyone! I delighted in both characterizations, however undeserved.

Of course, the world of business information technology did not stand still over the next decade. By 1995, distributed client/server computing models had taken hold, data storage was exploding, and the Internet Revolution was revving up. Against this increasingly complicated IT backdrop, many novice planners began to perceive disaster recovery planning as an activity beyond their grasp. Driven by repeated requests from readers of the first book to publish a new work that provided an illustration of how one might apply the methods and techniques discussed in the first edition of *Disaster Recovery Planning*, I did so—albeit, through gritted teeth. The number of books in print on the subject of DR had exploded since 1990 (a good thing), but so had the number of "canned plans"—boilerplate DR planning tools that sought to fit the disaster recovery requirements of all companies into a neat, one-size-fits-all template (a not-so-good thing).

I did not want the second book to fall into the latter category—and it didn't. Released by another publisher, book number two offered a sample implementation of the common-sense methodology described in the original book and added generic forms and checklists as a starting point for readers.

The decision to do the book was a response to two new "products" that had taken hold in the industry: "canned plans," as described above, and DRP certification programs, which were addressed in an earlier chapter. The approach favored by vendors in marketing these "products" struck me as profoundly cynical: play on the lack of self-confidence that many novice planners have in their abilities to develop a testable plan. Prey on their fear, uncertainty, and doubt. It seemed a resurgence of the same technique used by some DR consultants to cultivate contracts with corporate clients in the late 1980s. All of my experience militated against what I considered to be a return to old DR mythology. The mission was rekindled and book two was published.

In the years that have followed, the advent of *n*-tier client/server application suites (ERP, MRP, and the like), the development of new storage architectures (storage area networks), and the growth of the Internet and intranet technologies (including server-centric computing, web-based infrastructure outsourcing, thin client computing) have changed the landscape of disaster recovery planning. In response to these changes and, in part, as a result of the "business process reengineering" craze of the late 1990s, DR has shifted its focus from system recovery to business process recovery and has acquired a more fashionable moniker in some quarters: "business continuity planning."

Jargon aside, the "new focus" of DR is the same as the old focus: recover critical business operations as expeditiously as possible following an unplanned interruption. The difference, however, is that the complexity of business computing technology has increased, while corporate tolerance to downtime has decreased.

These facts are driving the first real changes in the scope and mission of disaster recovery planning since the discipline first appeared. As the millennium dawns, it is no longer sufficient for DR coordinators to follow behind business and IT decision makers, discovering ways to ensure the continuity of the processes and infrastructures that they leave in their wake. Given the increasing dependence of business on technology and its near-zero tolerance for outages, DR considerations need to become part of the business and IT decision-making process. Coordinators need to develop a new presence: helping to guide the risk calculus of business managers and influencing the application designs of corporate IT architects. In short, coordinators need to find ways to become more proactive.

As indicated in the forewords to this book, the DR industry takes many views on this topic. Understanding that modern DR coordinators have a broader mission than in the past, systems recovery service vendors such as IBM and Hewlett Packard Company are developing menu-based service portfolios to simplify certain aspects of recovery planning. With the right service selections, most vendors claim that they can recover systems without any on-site presence by company personnel whatsoever. Automatic recovery is possible, they claim, with the right combination of data mirroring or vaulting, automatic network rerouting, and top-notch operations support from your friendly service provider.

Meanwhile, web-based infrastructure outsourcing providers, like Exodus Communications, are insisting that companies concerned with potential interruptions are best served by the site replication services offered by the new breed of web-based outsourcing companies. The best disaster recovery plan, they argue, is an instantaneous, transparent failover from an interrupted system to a fully replicated, "hot" standby. Leave it to web guys, they argue, who have elevated site mirroring to an art form.

Even Paradyne Corporation's approach to Frame Relay network replacement by ISDN safety net facilities embodies a notion of hassle-free, machine-intelligent guarantees of process continuity. Disaster recovery has begun to blend with high availability, which concerns itself not with speedy restoral from outages, but with the preservation of "five nines" (99.999 percent uptime).

When and if this transition is ever complete, disaster recovery planning may fade away in its current form and become a component of corporate stewardship. However, for the foreseeable future, a mixed scenario will persist.

That, in a nutshell, is what prompts this second edition of *Disaster Recovery Planning*. In this period of rapid technological innovation, there are new challenges and new risks that call into question older, mainframe-centric methodologies and recovery techniques. At the same time, however, DR coordinators cannot afford to be distracted by the promises of a forthcoming disaster recovery "nirvana," described by both new and old vendors of DR products and services.

DR coordinators need to turn their attention to new challenges and meet them with a combination of time-tested techniques as well as innovative approaches that are appropriate to the modern business. In this endeavor, there are no experts, only fellow novices. What was true in 1990 persists today.

Conclusions serve two purposes. One is structural, as the book must have an ending.

The ending of this book is hopefully a beginning. Newcomers to the field of disaster recovery planning are now, I hope, a little better oriented to the task that is before them. Maybe this book will confirm that they do not labor alone and, just maybe, it will give them some added confidence that their self-made efforts are at least as valid as those of any self-styled expert.

Pragmatism dictates that this book must also end with a sobering thought. It is this: No amount of planning can cover every contingency. When a disaster strikes, even the best plans may prove unequal to the challenge. In an actual disaster, creativity, improvisation, and hard work will determine whether the business will recover.

What then is the value of disaster recovery planning? Just this: A company's chances of survival are better if it has a plan than if it doesn't.

The enterprise of disaster recovery planning, involving as it does numerous company employees, forces the company as a whole to face a reality that most would prefer to ignore. This has the effect of sensitizing persons to the causes of disaster, and perhaps helping to avoid one.

The second purpose of a conclusion is to serve as a repository for all the justifications of those quiet judgments that were rendered in the earlier chapters. It is where the author tries to comment on observations that he is sure will come in response to the book (although sometimes he only rationalizes his own complaints).

These are some of the issues that require closure.

1. *"Short shrift was given to quantitative risk analysis techniques."* This is true. I have dealt with the subject of quantitative risk analysis methods at some length elsewhere.[1] Those who know me know that I am not an adherent of any quantitative methods, and since there are already so many books dedicated to the subject, readers are directed to bookstores or The Rothstein Catalog on Disaster Recovery (www.rothstein.com/catalog.html) for further research.

2. *"Some disaster scenarios were brushed over in the book—for example, what if senior managers or other key corporate decision makers are lost in a disaster?"* This comment was actually received from a reader of the first edition in the UK. He will, no doubt, be disappointed by the absence of a treatment of the issue in this edition. While the loss of a key decision maker is a potential hazard faced by all companies, this book assumes that, in the majority of cases, some management element will be intact to facilitate the recovery process. The sharp decline, in the United States at least, in human casualties associated with business interruption events suggests the validity of this assumption. However, it would be relatively easy to integrate this consideration into a disaster recovery scenario should a coordinator wish to do so. From a political standpoint, it will probably be a difficult proposition in any case to sell management on a disaster recovery capability premised on its own demise.

3. *"You have not fully explored systems/network/user recovery options that are most appropriate to my company."* Again, this statement may be true. However, this book has sought to devote the greatest attention to those options that the apparent majority of companies with backup capabilities are using and also to introduce evolving strategies that are likely to become favored approaches over the next five years or so. Of course, companies with tested disaster recovery capa-

bilities, as stated in the Introduction and elsewhere, comprise only a small percentage of all companies in North America. If coordinators who read this book determine that a different recovery more closely meets their backup requirements than those strategies explored here, then, by all means, pursue the strategy. Different companies clearly have differing needs. The recovery options presented here are just that: options to consider when formulating a suitable approach. If cautions associated with specific options are viewed as inapplicable in a given case, coordinators should go with their best judgment.

4. *"If I have only twenty employees, how can I have ten to twenty recovery teams?"* or *"I run my entire company on a single server and a handful of local and long distance lines, so why do I need to use teams to perform tasks that a single individual could do blindfolded?"* The size of a disaster recovery team should be guided by the following considerations.
   - *Complexity of the task.* If a task can be performed by a single person within an acceptable timeframe, no team may be needed. If the task is somewhat complex, at least one other individual should be available to assist in the event of a problem. Very complex tasks may require several persons.
   - *Extent of preplanning.* If a task has been clearly defined, and no improvisation is required or expected, and one person can perform the task, designate a one-person team. If the strategy is not formalized, and/or the task is to be performed by "the seat of the pants," it may be necessary to allocate more than one person to the team assigned to perform the task.
   - *Availability of trained backup personnel.* If the person responsible for performing the task cannot be reached in a recovery situation, is there another qualified individual to whom the task can be assigned? If the answer is no, then a team approach—with cross training of team members—may be required.

5. *"You did not describe in any detail the way in which the financing of a recovery will be accomplished."* True. In this edition, based on experience, I made a conscious decision to relegate recovery finance to the amorphous category of tasks belonging to the Emergency Management Team. In my experience, companies vary greatly in terms of their approach to handling the ongoing accounts payable/accounts receivable processes during an emergency. After Hurricane Andrew, one national company actually paid employees out of a "war chest" without so much as recording the monies taken by employees during the emergency. They found that employees worked very cheaply and that payroll costs were actually lower during the post-disaster

period. In other cases, formal arrangements have been made with third-party providers or through branch operations to handle finances following a disaster. It will be necessary to document how management will prefer to handle the financing of emergency operations. However, little guidance of a generic nature can be offered on this point, so it was omitted for the discussion.

6. *"You said that there is no such thing as a failed test. Considering the money, time, and effort spent in developing a plan, wouldn't the plan be a failure if the test proved the plan inadequate?"* Personal embarrassment aside, coordinators need to view as beneficial any information that a test provides. If the plan fails in testing, the test is not a failure. It has succeeded in identifying areas of the plan that need to be reviewed and revised to make the plan better.

With those issues addressed, all that remains is to preview the companion web site for this book. The first edition of *Disaster Recovery Planning* featured multiple appendices including resource lists that were rendered obsolete over the course of time. What is needed to keep a resource list up-to-date is a "living appendix." That is what readers of this book will find on the World Wide Web at HTTP://WWW.DRPLANNING.ORG. This site offers a vendor-neutral clearinghouse for the latest thinking on disaster recovery planning as well as listings of products, services, and informational site links that may be of use to DR coordinators. If you are a vendor, feel free to contribute information about your products or services to the site. If you are a coordinator or someone interested in disaster recovery, feel free to join in the discussion groups that will be established on the site.

One final issue needs to be addressed: "When should I start to develop a disaster recovery plan?" The question is typically followed by a lengthy list of all of the reasons why now is not a good time. Here is a brief summary of the rationalizations and how I respond to them.

- *"We're just in the planning stages for bringing IT in-house. We have no computers yet, except a few workstations. Most of our processing is done by a service bureau or outsourcing agent and they have a plan."*

  In this instance, the disaster recovery coordinator is afforded a rare opportunity. Not only can current business processes be documented fairly quickly, but the coordinator is in on the ground floor of a IT migration project and may be able to influence how that project develops in order to favor disaster recovery considerations.

Second, the coordinator should participate in the service bureau's or outsourcing agent's disaster recovery tests. This can provide some useful information about recovery requirements for applications as presently configured.

Third, if facilities are being developed to house the company's new IT capability, the coordinator should attempt to become involved in planning disaster avoidance capabilities for the new facility.

Finally, disaster recovery planning is not planning for the recovery of IT infrastructure alone; it is planning for business recovery. Thus, all other components of the plan can be developed, leaving the systems recovery strategy for last.

- *"We've been changing over to a new software package (or to new hardware) and I wonder if we shouldn't wait until the conversion is successful and complete before we take on disaster recovery planning."*

Again, the coordinator has much more to protect than one system or application. Development of user and network recovery strategies should proceed, even if the systems recovery strategy cannot be finalized at this point.

Additionally, conversions are not only destabilizing, they can also create disasters if not properly managed and controlled. Thus, a disaster recovery plan should be written before a conversion begins to handle the possibility of a disaster involving the conversion project.

- *"We've had a shaky quarter, lots of expenses. I don't think that management will underwrite the costs of disaster recovery planning until maybe next quarter or next year."*

Disaster recovery planning need not be a cost born solely by corporate IT. It is the protection of corporate assets from loss that may result in savings in the cost of business interruption insurance. Even in difficult financial periods, the coordinator may be surprised to find management receptive to the notion of disaster recovery planning, especially if such planning seeks to leverage existing capabilities as dual-use disaster recovery capabilities. Financial hard times provide an excellent time for DR planning, since the pace of business change often slows somewhat during these periods affording the opportunity to complete "housekeeping" tasks—an unfortunate categorization that is often applied to DRP.

- *"We're putting out daily fires. There's not much time for disaster recovery planning and no personnel are available for the job."*

This comment suggests two things. One, the coordinator is saying, "What we have right now is such a headache, I'm not sure that it's worth saving." If systems and networks provide critical functions for the company, they are worth something. Discerning that value and creating a plan that is commensurate with it is prerequisite to good management. If the DR coordinator or IT manager doesn't agree, he or she is in the wrong job.

The second comment, regarding the availability of personnel, is a valid one. Unless a full-time employee is available or can be hired for the purpose of coordinating the disaster recovery planning project, the project will probably not yield a workable plan. Assigning or hiring such a person should be a higher priority than hiring a new programmer or analyst, since an investment in disaster recovery protects an investment in new software.

The bottom line is that the time to begin developing a disaster recovery capability is now. Stop reading about it. The way to write the plan is to sit down and write it.

ENDNOTES

1. Jon William Toigo, *Disaster Recovery Planning for Computers and Communications Resources* (John Wiley and Sons: New York, 1995).

GLOSSARY

ACCESS CONTROL: The process of limiting access to the resources of a system only to authorized programs, processes, or other systems (in a network). Synonymous with controlled access and limited access.

ACCESS CONTROL MECHANISM: 1. Security safeguards designed to detect and prevent unauthorized access, and to permit authorized access in an IT (information technology) product. 2. Hardware or software features, operating procedures, management procedures, and various combinations of these designed to detect and prevent unauthorized access and to permit authorized access in an automated system.

ADVANCED PROGRAM-TO-PROGRAM COMMUNICATIONS (APPC): A set of IBM protocols also known as LU 6.2 and Type 2.1 architectures. It functions within SNA's APPN to support peer-to-peer communications between workstations attached to SNA LANs and the applications running on those workstations. It was added to SNA as part of the "new" SNA to support peer-to-peer networking, unlike the traditional hierarchical SNA approach in which the mainframe acts as host or master and treats the other computer as a terminal or slave.

AGENT: A software-driven process running on a communications or networking device that allows that device to participate in a management system. For example, an SNMP agent running on a router provides the ability for the router to exchange information with an SNMP network management system through the use of the SNMP protocol.

ALTERNATE ROUTING: Safety technique enabling communication to continue in the event of node failure or congestion. The network design allows for alternate paths through the network to arrive at the same destination.

ALTERNATING CURRENT (AC): An electric current that reverses its direction at regular intervals. *See* DIRECT CURRENT.

AMERICAN NATIONAL STANDARDS INSTITUTE (ANSI): A group that defines U.S. standards for the information processing industry. ANSI participates in defining network protocol standards and represents the U.S. on other international standards-setting bodies like ISO.

APPLICATION PROGRAMMING INTERFACE (API): An interface between the operating system and application programs, which includes the way the application programs communicate with the operating system, and the services the operating system makes available to the programs.

APPLICATION SERVICE PROVIDER (ASP): An Internet-based application service bureau.

APPLICATION SOFTWARE: A set of programs that provides a specific function or set of functions.

ARCHITECTURE: The design of a system, network, or application.

ARCHIVAL BACKUP: A data backup that will be stored for a long time.

ARCHIVE: 1. To transfer files off the computer into long-term storage. 2. A file that has been archived. 3. A group of files which must be extracted and decompressed in order to use them; software to be installed sometimes comes in this format. 4. A file stored on a computer network, which can be retrieved by FTP or other means.

ARMA: Association of Records Managers and Administrators.

ARRAY: A group of disk drives that have been combined into a common array and appear as a single LSU (Logical Storage Unit). (*See also* DISK ARRAY.)

ASYNCHRONOUS TRANSFER MODE (ATM): A type of fast packet switching that uses a fixed size packet called a cell. This technique makes it possible to transmit data at great speed, and can make voice, multimedia, full-motion video, and video conferencing available to all users. It also makes dynamic allocation of bandwidth possible; telephone and cable TV companies can charge individual customers based on the amount of bandwidth they use.

AUTOMATIC REROUTING: A method of re-terminating wide area or local telecommunications traffic at alternate facilities in the event of a disaster. Automatic suggests that the rerouting of traffic may be accomplished rapidly by preplanning the alternate traffic routes with a carrier service vendor.

BACK END: A computer that does the main processing but has a smaller, more-friendly computer that the user interacts with (called the "front end"). Or, a program that takes care of details behind the scenes, performing tasks not directly controlled by the user.

BACK UP: To make copies of important files in case the originals are damaged. Data can be backed up on secondary hard drives, floppy disks, optical media, tape, etc.

BACK-UP SERVER: Software or hardware which copies files so that there are always two current copies of each file. Also known as a shadow server.

BANDWIDTH: A characteristic of a communication channel that is the amount of information that can be passed through it in a given amount of time, usually expressed in bits per second.

BAUD: A baud is a unit that measures the speed of data transmission. The baud rate of a data communications system is the number of symbols per second transferred. A symbol may have more than two states, so it may represent more than one binary bit (a binary bit always represents exactly two states). Therefore the baud rate may not equal the bit rate, especially in the case of recent modems, which can have (for example) up to nine bits per symbol.

BIOMETRICS: Technologies for authenticating the identity of an individual by using fingerprints, palm prints, retinal scans, or other biological signatures.

BIT: Short for binary digit.

BITS PER SECOND (bps): Bits per second, a measure of data transmission.

BRIDGE: A device that connects two local-area networks (LANs), or two segments of the same LAN. The two LANs being connected can be alike or dissimilar. For example, a bridge can connect an Ethernet with a Token-Ring network. Unlike routers, bridges are protocol-independent. They simply forward packets without analyzing and re-routing messages. Consequently, they're faster than routers, but also less versatile. Brouters, or Bridge-Routers, are devices that functions as both a router and a bridge. A brouter understands how to route specific types of packets, such as TCP/IP packets. Any other packets it receives are simply forwarded to other network(s) connected to the device (this is the bridge function).

BUSINESS CONTINUITY PLANNING (BCP): A re-casting of traditional Disaster Recovery Planning that focuses on business process (rather than IT infrastructure) as the central objective of recovery planning.

BUSINESS PROCESS: A routine or standard process or procedure for accomplishing a business-related task.

BUSINESS PROCESS REENGINEERING: To change business processes with the objective of improving performance and/or making more efficient use of resources. The concept of BPR generally includes the use of computers and information technology to organize data, project trends, etc.

BUSINESS RECOVERY SERVICES: Vendor provided services intended to aid businesses in recovering critical business processes following an unplanned interruption. IBM and HP both provide a BRS offering.

BYTE: The amount of memory space used to store one character, which is usually 8 bits. A computer that has 8-bit bytes (most large and small computers today) can distinguish 28–256 different characters.

CANNED PLANS: Somewhat disparaging term applied to fill-in-the-blanks DR planning software tools.

CENTRAL OFFICE (CO): A telephone company facility that joins subscriber telephone lines to switching equipment. This allows subscribers to connect to one another, through local and long distance connections.

CHANNEL EXTENSION: A set of technologies used to extend a mainframe (typically) channel across a Wide Area Network connection.

CHANNEL LATENCY: The waiting time for a communications channel to be available to transmit data.

CHECKLIST TESTING: The team reviews the plan and identifies key components that should be current and available.

CIRCUIT: A single communications facility or combination of facilities including satellite, microwave, fiber optics, or copper wire.

CLEAN AGENT: One of several replacements for halogenated fire suppression agents thought to be less detrimental to the environment and the ozone layer.

CLIENT/SERVER: An application architecture client/server in which applications are divided into discrete client and server components that may coexist on the same host platform or be divided among several hosts. A client machine sends a request to a server machine, which provides files, database searches, and other services.

COLD SITE: Cold site is a synonym for a shell site. It is a facility that is prepared to receive computer hardware and that may be used on an on-going basis for emergency system operations if a primary computer facility is destroyed or rendered uninhabitable.

COMMUNICATIONS CHANNEL: The physical media and devices which provide the means for transmitting information from one component of a network to (one or more) other components.

COMMUNICATIONS LINK: The physical means of connecting one location to another for the purpose of transmitting and/or receiving data.

COMMUNICATIONS PROTOCOL: A standard way of regulating data exchange between computers, including the rules for data transmission and the formatting of messages. Some communications protocols are TCP/IP, DECnet, AppleTalk, SNA, and IPX/SPX.

COMPUTER EMERGENCY RESPONSE TEAM (CERT): An organization formed by DARPA in 1988 after the Internet worm incident. CERT watches for threats to Internet security, educates the public about computer security issues, and conducts research to improve the security of existing systems. CERT issues advisories and provides 24-hour technical assistance in response to computer security emergencies.

CONCENTRATOR: A programmable device that combines the functions of a multiplexer with a data storage buffer, message error checking capability, and device polling capability.

COMMON OBJECT REQUEST BROKER ARCHITECTURE (CORBA): An architecture that enables pieces of programs, called objects, to communicate with one another regardless of what programming language they were written in or what operating system they're running on.

CUSTOMER RELATIONSHIP MANAGEMENT (CRM): Software that allows companies to manage every aspect of their relationship with a customer. The aim of these systems is to assist in building lasting customer relationships—to turn customer satisfaction into customer loyalty. Customer information acquired from sales, marketing, customer service, and support is captured and stored in a centralized database. The system may provide data-mining facilities that support an opportunity management system. It may also be integrated with other systems such as accounting and manufacturing for a truly enterprise-wide system with thousands of users.

DATABASE: 1. A large collection of data organized for rapid search and retrieval. 2. A program that manages data, and can be used to store, retrieve, and sort information.

DATA COMMUNICATION: The transfer of data from one computer to another.

DATA COMPRESSION: The encoding of data so that it consumes less storage space or transmission bandwidth.

DATA ENTRY: The process of entering data into a computer.

DATA PACKET: A format in which data is transmitted over a network. A packet contains the data itself as well as addresses, error checking, and other information necessary to ensure the packet arrives intact at its intended destination.

DATA PORTABILITY: The possibility for a set of data to be transferred from one operating system to another.

DATA RECOVERY: Salvaging data stored on damaged media, such as magnetic disks and tapes. There are a number of software products that can help recover data damaged by a disk crash or virus. In addition, there are companies that specialize in data recovery. Of course, not all data is recoverable, but data recovery specialists can often restore a surprisingly high percentage of the data on damaged media.

DATA WAREHOUSE: A large centralized database designed to hold and manage a company's information over a long period of time. Data warehouses are often used to mine key data for reference, for example, to detect trends, spot new market opportunities, and monitor business results.

DE FACTO STANDARD: A standard that is widely used and accepted even though it is not official.

DEFENSE ADVANCED RESEARCH PROJECTS AGENCY (DARPA): The Federal agency that began as ARPA, and created the Internet. It became ARPA again in 1990.

DEBUG: To fix problems in hardware or software.

DEDICATED LINE: A telecommunications line that lets your computer have a direct, permanent connection to the Internet or some other network. Different from a dialup connection which is only opened for temporary use. A dedicated line is assigned to only one purpose, and is always connected to the same equipment.

DIAL BACKUP: A technique for backing up a dedicated line or connection using a dial-up connection.

DIALUP CONNECTION: A temporary network connection usually established through Dual Tone Modulation Frequency (DTMF) "touch tone" telephone signaling.

DIGITAL SERVICE UNIT/CHANNEL SERVICE UNIT (DSU/CSU): A way of connecting a communications line to an external digital circuit.

DIRECT CURRENT (DC): An electric current flowing in one direction only. *See* ALTERNATING CURRENT.

DISASTER: An unplanned interruption of mission-critical business processes for an unacceptable period of time.

DISASTER RECOVERY PLANNING: Advanced planning intended to provide an organization with capabilities for preventing avoidable disasters and for mitigating the impact of disaster potentials that cannot be avoided.

DISK ARRAY (or ARRAY): A linked group of small, independent hard disk drives used to replace larger, single disk drive systems. The most common disk arrays implement RAID (redundant array of independent disks) technology. (*See also* RAID.)

DISTRIBUTED ARCHITECTURE: A set of interacting computer systems, databases, and workstations situated in different locations, typically dispersed across a department or enterprise-wide network.

DISTRIBUTED COMPONENT OBJECT MODEL (DCOM): A Microsoft developed system for exchanging objects over a client/server network.

DISTRIBUTED COMPUTING ENVIRONMENT (DCE): A set of middleware standards that defines the method of communication between clients and servers in a cross-platform computing environment; enables a client program to initiate a request that can be processed by a program written in a different computer language and housed on a different computer platform.

DLT TAPE: Quantum Corporation's widely installed Digital Linear Tape format. A type of 1/2" wide magnetic tape used for backup.

DOCKING STATION: A piece of hardware that a portable computer can be plugged into when it is at a fixed location. The docking station makes available devices that the portable computer is not able to support, such as a battery charger, a larger screen, additional drives, or a network.

DOWNLINK: 1. In satellite communications, a link from a satellite to one of its earth stations. 2. To receive data through a downlink.

DOWNLOAD: To transfer files or data from one computer to another. To download means to receive; to upload means to transmit.

DOWNSIZE: 1. To reduce the size of staff at an organization. 2. To move to a smaller host platform. 3. To reduce an operating budget.

DOWNTIME: The time during which a computer is nonfunctional because of problems with hardware or system software, etc.

DOWNWARD COMPATIBILITY: The characteristic of hardware, software, or standards to coexist or be compatible with older versions of the hardware, software, or standard. Also called backward compatible.

E-BUSINESS: Business use of the Internet and World Wide Web.

E-COMMERCE: The use of computers and electronic communications in business transactions. E-commerce may include the use of electronic data interchange (EDI), electronic money exchange, Internet advertising, websites, online databases, computer networks, and point-of-sale (POS) computer systems.

ELECTROSTATIC: Relating to static electricity, or nonmoving electric charge.

EMERGENCY OPERATIONS CENTER (EOC): A location from which an Emergency Management Team controls the execution of a disaster recovery plan.

ENCAPSULATION: The process of sending data encoded in one protocol format across a network operating a different protocol, where it is not possible or desirable to convert between the two protocols. For example, where Ethernet LANs attach to an FDDI backbone, it is not possible to convert between the different packet formats, so the Ethernet packet is encapsulated in its entirety inside an FDDI packet as it crosses the bridge on to the FDDI network. When the encapsulated Ethernet packet reaches the bridge connecting the destination Ethernet LAN to the FDDI network, the Ethernet packet is stripped out of the FDDI packet and put, unchanged, on to the destination Ethernet LAN. Also known as protocol tunneling.

ENCRYPTION: A method of defeating attempts to eavesdrop on data communications by encoding the data according to a scheme known only to the originator and recipient of the transmission.

ENTERPRISE: An enterprise consists of all functional departments, people, and systems within an organization. In some cases, the enterprise can include partners—even vendors and customers.

ENTERPRISE RESOURCE PLANNING (ERP): Typically, software designed to tie together all of an enterprise's various functions including human resources, finance, manufacturing, sales, etc. This software also provides for the analysis of this data in order to plan production, forecast sales, analyze quality, and so on.

EPCOT CODE: A set of building codes, including a fire code, developed in conjunction with the construction of the EPCOT Center at Walt Disney World in Orlando, FL. Considered one of the most advanced codes in existence.

ETHERNET: The most popular type of local area network, which sends its communications through radio frequency signals carried by a coaxial cable. Each computer checks to see if another computer is transmitting and waits its turn to transmit. If two computers accidentally transmit at the same time and their messages collide, they wait and send again in turn. Software protocols used by Ethernet systems vary, but include Novell Netware and TCP/IP. Named after the "ether" which was thought to be the medium through which electromagnetic waves propagated. The medium was initially a thick (about 1 cm in diameter) coaxial cable, usually yellow, and specially designed for the purpose. Today, there are several varieties of the Ethernet standard including 10Base-T, 100Base-T or Fast Ethernet, and 1000Base-T or Gigabit Ethernet.

EXTRANET: The part of a company or organization's internal computer network which is available to outside users, for example, information services for customers.

FAILURE: The malfunction of a system or component; the inability of a system or component to perform its intended function. A failure may be caused by a fault.

FAST ETHERNET: A local area network that transmits data at 100 Mbits/s. Officially, IEEE 802.3u, Fast Ethernet is an implementation of 802.3 "Ethernet" that uses 100 Mbits/s transmission and different bit encoding but otherwise is identical to 10BASE-T (same frame and message lengths, same collision detect scheme, same Ethernet drivers). Fast Ethernet is promoted by the Fast Ethernet Alliance, whose main members are 3Com, Intel, Standard Microsystems (SMC), Sun Microsystems, Lucent Communications, and Cabletron Systems. Also supported by Cisco Systems.

FAT CLIENT: Somewhat derogatory reference to the Windows/INTEL desktop PC architecture. PCs are called fat clients because of their large memories and hard drives. They store information and run programs locally from software loaded on hard drives. Fat clients are typically deployed in client/server environments, where they enable local execution of client applications. As a rule, fat clients are much more customizable than thin clients.

FAT SERVER: In a client/server environment, a server that does most or all of the processing leaving little or none that must be done by the client.

FIBER DISTRIBUTED DATA INTERFACE (FDDI): a high-speed (and usually local) networking technology. A 100 Mbits/s user data rate, dual ring (for redundancy), connectionless LAN. With configurable distances of up to 2 kilometers, some would say that this is also a Metropolitan Area Network (MAN) technology.

FIREWALL: A system designed to prevent unauthorized access to or from a private network. Firewalls can be implemented in both hardware and software, or a combination of both. Firewalls are frequently used to prevent unauthorized Internet users from accessing private networks connected to the Internet, especially intranets. All messages entering or leaving the intranet pass through the firewall, which examines each message and blocks those that do not meet the specified security criteria. There are several types of firewall techniques: (1) Packet filter: Looks at each packet entering or leaving the network and accepts or rejects it based on user-defined rules. Packet filtering is fairly effective and transparent to users, but it is difficult to configure. In addition, it is susceptible to IP spoofing. (2) Application gateway: Applies security mechanisms to specific applications, such as FTP and Telnet servers. This is very effective, but can impose a performance degradation. (3) Circuit-level gateway: Applies security mechanisms when a TCP or UDP connection is established. Once the connection has been made, packets can flow between the hosts without further checking. (4) Proxy server: Intercepts all messages entering and leaving the network. The proxy server effectively hides the true network addresses. In practice, many firewalls use two or more of these techniques in concert. A firewall is considered a first line defense in network security and is typically used in conjunction with encryption.

FIRMWARE: Vendor-written software usually stored in Read Only Memory (ROM) on a vended product.

FRAME RELAY: A protocol for sending small packets of data over a network. Frame relay uses packets of variable length, unlike cell relay, and requires less stringent error detection than other forms of packet switching because it is designed to take advantage of the more reliable circuits that have become available in recent years. Frame relay is often used for wide area networks, where it can transmit data at high speed more efficiently than point-to-point services. Frame relay is used with digital lines.

FRAME RELAY ACCESS DEVICE (FRAD): A combination of hardware and software that is used to convert communications packets from formats like TCP, SNA, IPX, and others into frames that can then be sent over a frame relay network.

FRONT END COMMUNICATIONS CONTROLLER: A programmable device that interfaces a communications network with a host computer. Some controller functions may include polling, speed control, code conversion, error detection, data buffering, and security authorization checking.

FULL-INTERRUPTION TESTING: Testing the DR plan by interrupting normal operations. This test is costly, could disrupt normal operations and should be used and scheduled with extreme caution.

GATEWAY: Gateways are points of entrance to and exit from a communications network. Viewed as a physical entity, a gateway is that node that translates between two otherwise incompatible networks or network segments. Gateways perform code and protocol conversion to facilitate traffic between data highways of differing architecture. In OSI terms, a gateway is a device that provides mapping at all seven layers of the OSI model. A gateway can be thought of as a function within a system that enables communications with the outside world.

GIGABIT ETHERNET: (1000Base-T) A standard for a high-speed Ethernet, approved by the IEEE (Institute of Electrical and Electronics Engineers) 802.3z standards committee in 1996. It supports the extension of existing Ethernet and Fast Ethernet standards, providing increased network bandwidth and interoperability among Ethernets at operating speeds from 10 Mbps to 1000 Mbps. Gigabit Ethernet can be used in backbone environments to interconnect multiple lower speed (10 and 100 Mbps) Ethernets.

GIGABITS PER SECOND (Mbps): 1000 bits per second, a measure of data transmission.

GIGABYTES PER SECOND (MBps): 8000 bits per second, a measure of data transmission.

HEAD CRASH: A serious disk drive malfunction. A head crash usually means that the head has scratched or burned the disk platter. In a hard disk drive, the head normally hovers a few microinches from the disk. If the head becomes misaligned, if platters warp as a result of heat, or if dust particles come between it and the disk, read/write heads can contact or crash the disk platter. Data loss is often the result. For this reason, it is important to operate disk drives, particularly hard disk drives, in as clean an environment as possible. Even smoke particles can cause a head crash. Head crashes are less common for floppy disks because the head touches the disk under normal operation.

HOST: Any computer-based system connected to the network and containing the necessary protocol interpreter software to initiate network access and carry out information exchange across the communications network. This definition encompasses typical "mainframe" and "midrange" hosts and workstations connected directly to the communications subnetwork and executing the intercomputer networking protocols. A terminal is not a host because it does not contain the protocol software needed to perform information exchange; a workstation (by definition) is a host because it does have such capability.

HOT SITE: A commercial systems backup facility. A vendor-provided facility equipped with computer host hardware, telecommunications hardware and personnel to aid subscribing companies in restoring critical business application processing following an unplanned interruption of normal IT operations.

HYBRID PRIVATE/PUBLIC NETWORKING: The creation of a network using both private leased lines and public switched facilities (digital dial-up bandwidth). The goals of combining both networking technologies are increased performance and flexibility at reduced cost.

INCREMENTAL BACKUP: A routine that makes it possible to back up only the files that have changed since the last backup, instead of backing up every file.

INSTITUTE OF ELECTRICAL AND ELECTRONICS ENGINEERS (IEEE): An organization that maintains the standards for 10BaseT and other communications standards.

INTEGRATED SERVICES DIGITAL NETWORK (ISDN): An international communications standard for sending voice, video, and data over digital telephone lines or normal telephone wires. ISDN supports data transfer rates of 64 Kbps (64,000 bits per second). Most ISDN lines offered by telephone companies provides two lines, called B channels. One line for voice and the other for data, or both lines, when used for data, provide data rates of 128 Kbps, three times the data rate provided by today's fastest modems. The original version of ISDN employs base band transmission. Another version, called B-ISDN, uses broadband transmission and is able to support transmission rates of 1.5 Mbps. B-ISDN requires fiber optic cables and is not widely available.

INTER EXCHANGE CARRIER (IXC or IEC): Common carrier providing communications channels between local telephone companies (LECs, or Local Exchange Carriers). Also known as long distance carriers, such as AT&T, WorldCom (Sprint and MCI WorldCom), WilTel, etc.

INTERNET: A global network connecting millions of computers. As of 1998, the Internet has more than 100 million users worldwide, and that number is growing rapidly. More than 100 countries are linked into exchanges of data, news, and opinions. Unlike online services, which are centrally controlled, the Internet is decentralized by design. Each Internet computer, called a host, is independent. Its operators can choose which Internet services to use and which local services to make available to the global Internet community. Remarkably, this anarchy by design works exceedingly well. There are a variety of ways to access the Internet, including the use of a commercial Internet Service Provider (ISP).

INTERNET SERVICE PROVIDER (ISP): A company that provides access to the Internet. For a monthly fee, the service provider provides the user a software package, username, password, and access phone number. Equipped with a modem, the user can then log on to the Internet and browse the World Wide Web and USENET, and send and receive e-mail. In addition to serving individuals, ISPs also serve large companies, providing a direct connection from the company's networks to the Internet. ISPs themselves are connected to one another through Network Access Points (NAPs). ISPs are also called IAPs (Internet Access Providers).

INTRANET: A network based on TCP/IP protocols (an internet) belonging to an organization, usually a corporation, accessible only by the organization's members, employees, or others with authorization. An intranet's Web sites look and act just like any other Web sites, but the firewall surrounding an intranet fends off unauthorized access.

LAST MILE SERVICES: A circuit, facility, or service used to connect an intercity cable, microwave system, and so forth to a customer of a point of presence (POP).

LAYER TWO FORWARDING: Often abbreviated as L2F, a tunneling protocol developed by Cisco Systems. L2F is similar to the PPTP protocol developed by Microsoft, enabling organizations to set up virtual private networks (VPNs) that use the Internet backbone to move packets. Recently, Microsoft and Cisco agreed to merge their respective protocols into a single, standard protocol called Layer Two Tunneling Protocol (L2TP).

LAYER THREE SWITCH: *See* ROUTING SWITCH.

LOAD BALANCING: The practice of splitting communications on one route into two or more routes to balance traffic on each route. Load balancing makes communications faster and more reliable. In remote internetworking, bridges and routers perform load balancing by splitting local area network (LAN)-to-LAN traffic among two or more wide area network (WAN) links. This permits a combination of several lower speed lines to transmit LAN data simultaneously.

LOCAL AREA NETWORK (LAN): A communications system that links computers into a network, usually via a wiring-based cabling scheme. LANs connect PCs, workstations and servers together to allow users to communicate and share resources like hard disk storage and printers. Devices linked by a LAN may be on the same floor or within a building or campus. It is user-owned and does not run over leased lines, though a LAN may have gateways to the PSTN or other, private, networks.

LOCAL EXCHANGE CARRIER (LEC): Local telephone company, providing connections between local points or to long distance carriers for extended connections. Examples are Pacific Bell in California, Illinois Bell in Illinois, GTE in Hawaii, etc.

LOCAL LOOP: A channel between a customer's terminal and a central office (CO). The most common form of loop, a pair of wires, is also called a line.

MATERIAL RESOURCE PLANNING (MRP): software for effectively managing material requirements in a manufacturing process. MRP II is better known as Manufacturer Resource Planning, a system based on MRP which allows manufacturers to optimize materials, procurement, manufacturing processes, etc., and provide financial and planning reports.

MESSAGING MIDDLEWARE: A middleware architecture where clients can send and receive higher-level messages—accomplishing an entire transaction or even a complete set of transactions with multiple servers.

METADATA: (1) Data referring to other data; data (such as data structures, indices, and pointers) that are used to instantiate an abstraction (such as "process," "task," "segment," "file," or "pipe"). (2) A special database, also referred to as a data dictionary, containing descriptions of the elements (e.g., relations, domains, entities, or relationships) of a database.

METROPOLITAN AREA NETWORK (MAN): A network established to serve a specific metropolitan area. AT&T INC and Sprint ION are two examples.

MICRON: A unit of length equal to one millionth of a meter or 39.3 microinches.

MIDDLEWARE: Software that connects two otherwise separate applications.

MIRRORING: A method of storage in which data from one disk is duplicated on another disk so that both drives contain the same information, thus providing data redundancy. A popular term for RAID-1.

MISSION CRITICAL: Any computer process that cannot fail during normal business hours; some computer processes (e.g., telephone systems) must run all day long and require 100 percent uptime.

MISSION CRITICAL DATA: Data or information considered to be so important that its loss would cause grave difficulty to all or part of a business. For example: customer account information at a bank, or patient information at a hospital.

MODEM: A peripheral device that connects computers to each other for sending communications via the telephone lines. The modem modulates the digital data of computers into analog signals to send over the telephone lines, then demodulates back into digital signals to be read by the computer on the other end; thus the name "modem" for modulator/demodulator. Modems are used for sending and receiving electronic mail, connecting to bulletin board systems, and surfing the Internet.

MULTIDROP CIRCUIT: A configuation for connecting communications devices that allows the sharing of a communications facility. Like a party line, several devices share a single line. Generally, only one device can be active at a time.

MULTIPLEXER: A device that combines different data streams into a single stream for transmission at high speed. Multiplexed transmissions are commonly received by a multiplexer at the destination site, where they are separated back (demultiplexed) into their component data streams.

MULTI-TIER TRANSACTION PROCESSING: The use of a two-, three-, or n-tier application architecture to perform transaction processing functions.

NATIONAL FIRE PROTECTION ASSOCIATION (NFPA): An organization that develops standards related to fire protection.

***n*-TIER CLIENT/SERVER:** A client/server application architecture using more than three tiers.

NETWORK ARCHITECTURE: The communication equipment, protocols, and transmission links that constitute a network, and the methods by which they are arranged.

NETWORK ATTACHED STORAGE (NAS): This is the provision of storage in a form that is readily accessible on a network. A disk array storage system that is attached directly to a network rather than to the server. NAS devices typically present a networked file system in accordance with a protocol such as NFS or CIFS/SMB. These devices are often referred to as thin servers as they have the functions as a server in a client/server relationship. A typical NAS thin storage server has a processor, an operating system or micro-kernel, and processes file I/O protocols.

OBJECT REQUEST BROKER (ORB): A component in the CORBA programming model that acts as the middleware between clients and servers, receiving, redirecting, and routing real-time inter-object messages.

100BASE-T: *See* FAST ETHERNET.

OPTICAL CARRIER LEVELS (OC): Used to specify the speed of fiber optic networks conforming to the SONET standard. The following table shows the speeds for common OC levels.

OC Level	Speed
OC-1	51.85 Mbps
OC-3	155.52 Mbps
OC-12	622.08 Mbps
OC-24	1.244 Gbps
OC-48	2.488 Gbps

OSI ARCHITECTURE: The Open Systems Interconnect Architecture advanced by the International Organization for Standardization (ISO) provides a framework for defining the communications process between systems. This framework includes a network architecture, consisting of seven layers. The architecture is referred to as the Open Systems Interconnection (OSI) model or Reference Model. Services and the protocols to implement them for the different layers of the model are defined by international standards. From a systems viewpoint, the bottom three layers support the components of the network necessary to transmit a message, the next three layers generally pertain to the characteristics of the communicating end systems, and the top layer supports the end users. The seven layers are: (1) Physical Layer: Includes the functions to activate, maintain, and deactivate the physical connection. It defines the functional and procedural characteristics of the interface to the physical circuit: the electrical and mechanical specifications are considered to be part of the medium itself. (2) Data Link Layer: Formats the messages. Covers synchronization and error control for the information transmitted over the physical link, regardless of the content. "Point-to point error checking" is one way to describe this layer. (3) Network Layer: Selects the appropriate facilities. Includes routing communications through network resources to the system where the communicating application is: segmentation and re-assembly of data units (packets); and some error correction. (4) Transport Layer: Includes such functions as multiplexing several independent message streams over a single connection, and segmenting data into appropriately sized packets for processing by the Network Layer. Provides end-to-end control of data reliability. (5) Session Layer: Selects the type of service. Manages and synchronizes conversations between two application processes. Two main types of dialogue are provided: two-way simultaneous (full duplex), or two-way alternating (half-duplex). Provides control functions similar to the control language in computer system (6) Presentation Layer: Ensures that information is delivered in a form that the receiving system can understand and use. Communicating parties determine the format and language (syntax) of messages: translates if required, preserving the meaning (semantics). (7) Application Layer: Supports distributed applications by manipulating information. Provides resource management for file transfer, virtual file, and virtual terminal emulation, distributed processes and other applications.

OUTSOURCING: Outsourcing is the third-party performance of functions once administered in-house. Outsourcing is really two types of service: ITO—IT Outsourcing, involves a third party who is contracted to manage a particular application, including all related servers, networks, and software upgrades; and BPO—Business Process Outsourcing, features a third party who manages the entire business process, such as accounting, procurement, or human resources.

PACKET SWITCHING: A data communications technique that allows messages to be divided or segmented into packets and routed dynamically through a network to a final destination point.

PACKOUT: A stage of records salvage in which specific cleaning, packaging, labeling, and storage procedures are performed.

PARTICULATE: A small particle of organic or mineral material that can collect in sensitive electronic equipment resulting in damage or destruction.

PASSWORD: A character string, often a word, that must be entered by the user and validated by the system or network before the system or network may be accessed.

PERMISSIONS: Read and write privileges assigned to users by the system administrator for programs and data sets. Permissions are often linked, via software, to device identifiers or user passwords.

POINT OF PRESENCE (POP): A location (and telephone number) that provides users dial-up access to the Inter Exchange Carrier network, to value added network services, or to the Internet.

POINT-TO-POINT CIRCUIT: A method for connecting communications devices in which a dial-up or dedicated circuit provides the connection between two communicating devices.

POTS: Plain Old Telephone Service.

PRIVATE BRANCH EXCHANGE (PBX): A leased or owned programmable device that facilitates communications between numerous voice and data communications devices at the customer premise and the public switched telephone network (PSTN).

PROTOCOL: Software-controlled rules that govern data transmission between communicating devices.

PUBLIC SWITCHED TELEPHONE NETWORK (PSTN): The name for a generic telephone network. One of the few acronyms consistently spelled out when spoken.

RAID (Redundant Array of Inexpensive Disks): A method of combining hard disks into one logical storage unit which offers disk-fault tolerance and can operate at higher throughput levels than a single hard disk.

REDUNDANCY: (Of a network) There are no perfect methods of transmitting signals—each one has inherent error rates, and all physical media is subject to damage. To safeguard against line and equipment failure during a transmission, a second, redundant line or unit can be active in the background to take over at any time. Network administrators always have a redundant (backup) module for multiplexers and other critical equipment.

REGIONAL BELL OPERATING COMPANY (RBOC): Any of the child companies created by the 1984 break-up of AT&T.

REMOTE ACCESS: The ability to log onto a network from a distant location. Generally, this implies a computer, a modem, and some remote access software to connect to the network. Whereas remote control refers to taking control of another computer, remote access means that the remote computer actually becomes a full-fledged host on the network. The remote access software dials in directly to the network server. The only difference between a remote host and workstations connected directly to the network is slower data transfer speeds.

REMOTE ACCESS SERVER (RAS): A server providing connectivity in the form of modems or other devices and software, to facilitate remote access to internal networks. RAS is also short for Remote Access Services, a feature built into Windows NT that enables users to log into an NT-based LAN using a modem, X.25 connection or WAN link. RAS works with several major network protocols, including TCP/IP, IPX, and Netbeui. To use RAS from a remote node, you need a RAS client program, which is built into most versions of Windows, or any PPP client software. For example, most remote control programs work with RAS.

REMOTE MIRRORING: Mirroring disk writes to a duplicate disk array located at an off-site facility using an WAN or Internet link.

REMOTE PROCEDURE CALL (RPC): A type of protocol that allows a program on one computer to execute a program on a server computer.

REMOTE TAPE VAULTING: Writing data backups to a tape library or loader located at an off-site facility via a WAN or Internet connection.

ROUTER: A device that connects any number of LANs. Routers use headers and a forwarding table to determine where packets go, and they use Internet Control Message Protocol (ICMP) to communicate with each other and configure the best route between any two hosts. Very little filtering of data is done through routers.

ROUTING SWITCH: A switch that also performs routing operations. Usually a switch operates at layer 2 (the Data Link layer) of the OSI Reference Model while routers operate at layer 3 (the Network layer). Routing switches, however, perform many of the layer 3 functions usually reserved for routers. Because the routing is implemented in hardware rather than software, it is faster. The downside of routing switches is that they are not as powerful or as flexible as full-fledged routers. Because they perform some layer 3 functions, routing switches are sometimes called layer-3 switches.

SERVICE BUREAU: A computer facility that provides processing services to subscribers on an on-going basis. In the context of disaster recovery planning, the vendor of a software package may be willing to make software available on its own hardware platform for emergency use by the customer.

SHELL SITE: *See* COLD SITE.

SIMULATION TESTING: A disaster is simulated so normal operations will not be interrupted. Hardware, software, personnel, communications, procedures, supplies and forms, documentation, transportation, utilities, and alternate site processing are thoroughly tested in a simulation test. Extensive travel, moving equipment, and eliminating voice or data communications may not be practical or economically feasible during a simulated test.

SOFTWARE: *See* APPLICATION SOFTWARE.

STORAGE AREA NETWORK (SAN): A network comprising multiple hosts and storage peripherals, currently conceived as Fibre Channel/SCSI Command Set-based. However, any interconnect and any network protocol could be used, theoretically, to establish a SAN, provided that the strict latency and throughput requirements of storage are met.

STRUCTURED WALKTHROUGH TESTING: Team members verbally "walk through" the specific steps as documented in the plan to confirm effectiveness of the plan and identify gaps, bottlenecks or other weaknesses in the plan.

SWITCH: In networks, a device that filters and forwards packets between LAN segments. Most switches operate at the data link layer (layer 2) of the OSI Reference Model and therefore support any packet protocol. However, increasing use is being made of ROUTING SWITCHES, which combine layer two and layer three operations. LANs that use switches to join segments are called switched LANs or, in the case of Ethernet networks, switched Ethernet LANs.

SYNCHRONOUS OPTICAL NETWORK (SONET): A standard for connecting fiber-optic transmission systems. SONET was proposed by Bellcore in the middle 1980s and is now an ANSI standard. SONET defines interface standards at the physical layer of the OSI seven-layer model. The standard defines a hierarchy of interface rates that allow data streams at different rates to be multiplexed. SONET establishes Optical Carrier (OC) levels from 51.8 Mbps (about the same as a T-3 line) to 2.48 Gbps. Prior rate standards used by different countries specified rates that were not compatible for multiplexing. With the implementation of SONET, communication carriers throughout the world can interconnect their existing digital carrier and fiber optic systems. The international equivalent of SONET, standardized by the International Telecommunication Union (ITU), is called Synchronous Digital Hierarchy (SDH).

SYSTEMS NETWORK ARCHITECTURE (SNA): IBM's layered communications protocol for sending data between IBM hardware and software. Shortly to celebrate its Pearl anniversary (it was first announced way back in September 1974), it is defined today in terms of a stack of seven layers. While there is some commonalty between the layers of OSI and SNA, it is difficult to make a direct mapping. SNA has traditionally been a hierarchical network architecture for homogeneous networking between IBM systems, but in the 'new' SNA IBM has added increasing support for peer to peer networking through the development of Advanced Peer to Peer

Communications. SNA is managed through the NetView network management system.

T-1 CARRIER: A dedicated phone connection supporting data rates of 1.544 Mbits per second. A T-1 line actually consists of 24 individual channels, each of which supports 64 Kbits per second. Each 64 Kbit/second channel can be configured to carry voice or data traffic. Most telephone companies allow customers to buy just some of these individual channels, known as fractional T-1 access. T-1 lines are a popular leased line option for businesses connecting to the Internet and for Internet Service Providers (ISPs) connecting to the Internet backbone. The Internet backbone itself currently consists of faster T-3 connections. T-1 lines are sometimes referred to as DS1 lines.

T-3 CARRIER: A dedicated phone connection supporting data rates of about 43 Mbps. A T-3 line actually consists of 672 individual channels, each of which supports 64 Kbps. T-3 lines are used mainly by Internet Service Providers (ISPs) connecting to the Internet backbone and for the backbone itself. T-3 lines are sometimes referred to as DS3 lines.

TELECOMMUTER: A work-at-home computer user who connects to the corporate LAN backbone using remote access technologies (for example, using a modem over analog lines, ISDN Terminal Adapter (TA) or ISDN router over ISDN lines, or CSU/DSU over Switched 56 lines).

10BASE-T: A local area network that transmits data at 10 Mbits/s over copper cabling. An IEEE 802.3 media option that supports 10 Mbits/s Ethernet over UTP. A non-standardized full-duplex version (sometimes called full duplex switched Ethernet, FDSE) is available from Compaq and a few other vendors.

TERMINAL EMULATION: Software that allows a PC to mimic the attributes of a dumb terminal normally attached to a mainframe or minicomputer, giving the user with access to function keys and control sequences which the host applications normally use when communicating with one of their own dumb terminals. The most commonly emulated terminals are Digital Equipment Corporation's VT100 terminal and IBM's 3270.

THIN CLIENT: In client/server applications, a client designed to be especially small so that the bulk of the processing occurs on the server. The term has also become symbolic of a dividing line within the computer industry between Sun Microsystems advocating Java-based thin clients running on network computers, and Microsoft and Intel advocating large applications running locally on desktop computers. Although the term thin client refers to software, it is increasingly used to describe computers, such as network computers and Net PCs, that are designed to serve as the clients for client/server architectures. A thin client is a network computer without a hard disk drive, whereas a fat client includes a disk drive.

TRUNK GROUP: A group of circuits in a telecommunications network.

TUNNELING: A technology that enables one network to send its data via another network's connections. Tunneling works by encapsulating a network protocol within packets carried by the second network. For example, Microsoft's PPTP technology enables organizations to use the Internet to transmit data across a virtual private network (VPN). It does this by embedding its own network protocol within the TCP/IP packets carried by the Internet. Tunneling is also called encapsulation.

UNINTERRUPTIBLE POWER SUPPLY (UPS): A battery power backup for utility-provided electrical power.

VALUE ADDED NETWORK (VAN): A data transmission network that guarantees data security and integrity through added computer control and communications from the sender to the recipient, often in the manner of a door-to-door courier or freight forwarder.

VIRTUAL CIRCUIT: A link that seems and behaves like a dedicated point-to-point line or a system that delivers packets in sequence, as happens on an actual point to point network. In reality, the data is delivered across a network via the most appropriate route. The sending and receiving devices do not have to be aware of the options and the route is chosen only when a message is sent. There is no prearrangement, so each virtual connection exists only for the duration of that one transmission.

VIRTUAL PRIVATE NETWORK (VPN): A network that is constructed by using public lines to connect nodes. Many VPNs use the Internet as the medium for transporting data. These systems use encryption and other security mechanisms to ensure that only authorized users can access the network and that the data cannot be intercepted.

VIRUS: (1) Malicious software, a form of Trojan horse, which reproduces itself in other executable code. (2) A self-propagating Trojan horse, composed of a mission component, a trigger component, and a self-propagating component. (3) Self-replicating malicious program segment that attaches itself to an application or other executable system component and leaves no external signs of its presence.

WEB-ENABLED APPLICATION: An application provided with an HTML interface to facilitate web access.

WIDE AREA NETWORK (WAN): A network which covers a larger geographical area than a LAN and where telecommunications links are implemented, normally leased from the appropriate IXCs. Examples of WANs include packet switched networks, public data networks and Value Added Networks.

WIRELESS LOCAL LOOP: Wireless service systems that compete with or substitute for local fixed-line phone service.

WORKSTATION: Term used freely to mean a PC, node, terminal or high-end desktop processor (for CAD/CAM and similar intensive applications)—in short, a device that has data input and output and operated by a user.

WORLD WIDE WEB: A system of Internet servers that support specially formatted documents. The documents are formatted in a language called HTML (HyperText Markup Language) that supports links to other documents, as well as graphics, audio, and video files. This means users can move from one document to another simply by clicking on hot spots. Not all Internet servers are part of the World Wide Web.

WRITE ONCE READ MANY (WORM): An optical storage technology that burns pits into the recording layer of an optical disk, allowing the disks to be written just once but read without limit. WORM drives write directly to an optical disk from a host computer. Both the drives and disks include built-in safeguards to assure that data, once written, cannot be erased, overwritten or altered. Tape-based WORMs have just begun to enter the market.

YEAR 2000 (Y2K) PROBLEM: The Year 2000 problem refers to the inability of software to handle dates beyond 1999.

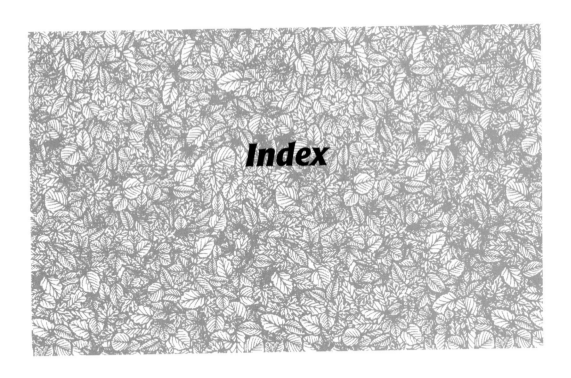

Index